affinities

ESSAYS IN GERMAN AND ENGLISH LITERATURE

OSWALD WOLFF
(1897–1968)

affinities

ESSAYS IN GERMAN AND ENGLISH LITERATURE

Dedicated to the memory of

OSWALD WOLFF

(1897-1968)

*

EDITED BY

R. W. LAST

OSWALD WOLFF

LONDON

MADE AND PRINTED IN GREAT BRITAIN BY
THE GARDEN CITY PRESS LIMITED
LETCHWORTH, HERTFORDSHIRE SG6 1JS

CONTENTS

FRONTISPIECE OSWALD WOLFF

INTRODUCTION vii

TRIBUTE TO OSWALD WOLFF ix

ACKNOWLEDGMENTS x

PART ONE—*German-English literary relations*

1. Between the idyllic and the sublime—some aspects of the reception of Milton in Switzerland (J. H. Tisch) 3
2. Schiller and Shakespeare—some points of contact (W. F. Mainland) 19
3. Germany, German literature and mid-nineteenth-century British novelists (L. H. C. Thomas) 34
4. Enoch Arden in the German Alps: a comparative study of Tennyson's *Enoch Arden* and Duboc's *Walpra* (M. J. Norst) 52
5. The strong enchanter: W. B. Yeats and Nietzsche (P. Bridgwater) 68
6. Gerhart Hauptmann and Hamlet (H. F. Garten) 88
7. Ashley Dukes and the German theatre between the wars (J. M. Ritchie) 97
8. Vernon Watkins and German literature (H. M. Waidson) 110
9. The Chatterton theme in modern German literature (B. Keith-Smith) 126
10. The 'comedy of politics': Dürrenmatt's *King John* (A. Subiotto) 139
11. Tradition and nightmare—some reflections on the postwar novel in England and Germany (W. E. Yuill) 154
12. H. C. Artmann and the English nonsense tradition (J. C. Alldridge) 168

PART TWO—*German themes*

1. Lavater, Mendelssohn, Lichtenberg (E. J. Engel) 187
2. Goethe's *Unterhaltungen deutscher Ausgewanderten* (H. Popper) 206
3. Mörike and Hölty (R. B. Farrell) 246
4. Herder and Nietzsche (D. Williams) 256
5. 'Maria Stuart': Agnes Miegel's originality as a ballad-writer (G. Rodger) 270
6. The 'twenties and Berlin (A. Natan) 280
7. A letter from Barlach to Kokoschka (L. Forster) 290
8. German men of letters (B. E. Schatzky) 296

PART THREE—*Translations into English*

1. Theodor Fontane on Laurence Sterne (D. Turner) 307
2. 'Ophelia': Variations on a theme (Ian Hilton) 318
3. Gertrud von le Fort and Graham Greene (J. Foster) 321
4. Koeppen: Red buses in an enchanted forest (M. A. L. Brown) 330
5. Eliot, Poe and Usinger (R. W. Last) 346

facsimile letter Barlach *oppos.* 290

INTRODUCTION

It is customary to pay tribute to the passing of a great figure in the academic world through the medium of a volume of papers dedicated to his memory; but the essays presented here are exceptional in that the man whose memory they honour, Oswald Wolff, did not hold any academic position. Yet German scholars throughout the world have come together in these pages to pay him their last respects, and this fact alone bears eloquent testimony to the very special position he held in the sphere of German scholarship.

Oswald Wolff had left Germany immediately before the outbreak of the Second World War to make his home in England, there to campaign for a wider recognition and understanding of German culture in the English-speaking world. Founding a publishing house to advance this purpose in 1959 was a natural culmination of his enterprise. From that point until his untimely death in 1968, Oswald Wolff set about the production of an impressive array of publications—the 1969 catalogue announces some fifty volumes in all—dedicated to this end.

It would be no exaggeration to term Oswald Wolff a pioneer: for the first time, scholars had the opportunity of publishing in English on a wide range of German themes, from sociology and history to critical studies of literature and translations from the German; and, equally for the first time, both students of German and the public at large had access, not just to isolated works, as had hitherto been the case, but to whole series of studies: *German Men of Letters* paved the way, followed by *German Narrative Prose*, and, more recently, *Periods in German Literature* and *Modern German Authors*, all of which are now taking their place alongside scholarly productions in German as standard works on German literature and culture.

Oswald Wolff's publishing enterprise was an act of faith: not only in the scholars who wrote for him, to many of whom he gave the chance of publishing an extended work for the first time, but also in bringing to the attention of the English-speaking world the rich and varied achievements of German culture. There is still a long way to go before German culture receives the recognition it deserves, but Oswald Wolff made the first significant advance away from the myth that France is the only country on the European continent whose culture and literature merit serious and extensive attention.

The essays in this volume, which are contributed by many of those who have written for Oswald Wolff in the past, seek to demonstrate as much as possible of Oswald Wolff's achievement in the field of German literature. Part One is devoted to comparative studies, reflecting some of the many correspondences between English and German men of letters; Part Two concerns itself with a selection of German themes of special interest to Oswald Wolff, or are representative of the kind of works whose knowledge and understanding he was seeking to promote; and Part Three offers in its translations from the German both a reminder of Oswald Wolff's achievements in this sadly neglected area and a brief glimpse of some of the fascinating and important work that still remains unknown to the English reader with no knowledge of German.

The editor is deeply grateful to those who so readily offered material for inclusion in this volume: the almost overwhelming response demonstrates beyond doubt our admiration and respect both for Oswald Wolff the man and also for his substantial contribution to the spread of knowledge of German culture in the English-speaking world. Our loss is great; but we are consoled by the fact that his widow, Ilse Wolff, is continuing the invaluable work which he initiated.

TRIBUTE TO OSWALD WOLFF
(1897–1968)

The death of Oswald Wolff on 14 September 1968 has deprived German studies in Britain of one of their few truly independent publishers and a personality appreciated by countless friends in both Germany and other countries throughout the literary world.

Oswald Wolff was born in Berlin into a middle-class business family, was invalided out of the army in 1914, and spent seven years studying philosophy, literature and law at Heidelberg University, at the end of which time he gained two doctorates. Married in 1925, he spent a number of years working in his father's business, but gradually devoted more of his time to helping German Jews to transfer their assets abroad, in order to escape the effects of Nazi economic policy, and later at considerable personal risk he obtained the release of many arrested after the 1938 *Kristallnacht*. In the same year, his wife died after a long illness, and he finally emigrated to Britain in August 1939 with his son and members of his wife's family. For ten years he tried his hand in the City and in industry, and finally, after publishing a one-year periodical of twelve monthly issues—*Goethe Year*—he started Interbook Ltd., an import-export business with a small group of devoted staff. He remarried in 1954, and in 1959 he was able to realise his 'pet ambition' to open a publishing house which has since achieved the unique distinction of being the sole specialist concern outside Germany for the publication of books on German literature, history, biography and economics. In this he was able to rely on his own wide knowledge of German affairs and culture and needed no university or other professional advisers. This independence had for him all the advantages and excitements of launching new ventures and encouraging many unknown writers. For those who worked with him it meant a personal interest in one's contributions, the feeling that one was a partner rather than an employee in an enterprise, and a unique blend of frank and constructive criticism which was always used to encourage rather than censure. Writing for Oswald Wolff was never an arid economic affair, but had the advantage that one always felt the publisher was going to read and digest one's work as carefully as the most demanding reviewer.

His continued activities for the promotion of Anglo-German relations led to his appointment to the executive of the Anglo-German Association. In 1958 his work was recognised by the award of the *Bundes-Verdienstkreuz 1st Class*. But no award could pay full justice to the humanity and openminded character of this determined, most warm-hearted personality of the publishing world. A whole generation of teachers and students of German studies in the English-speaking world owe him a great deal—not just because of the books he published, but because he succeeded in keeping the cause of independence from big impersonal business alive.

B.K.–S.

ACKNOWLEDGMENTS

Mrs. Ilse R. Wolff wishes to thank the following authors and publishers for their kind permission to use copyright material:

Eugen Diederichs Verlag (MARIA STUART by Agnes Miegel, from *Gesammelte Balladen*),
Henry Goverts Verlag (ZAUBERWELT DER ROTEN OMNIBUSSE by Wolfgang Koeppen, from *Nach Russland und Anderswohin*),
Peter Huchel (OPHELIA first published in *Neue Deutsche Hefte*),
Verlag der Arche (Gertrud von le Fort's introduction GRAHAM GREENE to *Graham Greene: Vom Paradox des Christentums*).

She also acknowledges with grateful thanks the ready co-operation of all contributors to this volume and for the high standard of their essays. (One of whom, Mr. Alex Natan, the Editor of our *German Men of Letters* series, unfortunately died before publication of this book; Volume VI of the series will be published posthumously.) Thanks are also due to Mr. Elwyn Blacker who designed the jacket, to Mr. Denys Middleton of The Garden City Press for the personal interest he took in the production, but above all to Mr. R. W. Last, without whose enthusiasm and devoted work this book would not have seen the light of day.

The book is a proud achievement and a permanent and fitting tribute to Oswald Wolff.

PART ONE

German-English literary relations

I

BETWEEN THE IDYLLIC AND THE SUBLIME—SOME ASPECTS OF THE RECEPTION OF MILTON IN SWITZERLAND

By J. H. Tisch

'Since Professor Bodmer through his excellent translation of Milton's *Paradise Lost* has made the merits of the poetic writings of that great man more widely known among the Germans, they complain not without cause that they are being deprived of the pleasure of reading also other works by that author in their language.'[1] These opening words from the preface to the first German translation of *Paradise Regained* by Simon Grynaeus fittingly pay tribute to the dynamic personality who virtually rediscovered *Paradise Lost* half a century after it had first been rendered into German and whose impressive achievement as a translator has been grossly underrated from his antagonist Gottsched down to modern critics.[2] Johann Jacob Bodmer (1698–1783) of Zürich, a vicar's son, by dint of a rare combination of untiring revisional labour, polemical zeal and the skill of an impresario, disseminated a knowledge of Milton in the German-speaking regions. His endeavours should be viewed against the wider background of the substantial contribution made by Switzerland to the cultural and literary discovery of England in the eighteenth century, to the 'English revolution' of German letters, a contribution reaching from Muralt's *Lettres sur les Français et les Anglais* to the activities of the gifted polyglot group that gathered around the champion of Milton, Bodmer. This 'Bruthenne für Talente' (Goethe) turned Zürich, then a city of around 10,000 inhabitants, into a cosmopolitan intellectual centre and, together with other sons of clergymen, and young theologians, proceeded to create a new type of secular but morally edifying literature and to mediate, like Grynaeus in Basle, between Protestant orthodoxy and *belles-lettres*. Was Bodmer's life-work then nothing but 'applied poetry', cure of souls, secularised literature for edification? Was this the central impulse that activated the Swiss to inaugurate, in the name of

Milton as it were, a new literary era, characterised by far-reaching transformations of style and artistic creed? The view that the new aesthetics arose purely from a theological background may be an extreme one, but one can hardly overlook the marked didactic, Christian orientation in the attitudes of the Swiss critics. If, as Pascal says, 'the great mass of criticism in Germany was religious and moralistic', then this becomes particularly manifest with regard to Milton. There is evidence that the vigorous rise of the literary Zürich in the eighteenth century should be understood as a direct continuation and gradual replacement of the 'theological' Zürich.[3] In the seminal work of the Zürich critics, theology and aesthetic theory sustained each other. Bodmer and his able collaborator Breitinger did not find it an easy task to reconcile their experience of Milton's elevated art with their tenets, which, like Gottsched's sober doctrines, were originally rooted in the common soil of Wolffian rationalism. But Bodmer in particular, deeply concerned with the freedom of religious imagination, produced theories made to measure for the defence of sacred poetry that extols deeds 'more Heroic then the wrauth/ Of stern Achilles'. Bodmer's 'recommendation of imaginative poetry remains in the service of Christian doctrine, of a religious didacticism'.[4] He regarded Milton's sublime style and message as a peak above which the human mind can hardly soar, and he proclaimed that the poet has as his avowed main objective 'to justify the ways of God to men'.[5]

The German enthusiasm for Milton who in Pyra's telling phrase 'has led Poetry/From the pagan Parnassus to Paradise' was strongly tinged with non-aesthetic, even irrational elements. Theological and pietist circles were prominently involved in the reception of the 'Christian Homer' in Germany and Switzerland. Apart from Pyra and Herder, this religious and spiritual undertone of the admiration for *Paradise Lost* was perhaps nowhere more audible than in Switzerland where men like Bodmer vindicated Milton's 'poetic theology'[6] with conviction.

These processes were aided by political affinities the republican Swiss felt with the 'free Britons'. There were also Protestant sympathies and connections reaching back several centuries; Milton himself refers to this feeling of kinship when in his capacity as Secretary for Foreign Tongues he writes (on 28 November 1653) on behalf of the English Parliament to the 'Most Illustrious and Noble Senators ... of the Evangelick Cantons of Switzerland . . . our dearest friends'. (As early as 1656 Milton's name appears in the autograph book of a Swiss traveller to England, a certain Johann Zollikofer who also obtained the signature of Th. Haak, the first translator of *Paradise Lost* into German.) While even the German Protestants, who otherwise looked across longingly to 'beatissima Anglia, quae puritate doctrinae gaudes', to the happy country of justice and peace,[7] were deeply shocked by the execution of Charles I—for decades Milton was stigmatised as the militant spokesman of the Regicides—the reaction among the Reformed Swiss was not unfavourable.

The legend of the idyllic happiness of Switzerland, of the incomparable freedom of her inhabitants, a well-worn topos of philhelvetism down to Schiller's *Tell*, was gradually losing status (Goethe mocks it as an old fairy tale preserved in methylated spirit). Among enlightened writers disillusioned with the political reality, these notions were ousted by the feverish glorification of the 'britische Freiheit'. The ties between English and Swiss Protestants (and humanists) however, were not a corollary of Anglomania. They go back—to give a symbolic date—to the visit to England in 1531 by the learned Simon Grynaeus (1493–1541, since 1529 Professor of Greek in Basle[8] and an ancestor of the Milton translator of the same name); they were strengthened when English refugees found shelter in Switzerland in the reign of Queen Mary. The Milton-Grynaeus approvingly notes that the ill-fated heroine of Bodmer's drama *Johanna Gray* would like to be 'in the pious city of Zürich' (the historical Johanna, Queen for twelve days in 1553, executed in 1554, corresponded with the Swiss reformer Bullinger), whereas the Johanna in Wieland's drama 'with her Guilford' hankers for a 'shepherd's hut'.[9] Cordial personal relationships as well as contacts and exchanges in the field of theological and devotional literature remained frequent and intensive, a prelude to the breakthrough of the creative discovery of English taste and thought in the eighteenth century which, at least in Zürich, was centred in Milton.[10]

Milton's poetry is mirrored in various German works in widely different facets. Bodmer who advocated 'elevated style' as an antidote to Gottsched's somewhat pedestrian notion of the poetic, was second to none in his awed appreciation of the sublime, majestic and heroic qualities of *Paradise Lost*. But his interest in the 'biblical' side of Milton's epic led him almost inevitably towards the patriarchal, idyllic aspect of Milton (which looms large in his theoretical writings too). The appeal of the timeless scenes in Eden was enhanced by the awakening *Naturgefühl* and the craving for unspoilt rustic simplicity and happiness that was in the air (and accounts for the international success of Gessner's *Idyllen*). Already Bodmer's first impressions of Milton[11] are coloured by a reaction against the narrowness of the 'dirty town'. In this nostalgic 'nature sentimentalism' which contains a strong Miltonic ingredient and imbues Bodmer's numerous works on biblical subjects, he can be regarded as a forerunner of Gessner and may have helped the latter to find his identity as a nature poet in prose.

Bodmer's indebtedness to Milton in his much-maligned *Noah* (1752) goes much beyond the invocation of Milton's muse, 'die Muse Sions' and the treatment of some of the prophecies from the final two books of *Paradise Lost*. Irredeemably dated, despite idyllic scenes of genuine beauty, *Noah* is historically noteworthy as the canonical model for the *Patriarchaden*. The strange alloy that went into its making throws light on the sensibility of the period: Old Testament subject matter, an attempt to reproduce, in the wake of Klopstock, the 'spacious' Homeric hexameter in German, the influence of 'sentimental' English poets, in particular of Young, and the products of an unadventurous but far from sterile imagination overheated by Miltonic visions. Especially in its infernal and pastoral highlights, *Noah* is permeated with phrases and details from Milton which have been painstakingly listed by researchers.[12] Relevant to the overall picture is the process itself, familiar to the student of Milton's reception on the continent: the emphasis on individual features, lifted from the complexity of *Paradise Lost* and given an independent existence, and the distortion of Milton's artistic image that results. The whole cult of the 'German Milton', Klopstock, was precariously based on a misunderstanding of Milton's intentions. The rapt response of Pfarrer Hess to *Noah*—'Behold, here is more than Milton!'—recalls utterances by enchanted contemporaries about the *Messias* of 'our more than Milton' as Schönaich maliciously describes Klopstock.[13]

The flowering of genres that hovered uneasily between poetry and edification and were mainly cultivated by authors with a theological background, such as the *Patriarchade* and the biblical drama, constitutes an important Protestant variation on the ubiquitous eighteenth-century predilection for the virtuous, the sentimental and the harmoniously idyllic. In this sphere the impact of Milton, discernible more in tone and style than in actual content, is softened, humanised, emotionally attuned. Milton's acute awareness of the nexus between the Christian paradise and the 'aetas aurea' of pastoral poetry lent support to the seemingly arbitrary identification of the world of biblical patriarchs with the Golden Age which underlies the spiritual Arcadia of Bodmer and his followers.[14] Little wonder then that Gottsched and his disciples aggressively mocked the 'sacral poets', the 'ätherischen' (a pervasive Miltonic loanword of the period) and 'sehraffischen Dichter', the 'alpinische Seuche der Hexametristen', above all Bodmer, the 'Syndfluthenbarden', 'Patriarchendichter' and 'Rabbinischen Mährchenerzähler' (as he is irreverently styled in the *Neologisches Wörterbuch*). Bodmer's Milton translation and his *Noah* indeed released a deluge of imitations in prose and verse, from *Der gepryfte Abraham* (1753) by Wieland who, then in his 'seraphic' phase, implored the Holy Muse to ordain him as her priest 'as you have ordained Bodmer' to Lavater's *Adam* (1781).[15] In his warm esteem of the idyllical passages in *Paradise Lost* and of Milton as a poet of God's glory through created nature, Bodmer did not stand alone: Brockes, Haller, Herder and others expressed profound delight over Milton's 'incomparable' morning hymn and 'the depiction of the innocent love of our First Parents' in his major epic. None other than Schiller, when critically assessing Gessner, celebrated Milton's 'magnificent' depiction of Adam and Eve and the state of innocence in Paradise as 'the most beautiful idyll in the sentimental genre'.[16] The 'Liebesfreiheit' (Petriconi), the fervent fulfilment, the purity and beauty of the love between Adam and Eve in Milton's Eden attracted the poets of the *Empfindsamkeit*. For decades, Milton's nuptial bower was endlessly imitated, from *Noah* to Maler Müller and Stolberg; also Abel and Thirza's 'Liebeslaube' of jasmine and roses in Gessner stems from this source. This bower 'is actually the symbol of the sentimental age, and it was borrowed on account of its idyllic connotations'.[17]

This brings us to a central document of Sentimentalism, *Der Tod Abels*, the most pleasing of the *Patriarchaden*. Its author, Salomon Gessner (1730–88) in his famous *Idyllen* endeavoured to invest the natural scenery with the perfection of Paradise. Conversely, in *The Death of Abel* he changed the framework but not the character of his poems: 'in the epic he remains the incomparable pastoral poet'.[18] But to view his excursion into the realm of the biblical epic merely as a fashionable manifestation of the Rococo spirit would fail to do justice to this serious but charming postlapsarian Arcadian vision that spread his fame to all corners of Europe. Gessner's *Abel* (written 1757), an elegiac-lyrical effusion on a tragic theme couched in a rhythmically pulsating prose, is unmistakably Klopstockian in the diffuseness of its contours, in its lacrymose emotionalism. But there is more than a touch of Miltonic grandeur about it.

Like his ancestors—scientists and printers—Gessner does not belong to the 'theological' stratum, the sociological group that became instrumental in the literary revolution of the eighteenth century. And yet underneath Gessner's Enlightenment concept of poetry as being governed by useful intelligibility and 'Vergnügen', in *Abel* there wells up a sense of mission, a belief in the dignity of religious poetry, a note of moral didacticism.[19] The exordium suggests Milton transposed into a pastoral key—'A sublime song I now desire to sing . . . be silent, soft rustic flute . . . assist me, Muse, or noble ecstasy'—and in stressing the flight of imagination towards the 'Wunderbare' and the 'Mögliche', it draws on the crucial terminology of the Zürich critics of Milton.[20]

A contemporary journal (referring to Adam and Eve's relation of their lives after the expulsion from Eden) states: 'Only Gessner was capable of carrying on where Milton left off'.[21] The author himself, as he writes to V. B. Tscharner in 1763, desired to be only himself, and not to compete with Milton. In this the 'matchless pastoral poet' certainly succeeds, but the cumulative effect of Miltonic echoes raises his *Abel* to a higher plane. While it is easy to pinpoint verbal parallels, analogies and similarities of mood and tone are less tangible, the more so as in the case of such 'idyllic' readings of *Paradise Lost,* they reflect the original at several removes.[22] Miltonic reminiscences in *Abel* range from the appearances of heavenly and demonic forces (the envious, ambitious Anamelech who in a dream instigates Cain to do the deed is a Satan in miniature) to the recurrent passages of hymnic elevation and praise and to the effective integration of pictorial situations or moving phrases. It is not the extent of these borrowings which is decisive, but the transfer of traits from the Puritan epic into the atmosphere of *Empfindsamkeit*, their emotional intensification and changed function, their amalgamation with their new context. In 'Da giengen wir, die ganze Erde lag . . .

vor uns: Hand in Hand giengen wir' for instance, the enigmatic beauty of Milton's closing lines is tempered by Sentimentalism, the untranslatable Klopstockian 'Oft weint' ich zurück', 'oft zurückweinend' taking the place of 'Som natural tears they dropd'.[23] This phenomenon makes Gessner's subtle biblical idyll a quintessential example of *Paradise Lost* filtered through a sentimental sensibility, poetic theology in anacreontic terms, painted delicately by a consummate Swiss craftsman. As Klopstock's reaction to *Paradise Lost*, and Milton's significance for Bodmer and Breitinger's postulate of the 'hertzrührende Schreibart', of emotive aesthetics indicate, the appeal to the heart was an important avenue for Milton's reception by German-speaking readers.[24]

'Not a female in the whole of Paris who does not have a copy of *la Mort d'Abel* on her dressing table': translations proliferated; a spate of English versions endeared 'the melodious Abel' (*Critical Review*, 1769) to readers and vastly enhanced the prestige of the poet of the *Idyllen* in the British Isles and in America.[25] Few texts could be more typical for the interplay and fusion of heterogeneous influences during this era (such as those of Milton and Young, inextricably merged in Bodmer's *Noah*) than the best English rendering of Gessner's epic: *The Death of Abel, A Sacred Poem* (London, 1763), translated by the Rev. Thomas Newcomb 'in the Stile of Milton' and dedicated to 'The Reverend and Very Learned Dr. Edward Young'. In his 'Advertisement', Newcomb claims 'the partiality of friends (too hastily perhaps) judged, that a piece so admired through the medium of prose translation [the first one was published in 1761] could hardly fail of pleasing in its present poetic dress, however negligent'. A brief quotation may illustrate how he conceives of 'Miltonic' style:

> ... Ardent, I now attempt my voice to raise,
> While in exalted strains, I strive to moan
> Our first sad Parents, drove from Eden's bow'rs.[26]

When Gessner tries to recapture Milton's 'exalted strains', his voice sounds less sonorous, but also less self-conscious.

Among the admirers of Milton in eighteenth-century Switzerland, none perhaps conforms more closely to the union of theological and literary interests we observed in Bodmer than the meek clergyman Simon Grynaeus of Basle, the first German translator of Milton's shorter epic, of *Samson Agonistes* (and also of Shakespeare's *Romeo and Juliet*). The work of this far-sighted mediator, today shrouded in obscurity, projects an image of Milton truly poised between the idyllic and the sublime and still merits closer scrutiny. Grynaeus (1725–99), for many years deacon at St. Peter's in Basle, was a direct descendant of his renowned sixteenth-century namesake. When he died after a painful illness borne with serene patience, the distinguished family of theologians and scholars became extinct. From the biographical documents and from his writings there emerges the profile of a self-effacing, deeply pious and tolerant personality, of a man in whom mildness and dignity, humility and wisdom, warm feeling and intellectual detachment were harmoniously mixed. A contemporary source ascribes to him 'an incredible proficiency in the English language' (there is corroborative evidence in his translations), and his journey to England (1749–50) seems to have galvanised him into becoming a prolific, popularising but sensitive translator.[27] Not that Grynaeus would necessarily have depended on a visit to England for such impulses: the intellectual milieu of Basle—where Haller too discovered his models among the English poets—was saturated with English influences. Grynaeus belonged to a circle that showed itself very much alive to English literature, and he had contacts with the English book trade, but his attention was focused on English letters by his theological teachers (who like the mathematicians in Basle kept abreast of English writings) *prior* to his journey to England and to his first contact with Bodmer. This is perhaps characteristic, because his copious translations of English religious works and his renderings of secular texts were motivated by the same force—by a fervent caritative urge to edify his readers and to win them back to Christian orthodoxy. Similar to Theodore Haak, F.R.S. (1605–90) with whom as a translator he shares a leaning towards theological material and the desire to communicate Milton to a large audience, but unlike his other seventeenth-century predecessors Berge and Wegleiter, he approached his task without literary ambition.[28] In the rural surroundings of Wintersingen, after his visit to England, Grynaeus undertook 'for my own pleasure' the translation of a number of works by Milton 'which as far as I am aware have never before been read in our language':[29] *Paradise Regained, Samson Agonistes*, and, full of the 'vitality and fire' of the poet's youth, *Lycidas*,

L'Allegro and *Il Penseroso* and *On the Morning of Christ's Nativity*—a formidable challenge for a beginner. In his 'Preface' he modestly admits to a lack of poetic talent (although his *Weynacht-Gesang* which emulates the metrical form of Milton's Nativity poem is a creditable performance) and wishes that even his errors will help his readers 'to gain a deeper insight into the beauties of the original'. Writing to Bodmer (to whom he is sending a copy) early in 1752, he is disarmingly self-critical and diffident. He confesses that 'this piece of work turned out very badly', emphasises his inadequate command of English and his neglect of the German language and predicts that his own 'rash enterprise' will remind the world at large of its debt of gratitude to Bodmer as the translator of *Paradise Lost*.[30] The hopes for a lenient verdict from such an established critic as Bodmer which Grynaeus obviously cherished were dashed, although Grynaeus himself may never have learnt how harshly Bodmer judged his translation. The 'father of the European Zürich', as he has aptly been called, displayed a curiously authoritarian and unsympathetic attitude towards rival translators of Milton: on the efforts of Gruner and Veiel (a vicar's son and a vicar respectively!) he commented 'not much good', 'very much a beginner's attempt', and on Grynaeus' volume 'very un-German and plebeian'. It is ironical that Bodmer who ten years earlier defied the risk of appearing 'undeutsch' in order to equal Milton's 'emphatic, concise and sublime style' should crush Grynaeus, who adhered to the same principle of faithful reproduction by that very expression.[31]

The erudite Grynaeus was conversant with the tenacious prejudices against Milton's shorter epic as being infinitely inferior to *Paradise Lost*. But like Herder (who preferred 'the hut to the palace of the fairies') he was not swayed by that widespread bias and perceptively defends the work against its detractors, mentioning also Milton's own reputed liking for the poem, reported with irritation by Elijah Fenton whose life of Milton, translated by Grynaeus, precedes his *Wieder-erobertes Paradies*.[32] Quietist by temperament, Grynaeus as an apologist of Milton does not command the polemical power of a Bodmer or the dialectical lucidity of a Pyra. But in his unhurried refutation of the strictures commonly levelled at *Paradise Regained*, he reveals real understanding of the epic's artistic discipline, of the reticence of its diction, and of the idiosyncrasies of Milton's style, his 'besondere Schreibart' in general. As a translator committed to an ideal of accuracy and clarity resembling Bodmer's, he strives in an 'inornate and yet noble prose [as a biographer remarked about his sermons] to follow my author as closely as possible and step by step, as it were'.[33]

Grynaeus was not a great translator, but then there is no German translation of Milton worthy of that epithet; no Schlegel or Tieck took up Milton's cause. Two brief excerpts may suffice to convey an idea of Grynaeus' not inconsiderable competence:

> Alles dasjenige ist das allerbeste (ob wir gleich oft daran zweifeln) was die unerforschliche Verordnung der höchsten Weisheit vollendet, und es wird allemal am Ende das beste erfunden. Oft scheinet er sein Antlitz zu verbergen, unerwartet aber kommet er wieder, und er hat an seinem Orte von seinem getreuen Helden herrlich gezeuget; Daher trauret Gaza, und alle die sich verbanden seiner unwidersprechlichen Absicht zu widerstehen. Seinen Knecht hat er nun, durch den Ausgang dieses großen Unternehmens, auf das neue bewährt erfunden; er hat ihn im Friede und wohl-geströstet beurlaubet; und alle seine ängstliche Sorgen haben sich in einer stillen Gemüthsruhe geendet.[34]

Mood and cadence of the supreme final chorus in Milton's Samson drama which the old Goethe praised as 'written in the spirit of the Ancients like no other play by any modern writer' are clearly beyond Grynaeus' modest potential although he translates fairly accurately and in the occasional phrase ('hat . . . herrlich gezeuget' for 'bore witness gloriously') even congenially. The wording of the closing lines accentuates the chasm between the original and the translator's mid eighteenth-century mentality.

Like Haak who in Barnett's words was 'much happier in Heaven than in hell', Grynaeus feels more at home in the familiar arena of theological argument than on imaginative heights. This is how he renders part of the complex and momentous debate on glory in *Paradise Regained*:

> Warum sollte sich aber der Mensch nach Ehre bestreben, welcher für sich selbsten nichts eigenes hat, und welchem nichts zugehöret, als Verdammung, Schmach und Schande? welcher, für so viele Gutthaten, abfallend, undankbar und falsch, sich von GOtt wandte, und sich also alles Guten selbst beraubete; Annoch wollte er, als ein Kirchenräuber, dasjenige zu sich nehmen, so GOtt allein von rechtswegen zugehöret. Dennoch besitzet GOtt noch so viele Güte, solche Gnade, daß er selbst diejenigen, welche

> seine Ehre befördern, nicht ihre eigene, zu Ehren bringen will. So sprach der Sohn GOttes; und hier hatte Satan abermals nichts einzuwenden, sondern er stuhnd geschlagen mit dem Verbrechen seiner eigenen Sünde; denn er selbst, unersättlich an Ehre, hatte alles verlohren . . .[35]

Unsophisticated and unpoetic, perhaps, but preserving the doctrine as well as the syntax, and not altogether unworthy of the ascetic austerity of Milton's epic that tells 'of deeds Above Heroic, though in secret done'.

Grynaeus' *Wiedererobertes Paradies* is surrounded by a cluster of other translations that—like Dryden's *State of Innocence* or Masen's *Sarcotis*—possess Milton associations of various kinds; well-informed as usual, Grynaeus knew about the accusations of plagiarism from Masen made by Lauder, 'a proven swindler' (Haller); a 'calumny' (Lessing) of Milton which Gottsched had exploited with relish. It is not entirely fanciful to bracket some of these translated texts together as an edifying series fostering Christian heroism and including *The Book of Job*, the *Psalms* and Steele's *Christian Hero*.[36]

From his tantalisingly one-sided correspondence with Bodmer (Bodmer's letters have not been preserved) we can infer that the tireless Grynaeus, under Bodmer's guidance, planned to produce a German version of *Paradise Lost* in hexameters (elsewhere he seems to consider a complete Shakespeare in German blank verse).[37] The eleven surviving letters, spread over the period February 1752–September 1763 afford vivid glimpses of the writer's personality—of his humility and unselfishness, his lively wit, his critical alertness, his childlike enthusiasm for his projects. Amongst the themes that recur, mingled with polite trivia, *Paradise Lost* deserves closer attention.

Grynaeus evidently looked up to Bodmer as to the older, more experienced man, occupying a commanding position at the very hub of Swiss literary life. Apart from a few cautious words of praise, Bodmer's remarks seem to have been predominantly critical. Grynaeus, forever depreciating his own 'miserable' efforts and apologising for his 'temerity', eagerly invites constructive comments, especially on questions of metrics. Bodmer had appreciatively adopted Klopstock's expansive 'new hexameter' for his *Noah*—a kind of prosodic manual for Grynaeus—and had hailed 'the full splendour' of the German heroic metre as the medium for the ideal translation of *Paradise Lost*. Grynaeus, whose hexameter versions of poetical works by Prior, Pope, Young and Glover (published 1757) were demolished by Lessing in a scathing review of not less than seven printed pages, was extremely conscious of the 'hard, rough, lame' quality of his verses. His letters are not entirely free from pragmatic calculation and diplomacy, but his reiterated thanks for his mentor's expert and detailed advice ('an eye opener') ring sincere.[38] But his imposing if unrealistic plan of presenting *Paradise Lost* in a splendidly illustrated bilingual edition was to remain a mirage after all. We can trace the fluctuations of his hopes, eventually frustrated by Bodmer's publisher Conrad Orell, who understandably refused to co-operate in a venture that commercially might have been detrimental to Bodmer's own Milton. In 1757 the excitable Grynaeus tackles Bodmer in the somewhat naïve words:

> If you consider a person like myself capable of giving the Germans a Milton in hexameters, then I request your further instructions on this task. However, if you are of the opinion, as I am almost myself, that I do not possess the ability for it, please tell me candidly and I shall dismiss it from my mind at once.

In 1759 he informs Bodmer that his enthusiasm has not cooled off, and early in 1760 he is still working on his version of *Paradise Lost*; however, there are symptoms of resignation:

> . . . but I am doing it only for my own use, since I hear that Mr. Zachariä has the same plan; for that reason I shall stay at home with mine, at least until I see what this gentleman will be offering to us.[39]

The role played by Bodmer—who himself had seen eight years elapse between the completion and publication of his Milton translation—cannot be determined with certainty. While it is unlikely that he sensed a serious and presumptuous rival in the submissive clergyman who faced the severe trial of his patience with equanimity, there is reason to believe that he fobbed Grynaeus off with promises and "Vertröstungstaktik".[40] Grynaeus' uninhibited facility in translating may have been incompatible with Bodmer's stringent standards. But the German Milton in hexameters was not to be a slapdash affair; in his letters, Grynaeus harps on the need to revise his text, to 'turn it on a lathe' so it would become readable at last.[41] His translation of Book I—the only part of the manuscript still extant—bears witness to the fact that Grynaeus (who in 1759 foreshadowed that 'without scruples' he was going to improve his own version with the aid of Bodmer's forthcoming new rendering) drew assiduously on Bodmer's earlier editions of 1732, 1742 and 1754. Whole stretches of Grynaeus' *Verlohrnes Paradies* consist of a colourful but in its effect surprisingly homogeneous mosaic from Bodmer (lines 19–20, quoted below, for instance blend expressions from all three versions), interspersed with some parallels with Zachariä's hexameter translation (published 1760 and ²1762). This is puzzling because Grynaeus had explicitly rejected the suggestion that his manuscript should be sent to Zachariä for perusal.[42] At its least inspired, Grynaeus' translation is hardly more platitudinous and unsuggestive than a considerable portion of Zachariä's; at its best, it offers testimony of an undeniable though not fully matured talent. The 'Swiss hexameters' (according to Lessing worse than bad prose), while not exactly vibrant with tension, do not strike the reader as quite so leisurely and padded as do the German writer's. Grynaeus' power of articulation does not match his admiration for Milton, and spiritually and aesthetically he is aiming at a wider audience than the select few. But he is never disloyal to his lofty original. His intense concern with *Paradise Lost* strikingly exemplifies how closely theological circles in Switzerland were associated with the reception of Milton. It is perhaps not incongruous to close with his translation of the lines that provided Bodmer with a formula commensurate with the high office of the poet 'to justifie the wayes of God to men':[43]

Und hauptsächlich du, O Geist, der du den prächtigen Tempeln
Ein Herz weit vorziehest, welches aufrichtig und rein ist;
Unterrichte mich; du weißest alles: du warest von Anfang
Gegenwärtig; Wie eine Taube die Flügel ausbreitet,
Saßest du brütend auf dem ungemäßenen Abgrund,
Und er ward fruchtbar. O erleuchte das, welches in mir noch
Finster ist; und was niedrig ist, unterstütze, erhöhe!
Daß ich düchtig sey zu der Hoheit meines Vorhabens
Um die ewigen Rechte der weysen Vorsicht zu schützen,
Und die Weege Gottes unter den Menschen zu retten.

NOTES

1. S. Grynaeus, *Johann Miltons wieder-erobertes Paradies . . .*, Basle, 1752, p. 3 f. (=*W.P.*).
2. W. Bender's relevant publications have done much to rehabilitate Bodmer; see his 'Nachwort' to *Johann Miltons Episches Gedichte von dem Verlohrnen Paradiese,* Deutsche Neudrucke, Stuttgart, 1965 (=*V.P.*), and my review, *AUMLA* XXVIII (1967) 92 f.
3. See H. Schöffler, *Das literarische Zürich 1700–1750,* Leipzig, 1925; cf. M. Wehrli: 'Das geistige Zürich im 18. Jahrhundert', *Schweizer Monatshefte* XXII (1942), 476; W. Bender: 'JJBodmer und Johann Miltons *VP*' *Jb. d. dt. Schiller-Ges.* XI (1967), 230, 249 f.; E. C. Mason: *The Mind of Henry Fuseli,* London, 1951, p. 16; R. Pascal, *The German Sturm und Drang,* Manchester, 1953, p. 291.
4. R. Wellek, *History of Modern Criticism I,* New Haven, 1955, p. 147 f.
5. Bender *V.P.*, p. 113.
6. Cf. Bender *V.P.*, p. 241; A. Sauer (ed.), *I. J. Pyra . . . Freundschaftliche Lieder,* Stuttgart, 1885, p. 115.
7. D. Tossanus (1636) cited in P. R. Barnett, *Theodore Haak,* 's Gravenhage, 1962, p. 18; Milton: see Columbia ed. XIII, N.Y., 1937, p. 119; Th. Ischer, *Die Gesandtschaft der protestantischen Schweiz bei Cromwell . . .*, Berne 1916, p. 58 f., 104 f.; Zollikofer: see A. Stern, *A.f.schweiz. Gs.* III (1878), 113 f.
8. See M. E. Welti, 'Der Gräzist Simon Grynaeus und England,' *Archiv f. Kulturgs.* XLV (1963), 232 f.; Milton, *Complete Prose Works II,* New Haven/London, 1959, p. 422.
9. Grynaeus, letter to Bodmer No. 8, p. 3 (17 April 1759), cp. Bodmer, *Drey neue Trauerspiele,* Zürich, 1761, p. 51; Th. Vetter, 'Englische Flüchtlinge in Zürich während der ersten Hälfte des 16. Jahrhunderts', *Neujahrsblatt. Stadtbibl. Zürich* (1893) p. 1 f.
10. cp. Bender, *Schiller-Jb.* 1967, p. 259; theological contacts: see L. Magon, 'Die drei ersten deutschen Versuche einer Übersetzung von Miltons *PL*' in: *Gedenkschrift für Ferdinand Josef Schneider,* Weimar, 1956, p. 39 f.
11. cp. H. Bodmer, 'Die Anfänge des zürcherischen Milton', *Studien zur Literaturgeschichte. Michael Bernays gewidmet,* Hamburg & Leipzig, 1893, p. 188 f.
12. on Bodmer's indebtedness to Milton and Young see C. H. Ibershoff, *JEGP* XVII (1918), 589 f., *PQ* I (1922), 110 f., *PMLA* XLIII (1928), 1055 f.; Th. Vetter, 'JJBodmer und die englische Litteratur', *JJBodmer. Denkschrift zum CC Geburtstag,* Zürich, 1900, p. 362 f.
13. A. Köster (ed.), C. O. Freiherr v. Schönaich, *Die ganze Aesthetik in einer Nuss . . .*, Berlin, 1900, p. 230; Hess, cited in G. Jenny, *Miltons Verlorenes Paradies in der deutschen Literatur des 18. Jahrhunderts,* St. Gall, 1890, p. 33.
14. cp. H. Petriconi, 'Die verlorenen Paradiese', *Romanist. Jb.* X (1959), 175 f.
15. Wieland 1753 ed. p. 2; cp. J. Wiegand & W. Kohlschmidt, 'Patriarchade', *RL,* ²II, 72 f.
16. L. Hirzel (ed.), *A. v. Haller: Gedichte,* Frauenfeld, 1882, p. 375; Schiller, *Sämtliche Werke,* Munich, 1959, V, 749.
17. J. Rothschild, *Kain und Abel in der deutschen Dichtung,* Würzburg, 1933, p. 70; cp. E. Pizzo, *Miltons Verlornes Paradies im deutschen Urteile des 18. Jahrhunderts,* Berlin, 1914, p. 40 (underestimates direct influence of Milton).
18. *Freymüthige Nachrichten* (=*Fr. Na.*) XVII (1760), 48 (quoting *Bibl. d. schönen Wiss.u.d.freyen Künste,* Leipzig, IV, 2).
19. cp. *Fr. Na.* XVI (1759), 119; Haller, *Göttinger Gelehrte Anzeigen* (1758), p. 1422 (cited in K. S. Guthke, *Haller und die Literatur,* Göttingen, 1962, p. 143.
20. S. Gessner, *Sämmtliche Schriften I,* Karlsruhe, 1795, p. 7 f.: cp. first ed. (1758) p. 3 f., 'Vorrede' (not in *Schriften*).

21. *Fr. Na.* (1759), 119.
22. On Gessner's approach to the Cain and Abel theme see A. Brieger, *Kain und Abel in der deutschen Dichtung,* Berlin & Leipzig, 1934, p. 55 f.; on Schiller's *Robbers* (where the motif coalesced with a strong interest in Milton) cp. my essay in R. Brissenden (ed.), *Studies in the Eighteenth Century,* Canberra, 1968, p. 226.
23. *Schriften* p. 26, 124; cp. *PL* XII, 646, 648 (Quotations from Milton's poetical works follow the edition by H. Derbishire, Oxford, 1952 and 1955); cp. P. Leemann-van Elck, *Salomon Geßner,* Zürich, 1930, p. 299; Gessner's only Milton illustration depicts the expulsion from Eden; for the parallels with Milton in *Abel* see *Schriften* pp. 8–11, 17, 37, 53 f., 62, 66 f., 74, 111 f.
24. cp. Bender, *V.P.*, p. 17* and *Schiller-Jb.* 1967, p. 258 f.; K.-L. Schneider, *Klopstock und die Erneuerung der deutschen Dichtersprache im 18. Jahrhundert,* Heidelberg, 1960, p. 20 f., 87 f.
25. 'Not a female . . .': *Fr. Na.* XVIII (1761), 371; on *Abel* in English tr. see B. Q. Morgan, *A Critical Bibliography of German Literature in English translation . . .,* Stanford, [2]1938, p. 143 f.; Leemann-van Elck, p. 217 f.
26. Newcomb p. 1 (lines 5–7); I have used the copy in the David Nichol Smith Collection in the Australian National Library, see W. J. Cameron and D. J. Carroll (eds.), *Short Title Catalogue . . .,* Canberra, 1966, No. 8359.
27. For biographical details see the solid thesis by H. Küry, *Simon Grynaeus von Basel 1725–1799,* Riehen/Basle, 1935 (not mentioned by Bender, *Schiller-Jb.* 1967, p. 228), also M. Lutz, *Nekrolog denkwürdiger Schweizer . . .,* Aarau, 1812, p. 186 f. and 'Zum Andenken Simon Grynäus', *Rauracis* (1830), p. 3 f., and the reference works listed in Küry which have been consulted for this study.
28. cp. his letter to Bodmer, no. 3, p. 2 (July 1758); Lutz, *Rauracis* (1830), p. 24; Haak: see Barnett p. 168, 186; on Grynaeus' orthodoxy cp. P. Wernle, *Der schweizerische Protestantismus im XVIII Jahrhundert I,* Tübingen, 1922, p. 568; Küry's remark about a 'curious dualism' of Grynaeus' theological and literary interests (p. 46) is misleading.
29. *W.P.* Preface p. 5, 12; Ernst Gottlieb von Berge, author of the first published German translation of *PL* (1682) also planned a translation of *PR.* But I know of no German versions of *PR* or *SA* earlier than Grynaeus'.
30. *W.P.* (Preface) p. 13 f., 21 f.; letter to Bodmer no. 1, p. 1/2 (February 1752).
31. 'sehr undeutsch und pöbelhaft': Bodmer, letter to Zellweger 23 March 1752, cp. J. Baechtold, *Geschichte der deutschen Literatur in der Schweiz,* p. 544 f. and notes p. 173; Bender, *Schiller-Jb.* 1967, p. 229; Schneider p. 16.
32. Prejudices: *W.P.* Preface p. 5 f.; cp. e.g. B. Markwardt, *Geschichte der deutschen Poetik I,* Berlin, [2]1958, p. 328 f. (on J. B. Mencke, 1710) or Gottsched, *Beyträge zur Critischen Historie . . .,* Leipzig, 1732, I, 4, p. 89; Herder: see O. Hoffmann (ed.), *Briefe an Hamann,* Berlin, 1889, p. 70.
33. *W.P.* Preface p. 17; biographer: Lutz, *Rauracis* (1830), p. 18.
34. *W.P.* p. 201, cp. *Samson Agonistes,* 1745–1758.
35. *W.P.* p. 51, cp. *Paradise Regained* III, 134–148; Haak: see Barnett p. 172.
36. Haller: Hirzel p. 292; Lessing: K. Lachmann/Fr. Muncker (eds.), *Sämtliche Schriften VIII,* Stuttgart, 1892, p. 170; cp. Grynaeus: *Sarcotis . . .,* Basle, 1780, p. 3; on Christian heroism see M. Y. Hughes, 'The Christ of *PR*', *SP* XXXV (1938), 267.
37. Letters to Bodmer: in Zentralbibliothek Zürich, *MS. Bodmer 2, 18.* The kind assistance of the *Handschriftenabteilung* of the ZB, and of Dr. M. Steinmann (Universitätsbibliothek Basle) and Mrs. H. Tisch-Giede

is gratefully acknowledged. I am preparing an edition of the letters and of Grynaeus' tr. of *PL* I.

38. Lessing, 39. *Lit. brief*: see Lachmann-Muncker VIII esp. p. 80 f. (cp. 40 *Lit. brief,* ibid., p. 86). Metre and verse: refs. to relevant passages in Grynaeus' letters to Bodmer (with dates unless previously given): no. 2, p. 1 (17 December 1757), no. 4, p. 1 (26 September 1758), no. 5, p. 2/3 (12 November 1758), no. 6, p. 1/2 (in Küry p. 43, this letter is erroneously dated '8 September 1758'—actually 8 December 1758), no. 7, p. 1 (9 January 1759), no. 8, p. 3; no. 10, p. 3 (11 January 1760), no. 11, p. 2 (17 September 1763).
39. Letter no. 10, p. 2; cp. no. 2, p. 2; no. 5, p. 4; no. 9, p. 2 (4 July 1759); bilingual ed.: letter no. 3, p.1.
40. Bender, *Schiller-Jb.* 1967 p. 229; L. M. Price, *Die Aufnahme englischer Literatur in Deutschland 1500–1960,* Berne & Munich, 1961, p. 110 (Bodmer 'disapproved' of Grynaeus' plan) cannot be documented.
41. see e.g. letter no. 9 p. 2/3. Only the manuscript of Book I has been preserved: *MS Bodmer 39, 29,* Zentralbibliothek Zurich (marked in Bodmer's writing 'Author Simon Grynaeus 1758').
42. letter no. 5, p. 1. In the projected ed. of Grynaeus' tr., an attempt will be made to unravel the filiation, if any.
43. See note 5. Quotation from Grynaeus' tr.: p. 1/2=*PL* I, 17–26. Some of the parallels with Bodmer: 1732 ed.: prächtigen, aufrichtig, rein, unterrichte, ungemäßenen Abgrund, erleuchte, niedrig, Weege Gottes; 1742 ed.: gegenwärtig, fruchtbar, unterstütze, erhöhe, Hoheit meines Vorhabens, unter den Menschen zu retten; 1754 ed.: von Anfang; Zachariä: Rechte der . . . Vorsicht zu[be]schützen.

2

SCHILLER AND SHAKESPEARE—SOME POINTS OF CONTACT*

By W. F. Mainland

'Shakespeare!—Our young gentlemen of today assume an air as if they were on very familiar terms with him. I would fain see what a state they would be in were the ghost of Shakespeare to do them the honour of appearing before them in its full heroic stature. Few of them, I think, could bear the presence.' Students of German eighteenth-century literature are aware of the image of Shakespeare, divine, heroic, inaccessible, conjured up by German critics and poets in the 1770's. 'If there is one man who evokes the huge figure "seated upon a towering cliff, storms and the sea raging at his feet, but his head in the light of the heavens", that man is Shakespeare! Yet I must add that in the deepest depth beneath that rocky throne there are murmuring multitudes, elucidating, redeeming, exonerating, adoring and slandering, translating and reviling him—and not one of them does he hear!'

These two expressions of admiration mingled with rebuke are typical of two great German writers who were largely responsible for the early phases of the Shakespearean invasion of their country: C. M. Wieland, a scholar of infinite resource, fine sensibility, and generous understanding; J. G. Herder, some ten years younger, impassioned, ecstatic, audaciously inventive, still retaining something of the youthful rhapsodist committed to a stormy voyage of spiritual adventure. Four years before starting work upon the first full pattern of Shakespeare translation, which was to be eagerly read and then attacked by Herder's generation, Wieland had written: 'With all his faults, I love Shakespeare. . . . Where would you find more bold and true designs, more novel, beautiful, sublime, and trenchant thoughts, more lively, happy, inspired expression than in this poet of incomparable genius?' The warmth of these words is part of the impulse behind the

* English text from a lecture prepared for the Pädagogische Hochschule, Essen, 1964.

labours of four years of translation (1762–66). And they *were* labours! No wonder Wieland was astounded in retrospect by his own temerity: 'Now that this Herculean task is over, I would not undertake it again for all the gods on Parnassus!' He had become aware of the elusiveness of Shakespeare's genius and was irritated by the thought of 'those wretched greenhorns who behave as if they were used to playing blind man's buff' with the great poet.

Some thirty years after Wieland's translation was launched, a younger Swabian writer composed a distich, *Shakespeare's Schatten:* 'Then at length I beheld the exalted might of Hercules. But 'twas only his shadow I saw. He himself, alas! was no longer in sight.' Among those whose attempts to grasp the substance of Shakespeare Schiller was criticising, Wieland as translator did not escape. But about this time Schiller revealed in his essay on naïve and reflective poetry how the vast, impressive and admired spirit of Shakespeare had hindered his approach and evaded his comprehension. He did not attribute the fault to other exponents or translators. He was looking back to his earlier years, when, as he admitted, he was given to seek in a literary work some contact with the author, some reflection of a subjective and moral order, and because he had not found this in Shakespeare, he had been baffled and alienated. But by the mid 1790's his view and practice of the literary art had developed in him the aesthetic discipline which will not tolerate excess of either intellect or passion or of moral preoccupation.

In 1923 there appeared in Germany a dynamic book destined to be widely read and to become for a time a standard work on the subject of Shakespeare in Germany. 'More than any other poet Shakespeare is the incarnation of the creative principle of life itself.' These are the words with which the author, Friedrich Gundolf, introduced the plan of his work. It was meant to offer 'not a chronicle of literary facts, or a psychological analysis of authors, but an account of vital action and re-action'. There is some therapeutic value in taking up again a book which one read a long time ago. To some extent it can revive and correct the memory. It can show on the one hand how some notions have persisted and on the other it chastises the presumed stability of our judgments, compelling us to think of the change in ourselves as well as in circumstance. One outcome of this is that we no longer see the book as an immutable thing in its relation to ourselves, but as potential diversity of encounter and experience. Almost fifty years ago Gundolf, in the climate of thought at that time, could claim to jettison the psychological discussion of authors and yet continue to see in Schiller, as central force and directive of his thought and art, a disposition to morality. 'To the logical dialectic of Lessing,' he wrote, 'corresponds in Schiller the moral rhetoric ... The effect of Schiller's verse depends not upon the innate poetic power but upon the power of the great man whose strong moral inspiration stirs and sustains the language even when the language itself has no wings to carry it.' Here we may recognise a core of traditional, almost static opinion, the acceptance of which may still be demonstrated by listening to school children and students in Germany and England, and even to some colleagues of various ages in both countries. Critical revision of it would seem to call for more of the pragmatic approach by which Levin L. Schücking enlivened Shakespeare studies in Germany and also for a furtherance of the aesthetic and historical studies of Schiller stimulated by Benno von Wiese, above all perhaps for an intensification of interest in formal structure and the poetic impulse in the plays of Schiller to which Gerhard Storz has contributed work of great value (and latterly also H. B. Garland).

The five years which have brought the Schiller and the Shakespeare celebrations close together in the compact orbit of our thoughts, tempts conjecture as to possible joint references in academic and popular addresses in the Shakespeare year. From Weimar there may be mention of the struggle of both Shakespeare and Schiller against feudal organisation and of their contributions to what must be called 'realistisch-human'. In Bochum or elsewhere in the Federal Republic there may be discussion of 'tragische Grenzsituationen' and the 'Absurdität des Daseins' in Shakespeare; if so, one or both of these rubrics would invite discussion of Schiller's *Maria Stuart, Braut von Messina, Demetrius.* Whatever of this sort emerges, it can be of present value to us, if we have the strength to defend a relativistic view. There is a limit to such strength, reached when one expresses the fervent hope that nothing we hear may suggest the frenzied travesty of scholarship which, in the 1930's, promoted Wilhelm Tell to the status of 'Führer', and Schiller to that of Hitler's comrade-in-arms.

The mid twentieth century has defeated many hopes and has deflated belief in progress in matters of great common concern. There may be comfort as well as frustration in the thought that, in the west at all events, literary interpretation is not all set on the same track. There is great discomfort to be expected in all pursuit of scholarship, and it will not be evaded even by the highly precarious illusion of progress engendered in exhaustive organisation of the life and thought of a modern community. Any kind of master plan to control study of the humanities may be devised with an eye to the conjectured needs of the immediate future and by skilled publicity attract increasing numbers of students, who will then, in their eager preoccupations, be content to know nothing of the rich and healthily disturbing diversity which the whole range of the humanities, by its very nature, has to offer. Hitler's 'Gleichschaltung' (a sort of national grid in the supply of political, social, and educational needs) may re-emerge under a different form and entirely different auspices, product of a further act of myopic secular faith.

As yet, few will deny that in both Shakespeare and Schiller there are exalted features of thought and diction. But in years of celebration such things are apt to be submerged beneath much tendentious and committed exposition. In an attempt at redress the fond academic may for a time subdue his particular formal interest in drama as pattern, and have recourse to the other character within him, the ordinary reader, who, like any maker of block-calendars, searches for 'golden thoughts' appropriate to the season, thereby of course admitting that he is himself in his way committed. He may say that the season through which we are living, with its busy make-shift and frightening dominance of the casual, induces one to turn, in Schiller and in Shakespeare, to such passages as have chastening or consoling relevance. They share the fear of chaos and the inarticulate, they establish by their art a semblance of control, and so momentarily strengthen the reader's will. 'As soon as you will, at any moment, you may prove your will is free.' With the echo of Schiller's exhortation in his ear, the reader, the ordinary reader in all of us, will find himself taken to task when he hears the even more searching injunction: 'Fear not the confusion without, but rather the confusion within'. Eventually we are enabled to contemplate for a time with renewed tranquillity those things which, with stabbing insistence, harrow us in our everyday life. Among these is the varied pace of time and its diverse significance, about which William Witte has written with fine perception in his essay *Time in Macbeth and Wallenstein*. We may perhaps not laugh 'sans intermission' at the fool, deep-contemplative in the forest, but at least as interpreter Jaques helps us to accept the inevitable decay which follows maturity:

> And so, from hour to hour, we ripe and ripe,
> And then, from hour to hour, we rot and rot.

Then, still fearful of time's tyranny, we shall be a little reconciled because the poet, in the elaboration of a loving conceit, has offered us a formula in a phrase about Time:

> whose million'd accidents
> Creep in 'twixt vows, and change decrees of kings,
> Tan sacred beauty, blunt the sharp'st intents,
> Divert strong minds to the course of altering things.

Preoccupation with the notion of change becomes in some periods of history so insistent that the expression of it turns uncouth. Such a period is our own time, in which the voices of political optimists are so strident. Does anyone know whether Shakespeare was an optimist? I think Schiller was, and I believe he may have been stimulated by the nature of his physical disorder. But I do not think either of them put his trust in any kind of economic miracle or in salvation by technology. No doubt their minds were possessed by the thought of change, and they were probably both aware of the benefits and scourges of their time, but their inspiration came from a realm beyond the Treasury and the laboratory. When they express their thoughts on the theme of change, they find phrases of such resonance that we can, in wonder, forget for a time some of the tawdry tunes of our own decade. A few years ago a book appeared in Germany under the title *Schiller in the Atomic Age*. We may think of Shakespeare in that same harsh context, but then we recall the lines: 'the great globe itself, yea, all which it inherit shall dissolve, and like this insubstantial pageant faded, leave not a rack behind'. We may be startled into pensive silence from which will emerge gratitude, even perhaps to our own epoch, that this great dramatic poem, judged by Stendhal in 1824 'mediocre', can beguile us with an acceptable cadence of dissolution. Schiller, in whom many lively and supercilious critics have seen little but the mediocrity of a moralist, introduces phrases of deceptive simplicity which gain a deeper meaning when read in their context today. 'This England of today is not what it shall be hereafter, even as it is no longer the England of the past.' We might dismiss these words of Shrewsbury in *Maria Stuart* as trite and humdrum, until we think of the moment and circumstance of their utterance in the play. 'Such fair days this isle has never seen, since our own princes ruled its destiny,' Shrewsbury has said, but then comes his admonition: 'Let not such prosperity be bought at the price of reputation.' Schiller saw the reign of Elizabeth I, enclosing part of Shakespeare's life, as an age of anxious experiment, with its uncertain probings of policy into the unknown void of the future. From the reading of history (he was for a time professor of history in Jena), and from shrewd observation of report from across the Rhine, he recognised the nature of change in political affairs, and saw the inevitable conflict of demands upon a community obliged by a culmination of troubles to act swiftly and save itself. 'Time in its passing brings a change of law,' says young Melchthal in *Wilhelm Tell*, and Schiller, with admirable restraint, does not suggest that the speaker is aware of the potency of his words beyond the episode which prompted them.

Wilhelm Tell can be read seriously as a satire on political behaviour. It is a fascinating drama of history in the making, in which the majority of the characters are aware that they are providing material for later chroniclers who must be able to give an edifying account of their deeds. The inner plot consists of the vicissitudes in the life of a community stirred by alien rapacity to proclaim solidarity in self-help, self-instruction, and the realisation of the strength of tradition as guide into a new life. Some details of the pattern are familiar, whether we approach it from Schiller's other works or from Shakespeare. There is, most notably, the theme of the usurpation of power, prominent in Shakespeare, continuous and almost constant in Schiller's plays. Without presuming to assert an influence, I will point out what seems to be a parallel of some significance. When, at the midnight meeting of men of the Swiss cantons, their elected Speaker has made his plea for an appeal to the Emperor before they unsheath the sword ('for even though the cause be just, 'tis ever fearful to resort to force') the forthright Konrad Hunn presents his report: 'I was there, at the Imperial palace, to raise our plaint against the governors' tyranny and request the patent of our ancient freedom which every king upon succession has renewed. . . . And I, your envoy, was bidden seek the counsellors, who straight dismissed me with words of shallow comfort, saying: the Emperor hath no time to see you now; later he may chance to think of you.' In *Henry IV* Part 2, IV, i, the Archbishop of York answers the remonstrance of Westmorland:

> . . . And have the summary of all our griefs,
> When time shall serve, to show in articles;
> Which long ere this we offer'd to the King,
> And might by no suit gain our audience:
> When we are wrong'd and would unfold our griefs,
> We are denied access unto his person
> Even by those men who most have done us wrong
> . . . . and the example
> Of every minute's instance, present now,
> Hath put us in these ill-beseeming arms,
> Not to break peace or any branch of it,
> But to establish here a peace indeed,
> Concurring both in name and quality.

The self-justification of group-intent, the declaration that constitutional efforts have been made and have failed, the profession of unwillingness to take up arms, the insistence that the purpose of attack is to establish peace and good order—these items, common to the passages quoted, are a tediously familiar ploy in present-day skirmishing before open conflict is voted inevitable. The dominant voice among Schiller's men of the cantons is that of Stauffacher, a cunning and persuasive orator, deeply versed in the history of his people and able to draw from it, with effective choice and exaggeration, those illustrations of valour, rectitude, and worthy custom which convince his companions of the justice of their cause. Then, with rousing crescendo he proclaims: 'There is a limit to the tyrants' power. When the oppressed can find no justice anywhere, and when at length the burden has become too great to bear, he will arise and, fearless, snatch from the heights of Heaven his eternal rights which rest, firm and constant as the stars themselves.' Stauffacher has had to resolve his own fearful doubts; or rather it is his wife Gertrud who has inspired him with resolution and purpose by giving shape to those thoughts he has not dared to utter. 'But,' he says, 'hast thou considered well whither thy councils lead? For thou dost summon discord and the noise of weapons into this vale where peace has reigned.'

Mention is often made in Schiller commentaries of the resemblance between Brutus and Portia in *Julius Caesar* and Werner and Gertrud Stauffacher in Schiller's play. Shakespeare's influence here is commonly recognised, and it is fairly safe to assume it, as Schiller greatly admired the play on the Roman conspiracy and mentioned it in correspondence when he was at work on *Wilhelm Tell*. There is a more obscure, but still enticing pattern of resemblance in the first scene of *Henry IV* Part 2, where Northumberland's retainer Mortimer speaks of the Archbishop as of a man who 'with a double surety binds his followers. . . . That same word, rebellion, did divide/The action of their bodies from their souls;/And they did fight with queasiness, constrain'd . . . for their spirits and souls,/This word, rebellion, it had froze them up,/As fish are in a pond. But now the bishop/Turns insurrection to religion : /Supposed sincere and holy in his thoughts,/He's followed both with body and with mind,/And doth enlarge his rising with the blood/Of fair King Richard. . . ./ Derives from heaven his quarrel and his cause;/Tells them he doth bestride a bleeding land,/Gasping for life. . . .' This cool appraisal of the Archbishop's schemes and methods, together with Scroop's own scathing comment on the fickle populace (I, iii) reveals a temperament skilled in the art of persuasion and ready to play upon the emotions and susceptibilities of those who listen to him.

Only those who cling to the traditional belief that Stauffacher is a patriot of complete integrity will greet with incredulous surprise the suggestion that he has considerable affinity with Shakespeare's cynical prelate. Nevertheless the affinity becomes apparent when we see in both Archbishop Scroop and Stauffacher men of superior intellect who can manipulate past and present circumstance to prosper the restorative action on which they are resolved. 'We are not founding a new league,' says Stauffacher. 'We are renewing the old covenant of our fathers.' Scroop is arrested for capital treason. Stauffacher, who has denounced private action, saves the reputation of the cause by acclaiming Tell as hero of the hour. Yet Tell has committed one of the three murders which have done more to free the cantons from tyranny than their vaunted solidarity.

In the character of Wilhelm Tell we may see a more subtle and profound influence of Shakespeare than in any other area of the play. To trace this through Schiller's growing addiction to the political theme, we must look back for a moment to *Don Carlos,* where we find in the Infanta a man who, without appropriate disposition or training, becomes involved, beyond the domestic tragedy of the royal household, in a scheme of tragic policy. By Schiller's own admission, the 'soul of Hamlet' is an ingredient of his Spanish tragedy. There followed now years of recession into history, philosophy, and investigation into the poet's craft and mission, years enfolding the French Revolution and the Terror, a period in Schiller's life rich in dramatic plans which culminated by the end of the century in the vast historical trilogy of *Wallenstein,* nearest among all his works to the amplitude and mystery of Shakespeare. The significance of crisis, corporate and particular, becomes more persistent in the dramas from *Wallenstein* to *Demetrius,* which, as construction and even (the *Braut von Messina*) as abstraction of political history, present the tension between personal disposition and communal function. The reluctance of the individual in the midst of doubt and abruptly changing circumstance to accept responsibility, is seen in those three plays where women are dominant—*Maria Stuart, Jungfrau von Orleans, Braut von Messina*; but there is no relaxation of concern for this matter throughout *Tell.*

> And still your fingers on your lips, I pray.
> The time is out of joint : o cursed spite,
> That ever I was born to set it right!
>
> (*Hamlet,* II, v)

Many will be ready to admit that the Prince of Denmark has a German kinsman in Don Carlos, but a Swiss kinsman in Schiller's Tell?—Surely not! Tell is so obviously the man of quick resolve, adroit in action. In the peaceful business of ordinary life, in the natural hazards of his lonely occupation as a chamois-hunter, and in the emergencies of the storm on the lake he proves his reputation. But when the political landscape is menaced by the gathering portents of tyranny, Tell is by nature unready, lacking in council of any constructive kind, and unwilling even to observe the signs. Stauffacher, seeing the builders at work on the new prison, laments: 'Oh that I had never lived to see this sight!' Tell's response is evasive: 'It is not good to stay here. Let us go.' At heart Tell is the countryman, whose antipathy to urban life is as traditionally devised as the holiday humour of Jaques in *As You Like It*. The more serious side of Tell's aloof nature (which has not escaped notice by the jealous governor Gessler) is apparent to us in the lines spoken to Walter, even in the modified text which Schiller sent to Iffland for the Berlin production: 'The land is free and open as the heavens. But those who live there are shut in behind the walls of large villages, which they call towns, where no man can trust his neighbour.' Swiftly the idyllic epic of the hero, at home in the remoteness of the natural scene, is again interrupted; Tell is jolted into the drama of men's politics, and for him, the unpolitical man, this drama becomes a tragedy. The countryman's native intensity goads him to seek personal revenge which the well-meaning politicians have been enjoined to foreswear. He has to argue his way into the defence of his cause and into a justification of the deed he has planned. The monologue before the assassination of Gessler is the cruel rehearsal of an abused and tortured mind, a kind of frenzied war-dance of a man whose conscience is challenged to redress a monstrous injustice and, for this, to suppress a principle of reverent living which has been his by nature and unquestioned custom. He never recovers, and the dual symbol of his tragic defeat is his silence amidst the plaudits of the people and the abandonment of the cross-bow which has been his livelihood and his companion.

Tell is much more than an individual character in the play. He has representative function. He embodies the concern of all the men of the cantons for the family and its wish to continue, unmolested, in the peaceful conduct of its everyday life. In their eyes, and so in his, this belongs to the natural order of things, which has now been violently disrupted. Unrestricted by the contract which rules the others, he is drawn to those extremes of thought and action towards which in similar isolation they would doubtless be propelled by events and their own passions. Baumgarten, much more closely and subtly associated with Tell than is commonly admitted, has already given earnest of such response. And Stauffacher, in the speech quoted above (which challenged the censors of Schiller's day) prefigures the very circumstance of Tell's final encounter with the tyrant: 'Nature in primitive state returns, when man faces man, and all else failing, takes to the sword.' But in a much wider sense it is with Tell as one belonging to the natural order that Schiller is concerned. His care to establish this is reflected in the abundance of reference to the natural environment. None other of Schiller's plays comes nearer than *Wilhelm Tell* to Shakespeare in the representation of man's awareness of the moods of nature, just as none other shows so clearly the assimilation of Shakespeare's lesson in the significance of crowds. Neither the crowd scenes nor the Alpine landscape can be thought of as mere experiments in dramatic decoration. Both are essential to the theme. The lowing of cattle on the high pasture, the moaning of the glaciers, the shrill storm and the beating of the waves on the lake-shore are echoed in our minds even as we read. And when, as in Shakespeare (*Lear, Julius Caesar*), disorder comes into human affairs, this finds its own echo, by a grandiose poetic conceit, in spectacular turbulence of the elements.

The monstrous intrusion of an alien tyrant is for Tell a negation of the order of nature. In the torment of his unnatural scheming to end this iniquity, hearing of the calamitous landslide in Unterwalden, he exclaims: 'Do the very mountains then begin to quake, the earth itself no longer firm beneath our feet?' Just so in Hamlet's mind the metaphor of unwholesome excess in nature is present when he cries:

> Fie on't! ah fie! 'tis an unweeded garden,
> That grows to seed; things rank and gross in nature
> Possess it merely
>
> (I, ii)

Hamlet, in a time out of joint, believes he is ordained to set it right. Tell, having killed the tyrant, proclaims that he has avenged the sanctity of nature.

I believe that we can see in these two men, behind the elaborate superficial variations, a kinship which belongs to the *individual* of the modern age. Lacking political skill or orientation, yet caught in the meshes of political event, he sees with increasing vividness his own implication, and whether he fails or is acclaimed as a hero, his struggle for outer freedom is found to have disturbed the balance within. If such an interpretation is applied to Schiller's characters, Fiesco, Carlos, Max Piccolomini,

Johanna may be readily accepted; but it can be extended to others not commonly thought of together: Elisabeth in *Maria Stuart*, Isabeau in the *Jungfrau von Orleans*, Isabella in the *Braut von Messina*. Thinking of these in relation to Hamlet we recall that it is said of him that he is one who

> May not, as unvalued persons do,
> Carve for himself, for on his choice depends
> The safety and health of this whole state,
> And therefore must his choice be circumscribed
> Unto the voice and yielding of that body
> Whereof he is the head.

The intention of these words of Laertes is narrowly limited as a warning to Ophelia against the trifling of Hamlet's favour (I, iii). But the words carry us beyond this limitation to the whole communal responsibility which Hamlet is expected to bear. The characters in Schiller which have just been mentioned are all, in some degree or other, 'valued persons'. Each of them has responsibility, and, as in Hamlet, there is in all of them a cast of mind which sooner or later allows emotional preoccupations to cloud and bedevil their communal function. They reflect upon their past, their tasks in relation to their private feelings, and upon their performance of these tasks. Wilhelm Tell is also a 'valued person'. But whereas the others have exalted status, Tell is valued among his equals for his outstanding qualities as a man in the everyday matters and the emergencies which may claim the attention of all. He is, unlike the valued persons of the other plays, the common man, but his virtues are in no common measure: skill, courage, and an abundance of good will. Whereas the confederates of the Rütli are enjoined to be forbearing in their treatment of the tyrants, and are yet ready without any qualms to rejoice in the benefit of a merciless assassination in the royal household, Tell seasons justice with mercy at his brief encounter with Johannes Parricida. The sources of his show of clemency are by no means as clear as the moralising, legalistic, anti-dramatic interpretations still widely prevalent would have us believe. Schiller may have his Chorus (in the Braut von Messina) declaim a curtain-line: 'Of all evils the greatest is guilt', but his concern as a dramatic artist was not to pronounce judgment from outside, but to body forth within the drama the troubled state of man. For him man seems to have been

> . . . an unperfect actor on the stage,
> Who with his fear is put besides his part,
> Or some fierce thing replete with too much rage,
> Whose strength's abundance weakens his own heart.

Not only in the maddening distraction of love which the context of the sonnet presents, but also in the fitful obsessions of hate and the fevers of doubt Schiller's characters reveal the frailties of man, forced to pay heed to the secret debate within himself between circumstance and what he fondly cherishes as personality, and sometimes, like Elisabeth in *Maria Stuart* or Wilhelm Tell making compact with God and then usurping His place. To this mysterious bedlam, into which in moments of crisis men sometimes probe by occult ways to discover meaning and guidance Schiller was drawn as a sensitive yet austere observer—in *Wallenstein*, the *Braut von Messina*, the *Jungfrau von Orleans*. The perils of prophecy and hazards of adventure beyond the bourne of reason were attractive to him as to other contemporaries of 'Count' Cagliostro; but no matter what heritage of popular fantasy yielded metaphor for forces which play upon human feeling and flatter the human will, it was (as it had been when he composed case-histories as a student of medicine) to the arena of the struggle—man's single state of being, obliged in the torture of uncertainty to make irrevocable decisions that Schiller applied his analytical zeal and his constructive imagination as a tragic dramatist. His great monologues of crisis from *Fiesco* with its two opposing versions through *Wallenstein*, *Maria Stuart*, *Jungfrau*, to *Wilhelm Tell* have this in common: they all have their origin in that state where 'function is smothered in surmise, and nothing is but what is not'. It is not surprising that among the plays of Shakespeare which most stirred his enthusiasm—*Lear*, *Othello*, *Julius Caesar*—the one he chose to translate was *Macbeth*. This task had previously attracted a number of German poets: Wieland 1765, Eschenburg 1776, F. J. Fischer 1777, H. L. Wagner 1779, G. A. Bürger, whose translation finally appeared in 1784, although it appears that F. L. Schröder had been able to use Bürger's version of the Weird Sisters' scene for production in 1777. It is Schiller's transformation of the Weird Sisters that has attracted most of the unfavourable criticism upon his version. The attacks seem to have started in the Schlegel circle: August Wilhelm for example wrote the crabbed little pastiche:

> Macbeth ist aus den Fugen. Schmach und Scham,
> Daß ich zur Welt ihn einzurichten kam!

(changing Hamlet's last phrase into 'to set *him* right'). But it must not be forgotten that the name of Schlegel is of the greatest significance in the history of Shakespeare interpretation, including collaboration on the German version of his plays which is used to this day and held in high esteem. The acuteness of Schiller's specific problem in the matter of the witches can best be appreciated by detailed comparison with the earlier translations to which reference has just been made, but this is a task too complex and lengthy for us at this time to undertake. It is relevant to note what Schiller wrote (3 July 1800) in reply to criticism from his friend Körner: 'Your comment on those clear statements inserted in the first Witches' scene may well be justified, but they seemed to me necessary for the stage performance, since the mass of the public is so inattentive that one has to do a little thinking for them in advance.' This strikes a harsh note, but it is not the first time, or the last, that he reveals a measure of contempt for the intelligence of his audiences. What he had done was to introduce dialogue to point the motive of the Weird Sisters, partly by question and answer, concluding: 'If the good man stumbles and the just man falls, the powers of Hell rejoice.' Schiller was more easily confident and nearer accuracy in rendering such lines as those of Macbeth as he observes the feigned approach of Birnam wood. The 'equivocation of the fiend' becomes 'Doppelsinn des Teufels!' 'Doppelsinn' (equivocation or ambiguity) was so dominant in those anxious meditations which inspired all his mature plays.

It may well be that the translation of a play was not his most appropriate or successful recognition of the genius of Shakespeare as inspiration or even of the measure of affinity which they share. Both have the power to lead us through excess of apprehension and of pity to a reverential awe before the mysteries of our human state. And, in both Schiller and Shakespeare we hear, between the contests of dominant characters the words of minor figures which find resonance in our minds. Thus, when the fantastic astrologer Seni (*Wallenstein, Piccolomini*) is murmuring his occult mathematic—'Five is the soul of man. For inasmuch as man is compounded of good and of evil, five is the first digit which holds the even and the odd'—a servant mutters 'the old fool!' But his fellow-servant says 'Nay, let him speak. I like to listen, for many a thought is set a-going by his words.' And then, from very close at hand, it seems, the modest assurance of a poet comes to us through the words of the soothsayer in Shakespeare's *Antony and Cleopatra*:

> In Nature's infinite book of secrecy
> A little I have read.

3

GERMANY, GERMAN LITERATURE AND MID NINETEENTH-CENTURY BRITISH NOVELISTS

By L. H. C. Thomas

Oswald Wolff will be remembered as a pioneer in our times of Anglo-German cultural relations through the publication of translations from the German and dissemination of information about German literature in a series of stimulating books by several hands. Today a serious interest in German life and thought is the exception among English novelists. Almost invariably Germans and their way of life are only portrayed from a negative point of view. German literature of the eighteenth or nineteenth centuries is largely unknown to the English-speaking public and few references are to be found to it in modern English novels. In *At Lady Molly's* (1957) Anthony Powell refers to German literature as a modish but ephemeral interest of his character Mark Members:

> Now he tended to be associated with German literature. Kleist: Grillparzer: Stifter: those were names to be caught on the echoes of his conversation. Latterly, he was believed to be more taken up with Kierkegaard, then a writer not widely read in this country. Members, no fool, was always a little ahead of the fashion.

John Le Carré studied modern languages, including German, at Oxford and might be expected to evince a more informed interest. In *Call for the Dead* (1961) the agent hero Smiley is portrayed as having worked on 'the literary obscurities of seventeenth-century German literature': there is also mention of Goethe's *Faust* and 'metamorphoses of plants', Heinrich von Kleist, Herder, Stefan George and, of course, Brecht. In *A Murder of Quality* (1962) there is even a reference to Georg Büchner, while in *The Looking-Glass War* (1965) Smiley, reappearing briefly, learns from a young agent Avery that he too has studied German at Oxford:

'When you were reading German, did you touch on the seventeenth century by any chance?' Smiley inquired hopefully as Avery rose to go. 'Gryphius, Lohenstein; those people?' 'It was a special subject. I'm afraid I didn't.' '*Special*,' muttered Smiley. 'What a *silly* word. I suppose they mean extrinsic; it's a very impertinent notion.'

In this reference German literature appears as a harmless, if useless and eccentric study. The novelist swiftly reverts to the kind of image of Germany his readers are supposed to prefer in the recent success *A Small Town in Germany* (1968), the hostile tone of which is strongly reminiscent of that of thrillers written during the last war.

A century and more ago the attitude to Germany was very different among English novelists and it was not necessary to dig so deep for impressions of the German scene among them. Prominent English writers were better informed about German literature than is the case today. If the cultured Englishman of the eighteenth century had tended to acquire the polish of the French, his counterpart in the nineteenth, perhaps more sentimental in outlook, turned his interest to German-speaking countries. Up to that time there had been no serious political rivalry between Britain and the German states, nor had there been two wars of attrition, involving most of the national populations, conflicts in which each side had used propaganda against the other with an effect which survived the wars themselves for a quarter of a century.

There was a certain contempt for Germany as a disunited political area in which the inhabitants had been unable to form themselves into a proper nation like the British, happily united under Queen Victoria. German achievements in philosophy, education, medicine and other spheres involving efficient organisation, diligence and trustworthiness were recognised by the more understanding and fair-minded British, but many still adopted a condescending attitude towards German scholarship, even when it was admitted to be superior to what the British could offer. The usual excuse was that an Englishman (a general term used for the British) lacked the time or patience to apply himself to minute study of petty detail or speculation about the abstract. Germany was not felt to be a political threat, however, and thus the grudging admiration of some of the British was unmixed with hatred or fear. At the worst the German was regarded as a dull fellow with coarse manners. In nineteenth-century Britain the traditional villain was usually French or Italian in origin, Rigaud in Dickens's *Little Dorrit* (1857–58), Madame Rubelle and Count Fosco in Wilkie Collins's *Woman in White* (1859) or the sinister Madame de la Rougière in Le Fanu's *Uncle Silas* (1864).

In his valuable historical survey A. R. Hohfeld[1] has demonstrated that the number of references to German literature in British magazines reached its highest point in 1845, afterwards sinking until 1860, mainly because of the British reader's greater political interest in other countries such as France, Russia, India and the United States. From as far back as the 1790's there had been a reasonably sustained interest in German publications among the readers of British literary periodicals and, this solid preoccupation with German culture having once been achieved, it was maintained in its essential character, even though the literary worth of much German literature of the 1850's and 1860's was ignored or misunderstood. Queen Victoria's marriage to Prince Albert in 1840 must have stimulated interest in German life and culture for some further sections of the British community.

In a short study of this kind it is impossible and probably undesirable to be absolutely comprehensive even about a few selected authors, but at least some indication can be given of the level of interest in Germany as a cultural area which can be traced in the case of some of the more gifted novelists in mid nineteenth-century Britain. Nevertheless there must be some starting-point for the investigation. Leaving aside the claims of Wordsworth, Coleridge and many other pioneers in Anglo-German cultural relations the best is undoubtedly the work and personal example of Thomas Carlyle (1795–1881) who was led to a study of German literature by reading Madame de Stael's *De l'Allemagne* in 1817: within six months he was learning German, teaching himself with a grammar and dictionary and also taking lessons. By 1821 he was deep in the study of Schiller, Kant, Schelling and Fichte. In 1824 his translation of *Wilhelm Meisters Lehrjahre* appeared, a remarkable achievement for its time, coming from a man who had learnt German only as a book language. Carlyle was worried about how the work would be judged by English readers, both from the literary and the moral standpoint. His life of Schiller (1825) was well received and Goethe wrote a laudatory preface to the German translation. Carlyle wanted to visit Goethe but was too poor to do so; however, there was an exchange of letters, Goethe even providing a testimonial for Carlyle's application for a Chair at the University of St. Andrews which was unsuccessful. Goethe saw Carlyle as his interpreter and that of German literature in general. Up to 1831 Carlyle had written on 'German Romance', Jean Paul, Zacharias Werner, Novalis, the state of German literature, the *Nibelungenlied*, German literature of the fourteenth and fifteenth centuries, German dramatists and German poetry. In December 1829 he was writing enthusiastically to Goethe, whom he was never to meet personally, of the rapid spread of knowledge and appreciation of foreign and especially German literature in English-speaking places. On Goethe's birthday in 1831 fifteen people from Great Britain including Carlyle presented Goethe with a seal. This was designed by Janet Carlyle and bore the dedication 'To the German Master, from Friends in England'. In 1837 Carlyle gave a series of public lectures on German literature which he was never, however, to sell in print, for histories of German literature, then as now, sold badly. In his lectures he spoke of valour as the outstanding characteristic of the German, defining valour in this context as indomitable perseverance.

Carlyle took to the German language and German thought to such a degree that he frequently introduced German phrases and quotations, sometimes slightly incorrectly, into his letters and journal, e.g. 'Kraftmann' (for 'Kraftmensch'), 'Festen Muth's und frohen Sinn's', 'Das hole der Teufel', 'Gott hilf Ihnen' or 'Ich zittere nur, ich stottere nur, und kann es doch nicht lassen'. He popularised Goethe and Schiller as great literary figures, even drawing a distinction between them. For him Goethe was comparable with Shakespeare, catholic in outlook, tolerant, peaceful, collected; Schiller was more like Milton, sectarian, earnest, devoted, intense, at war with one half of things, in love with the other half. Carlyle regarded Goethe's work as important because it belonged to the modern world and because Goethe was a positive writer intent on building rather than destroying, not only witty but also wise, a teacher with a reverence for the significant. An early essay (published in the *New Edinburgh Review* in 1822) had been devoted to Goethe's *Faust*. Carlyle was a sympathetic interpreter of most of the German writers he studied except Heine and probably gained most inspiration from his reading of Novalis. He did not visit Germany until 1858, when he toured the battlefields of Frederick the Great as preparation for his historical study of the Prussian king, which appeared from 1858 to 1865. The real Germany did not live up to his ideals, as his bitter complaints about the beds, the noise in the hotels and the food testify.

Few of the important novelists considered below have such a well-informed and deep-rooted interest in German culture as Carlyle. Charles Dickens (1812–70) was undoubtedly the most widely read and known English novelist of the mid nineteenth-century. His works were read both in the original and in translation in Germany soon after they first appeared. In 1838 Dickens wrote to Dr. Heinrich Kuenzel of Darmstadt offering his support for a new Anglo-German periodical *Britannica* which was to be published in Germany. After expressing his admiration for the Germans and referring to them as 'with their great intellectual gifts and culture . . . the chosen people of the earth' he waxes even more enthusiastic:

> I was never prouder and happier than when I first learnt that my writings had been favourably received by [the Germans]. I can be indifferent to nothing that links English literature with Germany . . . I wish to Heaven I could speak German, however badly. If I could, I should be with you in six months.[2]

We cannot believe that Dickens lacked the energy to learn German: it must have been a question of priorities. References to Germany, its literature or way of life scarcely play any role in his novels, which are mainly concentrated on the English scene. We do not know whether he ever learnt any German. In his library at his death[3] there were presentations copies, both of translations of his own novels into German sent him by publishing firms, and of English versions of works by Goethe, Schiller, Freytag and Lessing's *Laokoon*, also a translated collection *German Novelists* (1822), containing popular stories and legends, Schiller's *Verbrecher aus verlorener Ehre, Der Geisterseher* and other prose pieces, Tieck's *Der blonde Eckbert, Der getreue Eckart* and other tales, stories by Langbein, Engel, Fouqué and others, four volumes in all. Dickens also had two guides to Switzerland, both in English, and Flügel's English-German and German-English dictionary.[4] Only the dictionary suggests that he tried to learn German and there is no direct evidence that his reading of German literature influenced his own writing. In the summer of 1846, when he took his family on a holiday to the Rhineland which included visits to Coblenz, Mannheim and Mainz, many Germans read of this with interest and tried to get a sight of him, for he was a literary celebrity.

Charles Lever (1806–72), an Anglo-Irish novelist from Dublin, had a less tenuous link with Germany. In his youth he had known J. J. Anster, the first translator of Goethe's *Faust* and Professor of Laws at Trinity College, Dublin, where Lever was a student. In 1828 he went to Göttingen to study medicine, publishing an account of his experiences in 1830.[5] He visited Heidelberg and Vienna, later staying for a period in Weimar where he met Goethe. Then he travelled homewards via Bavaria and Strasbourg. Lever later told a friend that he had quite literally walked through Germany, exploring wherever possible and selling a German *Lied* he had translated. Scenes in the novels *Harry Lorrequer* (1840) reflect his impressions of Bavaria. On returning to Dublin he established there in 1830 a *Burschenschaft* devoted to things German on the German pattern except that the contests were with the brain instead of the sword. The members sang 'Ein freies Leben' from *Die Räuber*, in some ways the German work which makes the greatest impact among writers in the British Isles. In the spring of 1854 Lever made another trip to Germany, staying in Bonn, Coblenz, St. Goar and Baden-Baden where he lost money gambling but found copy for his story *Roland Cashel* (1850). He particularly enjoyed visiting Wiesbaden and Karlsruhe and wrote about his experiences in magazine articles.[6] His special friend was the secretary to the Russian embassy Otto von Kotzebue. Passing on to Bregenz he rented a castle in the Alps and spent the Christmas of 1846 there. Here he began writing *The Knight of Gwynne* (1847) and stayed on into the summer of the following year, making excursions into Switzerland and planning a series of stories about the Tyrol which never appeared.

When Lever used German words or phrases in *Harry Lorrequer* he made many mistakes. His friend Dwyer declared:

> Lever was never very accurate in foreign tongues, all his sympathies were at first in favour of Germany and its language and I remember perfectly him saying to me in 1830 that although an Englishman may reasonably hope to become a tolerably perfect German scholar he can never become a really good French one.[7]

According to his biographer Fitzpatrick his defective knowledge of German strong verbs caused embarrassment on at least one occasion.[8]

One of Lever's most ambitious attempts at novel-writing is *The Daltons* (1852). This complicated story extends to some six hundred pages and is mainly staged on the continent with a good opening section on Baden-Baden out of season. The tale begins in the 1820's and includes a revolution in Italy. The main characters are English-speaking, the Daltons being a dispossessed Irish family. A fair amount of German is introduced in conversation, often unidiomatic German: for example, 'Gerichtsruf' as a literal translation for a legal summons. Songs appear both in the original German and in English renderings. The principal German character, the loveable toymaker Hänserl Roeckle, epitomises an attitude to the Germans probably influenced by the spread of the German fairy-tale.

William Makepeace Thackeray (1811–63) is a fairly profitable subject for this investigation, despite the conclusion by Heinrich Frisa[9] that he is no pioneer in this field and that his work scarcely shows the influence of German literature. At least Thackeray had at his disposal a knowledge of Germany, its language and literature which enabled him to avoid the worse pitfalls of ignorance in references to things German. His letters and private papers[10] are a useful source of information. He developed a hearty dislike of the Prussians and was at one stage plagued through the well-meaning help of a German lady with 'governidges calling at all hours with High Dutch accents and reams of testimonials'. Yet these small annoyances did not create an all-embracing prejudice. After finishing his studies at Cambridge he took a brief series of German lessons in London from a Herr Troppeneger before embarking on a longish stay in Germany (from July 1830 to March 1831). Beginning with a month at Bad Godesberg, where he seems to have devoted nearly all his waking hours to improving his German and where he bought, perhaps even read, Schiller's collected works in German, Thackeray moved on to Dresden before settling at the end of August for a prolonged stay in Weimar. He met Goethe in October 1830 and claimed to have seen him three times. There is no mention of Thackeray in Goethe's diaries. A necessary but not entirely reliable source for Thackeray's contact with Goethe and Weimar is the letter Thackeray wrote to George Henry Lewes to help Lewes with his biography of Goethe in 1855.[11] In November 1830 Thackeray was writing to a correspondent: 'I am disappointed in German. I begin now to comprehend it a little, and must say that I have met with nothing which comes up to my expectation of the language. I have read Faust with which of course I was delighted but not to that degree I expected.' On 3 December he records: 'I have read a good deal of Goethe and Schiller, the latter is by far the favourite here—Goethe is by practice and profession a libertine, Schiller was on the contrary a man whose religion and morals were unexceptionable.' Thackeray's acquaintance with Goethe was largely brought about through the great man's daughter-in-law, Ottilie von Goethe, who held a literary salon and was attracted to young Englishmen. As time passed Thackeray grew ever more enthusiastic about Schiller's qualities in contrast to Goethe's and in February 1831 he wrote:

> I have been reading Shakespeare in German [probably the Schlegel-Tieck translation], if I could ever do the same for Schiller in English I should be proud to have conferred a benefit on my country—Goethe is a noble poet, and as interesting an old man to speak to and look upon as I ever saw, but alas that I must say it—I believe he is little better than an old rogue—It was a character which I was very unwilling to give him, but it is the strict and uncomfortable truth—one would have thought that genius so extraordinary as his would have been exempt from the little mean money-getting propensities to which it appears he is addicted.

The living Goethe cannot measure up to the ideal of the dead Schiller.

By December 1830 Thackeray is expressing a fondness for Weimar. He can now understand German 'pretty well', has translated poems by Theodor Körner and Goethe and a play by Kotzebue. He also plans to translate a short history of Germany, *Kompendium der deutschen Reichsgeschichte*, 'which will instruct me both in history and in German'. In the new year he makes the acquaintance of the famous actor Ludwig Devrient whom he sees playing Franz Moor at a performance of *Die Räuber* in Erfurt. Thackeray found the play 'a little too patriotic and free for our own court theatre' but he was greatly impressed by Devrient's performance, having 'never seen anything so terrible', particularly in Franz's prayer when the castle is attacked 'which has the most awful effect that can well be fancied—I am no common murderer mein Herr Gott etc'. Thackeray was a gifted amateur artist and made an attempt to sketch Devrient in this role and also as Shylock. By February he is thinking of returning to Germany for another stay and preparing a sketch book of the German scene for publication: 'the People of Germany are not known in England, and the more I learn of them the more interesting they appear to me'. The enthusiasm for Schiller continues with a translation of Thekla's song in *Die Piccolomini* and the delightful if naïve comment 'Talking of Schiller—I am in possession of his handwriting and his veritable court-sword and I do believe him to be after Shakespeare The Poet'. A love affair during the stay in Weimar is probably reflected in the Miss Löwe episode of the *Fitzboodle Papers* (preface dated May 1842). This is staged in a Germany presented in a humorous light and is possibly to be interpreted as the kind of sketch which Thackeray had in mind for his German sketch-book—if this was to consist of literary pen-sketches as well as drawings. The heroine of 'Ottilia' in the *Fitzboodle Papers* is said to be modelled on Jenny von Pappenheim to whom Thackeray was attracted during his stay in Germany.[12]

Thackeray returned to Germany for a short visit in 1851, but in the meantime he had extended his knowledge of its literature, mainly in English translation, as his diary for July 1832 testifies:

> Today was occupied in reading Wilhelm Meister [probably Carlyle's translation, published 1824] and a wretched performance I thought it—without principle and certainly without interest—at least the last volume—neither delicacy, morality or philosophy as I thought. . . . It is a mean book I think and have done with it—can a man with impure views of human nature be a philosopher?

Clearly Thackeray is arguing against the book on moral rather than aesthetic grounds. With regard to the German Romantics Thackeray had been interested in A. W. v. Schlegel's 'Die Kunstlehre', the first part of the *Vorlesungen über schöne Literatur und Kunst* (1801–5) which he had tried to read, probably with very little German, as early as September 1830, and he had not pursued a plan to translate it, though he was still persevering with the author in October 1832 ('I am going to compose myself to sleep over a German book of Schlegel's which I find excellent to that purpose'). Likewise in 1831 he is intending to read Fouqué's 'Undinchen for an hour'. In his diary for July 1832 he has moved to further Romantics whom he is reading in Carlyle's *German Romance* (1827):

> Have been delighted with the goodness and humour of Jean Paul and much disappointed in an old favourite Hoffmann—the extravagance of fancy which I used to admire so much now appears to me neither agreeable nor extraordinary. The chief recommendation of the story I read (the Golden Pot translated by Carlyle) was the humour, which for a German is very great—not so good however as Jean Paul's which is very Rabelaisian—Read Tieck's Trusty Eckhart. It is a very fine subject but might be made more of—The wandering minstrel from the Venus hill is very fine I think and would be a good character for a play made very wild but not ludicrous, à la Hoffmann.

In the same year Thackeray records that he read 'a Canto or 2 of Wieland's *Oberon*'. A many-volumed collected edition of Wieland was found among a number of books in German in Thackeray's library at his death.[13] These included a collected edition of Schiller, almost certainly the one Thackeray bought in 1830, *Des Knaben Wunderhorn* (2 vols., 1819), Wolfgang Menzel's *Geschichte der Deutschen* (1837) and Eduard Vehse's gossipy *Geschichte der Höfe des Hauses Braunschweig in Deutschland und England* (Hamburg, 1853). Other books of German interest included guide-books, dictionaries, a German conversation grammar, a German cookery book, Goethe's poems and ballads in translation, *Luther's Tabletalk* translated by Hazlitt and Ludwig Bernstein's *Selections from the best German authors* (London, 1851). The text of the latter was in German with English notes; it comprised many short items in prose and poetry, mainly didactic in tone.[14] Thackeray also reviewed two German works in translation, Leopold Ranke's *History of the Popes* in 1840 which he read 'with much pleasure' and Willibald Alexis's *Burgomaster of Berlin* (London, 1843) in 1844. In his review of the latter, a historical novel, he found style, print and German names difficult but finally described it as 'a most curious and careful picture of German life' in which the reader was carried into 'quite a new country'. When David Masson published a comparative study of *Pendennis* and *David Copperfield* in 1851 he quoted Goethe's view that 'Art is called Art precisely because it is *not* Nature'.[15] Thackeray disagreed with this quoted maxim, 'holding that the Art of Novels *is* to represent Nature: to convey as strongly as possible the sentiment of reality'.[16]

Goethe's *Werther* must have been known to Thackeray in some form. A friend describes him in the United States before one of his public lectures in 1852, unshaven and unprepared but 'rapturously absorbed in making a pen-and-ink drawing to illustrate a passage in Goethe's Sorrows of Werther for a lady'.[17] The story of Werther was, of course, a fashionable subject for representation in various forms of art and in 1853 Thackeray published his amusing poem 'Sorrows of Werther' which ends:

Charlotte, having seen his body
Borne before her on a shutter
Like a well-conducted person,
Went on cutting bread and butter.

When objection was raised to this last line as a 'falsification' Thackeray replied in a style very typical of his cynicism:

> What is there in Goethe's text to show that after young Werther's suicide Charlotte did *not* continue to cut bread and butter? 'They feared for Lotty's life' I take to mean that she was at one time much affected by Werther's demise, but that she survived the circumstance: in which case as a good housewife, she would certainly resume those operations in which she was so charmingly employed when Werther first beheld her—Otherwise I should probably have written Charlotte *'left off cutting bread and butter'*—a fine line too, but not so pathetic, I still humbly think . . .[18]

Thackeray often refers to Goethe's 'Zueignung' in *Faust*: in 1853 he writes in a letter 'my bussom fühlt sich jugendlich erschüttert', while in 1857 he quotes it with reference to *A Shabby Genteel Story* designed seventeen years before. For Thackeray 'the memory of the past is renewed as he looks at it—die Bilder froher Tage,/Und manche lieben Schatten steigen auf'.[19] In a letter he declares that these lines are 'about the prettiest of Goethe's, and utter sweetly and naturally a selfish, honest feeling of grief'.[20] Lewis Melville suggests in his biography that the lines express Thackeray's distress at re-reading his own works which reminds him of friends long dead.[21]

Not only minor works like the humorous sketch *The Kickleburys on the Rhine* (1850) reflect an experience of German life and literature. In the major novels too there are references to German literature which most of today's readers would not understand, for example in *Vanity Fair* (1847–8) to the *Vehmgericht* or to the song rendered by Emmy 'Einsam bin ich nicht allein—a tender love-song of Weber's', offered without a translation. Similarly in the same novel the student Fritz is made to declare that 'saufen and singen do not go together', there is mention of 'Herr Graf Lord Sedley nebst Begleitung aus England' and the song from *Fidelio* 'Nichts, nichts, mein Florestan', while Dobbin's old cloak, we are told, 'had manchen Sturm erlebt, as a favourite song of those days said'.[22] The author also indicates ironically that the disgraced Becky Sharp can be received in high society in the small German state where part of the action of *Vanity Fair* takes place: it is implied that 'a country where Werther is still read and the Wahlverwandtschaften of Goethe is considered an edifying moral book' has a laxer moral standard than England: the allusion would be missed by most present-day readers who would not understand the reference to Goethe's novels. It is possible that the introduction to the novel 'Before the Curtain' was partly inspired by ideas in Goethe's *Vorspiel auf dem Theater* in *Faust*.

In *Pendennis* the actress Emily Costigan with whom the hero falls in love has never heard of Kotzebue who is the author of the play in which she is acting. Pen's novel, *Leaves from the Life-book of Walter Lorraine*, 'was of a very fierce, gloomy, and passionate sort—the Byronic despair, the Wertherian despondency, the mocking bitterness of Mephistopheles, of Faust, were all reproduced and developed in the character of the hero; for our youth had just been learning the German language, and imitated, as almost all clever lads do, his favourite poets and writers'. Pen, like the young Thackeray, is fond of translating the 'sentimental ballads' of Goethe and Schiller.

Of all Thackeray's novels *Pendennis* is closest to the *Bildungsroman* and there are some parallels with *Wilhelm Meisters Lehrjahre*. The actress Emily has a similar position to Marianne, both being encouraged by an older person to favour a promising young admirer. Blanche resembles Philine and shares with her a desire to please. Pen ends his 'Lehrjahre' in marriage to Laura, as Wilhelm does in his alliance with Natalie. *The Newcomes* (1853–55) has a young hero Clive Newcome who understands German, also a reference to the popular novels *Abällino* (1794) by Zschokke and *Rinaldo Rinaldini* (1797) by Vulpius.

Charlotte Brontë (1816–55) learnt German in Brussels in

the 1840's[23] and even wrote a letter in German to a friend: this is dated 5 June 1843 and though containing some anglicisms reflects considerable fluency. In *Jane Eyre* (1847) there is indication of the author's acquaintance with the German text of *Die Räuber*. The fugitive heroine overhears two young women trying to read a passage from the play. The line 'Da trat hervor Einer wie die Sternen Nacht' is quoted with enthusiasm: equal relish is displayed for the phrase 'Ich wäge die Gedanken in der Schale meines Zornes und die Werke mit dem Gewichte meines Grimms'. These lines are taken from the scene in Act V scene 1 in which Franz is telling old Daniel about a terrible dream, as one of the students explains. From the conversation the reader discovers that they cannot speak German, though they read lines to one another, but are learning laboriously 'this crabbed but glorious Deutsch', as one student calls it, with the aid of a dictionary. Jane the heroine did not understand German at the time but was later to know 'the language and the book', hence her ability to quote the original German in her account. In *Villette* (1853) the heroine also studies German.

Mrs. Gaskell (1810–65) made a tour of the Rhineland in the summer of 1841 and visited Heidelberg in the autumn of 1858 with her daughters. A further trip to Germany was taken in 1860. Comments in her letters[24] show her as generally sympathetic to the German scene, though she did not enjoy the food. There is one reference to Goethe but none to contemporary German writers. She had a number of useful contacts through the Bunsen family and Catherine Winkworth, the translator of German hymns. In several of her novels there are German allusions. At one stage the heroine of *Mary Barton* (1847) is revived from a faint by spirit smuggled out of Hamburg by the old seaman Sturgis: this is called 'Golden Wasser' and is presumably identifiable as *Danziger Goldwasser*. The novelist uses chapter mottoes, some of them English translations from German writers, for example, Gretchen's spinning-song from *Faust* ('My rest is gone, my heart is sore/Peace find I never, and never more') or the poem by Rückert beginning 'Like a bark upon the sea/Life is floating over death'.[25] In *Cranford* (1851–53) old Mr. Holbrook, who likes to quote from the poets, pronounced the name of Goethe strictly in accordance with the English sound of the letters—'As Goethe says, "Ye ever-verdant palaces," etc.'.

North and South (1855), like the other novels of Mrs. Gaskell, has no direct connection with the German scene yet here again the mottoes sometimes derive from literature in translation, from *Wallenstein,* Kosegarten, one of whose works was parodied by Keller in *Sieben Legenden,* Zacharias Werner, Rückert and Uhland. A German proverb also appears in English guise: 'There's nought so finely spun/But it cometh to the sun' which in the German version is a *leitmotiv* in Friedrich Halm's *Die Marzipanliese* (1856) and is quoted in Ludwig's *Die Heiterethei* (1855) and Fontane's *Unterm Birnbaum* (1884–85).

Genuine involvement with German culture is most clearly seen in the case of George Eliot (1819–81) who became interested in Germany at an early age and began to study German in 1840. As a result she was able to translate David Friedrich Strauss's *Das Leben Jesu* and Ludwig Feuerbach's *Das Wesen des Christentums*, the English versions appearing in 1846 and 1854 respectively. Interest in German writing was reinforced by her spiritual and intellectual 'marriage' to George Henry Lewes who published his life of Goethe in 1855 after ten years' work. Her essays[26] include 'Three Months in Weimar' which covers the period from August to November in 1854 which she spent there. Her impressions are conveyed graphically with attention to statues and buildings, clothes and food, quotations from *Heinrich von Ofterdingen* and *Dichtung und Wahrheit.* Another article 'Liszt, Wagner and Weimar' is mainly concerned with Wagner's operas and ends with a quotation from Goethe's 'Über allen Gipfeln . . .'. 'The Morality of Wilhelm Meister' is written under the stimulus of reading and discussing Goethe's work with Lewes (in November 1854 they read aloud to one another from *Wilhelm Meisters Lehrjahre*). She declares that most educated people would reject the novel as immoral and dull, but she prefers to defend it. Whereas the incidents portrayed may shock the English reader, 'Goethe's mode of treatment seems to us precisely that which is really moral in its influence'. Although she judges Goethe's success or failure partly on moral grounds, she is less dogmatic about moral principle than Thackeray and does make a distinction between the events depicted and the author's treatment of them. A long, detailed study of 'German wit: H. Heine' is further evidence of her position as what Pinney calls 'one of the leading sponsors of German thought and art in nineteenth-century England'. 'Translations and Translators' reflects her concern for accurate literate standards of translation from

German. 'The Future of German Philosophy' is mainly devoted to a work by Friedrich Otto Gruppe and, like many of her other articles, is basically a literary review. 'The Natural History of German Life' is based on a survey of works by W. H. Riehl (1823–97), a popular writer of historical tales and a contemporary of George Eliot. George Eliot is the only writer among those considered who is closely in touch with German publications of her own day. In 1858 she read Ludwig's *Zwischen Himmel und Erde* with Lewes at a time when she was writing *Adam Bede*.[27]

'A word to the Germans' appeared in 1865. George Eliot dislikes calling the German a 'cloudy metaphysician' but continues:

> It is true the German rarely writes well, rarely arranges his matter well, or manages it with economy and therefore seldom produces a good book in the fullest sense of the word. . . . Nevertheless the proportionate badness in German books is much exaggerated . . . there are more books in German of which the matter is valuable, and the style bad, than in any other tongue. Our own literature does not positively swarm with good writers. . . . In fact, if anyone in the present day can be called cultivated who dispenses with a knowledge of German, it is because the two other greatest literatures of the world are now impregnated with the results of German labour and German genius.

Charles Kingsley (1819–75) was persuaded by his parents to holiday in Germany in 1851. In August he wrote to his wife from Bad Ems giving first impressions of the Rhine. Later he made a walking tour in the Eifel and visited Renderscheid, Geroldstein, Birreborn, Treves and Bonn. He was a friend of Professor Max Müller, son of 'Griechenmüller' and Oxford professor in German, and attended Müller's wedding to his niece in 1859. In 1854 he provided a preface to Catherine Winkworth's *Deutsche Theologie* and in 1866 wrote to Müller praising the Prussians for fighting the Austrians; at this time, as he remarks, he is reading much German, apparently history.

Kingsley's *Alton Locke* (1850) is half novel, half socio-political tract. Written as an autobiography, it is the story of a poor tailor's apprentice who has the chance through a wealthy cousin to see something of undergraduate life in Cambridge. His friends include the Chartist Crossthwaite and the bookseller Mackaye. In the midst of much reflection and discussion of political and social problems there are references to German literature. Apart from allusions to the work of David Friedrich Strauss and the angels bearing Faust up to Heaven in Goethe's *Faust II*, we are told that the Dean's library in Cambridge includes Goethe's *Wahlverwandtschaften*. The Dean declares:

> I never read a word of Goethe's verse, but I am convinced that he must be the great poet of the day, just because he is the only one who has taken the trouble to go into details of practical science.

Elsewhere he reflects:

> I have felt deeply, and you will feel some day, the truth of Jarno's saying in *Wilhelm Meister,* when he was wandering alone in the Alps with his geological hammer, 'These rocks, at least, tell me no lies, as men do'.

In the chapter 'The Plush Breeches Tragedy' we find a parallel with a situation in Alexis's historical novel *Die Hosen des Herrn von Bredow* (1846): plush breeches worn by the hero for his lectures are associated with the cause and pretensions of the aristocrat. The hero is sent a pair anonymously by an ill-wisher and Crossthwaite puts at his disposal for lecturing garb a plain pair of black trousers.

Yeast. A Problem (1852) has no proper plot but a fair number of German references, many of them inaccurate or vague, for example, to 'Boehmen' (Jakob Boehme). On one occasion a character quotes Schiller and is told to beware of the Germans, 'for they are all pantheists at heart'. There is reference to 'talk of ours over Falk von Müller's *Recollections of Goethe* and how you materialists are often the most fantastic of theorists'. On two occasions sayings by 'the German sage' (unnamed) are quoted: 'Poor human nature! Always looking back to some fancied golden age' and 'The destiny of any nation, at any given moment, depends on the opinions of the young men under five-and-twenty'.

The 'Victorian Best-Seller' Charlotte Yonge (1825–1901)[28] is certainly worth considering briefly in our survey. She became so well known through her works in Germany as to become a legend and one English visitor was told in Ulm Cathedral that Charlotte had married a German officer. *Heartsease* (1854) is full of German phrases; Theodora is 'ein hoch beseeltes Mädchen' who inspires St. Erme's 'Heldensängergeist' and his idea of a proposal is through the medium of romantic German verse. The diary of Helen Fotheringham is called 'Bekenntnisse einer schönen

Seele'. Charlotte Yonge's famous 'Gothic' novel *The Heir of Redclyffe* (1853) shows the influence of Fouqué's *Sintram*. The hero Guy sees in Sintram a man pursued by a like fate and he works out his salvation in a way which parallels Sintram's expiation. The remarkable popularity of this very romantic and idealistic novel reveals the taste of the public of the 1850's. Elderly professors cried over it and army officers regarded a copy as part of their essential equipment. However, we must agree with the view that Charlotte 'had been caught up in the backwash of German medievalism after its greatest vogue was passed'.[29]

Since we have been mainly concerned with English writers active in the 1850's and works of that period or earlier, it would go beyond our terms of reference to include either John Ruskin (1819–1900) or George Meredith (1825–1909), though this would not produce negative results, particularly in the case of George Meredith who went to a Moravian school at Neuwied on the Rhine.

Some of the preoccupation with German culture recorded indicates blind uncritical devotion to the Romantic ideal, some reflects only superficial understanding of German life and thought. In the example of George Eliot, however, we find a better informed and more positively critical approach than is generally encountered among English novelists today.

NOTES

1. A. R. Hohlfeld, *German Literature in British Magazines 1750–1860*, University of Wisconsin Press, Madison, 1949, p. 66.
2. See W. Dexter (ed.), *The Nonesuch Dickens Letters*, London, 1938, I, pp. 168–9 and Frank A. Gibson, 'Dickens in Germany', *The Dickensian*, XLIII (1947), pp. 69–75.
3. J. H. Stonehouse (ed.), *Catalogue of the library of Charles Dickens . . . and of W. M. Thackeray*, London, 1935. Further details:
   (*a*) 5-volume translation of Goethe's works by John Oxenford (1867), containing *Dichtung und Wahrheit, Faust, Iphigenie, Tasso, Egmont, Wilhelm Meisters Lehrajahre* and other prose works;
   (*b*) *Schiller's Early Dramas and Romances*, translated by Henry G. Bohn (1849) and containing *Die Räuber, Fiesko, Kabale und Liebe* and *Demetrius*;
   (*c*) Translation of Freytag's *Bilder aus der deutschen Vergangenheit* by Mrs. Malcolm (1862–63);
   (*d*) English versions of Lessing's *Laokoon* (1836) and Murner's *Eulenspiegel* (1837).
4. Third edition, Leipzig, 1856.
5. See Lever's 'Logbook of a Rambler', *Dublin Literary Gazette*, 16 January 1830 (written 1829).
6. See W. J. Fitzpatrick, *The Life of Charles Lever*, London, 1896, the most useful source for Lever's contacts with Germany.

7. Quoted by Fitzpatrick, op. cit., p. 42.
8. Ibid., p. 47. 'On one occasion Lever [in Germany] was explaining what happened to victims of the agrarian law [in Ireland] and, using the verb totschießen, forgot to change the vowel in the past participle, to the astonishment and confusion of the ladies.'
9. *Deutsche Kulturverhältnisse in der Auffassung W. M. Thackerays,* Vienna and Leipzig, 1908, p. 77.
10. *Letters and Private Papers of W. M. Thackeray*, collected and edited by Gordon N. Ray, 4 vols., London, 1945–46, the main source on which I have drawn below, apart from the collected works.
11. Ibid., iii, 442–5, also a sketch in the collected works, entitled 'Goethe in his old age'.
12. See Lili Braun, *Im Schatten der Titanen,* Stuttgart, 1910, p. 115.
13. See book mentioned in note 3 above.
14. Poets and authors include Klopstock, Rückert, Goethe, Gessner, Jean Paul, Hoffmann, Uhland, Schiller, Wieland, Herder, Haller, Gellert, Hebel, Hölty, Börne, Bürger, Körner, Tieck, Chamisso, etc. 312 pp. in 1842 edition.
15. David Masson 'Pendennis and Copperfield, Thackeray and Dickens', *North British Review*, May (1851), pp. 57–89.
16. *Letters and Private Papers of Thackeray*, op. cit., ii, 772.
17. J. T. Fields in *Yesterday with Authors*, London, 1872, p. 23.
18. *Letters and Private Papers of Thackeray*, op. cit., iii, 412.
19. In preface to vol. 4 of Thackeray's *Miscellanies,* dated 10 April 1857.
20. *Letters and Private Papers of Thackeray*, op. cit., iv, 48.
21. Lewis Melville, *Life of W. M. Thackeray*, London, n.d., p. 314.
22. The song is Karl von Holtei's once popular 'Mantellied' (1827) which begins 'Schier 30 Jahre bist du alt'.
23. See Winifred Gérin, *Charlotte Brontë,* Oxford, 1967, also for letter mentioned below (see p. 235).
24. See J. A. V. Chapple and A. Pollard (eds.), *The Letters of Mrs. Gaskell 1832–65*, Manchester, 1966.
25. Three four-line stanzas. Motto for ch. 26.
26. T. Pinney (ed.), *Essays of George Eliot*, London, 1963; see also for essays mentioned below.
27. See Lawrence Marsden Price, 'O. Ludwig's *Zwischen Himmel und Erde* and George Eliot's *Adam Bede', Dichtung und Deutung*: in K. S. Guthke (ed.), *Gedächtnisschrift für Hans M. Wolff,* Bern and Munich, 1961, pp. 113–15.
28. For the remarks below on Charlotte M. Yonge I am indebted to the stimulating book by Margaret Mare and Alicia C. Percival, *Victorian Best-Seller. The World of Charlotte M. Yonge,* London, 1947.
29. Ibid., p. 165.

4

ENOCH ARDEN IN THE GERMAN ALPS: A COMPARATIVE STUDY OF TENNYSON'S *ENOCH ARDEN* AND DUBOC'S *WALPRA*

By M. J. Norst

I

In establishing the ebb and flow of literary influences between England and Germany, no one as yet seems to have attempted a full length study of Tennyson in Germany. And yet, Tennyson would undoubtedly prove most rewarding in this regard. Like Carlyle, he absorbed much of the German Romantic tradition and was a known admirer of German literature. In his short critical biography of the poet, Edouard Duboc[1] makes a point of this: 'Tennyson in particular may be regarded as an expert in our German literature . . . his relationship with Prince Albert made this inevitable. . . .'[2] On the other hand, it was Prince Albert's support which gained for Tennyson the poet laureateship and so embalmed him forever as the compleat English poet. In his memoirs, Tennyson makes a very English and irreverent reference to the event, explaining that he dreamed Prince Albert came and kissed him on the cheek and that he said in his dream: 'Very kind, but very German.'[3]

By 1850, Tennyson was in the happy position of being acknowledged as the people's poet, most solemnly approved by the Establishment and lauded by the critics, who saw him 'as fulfilling the qualities which the Victorian critics looked for in poetry'.[4] A decade later, his reputation in Germany was almost as firmly established. His work had first been introduced into Germany in the 1830's in the form of selections by Freiligrath and Hertzberg, but, as so frequently happens with literary imports, it was not Tennyson's finest work which took Germany by storm, but a poem which even in the dawning of a Tennyson renaissance has failed to rouse any enthusiasm and seems to be regarded today as one of Tennyson's sentimental Victorian potboiling specials—namely, *Enoch Arden*.[5] By the strange law of selection which prevails in the matter of literary importation, it was precisely this poem which survived to become *the* work by which Tennyson is known in Germany. The German translators of Tennyson have offered some reasons for their rejection of other poems. Duboc excludes the longer lyrics: 'For German readers who, as we know, are unwilling to lend an ear to lyric poetry for more than a moment, "Lockseley's Hall" is far too long, a characteristic of most of Tennyson's poems.'[6] Curiously enough, Strodtmann maintains that it is the tendency to philosophise which will be unacceptable to German readers:

> Although individual sections of this work are marked by sublimity of thought and an elegiac charm in the treatment, the unvarying monotony of the metre and the longwinded philosophical reflections which make up the content would scarcely hold the interest of the German reader.[7]

This sentiment is echoed by Duboc in the selection he translated in 1870 under the title *Freundes-Klage*: 'one should refrain from transplanting [to German soil] those of his poems which by their very nature bear the marks of English religious zeal'.[8]

At all events, *Enoch Arden*—whether by virtue of its relative brevity, strong story-line and lack of philosophical flavour, or because it seemed to celebrate the domestic cosiness so cherished in the *Gartenlaube* Germany of the 1860's—enjoyed an immediate and popular success.

The best-known translation of *Enoch Arden* was the work of Edouard Duboc, better known under his nom de plume, Robert Waldmüller. This translation first appeared in 1867 and by 1897 the fortieth edition had been sold—evidence of its enduring popularity.[9] In 1869 Duboc's publisher, Grüning, sponsored a rival translation by Feldman of *Enoch Arden* and *Aylmer's Field* with an introduction by Geibel. An acrimonious correspondence between Grüning and Duboc shows the latter's reception of the news and by way of retaliation Duboc's third edition expressly states that it has been authorised by Tennyson himself.

Having thus familiarised himself with Tennyson's poetry and promoted his work in Germany, Duboc determined to write an original poem based on *Enoch Arden* yet definitely German in character. This poem he entitled *Walpra* and it appeared in 1874, ten years after the English original.

In the introduction, Duboc acknowledges his source and explains his intention. 'The inspiration for the narrative poem *Walpra* can be traced back to *Enoch Arden* . . . in which Tennyson tells the moving story of poor Enoch Arden.' Duboc explains that he was attracted by the idea of establishing 'that mode of narration which is not native to our shores and yet so very appropriate'. He would have his readers conscious of the link between the two poems in order to heighten their awareness of the essential differences:

> I have expressly referred to my classical model in order to make the thoughtful reader reflect on the peculiar nature of the task which has here been attempted and on the degree to which both works exhibit real or merely apparent resemblances.

He concludes by appealing to the national spirit, expressing the hope that

> the younger work may find a place of honour beside the older one, in whose shadow it grew and, even as the British Seaman has succeeded, and rightly so, in gaining for himself such a wide circle, so also may the German daughter of the mountains win herself friends.

The following discussion has been provoked by the challenge Duboc offers the reader to discover the 'real and apparent similarities' between the two poems. A comparison of *Enoch Arden* and *Walpra* seems to me peculiarly instructive, providing, as it does, particular insights into the national differences consciously and unconsciously revealed in the imaginative writing of that decade.

II

A necessary preliminary to any detailed analysis is a summary of the narrative of both poems. This will provide some orientation and serve as an introduction to Duboc's poem which is probably known to very few.

Enoch Arden—'a rough sailor's lad'—orphaned in childhood, Annie Lee—'the prettiest damsel in the port'—and Philip Ray, the rich miller's only son, grow up together in a coastal village. Both boys fall in love with Annie, and Enoch wins her. They marry and enjoy seven years together during which time two sons and a daughter are born. Enoch spends most of his time on the seas, fishing, to provide a living for them. Then misfortune strikes: the last baby, a son, is sickly; Enoch breaks a leg; trade falls off. As if in answer to a prayer, he is offered a job as boatswain on a cargo-ship sailing to China, and gratefully accepts it. He sells his fishing-boat, sets Annie up in a small shop, and, despite her pleas and forebodings, sets forth taking with him as a talisman a curl from his youngest son's head. For ten years there is no news of him.

Annie, left behind, fares badly: the shop fails miserably, the baby dies; the children run wild and seem to have no future. At the baby's funeral Philip Ray comforts her and offers to help with the education of the children ('for I am rich and well to do'). They 'call'd him Father Philip' and he is indeed a father to them. When ten years have passed, Philip asks Annie to marry him: 'I wish you for my wife. I fain would prove/A father to your children.' Reluctantly she consents, begging for more time, but a year and a half later there is still no news of Enoch. She prays for a sign from Heaven, and the Bible falls open at the lines 'Under the palm-tree'. She sleeps and in her dreams interprets the image not as Enoch on his island, but as dead Enoch in Heaven, singing 'Hosanna' for all eternity. She therefore marries Philip and, after an initially troubled period, eventually finds happiness with him when their child is born.

Enoch's story is then told. After a prosperous journey to the East, he suffers shipwreck on the journey home and with two companions is washed ashore on an island 'Eden of all plenteousness'. Five years later the others die and Enoch alone is left 'a shipwreck'd sailor, waiting for a sail'. Alone on his 'beauteous hateful isle' he thinks only of the 'dewy-glooming downs' of home and would have died 'of solitude' but for his faith in God.

At last a ship appears; Enoch by now 'looking hardly human' is rescued and safely landed in his own harbour. Discovering that his house is up for sale, he seeks refuge in an old tavern where he is unrecognised and hears 'the story of his house' from garrulous Miriam Lane. He secretly visits Annie's new home and, peering through the window, looks in upon a scene of domestic bliss with 'that other reigning in his place,/Lord of his rights and of his children's love'. He represses a cry of anguish and steals away determined not to 'shatter all the happiness of the hearth' and praying for the strength to carry out his resolve. He continues to live at the tavern, works hard at all manner of humble occupations and finds a measure of inner peace. Within a year, however, he falls ill and dies. Before dying, he reveals his story to Miriam Lane and asks her to tell his family after his death. The baby's curl, which he took with him on the journey, he begs her to give to his wife 'for it may be a comfort to her' and as 'a token to her,/That I am he'. Then he dies, crying: 'A sail! a sail!/I am saved'. The village honours him with a fine funeral.

It is essentially Enoch's story, though he is not on stage the whole time. More precisely, it is the story of his relationship with his wife. Early emotional tensions are resolved when he wins and marries her. Throughout the seven years of their marriage, he never ceases his travels 'on wrathful seas/Or often journeying landward', and all is well. Suddenly the broken leg forces him to face intolerable situations: the loss of his freedom and the realities of domestic life. Like Ulysses or a younger version of him, he is terrified of being chained 'by this still hearth, among these barren crags'. The island to which he journeys so eagerly is the same changeless island of enchantment which in *The Islet, Ulysses,* and *The Lotus Eaters* represents the temptation to escape from a burdensome changing reality into the exotic unchanging ideal.[10] Enoch nowhere admits his feelings, and we are given no indication that he is aware of his motives, for he provides only the acceptable rationalisations: he is undertaking the journey for the good of his family; he is sacrificing himself ('He not for his own self caring but her/Her and her children'); it is God's Will—since the offer of the journey has come in answer to a prayer. But all the evidence is against him. His joy at that particular answer to his prayer seems out of key: 'And Enoch all at once assented to it [i.e. the journey to the East]/Rejoicing at that answer to his prayer,' and as though his mind were already concerned with the island, in the very next stanza the word appears ('and isles a light in the offing'). He immediately organises his wife into the shopkeeping that he apparently never considers for himself, and is delighted because this will enable him to buy his freedom for many years to come:

> Should he not trade himself out yonder? go
> This voyage more than once? Yea twice or thrice—
> As often as needed. . .

But Annie, knowing better, fought against his will,

> Besought him, supplicating, if he cared
> For her or his dear children, not to go . . .

The change in pronoun 'her children'—'his dear children' is very significant. She views the shop as 'her own death-scaffold' and is in despair when he departs 'brightly and boldly' in the ship 'Good Fortune' to land on his 'isle at morn'.

Tennyson lavishes his best lines on the description of the island—it is what one remembers of the poem—but in *Enoch Arden* he writes as the moral realist and the island is exposed as an illusion. It is 'the loneliest in a lonely sea' and the 'eternal summer' leaves him 'ill content' and longing only for 'the smell of dying leaves'. The only intense awareness he attains is of his solitary state—he is 'the lonely man'. Because of his desertion, he has lost his identity. Faced by the opportunity to repeat the pattern and win against his rival a second time, he decides to expiate his guilt by accepting defeat, leaving the new family structure unharmed and leading the kind of life—alone—which he rejected as a way of existence before:

> and Enoch set himself,
> Scorning an alms, to work whereby to live.
> Almost to all things could he turn his hand.
> Cooper he was and carpenter, and wrought
> To make the boatmen fishing-nets, or help'd
> At lading and unlading the tall barks,
> That brought the stinted commerce of those days;
> Thus earn's a scanty commerce for himself . . .

He dies happy in the knowledge that he has redeemed himself ('I am saved'), and finally reestablishes his identity by sending back the token to his wife; a family token, meaningful only in terms of her relationship with him, since it is a part of the dead child.

If this interpretation of *Enoch Arden* seems rather unorthodox, the reason is to be found chiefly in the fact that the poem has not really received any critical attention in recent years. When it has been discussed, it has been rejected rather than reassessed.

No doubt for most of its Victorian readers *Enoch Arden* was simply the kind of pleasantly sentimental fare otherwise provided by the pious novelette. The pathetic tale of noble Enoch Arden, who when ill-used by a classical Greek fate shows decent Christian resignation (and a proper regard for family life) and after the requisite period of suffering, is released and rewarded by Divine Providence. Possibly, it was for them, as it was certainly for Tennyson himself, also a vigorous affirmation of the sanctity of the family and a tilt at the inhumanity of certain aspects of Victorian commercial life. (It is possible to read that infamous last line of the poem ironically and see it as part of this criticism.) But it seems to me that here we have a very clear case of that 'double awareness' of which F. Johnson speaks: 'an ability to satisfy the broad demands of the social spirit prevailing (with which obviously they had a certain sympathy), while also incorporating insights of different and sometimes contradictory import'.[11] Today *Enoch Arden* certainly makes more sense when read as a poem about a man's unsuccessful flight from reality and his painful re-establishing of his identity. To see it in these terms is not to read into the poem what is not there, for, though Tennyson would not have used this vocabulary, the problem was one with which he was deeply concerned in most of his writing.

III

A summary of *Walpra* reveals first of all a great increase in action which, as we shall see, cannot be explained entirely in terms of its greater length, though it is about a third longer than *Enoch Arden.*

The triangular relationship of Tennyson's poem is here given a pre-history. The poem opens with the description of four children—two boys: David and Joseph, and identical twin sisters: Walpra and Barbara, who grow up in an Alpine village in complete harmony. The boys, 'born in the same hour', are the sons of friends. They grow up 'like brothers' and are known as David and Jonathan—David is fair-haired and reserved, Joseph dark-haired and lively. The sisters and Joseph are Catholics while David is Lutheran, and the action takes place some 'four generations' ago. From earliest childhood, there is a natural affinity between David and Walpra, and Barbara and Joseph. Then Barbara dies. The triangular relationship which now emerges is full of tension. Eventually, Joseph can endure it no longer, and, when a recruiting sergeant appears, he joins up to fight in Italy. (Section I.)

David and Walpra try to dissuade him but to no avail. At his next meeting with Walpra, David, for the first time, speaks glowingly of their future together, to her evident delight. He leaves. A gypsy then appears with a child in her arms and announces that Walpra is to be married in a cathedral; to have taken from her what she loves and restored to her what she has lost and that, eventually, wounds will be healed and the star of peace shine over all. That night, Walpra dreams of the Cathedral in Milan, in which she walks as a bride and feels great joy. She wakes up to see David at her window and is totally bewildered when he tells her that he has decided to go with Joseph, leaving the decision about their rival claims in God's hand. He asks for her ring, saying: 'whichever one of us brings it back to you, refuse him not' and disappears. (Section 2.)

The third section shows Walpra's unhappy life as she waits. She is troubled by importuning suitors, including her master, a widower, who offers her protection in the approaching conflict between the Catholics and Lutherans. Walpra, no longer wanting marriage, despairs of seeing David again and dreads Joseph's return. (Section 3.) And, return he does—alone, bringing the report of David's death but no ring. The widower further corroborates the report, but the narrator makes it clear that both are mistaken. (Section 4.) Walpra and Joseph, troubled by feelings of guilt about David, accept the missing ring as an omen and determine to live as 'brother and sister'. (Section 5.) While on a pilgrimage, they pray for a miracle: 'that the ring may come back to us'. The monk who guards the miraculous picture of the Virgin Mary in the Chapel, assures them that Joseph's return and David's death are a clear sign, but Walpra still hesitates. They all kneel before the miraculous picture when suddenly there is a terrifying snow-storm which threatens to bury them alive. For five days and nights, they are walled in by ice and snow. The monk marries them, saying that their rescue will be the final sign for which they have been praying. Then he dies. (Section 5.) At this very moment, David, who has been a prisoner of war, returns to the village to hear the Chapel bell ringing out the news of their miraculous rescue. He sees the torchlight procession of rescuers and rescued wind its way down the hill and watches Walpra enter Joseph's house. Then, lacking Enoch Arden's restraint, he utters 'wild animal cries' which the mountains echo.

The threatened religious conflict now breaks out and edicts

are issued, demanding that the Lutherans return to the Catholic faith or suffer banishment. David, unrecognised because of his flowing red beard, and utterly transformed in character, now becomes the brilliant, eloquent leader of the oppressed Lutherans. (Section 6.)

Years pass. Three children are born to Walpra and Joseph: David, Barbara and Walpra. The family is rich and prosperous, troubled only by the plight of the Lutherans and the missing ring. One day, Joseph sees David and 'paralysed with horror' recognises him. He does not tell Walpra, avoids her and feels oppressed as though by blood-guilt ('Blutschuld'). When Walpra attempts to comfort him, he can speak only of omens of approaching calamity. (Section 7.) In the spring, David returns to the mountains near his own village, and only the thought of Joseph's unhappiness prevents him from visiting it. As he bends down to pick up the Bible, he sees Walpra's house and her children. Three times he calls her name and, as she comes out and looks up, she is convinced that she has been favoured by a vision and that David is blessing her from Heaven. She kneels ecstatically ('von Verzückung hingerissen') before the crucifix. Joseph is much alarmed when he is told of the 'vision' and fears for David's life. He resolves to save him, and persuades Walpra, who is unwilling to let him go, that it is God's will that he rescue the Lutheran preacher for David's sake. (Section 8.)

In an intensely emotional state, Joseph searches for David in the mountains ('his breast filled with passionate longing for his friend and yet oppressed by the thought of his nearness'). He loses his way in the impenetrable mist and, almost unconscious, falls to the ground, calling David's name. David answers his cries but is himself dying, half-buried in the snow, when Joseph crawls to his side. There is a passionate reunion ('Joseph's lips/ covered the hand and head of the dying man/with hot kisses') and Joseph begs for forgiveness—whereupon David gives him the ring. Both glimpse the celestial ladder, say the Lord's Prayer and die murmuring: 'Mein David'—'Mein Jonathan'—and the end is cosmic silence:

> Und dann war rings, so weit die Alpen-Welt
> In ihrer stillen Größe dalag, Schweigen.
> (And then, all about them, as far as the Alpine-World
> In its still majesty extended, was silence.)
> (Section 9.)

Unlike Tennyson's poem, which, as the title suggests, deals with Enoch Arden, *Walpra* is in fact not about Walpra at all, but about the relationship between David and Joseph. The poem begins with their birth 'at the same hour' and ends with their death 'at the same hour' and is essentially concerned with an account of their estrangement, their search for each other (Joseph becomes simply 'the seeker' ('der Suchende') and David 'the sought' ('der Gesuchte'), and final reunion. Two forces separate them: their religious differences and their rivalry in love for the same girl, and the poem shows how both of these are overcome. When David leaves Walpra to go with Joseph, we are told:

> thus in the difficult battle with love
> friendship had conquered

and the tension is finally resolved when Joseph, too, leaves Walpra and joyfully dies beside David:

> 'O the pity of it,' he cried
> 'You here, my David? And yet, o the joy of it,
> That having set out to find him, I now
> may die with him, here at his side.'

The ring, which is given and taken at the end, seems to be a token of their relationship rather than a bond between Joseph and Walpra. She has ceased to be an issue and in the whole of the last section is not even mentioned by name. Like Enoch, David is always present, even when he is not on stage, but, whereas in Tennyson's poem this only affects Annie, while Philip remains totally and stolidly unaware, in Duboc's version Joseph feels David's presence more than Walpra. He constantly expresses his feelings of guilt: 'I torture myself daily with bitter reproaches,' and these increase when he actually sees that David is alive and yet cannot bring himself to reveal the fact to Walpra. David's decisions about Walpra are also motivated only by his feelings for Joseph. He leaves her 'like a betrayer' for Joseph's sake and does not disrupt the marriage on his return because suddenly 'with great clarity Joseph's face appears to him wearing so sad an expression' that he cries: 'I may not! No, I may not!'

The ideological conflict, too, is finally resolved, but this will be discussed further in the next section.

IV

In comparing *Enoch Arden* and *Walpra*, it is useful to consider them first in a generalised form as basic myths perceived in universal images. While in *Enoch Arden* the essential image is the sea, in *Walpra* it is the mountain.

Enoch Arden is the fisherman, the Voyager, whose natural element is the sea with all its perils. Like Ulysses, he sets out on his Odyssey, but unlike him, finds on his return that Penelope has not waited. In his quest for 'eternal summer', he leaves his village set in a chasm, hollowed out by 'leaden-coloured seas', exchanges his own small boat for a larger one over which he has no control, and lands on the island set in the 'hollower-bellowing ocean'. The images are all of the sea and the sun. He has exchanged the 'darker isle beyond the line' for 'the isle at morn'. On this island, blazing in the sun, men die 'sun-stricken' and Enoch remains the lonely castaway. On his return, he follows the 'beacon-blaze' which leads him to the

> ruddy square of comfortable light,
> Far-blazing from the rear of Philip's house.

It is a 'comfortable' contained light, unlike the 'great mist-blotted light' which draws him to his former home, and when he approaches it, he sees the evergreen yew tree thriving in the small contained garden. The castaway has become the outcast in the barren 'waste', and in his despair 'dug/His fingers into the wet earth'. Enoch's quest has failed. He has returned to find that there is no escape from autumn and 'the dead weight of the dead leaf'.

In changing the setting from sea-side village to mountain valley, Duboc has fundamentally altered the myth. Here the Quester also bent on escaping from a narrow enclosed space, seeks first the turmoil of war and then the icy, remote mountain peak which towers above the sunny green valley. No woman can aspire to its heights—Barbara dies 'overcome by dizziness' when she climbs too far; Walpra fears it and begs Joseph :

> Do not I beg you climb the mountain,
> Do not cause me that pain.

Climbing the mountain here obviously involves abandoning

women. Like the sea for Enoch, the mountain is, however, David's element. He is the heroic leader who has renounced lesser joys and become 'der Erd-Entrückte' ('he who is removed from the Earth') and is in fact seen as a god by the earth-bound Walpra. Joseph, less certain in his quest, climbs up painfully to join him. The sun disappears, fearfully he throws away 'the happiness that was his . . . like a piece of burning coal', and terrified of falling, shivering with cold, he wanders lost in the mist unable to climb up or down. He is saved by his friend's voice. Their mystical union in death is shown as the Quest triumphantly fulfilled. The treatment of the image throughout demonstrates clearly that in the sacrificial death together, in the mist-covered heights, the two men have chosen the better part. The final scene shows the sharpest possible contrast to Enoch's death, alone, in that same village where Philip and Annie live happily united, maintaining and increasing the family which Enoch founded.

Both poems deal with an escape from the confines of family life, but, whereas Enoch always remains encompassed by the fertile sea; is to the end obsessed by his fatherhood; and finally, no longer a Voyager himself, makes fishing nets for others, in Duboc's poem the two men escape to die in the unfertile ice-bound mountain.

The attitude of the two poets to the choices their heroes make is very clear. Tennyson shows Enoch as a man who has erred, atoned and been saved. He provides a counterpart—Philip—who demonstrates the advantages of not erring, but leaves it open whether, in fact, Enoch could have acted differently. In Duboc's poem David is not shown to err. His decision to leave Walpra and to become a great religious leader has the poet's unqualified approval. It results in his being 'marvellously transformed' and possessing new powers. Joseph is the one who errs and is haunted by guilt, and he only redeems himself by also leaving Walpra and joining David on the mountain. Again the poet makes it very clear that it was the right choice, for the final scene is one of transcendental glory with all the stops pulled out.

There are also, of course, some basic resemblances. In each poem two men woo one woman, and the winner, despite the protests of the woman, leaves her. He thus deliberately becomes the loser but remains ghost-like to haunt the new relationship. Both women are most concerned to lay the ghost and do so by appealing for heavenly signs, which, ignoring more probable interpretations, they eagerly accept as evidence of their right to form a new relationship.[12] The winners-turned-losers are equally determined never to let the women forget—even in death. They use tokens to rouse memory and to re-establish their identity, rationalising this as a kindness to the women.[13] Though at the character level Walpra differs from Annie in her passivity, in defining the basic role of the woman, both poets seem to be in agreement.

While the comparison at this basic, and probably unconscious, level reveals the more startling differences, it is interesting also to note briefly what changes Duboc has made at the more conscious level where he specifically wanted to appeal to cultural differences.

Here the religious motif is particularly interesting, for, while religious belief is an integral part of both poems, it is very differently used. In *Enoch Arden* the Protestant ethos is simply an unquestioned part of the private lives of all the characters. In *Walpra* the religious conflict establishes the socio-political framework of the poem. It is the ideological conflict which first separates David and Joseph (when the priest refuses to allow him to be called Jonathan), and it is overcome in their death when they pray together, use the name Jonathan again and behold a celestial vision. Clearly, however, religion is introduced not merely as a personal issue but as a larger social one. Duboc was obviously concerned about religious differences in the Germany of the 1870's and argues for tolerance. He was himself the child of a French Catholic father and a German Lutheran mother, and is at pains to point out in *Walpra* that not the particular belief, but the general intolerance leads to conflict and misery. As the two men die, reciting the Lord's Prayer, 'they are reminded of the earth and the bloody religious conflict' and Joseph cries: 'O that there should be this dispute! / They have one prayer and yet quarrel'. One small scene suggests that Duboc sees in the new nationalism the over-riding idea capable of healing the religious rift. This involves the apparently unmotivated introduction of Hermann the Cherusker. While Walpra and Philip are talking, Walpra's master, the Catholic widower, sits in his corner, reading a book about Hermann which has been lent to him by a Lutheran and tells of his victory over the Roman legions. There is no further comment, and the function of the passage is simply to link the two ideas. The idea of Nationalism is also introduced in those episodes which carry overtones of the Franco-Prussian War. David speaks in Darwinian terms of the necessity of war, and Duboc uses descriptions of David and Joseph's war service to evoke memories of the recent war.

There is a strong appeal to Romanticism and this is underlined by some clear literary borrowings. David, the charismatic leader, is modelled on Michael Kohlhaas and the scene in the snow-bound Chapel and the gypsy's prophecies also owe much to Kleist. In defining the relationship of the four children, David refers to the four natural elements and elective affinities in terms very reminiscent of the late Goethe and the Romantic philosophers. One is also reminded of the lesser Romantic writer's obsession with certain aspects of medieval Catholicism: rosary beads, visions, miracles, a dying monk; all these pieces of standard Romantic equipment have their place in *Walpra* without serving any real function. The final section is the apotheosis of Romanticism and might well have been orchestrated by Wagner.

While Tennyson's *Enoch Arden* is in some sense a sad but firm farewell to Romanticism, and shows that idealisation of the unheroic world of the hearth, which also characterises German *Biedermeier* writers, Duboc deliberately invokes the Romantic tradition.[14] He operates with the Romantic notions of polarity and synthesis, and takes his place in the traditional writing after 1870 which Ronald Gray in his *German Tradition in Literature 1871–45* has characterised so well.

In discussing the poems, no account has been taken of their relative literary merit, since this does not affect their value for the kind of analysis attempted here. The comparison was made in the belief that Duboc in transplanting the British Seaman to the German Alps, reveals significant differences in attitude between Victorian England and Wilhelmine Germany in the 1870's, and, moreover, makes us aware once again—here by way of poetic images—of fundamental differences between the English approach to life and the German *Weltanschauung*.

NOTES

1. Edouard Duboc (ps. Robert Waldmüller) 1822–1910 was born in Hamburg of a French father and German mother. He studied art in Düsseldorf and Italy and after 1850 settled in Dresden and began writing. He published more than forty works—lyric and narrative verse, *Novellen*, novels, dramas and translations, and carried on a wide correspondence with most of the German literary figures of the day. A collection of his

works and papers and those of his brother, the philosopher Julius Duboc, was discovered in Australia and presented to the Public Library of New South Wales. An account of these papers is to be found in M. J. Norst and J. M. Ritchie, *Aus der "Sammlung Duboc" in Australien, Euphorion* LIX (1965), 416–48.

2. E. Duboc, *Zur Charakteristik Alfred Tennysons*, p. 116: in *Freundes-Klage, nach Alfred Tennysons 'In Memoriam' frei übertragen*, Hamburg, Grüning, 1870. cf. C. Tennyson, *Alfred Tennyson*, London, Macmillan, 1950: 'He had all his life been an assiduous student . . . of the romantic drama of Goethe and Schiller.'
3. Memoir, I, 335 quoted by E. Shannon, *Tennyson and the Reviewers*, Massachusetts, Archon, 1967, p. 219, note 36.
4. Ibid., p. 155.
5. cf. Steane, J. B.: *Literature in Perspective*, London, 1964; p. 132: 'Too unrestrainedly tearjerking. . . . A Victorianism that cannot resist a touch of warm intimate prettiness'; J. Buckley, *Tennyson: The Growth of a Poet*, Massachusetts, 1967, p. 157: ' "Enoch Arden" has no real social or moral theme at all. Indeed it has few larger overtones of any kind.'

   V. Pitt, *Tennyson Laureate*, London, 1969, p. 152 does suggest another reading, but does not elaborate; 'it is worth noting, however, that *Enoch Arden*, that poem most used by critics to demonstrate Tennyson's subservience to the values of his age, is a poem in which the central themes are death and exile, desolation and an unendurable solitude.'
6. E. Duboc, op. cit., p. 105.
7. A. Strodtmann, *Alfred Tennysons ausgewählte Dichtungen*, Hildburghausen, Bibliog. Inst., 1867, p. 7.
8. E. Duboc, 'Alfred Tennyson' in: *Westermanns Jahrbuch der Illustrierten deutschen Monatshefte*, Braunschweig, Westermann, 1869, p. 221.
9. In advertising the 24th edition in 1884, the publisher stresses the fact that this popularity is remarkable: '. . . thus after only 18 years, the twenty-fourth edition is appearing. A success of this kind is extremely rare in Germany.' He goes on to say that while in the interval Duboc's translation has had many competitors, it has not lost in popularity and is the one which is particularly preferred for public readings.
10. The emphasis in *The Lotus Eaters*, *The Islet* and *Enoch Arden* is on the island as a place of escape from inevitable change. In *Enoch Arden* this desire to escape is represented as an attempt to opt out of the human condition, and the consequences of such an attempt are shown. In the beginning the narrator states: 'Then came a change, as all things human change'; then, after his years on the island, Enoch is described as 'scarcely human'.
11. A summary of E. Johnson's notion of 'double awareness' in *The Alien Vision of Victorian Poetry* (Princeton, 1952) is provided by J. Kilham (ed.), *Critical Essays on the Poetry of Tennyson*, London, 1960, p. 17.
12. In this connection, an image in *Enoch Arden* is worth noting. When Enoch rationalises his reasons for leaving Annie

    she heard,
    Heard and not heard him; as the village girl,
    Who sets her pitcher underneath the spring,
    Musing on him that used to fill it for her,
    Hears and not hears, and lets it overflow.

13. Both Enoch and Joseph state that the return of the tokens (curl and ring) will be a comfort to their wives; neither explains how. cf. Enoch's: 'Take, give her this, for it may comfort her' with Joseph's: 'a heart sad unto death will then be better able to bear its confused lot'.
14. It is incidentally interesting to find that contemporaries who were beginning to be out of sympathy with Romanticism levelled the same

criticism at Tennyson and Duboc: that the language in a poem dealing with fishermen and peasants was too high flown. cf. Walter Bagehot in *Wordsworth, Tennyson and Browning* (1864) quoted by J. Buckley, *Tennyson: The Growth of a Poet*, Massachusetts, 1967, p. 159: 'Walter Bagehot thinking it absurd that a fish basket should be called an "ocean-smelling osier", pointed to the ornateness of the passage as the characteristic defect of Tennyson's art' with Eduard Mörike's objection that a passage in *Walpra* 'almost goes beyond what a peasant would be capable of expressing' (quoted by Duboc in *Eduard Mörike, Erinnerungsblatt* in: *Westermanns Jahrbuch der illustrierten deutschen Monatshefte*, Braunschweig, 1876, Vol. 40. p. 60).

Quotations throughout refer to the following texts: *Tennyson Poems and Plays*, London, 1965. Robert Waldmüller (Ed. Duboc): *Walpra, Alpen-Idylle,* Leipzig, n.d. (1874) Universal-Bibliothek Nr. 496.

I am very grateful to Prof. D. G. Mowatt (German Department, University of Newcastle) who made me rethink a number of issues which this comparison raised, and to Dr. J. Couper and Miss C. Fernando (English Department, Macquarie University) for their willing help.

I am also very much indebted to the staff of the Frankfurter Universitätsbibliothek for the incredible speed and efficiency with which they made a copy of *Walpra* available to me in Australia.

5

THE STRONG ENCHANTER: W. B. YEATS AND NIETZSCHE

By P. Bridgwater

It was in 1902 that Nietzsche was discovered by the major English-language poet whom he was to influence most strongly: W. B. Yeats. Yeats, like Herbert Read ten years later, came to Nietzsche after an enthusiastic reading of William Blake, and in the context of his work the juxtaposition of Blake and Nietzsche is particularly significant. It may be assumed that he first became acquainted with Nietzsche's work through Havelock Ellis's brilliant series of articles in *The Savoy*, to which he was himself a leading contributor.[1] Havelock Ellis's conclusion was striking enough: that 'the nineteenth century has produced no more revolutionary and aboriginal force'; but there is no evidence that Yeats was prompted to pursue the subject. Yeats could also have heard of Nietzsche from the Scottish poet and supposed 'Nietzschian' John Davidson in their Rhymers' Club days. But in fact his real interest in Nietzsche's work dates from the summer of 1902, when John Quinn lent him Thomas Common's 'choice selections', *Nietzsche as Critic, Philosopher, Poet and Prophet* (London, 1901); the copy which he read, now in the possession of Northwestern University Library, contains extensive underlinings and several significant manuscript annotations.[2] Yeats was so enthralled by Nietzsche that in September 1902 he wrote to Lady Gregory:

> I have written to you little and badly of late, I am afraid, for the truth is you have a rival in Nietzsche, that strong enchanter. I have read him so much that I have made my eyes bad again ... Nietzsche completes Blake and has the same roots—I have not read anything with so much excitement since I got to love Morris's stories which have the same curious astringent joy.
>
> (W. B. Yeats, *Letters*, 1954, p. 379)

He added that Nietzsche's thought 'flows in the same bed as Blake's, but still more violently' (ibid.); the parallel seems to have struck him forcefully, for in the revised edition (1903) of his *Ideas of Good and Evil* he repeated the simile, writing of 'Nietzsche, whose thought flows always, though with an even more violent current, in the same bed Blake's thought has worn' (p. 201). He will have seen at once that Blake (with his 'Marriage of Heaven and Hell') and Nietzsche (with his 'Beyond Good and Evil') are at one in rejecting conventional moralities, and that the same antinomies which Blake celebrated are celebrated in Nietzsche's own 'prophetic book': *The Birth of Tragedy* (Yeats' favourite work by Nietzsche, to which he refers in several letters written in 1903). Later, in *A Vision*, he significantly referred to the 'antithetical wisdom' of men like Blake and Nietzsche who are 'full of morbid excitement'.

In a letter to John Quinn dated 15 May 1903, Yeats referred to Nietzsche's two art-sponsoring deities, Apollo and Dionysos:

> I have always felt that the soul has two movements primarily: one to transcend forms, and the other to create forms. Nietzsche, to whom you have been the first to introduce me, calls these the Dionysiac and the Apollonic, respectively. I think I have to some extent got weary of that wild God Dionysus, and I am hoping that the Far-Darter will come in his place. (*Letters*, p. 403)

It is clear from this that Yeats accepted Nietzsche's distinction between the principles of Dionysos and Apollo, passion and form. Indeed, he was already in the habit of referring to these 'two movements' of the soul in occult terminology as 'the Transfiguration on the Mountain and the Incarnation'. No doubt it was partly the many parallels between Nietzsche's work and the occult literature with which he was already familiar, that made Yeats so receptive to Nietzsche. In a letter to ('A.E.') Russell dated 14 May 1903, he made use of Nietzsche's distinction to describe his own changed aesthetic:

> I am no longer in much sympathy with an essay like 'The Autumn of the Body', not that I think that essay untrue. But I think I mistook for a permanent phase of the world what was only a preparation. The close of the last century was full of a strange desire to get out of form, to get to some kind of disembodied beauty, and now it seems to me the contrary impulse has come. I feel about me and in me an impulse to create form, to carry the realization of beauty as far as possible. The Greeks said that the Dionysiac enthusiasm preceded the Apollonic and

> that the Dionysiac was sad and desirous, but that the Apollonic was joyful and self sufficient. Long ago I used to define to myself these two influences as the Transfiguration on the Mountain and the Incarnation, only the Transfiguration comes before [? after] the Incarnation in the natural order." (*Letters*, p. 402)

Clearly Yeats is in part ascribing to Nietzsche's terms meanings of his own; his 'sad and desirous' 'nineties muse is an absolute travesty of Nietzsche's Dionysos, for, as Jane Harrison said, summarising Nietzsche: 'Dionysos breaks all bonds; his motto is limitless Excess, Ecstasy' (*Prolegomena to the Study of Greek Religion*, repr. 1961, p. 446). But Yeats has also understood Nietzsche well, for it is precisely the 'impulse to create form, to carry the realisation of beauty as far as possible' that Nietzsche's Apollo represents, while Dionysos stands for 'the contrary impulse', the impulse to 'transcend forms'.

In *The Birth of Tragedy* Apollo and Dionysos represent opposed human and artistic impulses. Nietzsche himself does not stress the idea of alternating Apolline and Dionysian cycles, though this follows from his cyclic view of history and the fact that he sees these two interacting artistic impulses as imparting character to the epochs which they dominate. It is therefore reasonable to conclude that on reading Thomas Common's 'choice selections' in 1902, Yeats will have accepted three cardinal principles:

> The great man is a protagonist in that drama which is the historical process; history alternates, in cycles of endless recurrence, between Dionysian (or anarchic) and Apollonian (or severely disciplined) epochs or civilisations; and each new age, the opposite to whatever it succeeds, brings with it a 'transvaluation of values'.
> (M. I. Seiden, *William Butler Yeats. The Poet as Mythmaker 1865–1939*, 1962, p. 49)

Although Seiden did not know which of Nietzsche's works Yeats read in 1902, his comment is confirmed by Yeats' own statement in *On the Boiler* (1939): 'When a civilisation ends, task having led to task until everybody was bored, the whole turns bottom upwards, Nietzsche's "transvaluation of values" ' (p. 25). The hour-glass metaphor suggests that Yeats was thinking here of Zarathustra's pronouncement of the doctrine of Eternal Recurrence (see below). Nietzsche's distinction between Apollo and

Dionysos as historical opposites is subsumed in Yeats' later terms 'primary' and 'antithetical'.

Although Nietzsche's basic thesis in *The Birth of Tragedy* is that 'art owes its continuous evolution to the Apollonian-Dionysiac duality', his 'Apollo' and 'Dionysos' represent not only artistic impulses, but basic forms of human consciousness—what Yeats, in his first reference to Nietzsche, called 'two movements' of the 'soul'. They are the two faces of 'the original Oneness, the ground of Being, [which] ever-suffering and contradictory, time and again has need of rapt vision and delightful illusion to redeem itself.' Nietzsche himself saw art as the only remaining hope or means of restoring the broken unity of man with nature. But art takes these two basic forms: the Apollonian art of masks, and the Dionysian art of tragic ecstasy. He regarded the ancient Greeks' Apollonian consciousness as 'a thin veil hiding from him the whole Dionysiac realm': Apollonian control and symmetry superimposed on Dionysian tragic awareness. In view of Yeats' statement that he felt an 'impulse to create form', it is Apollonian art which is immediately relevant here; we shall return to Dionysos presently in connection with Yeats' definition of tragedy. Now Apollonian art is the art of masks; unable to face tragic reality, the Apollonian artist masks it with illusion, the 'veil of Maya'; he is the 'objective' as opposed to the 'subjective' artist; he is the 'Apollonian poet' as opposed to the 'Muse poet', to use Robert Graves' terms which echo Nietzsche's. But, as I have said, the 'separate art realms of *dream* [Apollo] and *intoxication* [Dionysos]' ultimately stand for different types of human consciousness and therefore of personality. This is where we come back to Yeats, for it is clear that Yeats will have found his doctrine of psychological dualism—self and antiself—confirmed by Nietzsche; after all, Nietzsche's all-important doctrine of *Selbstüberwindung* ('self-overcoming') really means the overcoming of antiself by self. Nietzsche, like Yeats, is very much concerned with the relationship between the self and its mask; as Richard Ellmann has rightly said,

> According to Nietzsche, the superman wears a mask he has designed for himself, while 'the objective man', whom he (and Yeats after him) describes as a 'mirror', creeps into 'a God's mask'. In the one case personality is asserted, in the other rejected.
> (R. Ellmann, *The Identity of Yeats*, 1954, p. 93)

It is after his reading of Nietzsche that 'mask' becomes a favourite term of Yeats. There is an obvious parallel between (i) the dialogue between self (*Hic*) and anti-self (*Ille*) in the poem 'Ego dominus tuus' (cf. also the poem 'A Dialogue of Self and Soul'), and (ii) Zarathustra's communing with his own soul (=anti-self) in 'Of the Great Longing' (*Zarathustra*, III, 14) or his distinction between 'I' and 'Self', for, as Nietzsche says, 'Man is hard to discover, and hardest of all to himself; often the spirit belieth the soul'. More generally, both Nietzsche's view of Apollo as the 'divine image' of the individual self, and his view of the Superman (see below) as totally subjective man, will have confirmed Yeats in his view of the Self. Nietzsche will certainly have 'taught Yeats . . . to have confidence in his thought and in his subjective synthesis' (F. A. C. Wilson, *Yeat's Iconography*, 1960, p. 180), though it seems unlikely that he—of all people—taught Yeats to 'think calmly' (ibid.). Yeats even—at times—shared Nietzsche's premiss: that the individual creates his own world, what is known as reality being only a 'mythology' (Nietzsche) or 'phantasmagoria' (Yeats). In both cases this view goes back to Schopenhauer, whose philosophy lies behind the whole of *The Birth of Tragedy*, and whom Yeats greatly admired ('Schopenhauer can do no wrong in my eyes—I no more quarrel with him than I do with a mountain cataract', he wrote to Sturge Moore).

This brings us to the religious aspect of the question. Yeats was evidently disturbed by Nietzsche's rejection (in *The Birth of Tragedy*) of Platonic thought and his condemnation (in *Thus Spake Zarathustra* and elsewhere) of Christian spirituality. Beside the contrast of 'master morality' and 'slave morality', that is, of subjective and objective morality, in *Nietzsche as Critic . . .*, Yeats wrote:

Night {	Socrates Christ	one god—	denial of self in the soul turned towards spirit, seeking knowledge.
Day	Homer	many gods—	affirmation of self, the soul turned from spirit to be its mask and instrument when it seeks life.

This annotation shows both that Nietzsche helped Yeats to establish the pattern of opposition between self and soul which is implicit in much of his later work, and that Yeats has substituted Christ for Nietzsche's Dionysos. Yet when he came to write *The*

Resurrection in 1927, Yeats did so 'out of his confident belief that Dionysos worship, in its pure form as a mystery religion [= Orphism], was a more primitive faith of the same order as Christianity' (F. A. C. Wilson, *Yeats's Iconography*, p. 182). Though he later studied the whole Dionysos myth in more detail, Yeats' early interest in the myth—which came from Nietzsche—is shown by the poem 'The Magi' (1914), in which Dionysos-worship and Christianity are already juxtaposed:

Now as at all times I can see in the mind's eye,
In their stiff, painted clothes, the pale unsatisfied ones
Appear and disappear in the blue depth of the sky
With all their ancient faces like rain-beaten stones,
And all their helms of silver hovering side by side,
And all their eyes still fixed, hoping to find once more,
Being by Calvary's turbulence unsatisfied,
The uncontrollable mystery on the bestial floor.

(*Collected Poems*, p. 141)

The description of the Dionysian Mysteries here could well have come from *The Birth of Tragedy*; it shows the aesthetic fascination which Dionysos held for Yeats, for all his ultimate moral misgivings. Nietzsche, for his part, knew very well that the myth of 'the god who is destroyed, who disappears, who relinquishes life and then is born again' (Plutarch) is common to Orphism and Christianity; the Orphic adepts conferred on Dionysos' passion and resurrection a mystic sense that makes his identification with Christ understandable. It may well be that Nietzsche came to insist so desperately on Dionysos and Christ as being opposites because he knew that they were not opposites at all, and that his own Dionysian doctrine was a super-Christian doctrine.

More than anything else in Nietzsche, it will have been the vision of Eternal Recurrence, annunciated in *Thus Spake Zarathustra*, that caught and held Yeats' attention. In the third part of the book ('Of the Vision and the Riddle', cf. Yeats' *A Vision*) Zarathustra first tells of his shattering vision of eternity as a gateway with two paths leading from it in opposite directions, and later finds the courage to spell out the idea of Eternal Recurrence: at the end of a Great Year of Becoming the hour-glass of the universe is reversed so that all things run their course again. Now while it is true that Yeats' own cyclic theory is more elaborate than and in some respects quite different from Nietzsche's doctrine of identical recurrence, there can be little doubt that here as elsewhere Yeats received a considerable stimulus from Nietzsche, whose ideas were largely derived from the same sources as his own.

Nietzsche's myth of Eternal Recurrence is clearly indebted to Pythagoras' doctrine of the 'Great Year', and to Heraclitus, the 'dark' philosopher who 'seems to hint at a "cycle of life"' (W. K. C. Guthrie, *Orpheus and Greek Religion*, 2nd ed., 1952, p. 226). In his lectures on *The Pre-Platonic Philosophers* Nietzsche referred to the recurrence in his exposition of Pythagoras, and in the second of his *Unzeitgemäße Betrachtungen* he repudiated the Pythagorean doctrine of eternal recurrence—but only because in his view events do not recur within the span of *known* history. With this proviso he accepted Pythagoras' doctrine. Later, in the section on *The Birth of Tragedy* in *Ecce Homo*, he referred to Heraclitus, the prophet of 'eternal Becoming' whom he admired so deeply:

> The doctrine of the 'Eternal Recurrence', i.e. of the unconditional and infinitely repeated circulation of all things—this doctrine of Zarathustra *might* have been taught by Heraclitus. At least the Stoics, who inherited almost all their principal ideas from Heraclitus, show traces of it.

The last remark is particularly suggestive since Nietzsche was in the habit of referring to himself as the 'last of the Stoics'. Though the evidence is inconclusive, it seems fairly clear that Heraclitus believed in a cycle of life, though not necessarily in the idea of *identical* recurrence. There are also parallels between Nietzsche and various Indian religions (which he knew, though probably not as well as Yeats) on this point; quite apart from the symbolism of Buddha, there is a passage in the Theravada Scriptures from the Pali Canon which connects with Nietzsche's doctrine and provides an analogue for some of Yeats' ideas in *A Vision*:

> Verily, this world has fallen upon trouble! One is born, and grows old, and dies, and falls from one state, and springs up in another. And from this suffering, no one knows any way of escape, even from decay and from death.

In *A Vision* Yeats noted that in both the Vedas and the Upanishads there are analogues to his own cyclic theories. And of course this passage from the Pali Canon is remarkably close to Heraclitus:

> One and the same thing are the living and the dead, the waking and the sleeping, the young and the old; the former change and are the latter, the latter change in turn and are the former.
> (Quoted from Charles M. Brakewell, *Source Book in Ancient Philosophy*, N.Y., 1907, p. 33)

Another likely source for Nietzsche's idea of Eternal Recurrence is the Orphic doctrine of the 'circle of birth' or 'cycle of births' or 'wheel of fate and birth' (Simplicius on Aristotle, *De caelo*), the idea which is found as part of Plato's arguments for immortality in the *Phaido*: to Plato it was already an *ancient* doctrine that 'the souls of men that come Here are from There and that they go There again and come to birth from the dead'. The Wheel as such had its place in Orphic ritual. What is important is that in the case both of Orphism and of Nietzsche, this cyclic doctrine is the ultimate expression of our moral responsibility as human beings; for Orpheus the Wheel was a 'cycle of ceaseless purgation' (Jane Harrison). And of course Nietzsche's doctrine of Eternal Recurrence—a 'sorrowful weary Wheel' indeed—was essentially a private myth, a surrogate for the Christian concept of immortality in which he no longer believed. Pythagoras, Heraclitus, Orphism in general, Plato, Indian philosophy—these are also among Yeats' main sources for his esoteric cyclic philosophy which of course differed sharply from Nietzsche's in that Yeats believed that it was possible—exceptionally—to escape from the Great Wheel of Incarnations.

One of the basic ingredients of Yeats' personal myth is the eternal conflict between Being and Becoming (the supernatural and the natural). Here too he will have found his ideas part confirmed, part contradicted by Nietzsche who is also very much concerned with just this conflict, though Nietzsche tends to reject the idea of Being in favour of 'the eternal and exclusive Becoming, the total instability of all reality, which continually works and becomes and never is' (Heraclitus, quoted by Nietzsche in his *Philosophy in the Tragic Age of the Greeks*). For Nietzsche the replacement of stable Being by a totally instable and ever haphazardly changing Becoming is an inevitable consequence of the 'death of God'.

After this outline of the main basic ideas which Yeats obtained from, or found confirmed by Nietzsche, let us turn to the Nietzschean echoes in his poetry and verse plays. So far as Yeats' plays are concerned, the influence of Nietzsche is seen most clearly in the years 1903–10; but there are echoes of Nietzsche right through to 1935. There seems little doubt that Yeats will have had his mind wonderfully cleared by Nietzsche's theory of the Dionysian 'mystery doctrine of tragedy'. This is where 'Nietzsche completes Blake' in Yeats' own words, for both Nietzsche and Blake see art as the means, or hope, of restoring the original oneness between man and nature. After referring to the rebirth of Dionysos, whose ritual passion tragedy once celebrated, Nietzsche writes of

> a profound and mystic philosophy [Orphism] and . . . the mystery doctrine of tragedy; a recognition that whatever exists is of a piece, and that individuation is the root of all evil; a conception of art as the sanguine hope that the spell of individuation may yet be broken, as an augury of eventual reintegration.
> (*The Birth of Tragedy,* X)

This Dionysian definition of tragedy appears to have influenced Yeats' *Where There Is Nothing*; it is also reflected in the essay 'Poetry and Tradition' (1907), where he defines tragic emotion in terms of Nietzsche's 'Dionysiac rapture':

> Shakespeare's persons, when the last darkness has gathered about them, speak out of an ecstasy that is one-half the self-surrender of sorrow, and one-half the last playing and mockery of the victorious sword before the defeated world.
> (Yeats, *Essays and Introductions,* 1961, p. 254)

This appears to reflect Nietzsche's view that it was the combination of tragic terror and the *comic* spirit that was the salvation of Greek art. In another essay, 'The Tragic Theatre' (1910), we find Yeats distinguishing between 'an art of the flood' or 'tragic art', and 'an art that we call real'. The latter, 'the daily mood grown cold and crystalline', apparently derives from Nietzsche's 'Apollonian sphere', 'that artificially restrained and discreet world of illusion', the world of the (Apolline) art of dream (with which Yeats was so much concerned); but it is surely Nietzsche's Dionysos, god of tragic passion, who inspired Yeats' definition of tragic art in 1910:

> Tragic art, passionate art, the drowner of dykes, the confounder of understanding, moves us by setting us to reverie, by alluring us almost to the intensity of trance. The persons upon the stage . . . greaten until they are humanity itself. (ibid., p. 245)

Yeats' basic view in the same essay, that 'tragic ecstasy . . . is the best that art—perhaps that life—can give,' and that the audience participates in the discovery of a place 'where passion . . . becomes wisdom', also exactly parallels Nietzsche's view in *The Birth of Tragedy.* And the essays contain other echoes of Nietzsche, for example, the statement that 'the nobleness of the arts is in the mingling of contraries, the extremity of sorrow, the extremity of joy' (ibid., p. 255), the reference to Hesiod and Homer as 'those pure first artists' (ibid., p. 298), and so on. But such echoes and parallels are incidental, as even the Dionysian definition of tragedy is incidental. What matters in the last analysis is that Yeats shares Nietzsche's belief in art as the only remaining means of saving an otherwise doomed world. As Erich Heller has pointed out ('Yeats and Nietzsche', *Encounter*, December 1969), the 'artifice of eternity', of which Yeats writes in 'Sailing to Byzantium' (1927), springs from the same view of art and reality as Nietzsche's definition of art as 'the last metaphysical activity within European nihilism' and of the world as an 'aesthetic phenomenon'. Nietzsche and Yeats are so closely linked because they both believe in the religion of Art and therefore tend to confuse the aesthetic and the moral spheres.

Turning to individual plays, echoes of Nietzsche are first found in *The Hour Glass* (1903), the title of which may derive from Zarathustra's definition of Eternal Recurrence, where the metaphor of the hour-glass ('sand-glass' in the translation Yeats read) of the universe is used. The theme of *The Hour Glass* is thoroughly Nietzschean, and surely reflects Yeats' reading of *The Birth of Tragedy*: the antinomy of Socratic and Tragic man, named by Yeats the Wise Man and the Fool respectively.

If *Where There Is Nothing* (1903) is based on Nietzsche's Dionysian definition of tragedy, Yeats is no less interested in the Apolline element ('the dream itself,' as he calls it in *On Baile's Strand*). *Where There Is Nothing*—like *On Baile's Strand* (1903), *The King's Threshold* (1904), and *The Unicorn from the Stars* (1908)—shows Yeats' preoccupation with spiritual heroism of the type embodied in Zarathustra; the Nietzschean hero of the play, Paul Ruttledge, becomes a Zarathustra-like Wanderer searching for 'lawless' freedom and Dionysian laughter. Cuchulain in *On Baile's Strand* is 'an heroic great man, drawn probably out of an admiration of Nietzsche's theories which were constantly in W.B.'s head at the time' (A. Norman Jeffares, *W. B. Yeats, Man and Poet*, 1949, p. 152); in 1906 Yeats' father found it necessary to criticise 'the theory of the overman' as 'but a doctrinaire demi-godship', and two years later he wrote of Nietzsche as 'malign'. *The King's Threshold* opens with the King speaking of 'two kinds of Music: the one kind/Being like a woman, the other like a man', which is presumably an echo of the first sentence of *The Birth of Tragedy*, where the 'Apollonian-Dionysiac duality' is likened to 'the duality of the sexes'; the play ends with the Youngest Pupil echoing *Thus Spake Zarathustra* in a reference to 'the great race that is to come'.

Yeats accepted the idea that the great individual is the protagonist in the drama of history, but he remained critical of Nietzsche's Superman; he saw man through Blake's eyes rather than Nietzsche's, as something to be restored to his former estate rather than surpassed. Though he deeply admired spiritual heroism of the type represented for him by Nietzsche, and shared Nietzsche's ideal of *Vornehmheit*, he rejected the arrogance of the Superman. He approved Nietzsche's statement that 'The noble type of man regards *himself* as the determiner of worth' on a superficial level, without in any way approving the solipsism that lies behind Nietzsche's words. He therefore disapproved of Nietzsche's *Herrenmoral* ('master morality'): '[Nietzsche's] system seems to lack some reason why the self must give to the selfless or weak, or itself perish or suffer diminution' (Yeats' annotation in *Nietzsche as Critic . . .*).

Yeats' moral and historical reservations were strongly challenged by the deep aesthetic fascination which the Superman held for him (cf. the case of C. F. Meyer); as late as 1919 he suggested that Nietzsche might have taken his conception of the superman in history from Balzac's *Catherine de Medici*, which, although most unlikely, shows his mind still preoccupied by the idea. But he certainly never accepted the Superman idea in toto; there is therefore no reason to doubt what F. A. C. Wilson says about *The Unicorn From The Stars*, a revised version of *Where There Is Nothing*:

> *The Unicorn From The Stars*, where the hero is made to turn from a life of anarchic action to one of mystical contemplation, seems... a clear sign of his rejection of the superman theory, and was probably written in his reaction from it.
>
> (*Yeats's Iconography*, p. 177)[3]

By the same token Yeats' next relevant play, *At The Hawk's Well* (1918), marks something of a reaction against Nietzsche himself. Cuchulain, the hero of the play, belongs to the same phasal type (the twelfth incarnation) as Nietzsche: the so-called 'heroic' phase or type. Yeats' comments on this type in *A Vision*, where he says that this type of man wears a 'lonely, impeturbable proud Mask' in self-protection because he is 'overwhelmed with the thought of his own weakness' (*A Vision*, 1937, p. 128), can be applied back to Cuchulain and thence to Yeats' view of Nietzsche in 1918. The parallel strongly suggests that by 1918 Yeats was at last seeing Nietzsche pretty objectively. Cuchulain is the would-be Superman who is thwarted by his 'all-too-human' limitations and therefore fails to gain the Dionysian Unity of Being for which he quests.

In *The Only Jealousy of Emer* (1918) too, man is seen as 'human, all-too-human' in the final chorus which again seems to echo Nietzsche:

> He that has loved the best
> May turn from a statue
> His too human breast.

The last four plays in which the influence of Nietzsche is discernible are all concerned with the Dionysos myth, to which Yeats was introduced by Nietzsche in 1902. At some time between 1903 and 1925 Yeats appears to have studied the Dionysian mysteries in detail, almost certainly via Thomas Taylor's *A Dissertation* (1790). If he read Taylor, and it seems that he did, then it was most likely between 1918 and 1920 since *Calvary* (1920) is the first play in which a fairly detailed knowledge of the Mysteries is in evidence. In general, however, it is difficult to know when Yeats' allusions to the Dionysian mysteries derive from *The Birth of Tragedy*, and when they derive from elsewhere.

F. A. C. Wilson, the critic who has examined Yeats' debt to Nietzsche most thoroughly, wrote in his *W. B. Yeats and Tradition* (1958, p. 10): 'The play which owes most to Nietzsche is . . . beyond doubt *Calvary*.' This I find hard to accept, not only because there is surely much more of Nietzsche in *Where There Is Nothing*, but also because in *Calvary* there is very little that seems to come specifically from Nietzsche: the conflict between the objective Christ and his Dionysian antagonists *need* not be

Nietzschean. *The Resurrection* (1927), also concerned with the transition between subjective (Dionysian) and objective (Christian) historical cycles, is interesting for the parallels it draws between the Orphic and the Christian Mysteries; in asserting the identity of these two myths Yeats is closer to Hölderlin than to Nietzsche, while the *detailed* symbolism of *The Resurrection* could *not* have come from Nietzsche. The same is true of Yeats' other treatments of the Dionysos-myth, *The King of the Great Clock Tower* (1934) and its revisal *A Full Moon in March* (1935), although the refrain sung by the Severed Head at the end of *The King of the Great Clock Tower* may well be indebted to Zarathustra's 'Drunken Song'. Finally, in *Purgatory* (1939), the old man's final prayer—

> Dear God,
> How quickly it returns—beat—beat!
>
> Her mind cannot hold up all that dream.
> Twice a murderer and all for nothing,
> And she must animate that dead night
> Not once but many times!
> O God,
> Release my mother's soul from its dream!
> Mankind can do no more. Appease
> The misery of the living and the remorse of the dead.

may once again reflect Nietzsche's nightmare of eternal recurrence: but it may equally reflect the 'sorrowful weary Wheel' of Orphism, and this prayer for release is addressed to the *Christian* God. So far as the last five plays are concerned, then, it seems fair to say that while they all centre on the Dionysos-myth in which Nietzsche first interested Yeats, their main sources lie beyond and behind Nietzsche, and are probably to be found in the works of Thomas Taylor ('Sipsop the Pythagorean', as Blake called him), including his translations of Heraclitus and Plotinus.

Nietzsche had less impact on Yeats' poetry than on any other part of his work; but here too there are clear echoes of Nietzsche. It was after reading *The Birth of Tragedy*, in which Nietzsche speaks of 'Homer the magnificent' as a naïve artist nurtured in the bosom of nature, one of the very rare instances of true naïveté, that Yeats adopted Homer as his own poetic model. His line 'Homer is my example and his unchristened heart' in the poem 'Vacillation' (1932) exactly reflects Nietzsche's view of

Homer. Similarly Nietzsche's attack on Plato's Socrates as representing 'the absolutely perfect man, good, wise, just, a dialectician—in a word, the scarecrow' may be echoed in the line 'Old clothes upon old sticks to scare a bird' in 'Among School Children'.

Yeats instinctively shared Nietzsche's ideal of *Vornehmheit*; as G. S. Fraser has said,

> What may be called [Yeats'] morality was . . . a morality of 'style'. It very much resembled (given that Yeats had a more genial and generous temperament) the morality of Nietzsche. Yeats' instinctive sympathies were with the strong and proud, not with the weak and humble; with the brilliant rather than with the stupid, with the exceptional rather than the average.
>
> (G. S. Fraser, *W. B. Yeats*, 1958, p. 8)

Confirmation of this is found in the fact that in the volume of Nietzsche which he read in 1902, Yeats marked the passage 'The noble type of man regards *himself* as the determiner of worth'. He was also fond of quoting Zarathustra's 'Am I a barrel of memories that I should give you my reasons?' (for example, in letters to his father in June 1918, and to Mrs. Llewelyn Davies in March 1937). The theme of aristocratic morality then becomes the subject of the poem 'To A Friend Whose Work Has Come To Nothing' (1913):

Now all the truth is out,
Be secret and take defeat
From any brazen throat,
For how can you compete,
Being honour bred, with one
Who, were it proved he lies,
Were neither shamed in his own
Nor in his neighbours' eyes?
Bred to a harder thing
Than Triumph, turn away
And like a laughing string
Whereon mad fingers play
Amid a place of stone,
Be secret and exult,
Because of all things known
That is most difficult.

Yeats will no doubt have sympathised with Nietzsche's Zarathustra—the very embodiment of this secret and exultant morality—because his attitude towards Eternal Recurrence was so similar to Yeats' own attitude towards the cycles; but more generally, Zarathustra's whole philosophy is extraordinarily close to that of Yeats' aesthetic antiself (however much his moral self may be disapproved). Zarathustra's 'Dionysiac' attitude—'He who climbeth on the highest mountain laugheth at all tragic plays and tragic realities'—is echoed throughout Yeats' poetry from 1902 onwards, for example, in the line 'Who have lived in joy and laughed into the face of Death' in 'Upon a Dying Lady' (1912/13), and is seen particularly clearly in his last poems, for example, 'Lapis Lazuli' (1936):

> All perform their tragic play
> ...
> Gaiety transfiguring all that dread
> ...
> All things fall and are built again,
> And those that build them again are gay.
> ...
> There, on the mountain and the sky,
> On all the tragic scene they stare.
> One asks for mournful melodies;
> Accomplished fingers begin to play.
> Their eyes mid many wrinkles, their eyes,
> Their ancient, glittering eyes, are gay.

For such as these tragic knowledge, the knowledge of eternal recurrence, is indeed a 'gaya scienza'. The same theme is found in 'The Gyres' ('We that look on but laugh in tragic joy') and in 'A Crazed Girl' and 'News For The Delphic Oracle'. Of course, Yeats was not the first English-language poet to voice this Nietzschean idea of tragic joy, as can be seen, for example, in these lines by the American poet Morgan Shephard:

> Ye Gods and Men, shall I
> Bend low beneath the random soulless hand
> Of Fate? Or quail to see the blackened sky?
> All these are great, but I will fearless stand
> An Atom to defy—a sharp Comparison,
> And *laugh* with joy, and wait with teeth close set.

Nor is this the only or even the most significant Nietzschean motif in Yeats' later poetry. It is, for instance, Nietzsche's prophecy of 'What is to come' ('I foresee something terrible. Chaos everywhere') that informs the poem 'The Second Coming' (1921):

> Things fall apart; the centre cannot hold;
> Mere anarchy is loosed upon the world,
> The blood-dimmed tide is loosed, and everywhere
> The ceremony of innocence is drowned;
> The best lack all conviction, while the worst
> Are full of passionate intensity.
>
> ... I know
> That twenty centuries of stony sleep
> Were vexed to nightmare by a rocking cradle,
> And what rough beast, its hour come round at last,
> Slouches towards Bethlehem to be born?

No doubt this 'rough beast', slouching towards Bethlehem, is Dionysos-as-Antichrist (the selections from Nietzsche which Yeats read in 1902 included passages from *The Antichrist*); it is also reminiscent of the 'lion-monster' and the 'laughing lions' in *Thus Spake Zarathustra* (IV, 11: 'I wait for higher ones ... *laughing lions* must come!'). In the last of Yeats' 'Supernatural Songs' ('Meru') this same motif is combined with the no less Nietzschean antithesis of thought and life:

> Civilization is hooped together, brought
> Under a rule, under the semblance of peace
> By manifold illusion; but man's life is thought,
> And he, despite his terror, cannot cease
> Ravening through century after century,
> Ravening, raging, and uprooting that he may come
> Into the desolation of reality...

In the earlier 'Michael Robartes and the Dancer' (1921), Yeats saw thought—with Nietzsche and Bergson—as falsifying reality; now he sees it—again, with Nietzsche (the Nietzsche of *The Antichrist*)—as enabling man to view more or less objectively the 'desolation of reality', that same desolation (*Wüste*) which Nietzsche saw as growing.

In Yeats' poetry, as in his plays, key-concepts may come from Nietzsche, but the all-important elaborations and symbolical detail as often as not come from elsewhere, cf. these lines in the poem 'Byzantium' (1930):

> I hail the superhuman
> I call it death-in-life and life-in-death.

Here 'the superhuman' reflects Yeats' aesthetic fascination with the Superman; but the more important second line comes straight from Heraclitus.

Yeats' immediate reaction to Nietzsche's work in August 1902 speaks for itself: the German philosopher's myth-centred tragic aestheticism enthralled him, and it is reasonable to suppose that it was partly the ideas thrown out by Nietzsche, to say nothing of his fervid eloquence, that made the following year—1903—a turning-point in Yeats' art. Nietzschean ideas and echoes play an important part in his work from 1903 to 1921, and from 1930 to 1939; there are comparatively few references to Nietzsche in the 1920's. In his first Nietzsche phase Yeats would drag in this 'strong enchanter's' name on the slightest pretext. The Irish poet Austin Clarke, himself under Nietzsche's spell at that time, has reported that at a meeting commemorating the centenary of Thomas Davis in early 1915,

> [Yeats] brought in irrelevantly the name of Nietzsche, for the German poet and philosopher of the Superman was regarded with horror in all our pro-British press during the First Great War. I felt annoyed for I had been reading with guilty delight *Thus Spake Zarathustra, The Joyful Science* and *The Birth of Tragedy* with its fascinating theory of Dionysiac and Apollonian moods.
> (In: F. MacManus (ed.), *The Yeats We Knew*, 1965, pp. 86–7)

In the 'thirties Yeats had a second Nietzsche phase. Jeffares has written of 'Nietzsche, to whom Yeats had returned at the end of the nineteen-thirties' (op. cit., p. 294), but the Nietzschean echoes in his later work suggest that he in fact returned to Nietzsche —if indeed he had ever really left him—at the *beginning* of the 'thirties at the latest. His revived interest in Nietzsche may in fact date from those 'exultant weeks' in Rapallo in spring 1929, when he had decided that 'such leisure as he had should be reserved for the study of local memories of Nietzsche' (J. M. Hone, *W. B. Yeats 1865–1939*, 1942, p. 400). On 7 April 1930 too we find him writing to Lady Gregory:

> Just outside the gate of the hotel grounds there is a small restaurant and hotel which was once the lodging, or rather tenement house, where Nietzsche lived for some months and boasted to his friends of having found a place where there were eight walks.
> (*Letters*, p. 773)

Nietzsche had stayed in Rapallo from November 1882 to February 1883, and it was there that he began writing *Thus Spake Zarathustra*, a book that was written out of despair (cf. Yeats' later comment: 'My poetry is generally written out of despair').

Even the poet's thoughts on old age, surely a very personal subject, echo Nietzsche. The middle stanzas of 'An Acre of Grass' (1936/39):

> My temptation is quiet.
> Here at life's end
> Neither loose imagination
> Nor the mill of the mind
> Consuming its rag and bone
> Can make the truth known.
>
> Grant me an old man's frenzy,
> Myself must I remake
> Till I am Timon and Lear
> Or that William Blake
> Who beat upon the wall
> Till Truth obeyed his call...

echo the passage in *The Dawn of Day* in which Nietzsche criticises 'the old thinker' for savouring his life's work, infusing into it 'a certain amount of fantasy, sweetness, flavour, poetic mists, and mystic lights', rather than continuing it and testing it. John Davidson voiced the same view in his *Fleet Street Eclogues* (1893):

> But you are old; the tide of life is low;
> No wind can raise a tempest in a cup:
>   Easy it is for withered nerves and veins,
>   Parched hearts and barren brains
> To be serene and give life's question up.

Yet although Nietzsche had considerable influence on Yeats, he was a minor influence compared with, say, Plotinus. Yeats never really lost his head over Nietzsche, as Edwin Muir was to do in 1912, and it is significant that right from the start he was critical of the Superman-myth which proved to be the headiest of Nietzsche's ideas for other English-language writers. Yeats found many of his own ideas, interests, and even metaphors (for example, those of birds of prey) rationalised, confirmed, and justified by Nietzsche. He assimilated, criticised, and in several respects went beyond Nietzsche. Thus Yeats' view that there are two paths to the spiritual world, the objective (Christian) way and the subjective ('Dionysiac') way, was confirmed by Nietzsche; but his cyclic theory went far beyond Nietzsche's. Nietzsche confirmed Yeats in his view of the Self, of art, of myth, and encouraged him to claim for *A Vision* (in which Nietzsche appears as mythical Hero) the status of absolute truth. No doubt it was partly because his interests and sources (Plato, Heraclitus, Pythagoras, Goethe, Schopenhauer, Vico, Indian philosophy, etc.) were so extraordinarily close to Yeats' own, that Nietzsche proved to be such a 'strong enchanter' for the Irish poet.

It is precisely because Nietzsche held such a strong enchantment for Yeats, that it must be stressed that when all is said and done Yeats withheld his assent to Nietzsche's fundamental rejection of Socratic-Christian thought. In Thomas Common's *Nietzsche as Critic, Philosopher, Poet and Prophet* there are a number of passages from *The Genealogy of Morals* denouncing the 'Christian infamy'. In the margin Yeats wrote the rather 'old-fashioned' comment:

> Does Christianity create commerce by teaching men to live not in the continual present of self-revelation but to deny self and present for future gain, first heaven and then wealth?

And immediately afterwards he added the often-quoted question:

> But why does Nietzsche think that the night has no stars, nothing but bats and owls and the insane moon?

Yeats' comment reads like an echo of the lines 'Night—it was always night/And never a star above' from John Davidson's *New Ballads* of 1897. Nietzsche, of course, is all things to all men; but it is interesting to note that while the Scottish poet was attracted to Nietzsche because he seemed to offer a way out of his own pessimism, the Irish poet ultimately condemned Nietzsche for his pessimism—but only after spending much of his intellectual life in Nietzsche's company.

NOTES

1. No. 1 of *The Savoy* (January 1896) contained two love-poems and a story by Yeats; No. 2 (April 1896) contained the first part of Havelock Ellis's 'Friedrich Nietzsche', together with Yeats' 'Rosa Alchemica' and 'Two Poems Concerning Peasant Visionaries'; No. 3 (July 1896) included the second part of Havelock Ellis's 'Friedrich Nietzsche' and the

first part of Yeats' essay 'William Blake and His Illustrations to the Divine Comedy', as well as the poem 'O'Sullivan Rua to Mary Lavell'; No. 4 (August 1896) contained the third and last part of Havelock Ellis's essay on Nietzsche and the second part of Yeats' essay on Blake.

2. For information in this connection I am most grateful to Dr. Richard D. Olson, Curator of Rare Books and Special Collections in the University Library, Northwestern University, and to his successor, Mr. R. Russell Maylone.
3. G. Wilson Knight has said (in his *Christ and Nietzsche*, 1948, p. 185) that *The King's Threshold, The Player Queen*, and *The Unicorn From The Stars* are 'strictly Nietzschean in conception', and has pointed out that Yeats links the unicorn with the Superman.

6

GERHART HAUPTMANN AND HAMLET

By H. F. Garten

Gerhart Hauptmann came to England only once in his life—in 1905, when he was awarded an honorary degree by Oxford University. On that occasion, he also visited Stratford. There he broke a reed from the river Avon, which he reverently preserved to the end of his life. It was a symbol of his deep admiration for Shakespeare. On several occasions, he paid homage to the English dramatist: in a speech to the German Shakespeare Society ('Deutschland und Shakespeare' 1915); in an introduction to a volume of illustrations to Shakespeare's works (*Shakespeare-Visionen*, 1917); in an address delivered at a meeting of the Shakespeare Society in Bochum ('Shakespeare-Tagung in Bochum', 1927). These public utterances, for all their reverence for Shakespeare's work, scarcely go beyond generalities suited to the occasion. The only time Hauptmann probed more deeply was in his essay on *Hamlet* (1927), which accompanied his bold attempt to adapt, and in parts to complement, Shakespeare's play.

No other work attracted him so long and so persistently as *Hamlet*. His absorption in the Hamlet theme ranged over more than a decade, from 1924 to 1936. As always, it took the form of an intuitive appropriation of the foreign subject-matter, and its re-creation from his own poetic resources. His preoccupation resulted in three works: a free adaptation of Shakespeare's drama, an independent play, *Hamlet in Wittenberg*, and a novel, *Im Wirbel der Berufung*, centring on a theatrical production of *Hamlet*.

In his essay on *Hamlet*, based on a thorough study of the sources, the various editions and critical commentaries, Hauptmann sets out in detail his reasons for reshaping what he considered to be a mere 'torso' of the original play. The haphazard way Shakespeare's works were copied and edited, he argues, has caused errors and omissions which distort the original meaning.

His main contention is that owing to the carelessness of copyists, the vanity of actors, and so on, the text of Shakespeare's play, as we now have it, is seriously corrupt: lines have been exchanged, scenes transposed or omitted, gaps left unfilled. And so Hauptmann sets out to restore what he thinks may have been the original form of the drama, using throughout Schlegel's translation. He takes many liberties with the text, restoring lines to what he believes were their original speakers, and adding whole scenes of his own. All along, his approach is prompted not so much by academic considerations as by imaginative conjecture, by his desire to find what he calls 'the transcendent idea of the work, the logic of its form' (*Gestalt*).[1] It is in this light that we must judge Hauptmann's daring attempt to tamper with Shakespeare's play, an attempt which, from a scholarly point of view, was no doubt misguided. His adaptation does not add to our knowledge of Shakespeare but rather of Hauptmann himself.

It would be pointless in this context to trace Hauptmann's alterations in detail. His arguments are as follows: the whole complex connected with Fortinbras and his intervention in the affairs of Denmark is insufficiently motivated. Hauptmann therefore interpolates several scenes: one at the beginning of Act Two, where the King of Norway learns of the death of the Danish King, which rouses his hopes of bringing Denmark back into the Norwegian fold; another scene opening Act Three, which shows young Fortinbras already on Danish soil, eager to exploit the troubles of the royal family for his own purposes. The most far-reaching changes, however, are made in Act Four, which Hauptmann regards as a 'heap of rubble' ('Trümmerfeld'). He transfers Laertes' rebellion, challenging the King for the murder of his father, to Hamlet. His arguments for this change run as follows: Laertes, a nobleman highly favoured by the King, has no reason to suspect Claudius of Polonius's murder. Moreover, since he has no claim whatever to the throne, his challenge would be pointless and doomed to failure. Hauptmann even finds his view confirmed by Laertes' words

> ... brands the harlot
> *Even here*, between the chaste, unsmirched brows
> Of my true mother. (IV, 5)

This, he contends, can only refer to Hamlet's mother, the Queen, who is present. If it is Hamlet who challenges the King, this scene falls into place as a consistent link in the chain of events: after his return from the abortive journey to England and his meeting with Fortinbras, he is at last resolved to challenge Claudius publicly: 'O thou vile king, give me back my father!' This, of course, puts a very different complexion on Hamlet's character, as Hauptmann is well aware. He firmly rejects all interpretations which see the essence of the tragedy in Hamlet's irresolution, his unwillingness to act. Instead, he visualises the Prince as a man of action, thwarted merely by the insufficiency of the Ghost's evidence; as soon as he is sure of the King's guilt, he is prepared to act. Hauptmann finds his argument confirmed by the sources on which Shakespeare had drawn, *Saxo Grammaticus* and Belleforest's *Histoires Tragiques*, both of which describe Hamlet as a man of action who, after returning from England, openly challenges the King.

In Hauptmann's version, Hamlet's resolution falters only at the sight of Ophelia, who has been summoned by the King. He is thus present at the mad scene. Moved by Ophelia's derangement, he realises his own guilt and 'drops the sword from his hand'. Thus Ophelia's madness has a direct bearing on Hamlet's tragedy. For Hauptmann there is no doubt that she has been the Prince's mistress (he even suggests that 'in a freer adaptation' a balcony scene between the two, on the model of *Romeo and Juliet*, might be inserted!). Only this would account for her subsequent madness and the effect it has on Hamlet. Moreover, he exchanges the lines of Hamlet and Laertes in the graveyard scene: it is Hamlet who first jumps into Ophelia's grave, and Laertes who challenges him. Lastly, Hauptmann puts Hamlet's soliloquy 'To be or not to be' after this scene, as V, 2: only when the Prince has faced death and contemplates suicide in order to escape the net closing in on him, is he ripe for the ultimate question. In Hauptmann's words: 'Now the whole immense burden of what he has lived through weighs on his monologue.'[2]

This is not the place to scrutinise Hauptmann's bold interpolations on textual grounds. What is important is the fact that over many years he devoted much of his creative energy to a close study of Shakespeare's tragedy and felt inspired to come to grips with its manifold problems. His version was performed, under his own direction, in Dresden in 1927. Undaunted by the largely adverse criticism he met, he embarked on a second version which went even further. This was published, in 1930, in a luxury edition, with illustrations by Edward Gordon Craig.[3] The fact that Hauptmann included it in the *Ausgabe letzter Hand* of his collected works indicates to what extent he regarded it as a work of his own.

More important than the controversial attempt at rewriting Shakespeare's play are the two original works stimulated by the Hamlet theme: a novel, *Im Wirbel der Berufung*, and a play, *Hamlet in Wittenberg*. Both were begun simultaneously, in 1924, but not completed until 1935. *Im Wirbel der Berufung* revolves around a stage production of *Hamlet* in a small provincial theatre, with a mixed cast of amateurs and professionals. The parallel to Goethe's *Wilhelm Meisters Lehrjahre* is obvious, and no doubt intended. But while in Goethe's novel the discussion of Shakespeare's play forms merely an episode, it is the dominant theme in Hauptmann's work. The hero, Erasmus Gotter, is a young writer (clearly a self-portrait of the author in his early twenties), who is planning a performance of *Hamlet* on the Baltic island of Rügen, where he is spending the summer. As the rehearsals progress, there are long discussions on every aspect of the play. The views put forward correspond closely to the arguments of Hauptmann's essay, which also underlie his own adaptation, but now they are set out in lively exchanges between the various members of the company. Throughout, Gotter acts as the author's mouthpiece. However, there is one line of thought not touched upon in the essay. It concerns the apparition of the Ghost, who is seen as the motive force of the whole drama. Hamlet's tragedy, so the argument runs, has its mythical root in the *Totenkult*, the cult of the dead:

> The soul of a great dead man, especially if he has lost his life through murder or assassination, must be pacified, as otherwise his wrath and the power to carry it though are devastating. The *heros* [Hauptmann uses throughout the Greek word] has, as soon as he has died, a rank and power similar to those of the chthonic, that is, subterranean gods.[4]

Shakespeare's drama is a supreme example:

> The terrible ghost of the murdered King Hamlet, grown to a heros, demands atonement and vengeance on his enemy. He is fully armed and prepared to avenge himself, if need be, even on a tardy avenger. The only thing that can reconcile him, is blood.[5]

Seen in this light, the violent death to which all the characters involved, including Hamlet himself, succumb, takes on a new aspect: 'The offended demon destroys and crushes his own house.' Even the black of Hamlet's costume has symbolic connotations: it is the colour of the animals sacrificed to the heroes as well as of the priests entrusted with their reconciliation through blood. Thus the ghost of Hamlet's father assumes an overpowering importance: at the end, he towers over the scene of slaughter as a 'bloodthirsty, invisible, satisfied spirit of revenge'.[6] Hamlet himself is his victim. After the Prince's rebellion (according to Hauptmann's version) has been frustrated, 'everything around him grows macabre, dark, and confused, his will-power seems paralysed, until finally he too is crushed without mercy by the mailed foot of the raving demon'.[7]

It is evident that Hauptmann superimposes on Shakespeare's play his own ideas about tragedy, derived from his preoccupation with ancient Greek drama. His interpretation would apply to Aeschylus rather than to Shakespeare. Hauptmann himself is fully aware of this, indeed, he repeatedly stresses the close affinity of the Hamlet theme to the *Oresteia*. At one point, he speaks of 'Orestes-Hamlet', he calls Claudius the 'Aigisthos of the play' and compares Horatio to Pylades.[8] In several instances, he quotes verses from Aeschylus' drama to support his views. The atmosphere in which Hamlet lives is 'closely akin' to Aeschylus' *Libation Bearers*, which Hauptmann calls *Totenopfer* (Sacrifice to the Dead). He even speaks of the 'Erynnis' of the murdered King, lurking at the back of the Queen, and claiming his adulterous wife as a victim of his relentless vendetta. In this juxtaposition of Shakespeare and Aeschylus Hauptmann's approach is not that of the literary critic: it is an attempt to penetrate to the mythical substance which lies at the core of both dramas. What he sees in *Hamlet* is a manifestation of the *Urdrama*, the perennial struggle between light and darkness, heaven and hell, from which all great drama has grown.

Whatever the objective validity of these theories, they bear out how deeply Hauptmann, at that time in his life, was immersed in ancient Greek myth. In fact, his interpretation of *Hamlet* clearly foreshadows his last great dramatic work, the tetralogy of the *Atrides*.

In the novel *Im Wirbel der Berufung* the discussion turns

repeatedly on Hamlet's stay in Wittenberg, referred to early in Shakespeare's play. The Prince's wish to return to Wittenberg is interpreted as a desperate attempt to escape from the terrible spell of his father's ghost. 'The angry heros has power only within the orbit of his grave, his palace, his country, but not outside the country's borders. By fleeing abroad, Hamlet would have saved himself', one of the speakers argues.[9] Thus the Prince's brief reference to Wittenberg has a deeper significance in the context of the play. We learn that Gotter has written a tragi-comedy, *Hamlet in Wittenberg*. It is the title of Hauptmann's own play, on which he was working simultaneously with the novel, mainly between 1930 and 1935.

We can now follow from the published *Nachlaß*[10] the successive stages of the work. By setting his *Hamlet in Wittenberg* at the time of Luther, Hauptmann advances the period by several centuries. The Prince is thus caught up in the spiritual upheaval of the Reformation—a period which always held a special fascination for Hauptmann. In the early drafts of the play, he unfolds a broad picture of Luther's Wittenberg, introducing various historical characters such as Luther himself, his friend Melanchthon, Abrecht Dürer, Lucas Cranach, and others. In the final version, all this is reduced to a single scene between the Prince and Melanchthon, with the historical background only lightly sketched in.

Hamlet in Wittenberg forms a kind of prelude to Shakespeare's tragedy, showing Hamlet, aged nineteen, as a 'gentleman student' at the university of Wittenberg. In a preface Hauptmann states what prompted him to this work:

> I was tempted to imagine the world-famous Danish prince and his Sturm-und-Drang time in the town of Luther . . . I followed the temptation from a natural love for the figure of Hamlet and by no means with the ludicrous intention of challenging comparison with the towering genius of the immortal Briton.[11]

Despite its derivative character, the play holds its own. The only characters taken from Shakespeare, apart from Hamlet himself, are his friend Horatio and Rosencrantz and Guildenstern, sent by Claudius to spy on the Prince. The rest of the cast comprise a motley crowd of fellow-students, riff-raff, and gipsies—the company in which Hamlet mainly moves. Most of the scenes are set in various low taverns, frequented by students and all sorts of outcasts. The language, alternating between prose and blank verse, is clearly modelled on Shakespeare's, or rather, on the German translation. Hamlet, nicknamed 'Proteus' by his friends for his ever changing moods, is given to melancholy and gloomy introspection. Despite his youth, he feels old in 'this whole world of sorrows'. Time and again, he is haunted by images of torture, death, and man's inhumanity to man. 'For nights I am tormented by nightmares,' he confesses to his friends.

> Like infinite suffering itself, the sight of the bleeding God on the cross pursues me... At night I creep into the churches, but here too only the evil spirit awaits me. The vessels of holy water reek of blood, the candles smoke like piles of faggots. Not only the pictures of the martyrs tell of blood, torture, and death. I see everywhere gallows, executioner's axes, and wheels. In short: the seven days' creation seems to me a work of Satan, a foul and pestilent congregation of vapours...[12]

From these depths of gloom he tends to change, at a moment's notice, to youthful gaiety and exuberance. But his prevailing mood is an unfathomable sadness:

> Die Trauer bin ich der verweinten Welt,
> Der schwarze Mantel überm Himmelszelt.[13]
>
> (I am the sorrow of the weeping world,
> The inky cloak spread over heaven's vault.)

Subconsciously, he has dark forebodings of what the future holds in store for him. He feels at home in Wittenberg: 'If it were possible and Denmark had no objections,' he says to Rosencrantz and Guildenstern on their arrival from Elsinore, 'I should work for a master's of doctor's degree to end my life here, perhaps as a lecturer of poetics.'[14]

The main action centres on the Prince's love-affair with a gipsy girl, Hamida, whom he saves from the clutches of a brutal lover, and with whom he celebrates a mock-wedding in a students' masquerade, posing as King Cophetua with the beggar-maid. For some time, he lives with her in a friend's castle near Wittenberg, oblivious of everything around him, and even tries to persuade Melanchthon, the friend of Luther, to marry them. He is rudely roused from his dream when messengers arrive from

Elsinore, announcing the King's death. Even before the news is broken, he has seen his father's ghost, with blood streaming from his temples. Not unlike Prince Hal in *Henry IV*, he realises that the time for youthful revelries has passed; without a moment's hesitation, he dismisses Hamida to face what he feels lies in store for him:

> Die Kerzen sind herabgebrannt. Es riecht
> versengt, und so entlass' ich euch nun alle.
> Ihr kamt und bliebt und hieltet aus—ich dank'
> es euch, inwährend ich den Becher
> der Jugendtorheit bis zur Neige leerte...
> Und schon steht mir ein neuer Kelch gefüllt
> mit einem schwarzen Trank, der gärt und raucht,
> und muss getrunken sein.[15]
>
> (The candles are burnt out. It smells of burning,
> And so I now dismiss you all.
> You came and stayed and persevered—I thank you,
> Whilst I drained the cup of youthful folly to the dregs...
> Already a new chalice stands waiting for me, filled
> With a black potion which ferments and smokes,
> And must be drunk.)

The play ends with Hamlet being acclaimed as king of Denmark. The stage is set for Shakespeare...

Hamlet in Wittenberg is certainly not one of Hauptmann's major achievements. Since its first performance in 1935 it has only rarely been staged. No doubt its derivative theme has obscured its intrinsic merits. Yet its prose dialogue has a vigour rare in Hauptmann's later works, and some of the poetic passages are of great lyrical beauty. Above all, the figure of the Prince, seen in an entirely different context, carries conviction as a youthful incarnation of Shakespeare's enigmatic hero.

NOTES

1. 'Hamlet. Einige Worte zu meinem Ergänzungsversuch' in: *Ausgabe letzter Hand*, 1942, vol. xvii, 347.
2. Ibid., p. 362.
3. *Shakespeares tragische Geschichte von Hamlet Prinzen von Dänemark*, Weimar, 1930.
4. *Im Wirbel der Berufung*, A.l.H., xiii, 531.
5. Ibid., p. 532.
6. Ibid., p. 627.
7. Ibid., pp. 627–8.

8. Ibid., p. 588.
9. Ibid., p. 537.
10. Centenar-Ausgabe, vol. ix, 1401–20.
11. A.l.H., xiii, 178–9.
12. Ibid., p. 202.
13. Ibid., p. 307.
14. Ibid., p. 242.
15. Ibid., p. 313.

7

ASHLEY DUKES AND THE GERMAN THEATRE BETWEEN THE WARS

By J. M. Ritchie

The entry for Ashley Dukes (1885–1959) in the *Oxford Companion to the Theatre* describes him as an English dramatist, theatre manager and critic who wrote for the *Star* and the *Illustrated Evening News* and who acted as the English editor of the American *Theater Arts Monthly* for many years. It notes the significance of his work with the Mercury Theatre, a small playhouse in Notting Hill Gate which he opened in 1933, and in particular the way in which he used it in order to put on new and foreign plays. As far as the history of the British theatre is concerned his importance is felt to lie in his advocacy of poetic drama in place of naturalism; he was, for example, closely associated with the first productions of T. S. Eliot's *Murder in the Cathedral.* At the same time he is remembered for the ballet company associated with his theatre and directed by his wife Marie Rambert. This company had a significant part to play in the development of British ballet. The brief note in the *Oxford Companion* then gives a quick and necessarily incomplete account of Ashley Dukes' translations from French, German and Italian and lists his original works as well, some of which were phenomenally successful.

Seen in the context of such many-sided activities in all spheres of theatrical life, Ashley Dukes' translations and adaptations from the German may at first sight seem relatively unimportant. In fact, however, his association with Germany and the German theatre was a long, deep and important one. Good translations of German dramas are scarce and actable adaptations are even scarcer. It is this and much more from the German that Ashley Dukes had to offer. Without disparagement to his plays from the French like *The Man who Married a Dumb Wife* and *Mozart,* from the Italian, Machiavelli's *Mandragola,* and from the Spanish, e.g. *La Celestina,* a study of his life and work as revealed in his autobiography *The Scene is Changed* clearly shows that Germany was his first and lasting love. In the period between the wars he became the supreme mediator between English and German theatre.

The first real turning point in Ashley Dukes' life seems to have come in 1907 when he resigned from his post as a lecturer in science at the University of London and went off to live in Munich. In this great city of the arts he gradually abandoned his science, learned a great deal of German and saw everything the theatres had to offer, which meant the normal fare of the Residenztheater, the Schauspielhaus and the Hoftheater, not forgetting the intellectual cabarets like Simplizissimus. What a theatrical feast for a starving Englishman! From Munich he went to Zürich before returning to London to write plays. But even living in England at this time did not mean a complete break with the German theatre. For one thing he was soon busy with a translation from the German, namely Sudermann's *Midsummer Fires* which he did for Miss Horniman's theatre in Manchester. Besides, the Germans themselves were still raiding England. In 1911 the Reinhardt Company came to the London Coliseum with *Sumurun*, a theatrical extravaganza more notable for its Victor Holländer music and its acting and miming than for the literary quality of its text. Ashley Dukes was enchanted by its sheer theatricality and saw it over and over again. Later in the same year came the Reinhardt production which every contemporary history of the theatre, but no history of German literature ever mentions, namely Karl Vollmoeller's *The Miracle*, to the music of Humperdinck. As Ashley Dukes puts it:

> Both productions, very likely, had been conceived with the idea of making as much money as possible out of the English public, so that it could be spent on further Reinhardt productions in Berlin. In this they succeeded . . .[1]

But it was after the Great War, in which Ashley Dukes served as an officer with the artillery, that his contacts with the German theatre became really significant. As a German-speaking officer he was nearly seconded for special duties, but fortunately he found a relatively quiet position as commandant of a staging-post at Elsenborn Camp from which he was able to make play-going visits to Aachen, Cologne and Coblenz. The chief theatre in Cologne in particular included in its repertoire practically every play of merit written in German since 1914. Of these the one that impressed Ashley Dukes most was *Der Bettler* by Reinhard Sorge:

> It was the first expressionist drama, and perhaps the best because it never left the plane of poetry. The subject was modern yet timeless, just one of those German domestic dramas that in prose can be so boring; the verse irregular and strong, seldom lyrical, always dramatic. The staging showed an understanding of the expressionist mind; across the proscenium hung a fine gauze, that now familiar device for preventing the diffusion of light on a subdivided scene. Symbolic arrangements of pieces of furniture and a stove, café seats on a raised terrace, a high window and the shrubs of a garden, formed the sub-division. The lighting moved from one part of this scene to another, leaving all the unlighted part invisible.[2]

This was poetic, non-naturalistic drama indeed and the thought of Ashley Dukes in the uniform of an English officer attending such performances of avant-garde theatre in Cologne at this time is an intriguing one. Naturally the theatre management assumed he was from the British censorship and the ever-promenading German public in the foyers simply stared and stared in unbelief. For Ashley Dukes himself, however, this visit to Cologne in particular was a rewarding one for he came back from this leave full of his new theatrical experiences and loaded down with a library of expressionist drama. A little later in Cologne he saw Kaiser's *Von morgens bis mitternachts*, a play which seemed to him 'the most characteristic *prose* work the expressionists had produced, and so the best to translate for the English-speaking stage'. As a man of the theatre who had known the old Germany intimately Ashley Dukes was indeed in a uniquely favourable position to judge the revolutionary time that Germany was living through:

> ... a revolutionary time—for 1919 was so in every country more or less—the stage was making new and positive gestures of its own. I had the good fortune to see them in their full significance, because in Germany the theatre was a genuine reflection of a people's dramatic will; it was not as in post-war Soviet Russia or in the total state of today, an instrument of policy. It was still too early for some of the dramatic writing that came out of this time of struggle, though Toller's *Die Wandlung* and Fritz von Unruh's *Ein Geschlecht* were already written, besides Sorge's play which has been described.[3]

On returning to England Ashley Dukes' aim was then to enlist sympathy for this avant-garde theatrical movement of German origin, to make the English public aware of the revolution that had taken place since the days of *Sumurun*. As he clearly saw this was an extremely difficult task given the anti-German mood of England in the post-war period and the general hostility to all forms of modernism, German or otherwise. However, it was a task he accepted and so in this 'first civilian summer' he rose at six o'clock every morning and set about furnishing new material for the English stage. His first play to this end was a translation of Kaiser's *Von morgens bis mitternachts*. With this play German Expressionism made its first and most successful appearance on the British stage.

It was the summer of 1922 before Ashley Dukes returned to Germany and the exhilarating experience of a raging inflation that made even poor poets and translators like him into millionaires. In Berlin he saw the massive Reinhardt production of Ernst Toller's *Die Maschinenstürmer* in the huge circus-like arena of the Grosses Schauspielhaus. Clearly no production on this gigantic scale would ever be possible in England, and Ashley Dukes could envisage only a simple presentation in which the Engine should consist of shadows of wheels and crankshafts, and the more personal scenes would be given their full value. However, he was immediately captivated by 'the great theme' of man against the machine and determined to meet Toller and discuss with him the translation he felt had to be made to give back to the English this great theme drawn from Byron's speech of 1812 in the House of Lords against the Framework Bill. An interview with Toller was not so easily arranged, however, for he was by this time imprisoned in the fortress of Niederschönenfeld near Augsburg. Once again, however, Ashley Dukes' military rank stood him in good stead, for he presented himself at the gates of the prison, showed his passport which still described him as a major. He thereby outranked the puzzled governor of the prison who was only a captain and was admitted to see the political prisoner Toller. The brief interview with Toller was a very fruitful one for it ended with an agreement for the translation of both the play and the long poem *Das Schwalbenbuch*. The *Machine Wreckers* was performed in English in the spring of 1923 by the Stage Society at the Kingsway Theatre. Herbert Marshall played the leading role. The *Swallow-Book* was published by the Oxford University Press in the following year.

Easter 1926 saw Ashley Dukes' next contact with the German, or better, Austrian theatre for his own comedy *The Man with a Load of Mischief* was accepted for performance by the Burgtheater in Vienna which meant lengthy discussions with the director about various details of the German version. Visiting the Burgtheater and working with it gave him a valuable opportunity to enjoy the great range of theatrical activities in a city like Vienna but also a valuable insight into the quite un-English scope and range of facilities at the disposal of a great European theatre. He had discussions with his translator Felix Salten, the author of *Bambi*, and in his home had the first of many subsequent meetings with Max Reinhardt and the actress Helene Thimig who was later to be Reinhardt's wife. At this time the great professor was still at the height of his power, controlling four theatres in Berlin, the Viennese Theater in der Josefstadt and the dramatic side of the yearly Salzburg Festival. Ashley Dukes paid his first visit to the Salzburg Festival in that same year and from then on became a regular visitor accompanied by his wife, Marie Rambert. Gradually he adopted the custom of spending the summer in a high Austrian village walking and writing, and not surprisingly in this ambience, adaptations from the German came to play an ever increasing part in his work for the theatre. First among these was Alfred Neumann's *Der Patriot*, a Berlin hit play about the conspiracy of Count Pahlen against the crazy Paul I of Russia. This was given the Shakespearean title *Such Men are Dangerous* and in this guise became a great success in England and still enjoys regular revivals to this day. It was followed by an adaptation of Lion Feuchtwanger's *Jew Süss*. Feuchtwanger had originally written this as a drama, which he then turned into a novel when the drama caused no stir. Under the title *Power*, the novel became a best-seller in England and America. It was from this novel that Ashley Dukes made his dramatic version *Jew Süss*, which Feuchtwanger liked so much he had it translated back into German. With Matheson Lang, Peggy Ashcroft, and Felix Aylmer in the key parts the English version was a sensational hit in London in 1929. Then in 1931 the invitation came to make an English version of yet another German play which itself owed much to English history. This was Ferdinand Bruckner's *Elizabeth of England*. Once again the

German success was repeated in England under the direction of Reinhardt's successor at the Deutsches Theater, Heinz Hilpert, who came over from Berlin specially to recreate the original production though he could speak not a word of English. The result was a theatrical triumph. By 1934, though aware of the shadows that were falling over Germany, Ashley Dukes was still involved with adaptations from that country's successes, this time with Hans Rothe's version of the *Comedy of Errors.* (Brecht was not the only German playwright interested in bending Shakespeare his own way.) Ashley Dukes turned this into a play he called *They Wander in a Maze*. The resulting product, as he saw, was something very much akin to the contemporary American musical and screenplay *The Boys from Syracuse*. In the summer of 1935 Ashley Dukes returned to the London West End with yet another German play that proved very successful. This play, *The Mask of Virtue*, was a free English adaptation of Sternheim's *Die Marquise von Arcis.* As Ashley Dukes realised, this was 'entertainment for a sophisticated audience, balancing always on the fine razor-edge of irony and masquerade', and not therefore something which might normally have been expected to appeal to the English theatre-going public. However, he was fortunate in casting excellent comedians like Jeanne de Casalis and Frank Cellier. What he could not have anticipated was the personal performance of Vivien Leigh, a young actress whom nobody had ever seen before. She completely stole the show and this Sternheim production at least was a great success. Yet another English-German project for which Ashley Dukes was to be responsible for the English version was the plan for a dramatic version of *War and Peace*, to be written jointly by Alfred Neumann and Erwin Piscator and directed by Piscator himself with all the resources of stage mechanisation:

> The use of platforms and stage boxes for characters making their commentary on the play, of moving backgrounds for the personages within it, and of puppet soldiers amid artificial mists on the field of Borodino . . .[4]

The production came to nothing and the whole scheme only serves to show how well Ashley Dukes was managing to keep abreast of all the theatrical developments in Germany from Reinhardt's exotica through Expressionist poetic drama to Piscator's gadgetry. The only surprising thing is that Ashley

Dukes, the man who knew everybody in the German and Austrian theatre world never once mentions Brecht in his autobiography.

Looking back over all this active participation in the German theatre between the wars one is forced to admit that Ashley Dukes seems to have been enormously successful in forcing a rich and varied diet of German theatrical fare on a notoriously reluctant English public. Some of his adaptations from the German were even *financially* successful! Yet many might still feel inclined to dismiss him as a *mere* translator and adaptor. This might indeed be arguable if it were not for the particular significance attaching to his versions of Expressionist drama. Indeed, but for Ashley Dukes the English-speaking theatre might have remained almost totally unaware of the great Expressionist theatre revolution. In addition, Ashley Dukes' version of *From Morn to Midnight* in particular played an absolutely vital role in the little theatre movement in England, that 'Other Theatre' which provided the only outlet against the conservatism of the commercial theatre, the parochialism of London managers and audiences and the suffocating effects of censorship.[5] Based on clubs and Sunday Societies the little theatres made it at least possible for plays to be produced that did not have an immediate and general appeal. The oldest and most famous of these societies was the Stage Society, founded in 1900. It was in this society which had barely survived the 1914–18 war, that Ashley Dukes' version of *From Morn to Midnight*, the first example of the new expressionist drama and the first German play to be produced in England after 1914, was performed. Other examples of expressionist drama followed, notably his version of Toller's *The Machine Wreckers* in 1923. This is how Dukes describes the move from the old realistic drama to the new poetic drama in his introduction to that work:

> We have travelled far since Ibsen's *Ghosts*, Hauptmann's *Weavers*, and Shaw's *Widowers' Houses*. Much water has flowed under the bridges of drama, much blood has trickled from the wells of tribal hatred; and the pioneers of last generation are no longer pioneers, but ancient colonists. We respect them, we honour their work, but we know that their rallying cries will never stir our pulse, and that their forms are not the destined mould of our desires. The battles they fought are long since won; the world they knew is long since changed. The quiet theatre of the realistic

> drama, where the tranquillity of nature was broken only by the alarums and excursions of problematic man have given place to a restless and whirling scene where peace finds no anchorage but in the living heart. In Middle Europe the dramatic representation of this changing conflict has taken singular forms. The expressionists have sought to concentrate in graphic gestures and key-words the essence of the rapid movements that characterise their drama. Symbolists and neo-realists have joined in the pursuit of formulas. The air is thick with definition of this play or that as 'non-representational', 'dynamic', 'rhythmic', or 'ecstatic'. And we of Western Europe, who have less love of generalities, know that we also seek something the contemporary drama has not yet given. Naturalism has no more to offer us; that door is opened indeed, but the cupboard is bare. The drama of ideas, and nothing but ideas is dead. We famish as we sit over the walnuts and port of after-dinner comedy. The Elizabethans alone cannot save us; the poetry of our time must come to expression in the theatre.

The Stage Society certainly saw to it that some people at least were able to see something other than after-dinner comedy or Shakespeare. Following Ashley Dukes' initiative a whole series of German plays were produced there in the following years, notably Wilhelm von Scholz' *The Race with the Shadow*, Karl Schönherr's *The Children's Tragedy* and Wolfgang Moeller's *Douaumont: or The Return of the Soldier Ulysses*.[6]

But while Ashley Dukes' influence on the Stage Society was important his version of *From Morn to Midnight* was to play an even greater part in the life of the Gate Theatre. This tiny theatre, actually a loft in Floral Street which had been opened as a theatre club by Peter Godfrey was in a bad way until saved by German Expressionism! Godfrey, a completely professional man of the theatre had like Ashley Dukes become completely dissatisfied with the current theatrical fare of his time, especially after reading the new expressionistic drama that was being produced in Germany. Hence he opened his own little theatre to put on plays not just for one or two members' performances, but for nightly runs of two or three weeks. After opening on 30 October 1925 the Gate Theatre struggled along without success and near to dying until Peter Godfrey decided to put on a production of *From Morn to Midnight*. The review which James Agate gave changed the whole course of the Gate Theatre's future and perhaps that of the little theatre movement which till then had been ignored and passed over in silence by all the critics:

> In the West Central district of London there is a thoroughfare called Floral Street. Dejection reigns there, and the *décor* consists of humble entrances whose doors are studded with nails to facilitate suicide. It is a street after the heart of Edgar Allan Poe, and the most intrepid taxi-driver will think twice before leaving the comparative safety of St. Martin's Lane. Over the door of number Eleven hangs a mysterious sign, 'The Gate Theatre Salon', which may possibly repel more people than it attracts. But let not the man who has the theatre in his bones be deterred either by the sign, the crazy staircase, the barn-like appartment which houses both stage and auditorium, or the cheap sacking of which the curtain would appear to be composed. If the adventurer's courage does not fail him before the curtain goes up, he will assuredly stay till it falls.[7]

Agate was determined that this promising venture should not die and so he urged his readers to see the play at all costs before the theatre was forced to close. He not only gave full information on how to find the tiny theatre, he even included the theatre's telephone number in his review so that readers could apply for membership by phone. Immediately applications started pouring in and in no time every performance for the rest of the run of the play was completely sold out. At the end of its three weeks' run at the Gate the production was transferred to the Regent where Claude Rains took over the part of the Cashier played by Peter Godfrey who refused to leave the Gate. Agate who liked what the little theatre movement was trying to do but had no time for Expressionism then felt free to pan the play which he did:

> I tried with might and main to see the spiritual significance in Mr. Kaiser's turgid bombinations, but all I could see, or rather hear was a small cashier talking at enormous length through a very large hat.[8]

Clearly what interested the English critic and playgoer was not the play nor the playwright, but the 'expressionistic' production, though those who, like Ashley Dukes, had experience of contemporary German theatre were aware of the vast difference between the enormous theatrical resources on which the German producer could draw in his great theatres and the limited resources available to the producer of avant-garde theatre in a

Covent Garden loft. Hence there is a difference between Expressionism in Germany and in England. Expressionism in Germany was never the concern of a small coterie or an élite, it was a vast movement embracing everything from intellectual cabaret to circus arenas. Its plays were performed throughout the length and breadth of the country on the best stages with the best actors, producers and stage designers in Germany. And for a while at least it succeeded in attracting the best and biggest audiences. Lacking such great resources and such general acceptance of the aesthetic revolution, Ashley Dukes naturally reduced the scope of the play when he came to translate and adapt *From Morn to Midnight*. The Salvation Army band became a harmonium, the Sports Palace for the Six Day Cycle Race became the stewards' box, the big production effects with the skeleton tree and the snowy landscape were omitted. And generally speaking Ashley Dukes toned down and normalised Kaiser's expressionistic language. Instead of the abrupt, staccato effect of the Telegram Style, the hard, brutal, non-poetic note, Dukes gave smooth-flowing English. Similarly his stage directions all became tamer and everything which might be offensive to normal English good taste was omitted—for example the significant parallels between the Cashier and Christ on the Cross were removed. Also expunged were all grotesque images of the type which the Expressionists loved to develop, e.g. the five in the gallery pressed so tightly together that the man in the middle is squeezed out and plunges to his doom; or the bowler hat that lands on a lady's bosom and is there irretrievably indented into it. Hence the English *From Morn to Midnight* was already a much reduced version of the original and when he came to produce this Ashley Dukes' version Peter Godfrey had to reduce the play even more to make it manageable.

> Lack of money made any form of solid realistic scenery out of the question. Even if the money had been available the tiny stage made it impracticable. From the beginning his method had been to use a permanent black background, indicating the locale of the scene by the minimum of properties and furniture, relying for atmosphere and effect entirely on unrealistic lighting. Even his favourite method of opening a play by drawing the curtains on a pitch dark stage and then gradually bringing up the lights had a practical origin. The theatre could not afford curtains of material heavy enough to be impenetrable by light.[9]

Inevitably expressionism in the English theatre became associated with a certain meanness and starkness far removed from the startlingly theatrical (and often very expensive) effects demanded by the original German plays. Nevertheless even on this drastically reduced scale the power of a play like *From Morn to Midnight* was enormous and the Ashley Dukes' version was brought back again and again. When in 1944 Peter Godfrey opened a Gate Theatre in Hollywood one of the plays he chose for the opening was *From Morn to Midnight*. Hence because of Ashley Dukes' efforts and mainly because of this one play interest in German Expressionism grew until it eventually became a force to be reckoned with in the English-speaking theatre. Of course it would be an exaggeration to claim that what was happening in one or two little theatres could seriously affect the course of English theatre at this time. Arguably the influence of the German theatre revolution was greater in America than in England for it was only in the later 'twenties and 'thirties when Expressionism began to come back to England from America in the form of plays like Elmer Rice's *The Adding Machine* that the real discussion (and condemnation) of Expressionism began and James Agate could write his 'Case against Expressionism'![10]

Ashley Dukes' version of *From Morn to Midnight* was certainly in at the beginning of American interest in theatrical expressionism. The first American production of the play using his translation was the Theater Guild's from 31 May to 3 August 1922, 'the closest Kaiser ever came to a Broadway success'. The critical response to the play ran the full gamut from total bewilderment and rejection to unstinted praise.[11] The terms of the bewilderment are conventional and predictable, the words of praise and wonder in *The Dial* (lxiii (1922), p. 116) deserve to be quoted at least in part:

> Something akin to divine assurance was restored to our theatre when *From Morn to Midnight* was produced by the Theatre Guild. The certainty we had so long lacked that the theatre could give us anything hard and clear, swift and certain in its movement, had been insufficiently challenged in the last year or two; among Americans Mr. O'Neill alone made it advisable to wait and see. We understand fully that *From Morn to Midnight* is neither the best example of Georg Kaiser's work nor an exceptional example of expressionism on the stage. It is easy to quarrel with the occasional wearing thin of the material out of which the

> play is made. But one cannot question the profound conviction that this play is a way of revelation for the cluttered and floundering theatre of our time.

The review continues in this vein. No doubt the references to the 'wearing thin of the material' refer in part at least to Ashley Dukes' reduced version of the text, for the actual production seems to have been slightly more elaborate than the original Peter Godfrey production. The difficulty of the gnarled tree that changes into a skeleton was overcome by using a Linnebach projector and the velodrome sequence was as usual the great *coup de théâtre*.[12] Altogether Ashley Dukes' original description of the new expressionistic method as a filmic one whereby Georg Kaiser 'will appear to be a link between the three dimensional stage and the screen', was a point more deeply taken and understood in America than in England. But however theatrical expressionism is assessed (and a lot more still needs to be uncovered about performances of plays like *From Morn to Midnight* in England and America in the period between the wars) Ashley Dukes' own considered verdict is unquestionably a just one:

> When the dramatic history of our century comes to be written this movement may appear much more important than it appears now, a few years after its decline and virtual abandonment by dramatists. These nameless characters of the expressionist imagination, the Mr. and Mrs. Zeros or other numerical figments, played their parts in a fermentation of the creative mind which was the possible fore-runner of a new dramatic poetry. And in its wildest extravagances the actor and the director found stuff to work upon.[13]

BIBLIOGRAPHICAL NOTE

A select bibliography of books and translations by Ashley Dukes

Adaptations of plays from the German

From Morn to Midnight. A play in seven scenes by Georg Kaiser, translated from the German by Ashley Dukes, London, Hendersons, 66 Charing Cross Road, 1920.

The Machine Wreckers. A drama of the English Luddites in a prologue and five acts, by Ernst Toller, English version by Ashley Dukes, London, Benn Brothers Limited, 8 Bouverie Street, E.C.4, 1923.

Such Men are Dangerous. A play in eight scenes adapted by Ashley Dukes from 'The Patriot' [by Alfred Neumann], London, Victor Gollancz, 1928.

Jew Süss. A tragic comedy in five scenes by Ashley Dukes based upon the romance of Lion Feuchtwanger, London, Martin Secker, 5 John Street, Adelphi, 1929.

Elizabeth of England. A legend in twelve scenes by Ferdinand Bruckner [i.e. Theodor Tagger], English version by Ashley Dukes, London, Ernest Benn, 1931.

Mask of Virtue. A comedy in three acts, adapted from 'Die Marquise von Arcis' [of Carl Sternheim] by Ashley Dukes, London, Victor Gollancz, 1935.

Verse from the German

The Swallow Book by Ernst Toller, English version by Ashley Dukes, London, Oxford University Press, Humphrey Milford, 1924.

Books on the theatre

Modern Dramatists, London, Frank Palmer, 1911.
The Youngest Drama. Studies of Fifty Dramatists, London, Ernest Benn, 1923.
Drama. Home University Library of Modern knowledge, vol. 123, London, 1926.
The World to Play With. [Essays on the drama] London, Humphrey Milford, 1928.
The Scene is Changed. [Autobiographical reminiscences. With a portrait], London, Macmillan & Co., 1942.

NOTES

1. *The Scene is Changed,* p. 35.
2. Op. cit., pp. 51–2.
3. Op. cit., p. 57.
4. Op. cit., p. 238.
5. *See* Norman Marshall, *The Other Theatre* (London, 1947), especially chap. IV Peter Godfrey and The Gate and chap. VI The Sunday Theatre.
6. *The Other Theatre,* p. 74.
7. *The Other Theatre,* p. 44.
8. James Agate, *Red Letter Nights. A survey of the Post-Elizabethan Drama in Actual Performance on the London Stage, 1921–1943,* London, 1944. *From Morn to Midnight* by Georg Kaiser (Regent) Claude Rains, pp. 134–6.
9. *The Other Theatre,* p. 44.
10. James Agate, *Their Hour Upon The Stage,* Cambridge, 1930. The Case Against Expressionism. *The Adding Machine*: a play. By Elmer Rice, Court Theatre, 9 January 1928. pp. 30–4.
11. *See* R. A. Jones, German Drama on the American Stage: The Case of Georg Kaiser. *The German Quarterly,* XXVI (1964), 16–25.
12. *See* D. S. Dew, *Expressionism in the American Theater 1922–1936,* Yale University Ph.D. dissertation in Language and Literature, 1968. (Unpublished thesis on Microfilm in Hull University Library.)
13. *The Scene is Changed,* pp. 52–3.

8

VERNON WATKINS AND GERMAN LITERATURE

By H. M. Waidson

Vernon Watkins used to speak of some of the great names in English literature as the first models for his own poetry. He regarded the meeting with Yeats in Dublin in 1938 as very important, and the long poem *Yeats in Dublin* testifies to this. The friendship with Dylan Thomas, whom he met in 1935, he saw as being of major importance too, while T. S. Eliot's example meant much. The life and landscape of Gower and South Wales are an integral part of the experience of very many poems, but the contact with European scenes and writings plays also a considerable part. The Biblical and the Classical traditions frequently form the basis of poems.

The poet's interest in German thought and letters no doubt owed its initial stimulus to his mother, who had been at school in Germany, while his school education at Repton and the time he spent at Cambridge would provide the academic basis for his German studies. During the period between the wars he paid a number of holiday visits centring upon personal contacts in Bonn and Heidelberg; after 1945 there was less direct visiting. Vernon Watkins' concern for German poetry accompanied him throughout the years when he was publishing, that is, the second half of his life. Already in 1938 Vernon Watkins had sent to Dylan Thomas 'a free, rhymed translation of Novalis's hymn, "Wenn alle untreu werden" '; Dylan Thomas acknowledged the gift in a letter of 19 October 1938: 'That hymn must be great in the original, I wish I could read German.'[1] Another letter of Dylan Thomas to Vernon Watkins, thought to be probably from August 1940, says: 'You translate Holderlein [sic] and swear in German to the Home Guards'.[2] Commenting on a letter of 21 June 1941, Vernon Watkins writes: 'We had read Rilke's Duino Elegies to each other in the look-out of Laugharne Castle perched on the wall over the estuary. The poems excited Dylan deeply, though he called Rilke "a very odd boy indeed".'[3]

Vernon Watkins' concern for German imaginative writing was

expressed in translating and also in incorporating German literary and other associations into his own poetry. As the translations of poems have not appeared in a collection of Vernon Watkins', with the exception of Heine's *The North Sea* (New York, 1951; London, 1955), it may be useful to list them at this point. Following the list of 'Poems published in periodicals and anthologies not in *The Ballad of the Mari Lwyd and Other Poems*. Published Prose',[4] a version of Rilke's 'Autumn Day' appears to have been the first translation of German verse which the poet published, in *The Listener*, 2 October 1941. During the years 1944–51 there was a steady flow of translations of German poems which were for the most part first published in journals:

Hölderlin, 'Half of Life'	*Horizon,* April 1944; also in *Quarterly Review of Literature,* Hölderlin Number, 1959
Hölderlin, 'Hyperion's Fate-Song'	do.
Heine, Six Poems from *Die Nordsee*	*Life and Letters Today,* August 1944
Heine, Three Poems from *Die Nordsee*	*Life and Letters Today,* September 1944
Hölderlin, 'Memories'	*Life and Letters Today,* April 1945; also in *Quarterly Review of Literature,* Hölderlin Number, 1959; also in Angel Flores, *Anthology of German Poetry from Hölderlin to Rilke,* New York, 1960; also in Anne Fremantle, *The Protestant Mystics,* 1964
Hölderlin, 'Home'	*Horizon,* February 1945; also in *Quarterly Review of Literature,* Hölderlin Number, 1959; also in Angel Flores, op. cit.
Hölderlin, 'Patmos'	*Translation (First Series),* November 1945
Rilke, 'Archaic Torso of Apollo'	*Translation (First Series),* November 1945; also in *A Little Treasury of* in Rilke, *Rodin* (transl. Jessie Lemont *World Poetry,* New York, 1952; also and Hans Trausil, 1946
Rilke, 'Autumn'	*Translation (First Series),* November 1945
Heine, 'The Castaway', from *Die Nordsee*	*The Wind and the Rain,* Winter 1945
Hölderlin, 'Human Applause'	*Life and Letters,* August 1946; also in *Quarterly Review of Literature,* Hölderlin Number, 1959
Hölderlin, 'Sophocles'	do.
Hölderlin, 'The Good Belief'	do.
Hölderlin, 'Formerly and Now'	do.
Hölderlin, 'Sunset'	do.
Hölderlin, 'To the Fates'	do.

Heine, 'Sea-Sickness', from *Die Nordsee*	*Wales 25,* Spring 1947
Rilke, 'The Death of the Poet'	*The Gate,* May 1947; also as 'Death of the Poet' in *The Listener,* 18 December 1958; also in Angel Flores, op. cit.
Ricarda Huch, 'Peace'	*The Gate,* August 1947
Rilke, 'Love Song'	*Translation* (*Second Series*), ed. Neville Braybrooke and Elizabeth King, 1947
Heine, 'Night on the Beach', from *Die Nordsee*	do.
Hölderlin, 'The Unforgivable'	do.
Rilke, 'When the clocks are so near . . .'	*The Listener,* 26 August 1948
Walter von der Vogelweide, 'Under the Lime-Tree'	*Poetry* (*Chicago*), October 1948
Goethe, 'Anacreon's Grave'	*The Listener,* 7 July 1949; also in Stephen Spender, *Great Writings of Goethe,* New York, 1958
Goethe, 'The Godlike'	*Poetry* (*London*), September 1949; also in Stephen Spender, op. cit.
Goethe, 'Harpist's Song'	do.
Goethe, 'Song of the Spirits over the Waters'	*The Gate,* Goethe Bi-Centenary Number, 1949; also in Stephen Spender, op. cit.
Goethe, 'Limits of Human Nature'	do.
Heine, 'The Phoenix', from *Die Nordsee*	*Poetry* (*Chicago*), August 1949
Rilke, 'Sonnet to Orpheus IX'	*The Listener,* 27 April 1950
Hölderlin, 'Nature and Art, or Saturn and Jupiter'	*Review Fifty,* December 1950
Heine, 'Evening Dusk', from *Die Nordsee*	*The Nation,* 19 May 1951
Günter Eich, 'Think of This'	*Atlantic Monthly,* March 1957
Gottfried Benn, 'Fragments'	*Atlantic Monthly,* March 1957; also in E. B. Ashton (ed.), *Primal Vision, Selected Writings of Gottfried Benn,* Norfolk, Connecticut, n.d.
Rilke, 'A Young Girl's Tomb'	*The Listener,* 13 November 1958; also in Angel Flores, op. cit.
Goethe, 'A Likeness'	Stephen Spender, op. cit.
Goethe, 'Mignon'	do.
Goethe, 'Hope'	do.
Schiller, 'Elegy'	*Adam* (bi-centennial number), Winter 1959
Heine, 'Ah, your White-as-Lily Fingers'	Angel Flores, op. cit.
Heine, 'At the Crossroad Lies Buried'	do.
Mörike, 'In Spring'	do.
Hofmannsthal, 'Many Truly . . .'	Angel Flores, op. cit.; also in Hugo von Hofmannsthal, *Poems and Verse Plays,* ed. Michael Hamburger, New York, 1961

Hofmannsthal, 'The Youth in the Landscape'	do.
Hofmannsthal, 'A Boy'	Angel Flores, op. cit.; also in Hugo von Hofmannsthal, *Poems and Verse Plays,* ed. Michael Hamburger, New York, 1961
George, 'Come in the park they took for dead and see . . .'	*The Listener,* 15 February 1962
Storm, 'Cats'	*Times Literary Supplement,* 9 March 1962; second version, *Unicorn,* Autumn 1962
Kästner, 'Jardin du Luxembourg'	Erich Kästner, *Let's Face It,* ed. Patrick Bridgwater, 1963
Kästner, 'Real Romance'	do.
Kästner, 'Sadness Everyone Knows'	do.
Kästner, 'February'	do.
Kästner, 'May'	do.
Kästner, 'Old Woman in the Churchyard'	do.

Vernon Watkins admired Hölderlin, coming to prefer his poetry to that of Rilke. Here, as no doubt elsewhere, he appreciated the stimulus of Michael Hamburger, to whom he dedicated his poem 'Epithalamion' (in *The Death Bell*). The Goethe translations were provided for the bi-centennial occasion, and in the introductory note to the volume *The North Sea* the translator's sympathies are with the younger Heine in his meeting with the older poet. But it was the theme of the sea that particularly attracted Watkins to Heine's *Die Nordsee,*[5] and this theme plays a vital part in a considerable number of his own poems. Vernon Watkins' one translation of a play from German into English verse is that of Hofmannsthal's *The Salzburg Great Theater of the World,* contributed to Michael Hamburger's edition of Hugo von Hofmannsthal, *Selected Plays and Libretti,* New York, 1943. Among the seven poems by the Hungarian Attila József, which Vernon Watkins translated (in the volume Attila József, *Poems,* 1966), there is one entitled 'Welcome to Thomas Mann'.[6]

Writing on 'The Translation of Poetry' (in *Contemporary Literature in Translation,* University of British Columbia, Vancouver, vol. 1, no. 1, n.d.), Vernon Watkins speaks of the conveying of meaning as translation's first aim, and of the conveying of form as the second. '[The translator] must obey both meaning and form, and the better the form is, the more identical the two become: the form is the meaning.' In the translation of poetry there is the approach of the scholar, which would give the exact meaning in prose, and there is that of the poet who, having first established meaning, goes on to the task of creating from this an equivalent poem in his own language, where inevitably literal meaning and/or full formal equivalence may have at time to be left.

> Remember that every poem is a problem of unity. The original poet found it; the translator must find it, too. The choice, then, may lie between keeping exact detail and losing unity or finding unity by losing a detail or inventing a new one, for the exigencies of form.

Vernon Watkins, after quoting Shelley on 'the vanity of translation' in his *Defence of Poetry*, makes the point 'that the whole poem, not only a single line, can gain a new life in a new language'. He then asks Goethe 'to take Shelley's flower out of the crucible and show it to us in a vase', giving this rendering of 'A Likeness':

> I picked some flowers that I saw bloom
> In a field, and thoughtfully carried them home;
> But soon their heads, in the warm hand bound,
> Had fallen, and limply hung to the ground.
> I put them in water, in a fresh glass;
> Next, what a wonder came to pass!
> The little heads rose up straightway,
> And the stems of the leaves in green display;
> And altogether so healthy and sound
> As if they still stood on their mother-ground.
>
> So seemed it to me when miracle-sprung
> I heard my song in a foreign tongue.

The poet-translator looks for a rendering that shall be alive as poetry as well as close to the original. 'Only by reading the translation apart from the text can it be tested as a poem.' Difficult though such a task is, it is a creative and sustaining one. 'A poet needs, besides his inspiration, the role of interpreter, and besides his prophet's vocation, the care and manifestation of what is valid in the Past.' There is then the double role: the creative writer whose originality is essentially forward-looking, and the secondary author who cares for and displays what has already been found and esteemed. The translator combines the functions of conservation and creation; he recreates in another medium. His activity is part of tradition, and therefore an essential part of Watkins' poetic personality, if we accept Kathleen Raine's comment:

> [Vernon Watkins] chose tradition (vital memory) as against education, and inspiration as against the new positivist spirit of the age; he remained true, as Yeats said poets must, to 'certain heroic and religious truths, passed on from age to age, modified by individual genius, but never abandoned'.[7]

If Vernon Watkins was concerned in translations for a process of handing down which should be newly creative, this is applicable to various themes in his own poetry, and quite clearly so in those poems which take German poets as their subject. His first published volume of poetry, *Ballad of the Mari Lwyd and Other Poems* (1941), includes two poems in which he marks out a number of his interests in German literature. 'The Shooting of Werfel' notes beneath its title that it originated in a newspaper report claiming that 'Werfel has been shot in Paris'. Its eleven stanzas, each of four long lines, are an impassioned reaction to the imagined situation of a fellow-poet's violent death. After the first stanza, with its abrupt opening query 'Werfel dead?', the theme of the wronged poet responding with forgiveness to the lethal aggression is introduced:

> His early words creep back through the crisp, dead leaves;
> 'As great you are as death looks little before you';
> 'What sweeter joy on Earth than be wounded and say nothing!'
> —Werfel, who sought in each the return of the Saviour.

There is a comparison with Rilke, implied no doubt also in the fifth verse with its mention of Prague and Vienna before it speaks of 'Paris, the place of Heine's exile'. The vulnerability of the hunted artist before 'calculating bullets' and his longing for lost life do not detract from his god-like nature. In the same volume, the last of the shorter poems, 'Discoveries' presents a series of brief descriptions of poets and thinkers of the world in a cosmic setting. After Beethoven and von Hügel, two lines evoke Rilke, in the context of the latter's 'Autumn' which Vernon Watkins translated:

> Rilke bears all, thinks like a tree, believes,
> Sinks in the hand that bears the falling leaves.

In *The Lady With the Unicorn* (1948) is included the poem 'Swallows over the Weser' with its opening line: 'Dark in their dipping and rising the swallows fly over the Weser.' Lying on a meadow by the river's edge the protagonist and his companions look at the swallows; apart from the poet's private memory there is nothing in this poem that has specifically German associations. 'The Broken Sea' (in *The Lamp and the Veil*, 1945) a long poem in twenty sections, is inscribed 'For my Godchild. Danielle Dufau-Labeyrie, born in Paris, May 1940'. Vernon Watkins explained, in his lecture and reading on Swansea, that he began this poem in 1941, and that he, as godfather of the child, was to have gone to Paris for the christening, when news of the German invasion came and prevented this. The paradoxical association of birth with the chaos of war is seen with anguish, underlined by air-raids on Swansea which are the poet's immediate experience while he is looking back to May 1940. In Section 19 the poet pictures in his imagination the child in her cot, and invokes the 'holy witnesses' Taliesin, Dante, Hans Andersen and Blake, to be followed, at the opening of Section 20, by these lines :

Now that the years draw in
All death to a single mind,
The sweet adventure of dawn,
The words of Hoelderlin,
And the vision he divined
Of Greece, the Christian dawn,
Of Patmos, islands, hills
Proclaiming Christ aloud
Through all that Nature wills,
The work that he always signed,
Words secret and proud,
Like a lion, like a fawn,
Uniting the gentle and strong,
Though half his life was undone
By a bitter shaft and blind;
Though dust, his black words move
The stars that did him wrong
To his individual love,
The purity of his song.
Fixing his eyes upon
The stillness of aether, he
Man's nature lost and found.
The water leaps on the stone,
It follows its path to the sea,
But never forgets that sound.

The verse and person of Hölderlin are remembered again, in a prominent position, in *Affinities* (1962), the last collection of his poems which Vernon Watkins saw through the press himself. The ordering of the sequence is not without significance. It opens with 'Waterfalls', the recalling of a boyhood memory of rural Wales ('Always in that valley in Wales I hear the noise/Of waters falling'). The second poem links the craft of writing with the father's feelings for his young son ('The Precision of the Wheel'). The following ten poems are concerned largely with general themes connected with the inspiration and labour demanded by the creative imagination: the pause needed between productive spells, the strict demands of the Muse, 'Ironies of the Self', the slow emergence of the vine's leaves and fruit, the contrast between tradition and fashion, 'Demands of the Poet', 'Demands of the Muse', the living inspiration that is to be found in ancient poets, 'Muse, Poet and Fountain', the crane and his mate. 'Ode to Swansea', opening the second section, shows the place and its contribution ('Here is the loitering marvel/Feeding artists with all they know'). Memories of Dylan Thomas follow, then 'Ode to Nijinsky' (with analogies with French poets), 'A Bell Unrung', 'Three Sonnets for Charles Williams' and an ode to T. S. Eliot. The two poems comprising a third section centre upon D. H. Lawrence in Cornwall; in an earlier typescript draft of the contents page (in the possession of Mrs. G. Watkins) these poems appeared as the final ones of the volume, but the poet indicated in ink his wish to move them to their present position. The second stanza of 'Zennor Cottages (once sheltering D. H. Lawrence)' runs:

> ... shows one inhabiting
> A cottage, who gave wrongs
> A name, while he would sing
> His German songs.

'The Ballad of the Mermaid of Zennor', with its central dialogue between the boy and the mermaid, seems to have analogies with Goethe's 'Der Fischer', though a typescript of the poem contains a note implying that the poet was thinking rather of the Loreley legend:

> In the church at Zennor there is a carving in black teak of a mermaid who is reputed to have lured down to the sea and to his death by drowning a youth who sang in the choir. Cornwall's

Lorelei was different from the Rhine's. She was captivated by the boy's voice, and he by her beauty.

After 'Héloïse' come five poems devoted to five poets—Hölderlin, Heine, Wordsworth, Keats and Browning. 'To Hölderlin' consists of two sonnets, where the poet speaks directly to Hölderlin, evoking him in a numinous, mythical context and then summing up his qualities in the past tense, in a series of statements:

> Love was to you as to the birds their flight.
>
> You looked for constancy. Heroic power
> Greece gave you . . .
>
> The Christian and the Greek were reconciled . . .

The echoes of 'Hälfte des Lebens' in the final three lines encourage new images and thoughts to be associated with Hölderlin's poem:

> Smooth on the flowering lake, swans plunged their eyes
> Into a walled, a wintry world below,
> Where light was cloistered, and became unwise.

'To Heinrich Heine (on the centenary of his death)' also ascribes to this poet a mythical significance; his was a wisdom that was largely concealed from his contemporaries, though his own vision bestrode planets and penetrated through the earth's exterior. His Muse, like the Loreley, was 'cradled above the Rhine'. He remained elusive, whether concealed behind 'a subtle, mediaeval mask' or during his last period in Paris. The centre of the poem seems to lie in stanza ten, where the protagonist makes a direct comment:

> Hatred and wit engaged you;
> Your language was your sword.
> Yet you despised all words save one,
> And candour was that word.

The four concluding stanzas present further characterisation, but in an oblique manner, apostrophising a sculptor's interpretation of the poet. From the solidity of a corporeal presence in a specific place rises an awareness of the otherworldly, stressed by the juxtaposition of the adverbs 'deathward' and 'backward':

> Spirit with deathward gliding arms
> And backward glancing head.

and, two stanzas later, by the parallel in the additional dimension provided by the inclusion of the two German words:

> The statue stood in Frankfurt.
> On a rose-planted lawn
> Embodying there a double dream,
> Fliegender Geist, yet Faun.

It may be queried whether the short, regular measures of this poem are as congenial to the poet as the long, freer lines of 'The Childhood of Hölderlin'. In the volume *Fidelities* (1968) 'A Neglected Grave (for Heine)' takes up the appraisal of Heine once more, though in briefer, less developed measures. As Neville C. Masterman recalls, Vernon Watkins was primarily attracted by Heine's poetic style and manner, but was not interested in his approaches to love poetry, nor his attitudes in politics and philosophy.

The group of poems conjuring up poets leads to 'The Childhood of Hölderlin', which, opening with Hölderlin's 'To the Fates' and proceeding to a sequence of nine poems, clearly occupies a pivotal position in the collection and grants to this poet a wealth of appreciation which is unique in the volume *Affinities*. The first poem puts two questions, one indicating the difficulty of re-creating the childhood of Hölderlin, another which brings out the unusual quality of the poet who could be familiar with heaven and refuse to modify his vision when he returned to earth. Consequent upon the poet's closeness to heaven is the intermingling of joy and suffering. The experience of the proximity of these two is reinforced by 'Sophocles' music'. Presented twice already in the first poem, the theme of joy and suffering recurs subsequently: the second poem ends with the restatement of the double presence in a translation of Hölderlin's epigram 'Sophocles', while the last stanza of the fourth poem links together 'the deepest joy' with 'the deepest shadow in death'; the theme re-enters ('Grief keeping pace with joy') towards the close of the sequence, in the ninth poem.

In discerning a biographical pattern through 'The Childhood of Hölderlin', further traces of the paradox of the double presence may be noticed. The second poem shows infancy merging into boyhood, moulded by his mother, by nature and the reading of

Greek myths. Birth and death are linked; near the opening comes the statement 'Before birth / He had experienced death', while the longer quotation from Hölderlin in this poem ends with the line 'My words are silence. Orpheus plays to the Shades'. The third poem interprets 'Hälfte des Lebens' again, as in 'To Hölderlin', but now the division of youth and age marked by the surface of the lake is seen as prophetic of the poet's later, sadder phase of life. In the fourth poem Hölderlin is shown as moving towards a unification of Greek and Christian traditions in the creating of 'Bread and Wine' and 'Patmos'. The indifference of Goethe and Schiller to the younger poet (in the fifth poem) leads Vernon Watkins to claim the superiority of Hölderlin's poetry particularly through the quality of 'supernatural love' which, mentioned in the second poem, was developed in the fourth poem, and now receives a threefold stress in the fifth poem, finally in Hölderlin's words from 'Andenken', where France is recalled. After the sixth poem, where the poet's self-identification with what he described in nature is evoked, the theme of love, in the seventh poem, includes Diotima as a culmination of the fulfilment granted to the poet, closely associated with sacrifice and death. The eighth poem, looking towards late, cold night, portrays Hölderlin in the years after his breakdown. The theme of birth reappears in the final, ninth poem, where the rebirth of a flawless Adam is postulated as a precondition for the realisation of Hölderlin's ideal world. But the poet now 'speaks in fragmentary language', though Christian contexts appear. Sorrow interweaves with joy, sound with silence, and death with life.

Greek and Christian traditions have provided Vernon Watkins' Hölderlin with a duality of cultural, archetypal models, the Christian finally dominating in the ninth poem. Parallel with these influences, the awareness of nature is a constant experience of the poet. The poet has an intuitive, positive relationship with nature as a whole: 'In that pure instant he knew the workings of nature', 'Harmonious nature differed from exiled man' (first poem), 'If he touched a bud, he knew the secrets of nature' (second poem), 'the language of petals and leaves / His mother tongue' (fifth poem). He is 'poet of rivers and supernatural love' (fifth poem). 'Fountain' and 'river of light' are introduced into the first stanza of the first poem; Here follow the Rhine (second poem), the swan's lake (third poem), the Danube and the sea (fourth poem), waterfall, river and sea (fifth poem), rivers and cataract ('he *became* the river', sixth poem) sea, river and cataract (seventh poem), the Neckar stream (eighth poem), and rivers (ninth poem). The sun, the moon, the earth, birds, mountains, flowers and trees recur, frequently described in terms of praise and worship. The specific images of racing foal and violet are linked together in the opening stanza of the first poem, and again in the first stanza of the fifth poem.

After 'The Childhood of Hölderlin' follows 'Angelo's Adam', the last of the poems centred upon an individual creative artist, linked with the foregoing ninth poem of the Hölderlin sequence by the figure of Adam. The subsequent seven poems either have or might have a personal, Welsh setting. The childhood recollection in 'The Smoke of Cities Passed' might be in correspondence with the mood of the first poem in the volume, 'Waterfalls'. 'Taliesin and the Mockers' involves God's creating the world and man. 'Music of Colours—Dragonfoil and the Furnace of Colours' reintroduces Orpheus. With 'Quem Quaeritis' and 'Five Poems of Magdalenian Darkness' the poet concentrates on purely Christian themes. In the four poems of 'Revisited Waters (for the Quatercentenary of Repton School, founded in 1557)' memory associates transience with the stream, links nature and Christian themes, dispensing with the portrayal of specific individuals or works of art. The final poem 'Returning from Harvest' is an autumnal, evening close, evocative of a country scene, its issues expressed within this framework.

The ordering of some of the themes in the volume *Affinities* has been attempted here so that the relevance of German literary tradition to Vernon Watkins' poetic attitudes may be touched upon. Reference to preliminary drafts of the material that eventually comprised this volume opens up evidence of the often complex genesis of the poet's work. The manuscript and typescript material relating to Hölderlin in *Affinities* (as held by the British Museum, Add. 54165) is particularly rich; there are ten complete typescripts of 'The Childhood of Hölderlin', and apart from the title 'The Childhood of Hölderlin' there were a further eight separate titles which Vernon Watkins used in this context. To do justice to this material would require a detailed exercise that cannot be undertaken here. A few examples of the poet's earlier conceptions may, however, be of interest. For instance, one of the completed drafts of 'The Childhood of Hölderlin' is entitled

'Hölderlin' and subdivided into three headed sections: 'Childhood', 'Manhood and Death' and 'Reperception'. Then there is the second stanza of the fifth poem of 'The Childhood of Hölderlin'. Here Vernon Watkins speaks of Hölderlin's relationship with Goethe and Schiller, and the difficulty he had in finalising his words on this subject can be shown by quoting stages through which this stanza went. In the following quotations, the last one is the final, printed version:

(*a*) His crime was tenderness. Goethe was reigning in Weimar.
Schiller to him was surpassing, the last of the Hellenes,
An unapproachable star: the one an eagle
Level in light, the second an eagle plunging.

(*b*) Poet of rivers and supernatural love,
His crime was tenderness. Goethe was reigning in Weimar
Majestic, holding the court of what Europe had learned.
For Hoelderlin Schiller surpassed him, the last of the Hellenes,
An unapproachable star. Yet neither accepted
The eccentric course of their visitor, pledged to his myth.

(*c*) ... Goethe was reigning in Weimar
Majestic, holding for Europe his court, like the sun.
... Yet neither accepted
The eccentric course of their visitor, pledged to a loftier myth.

(*d*) ... Goethe was reigning in Weimar,
Holding, majestic, his court like a rational sun.

(*e*) [Final version]
Poet of rivers and supernatural love,
His crime was tenderness. Goethe was reigning in Weimar,
Holding, majestic, his court, like a classical sun.
For Hölderlin Schiller surpassed him, the last of the Hellenes,
An unapproachable star. Yet neither accepted
Their eccentric visitor, pledged to a loftier myth.

One of the completed drafts of 'The Childhood of Hölderlin' (signed, and with the words 'Finished June, 1953' added) contains six stanzas which are not included in the final, printed version of the poem. They are a translation of Hölderlin's 'Die Heimath' ('Home'), which Vernon Watkins had already published.

From the Hölderlin manuscript material it may be of interest to reproduce one poem (by kind permission of Mrs. G. Watkins) at this point:

A Late Wreath for Hölderlin

To whom do you carry those leaves? First, who has wound them?
For the laurel lives from the dawn of time on the fortunate,
It crowns his exultant labours,
And behind the foliage move the eternal dancers.

Men built on the slopes of the hill. From the rock rebounding,
The waterfall thunders, down-rushing. And over the river
Bridges like diving swallows
Hang; they are fledged by a thought, by the steeple striking.

'Rest. Our hero is laid. The shroud is upon him.
He, of all men alone enamoured of daybreak,
Sprang to the sacred fountain,
Blind to the shadows of earth, for the light had killed him.'

Vernon Watkins also wrote some light, occasional verse, for private family and other events. There is 'A Survey of the German Romantic Movement (as seen by an undergraduate, and after)', which bears the dating: May 1967 and earlier (3-vi-1925). 'Arrival in East Shelby', with its literary references, has as its last stanza:

'Dear God', I softly pray, as one does
Who fears the crash of balls through windows,
'May now that Storm is propped with Mörike,
Cricket appease North-West America.'

The poem 'Mozart at Zell-am-See', date January 1967, was published in *The New Yorker* and subsequently in the volume *Uncollected Poems* (with an introduction by Kathleen Raine, 1969); a preliminary draft has the title 'A Theme of Mozart'. There is a manuscript translation of Hölderlin's 'Human Applause'. The poem 'Farewell to Nürnberg', dated 1932 and 1949, is printed in this volume by kind permission of Mrs. Gwen Watkins, who points out that it is 'in his *earlier* pre-Mari-Lwyd style: I don't think it would have satisfied him now'.

At the end of these notes on Vernon Watkins and German literature, it may be mentioned that two poems, from *The Death Bell*, 'The Strangled Prayer' and 'Music of Colours: The

Blossom Scattered', have been included in *Von Hopkins bis Dylan Thomas. Englische Gedichte und deutsche Prosaübertragungen* (herausgegeben und übertragen von Ursula Clemen und Christian Enzenberger), Fischer Bücherei, Frankfurt and Hamburg, 1961; and that a verse translation, 'Christus und Charon', from *Cypress and Acacia,* by Agatha Horst, appeared in *Das Goetheanum*, Vol. 39, No. 16, 17 April 1960. Further, the poem 'To Hölderlin', translated into German by Joachim Uhlmann, is included in a collection of nine poems written in English on the subject of Hölderlin which was presented with an introduction by Michael Hamburger ('Englische Hölderlin-Gedichte mitgeteilt von Michael Hamburger', *Hölderlin-Jahrbuch*, XIII (1963–64) 80–103). Michael Hamburger also refers to Vernon Watkins in his essay 'Die Aufnahme Hölderlins in England', *Hölderlin-Jahrbuch,* vol. 14, 1965–66, pp. 20–34.

NOTES

1. Dylan Thomas, *Letters to Vernon Watkins* (edited with an introduction by Vernon Watkins), 1957, p. 47.
2. Dylan Thomas, op. cit., p. 100.
3. Dylan Thomas, op. cit., p. 105.
4. Photocopy of extracts from the working notebook of Vernon Watkins, made 20 July 1965. Copies in the British Museum and Swansea University College Library. The list of translations of German poems is based largely on this source.
5. This emerges in the translator's comment on the dust-jacket of *The North Sea,* New York, 1951.

This poem was drawn to my attention by Cecil Price. It first appeared in *Times Literary Supplement,* 26 June 1959.

Kathleen Raine, 'Vernon Watkins: Poet of Tradition'. *Anglo-Welsh Review,* vol. 14, no. 33, 1964, p. 21.

FAREWELL TO NUREMBERG

Nuremberg, I leave you; but I shall come again.
Slow pulls the Northbound train. Red the geraniums hung,
Faint on the wondering balcony. Last look; and then, O train,
Leave, gold, the window-glass, the musical-box that sung.

Leave far behind you the mountains of the vine.
Leave, small, the cobbled squares where fountain basins fill.
Pause not, nor give me rest until I see the pine
Standing alone in silence high on Glamorgan's hill.

There I shall clamber, above the scented fern,
Late, when the sunset sky changes to vivid green,
There see the seawave fall, and hear the wash return
Roaring through luminous caverns, secret and serene.

Strong Dürer toiling, with Eden in his brain,
Wrought there a pious path for noble feet to tread;
Hans Sachs's working lamp and last for eyes remain
Turning a shoe like parchment, stitched with a cobbler's thread.

Great Lorenzkirche, gloom of unearthly fire,
Raised wings of angels, poised in the trembling light,
Stilled wings, desire restrained, more true than wild desire,
Guarding a flying hush, a mute, perpetual flight.

Downcast, those angels gaze, carved in the gloom of prayer;
Downcast the Virgin's face, full of unspeakable love;
All, all of sweetness, all the swift heavens are there,
Stars in a drop of water, held by the wings of a dove.

Strawed market-bridges, your alleys close their eyes
Near lilac ramparts, to watch a petalled stream
Keep, caught in distance closed, like wings of butterflies,
Pensive, the spots of flight, the dawdling, wayward gleam.

Once, there, a Jewess lived, fond of the cobbled town,
Sought peace in crimson tiles where the wings of pigeons rest.
Poised, there, a fountain-boy calls the bright water down;
Like a joy just removed, he calls it to his breast.

Love, highest wisdom, a footstep from us lies;
Truth hides, is near us, at the heart of light and sound.
Once met, they catch our breath, and in that breath the eyes
Burn with immortal heaven, and we know what we have found.

Vernon Watkins
(1932 and 1949)

9

THE CHATTERTON THEME IN MODERN GERMAN LITERATURE

By B. Keith-Smith

"An ingenious man never starves unknown"
(Shaftesbury)

'Ja, Thomas Chatterton ist Thomas Chatterton. Das ist eine einfache Aussage für eine komplizierte Sache,' says the character Thomas Chatterton in Hans Henny Jahnn's tragedy on 'Bristol's poet' (p. 33). And well he might, to judge from both the complex real-life character and from the intricacies of the legends that have grown up about him, not to mention the variety of approaches taken by numerous critics to the Chatterton problem. The actual life and works of Thomas Chatterton are reasonably well documented, and both the works and the legend continue to arouse professional critical interest in this country.[1] The influence of Chatterton on French literature is well known because of the Romantic drama by Alfred de Vigny.[2] Less well known is his influence on the work of the father of Portuguese Romanticism João Baptista da Silva Leitão Almeida-Garrett. Equally little known is the influence of Chatterton on modern German literature, partly because there are no references to this in the standard bibliographical sources for comparative literature, but also because at first sight the Germans might be expected to have found sufficient material on the problem of the artist and society and that of the young man's suicide in their own literature. This article is limited to a discussion of the three twentieth-century works: Ernst Penzoldt's novel *Der arme Chatterton*,[3] Hans Henny Jahnn's tragedy *Thomas Chatterton*,[4] and Johannes Bobrowski's Sapphic ode *Ode auf Thomas Chatterton*.[5] It will also consider one nineteenth-century drama: Heinrich Blau's tragedy *Thomas Chatterton*[6] and refer to three critical works in German.[7]

Ernst Penzoldt's novel presents Chatterton as a disturbing influence on all those who come into contact with him. Through his crises they are led to revaluations of their situation and of his. The first hundred pages could be compared with a dream in which Chatterton drifts along through life with nothing but an opportunist's outlook on every problem. The past—represented by his father's name carved in a chair, by the coats of arms on the tombs, by the strange presence of St. Mary Redcliffe, by the traditions of the Colston's School, by respect for old parchments, by emphasis on ceremonial, and by the tradition-bound trust on which Bristol life is shown to be based—all becomes the central process by which Chatterton is brought up into the world. At first an inescapable necessity, it becomes a challenge for him to make mockery of, and against which he rebels more and more. The description of St. Mary Redcliffe represents the point of departure from which Chatterton sets out to conquer Bristol for himself. Seen through his eyes, the way the tower is described suggests precisely how Chatterton himself will become:

> The tower was broad, heavy and red and not built as if by petty complaisant human hands, not by creatures of suspect flesh, but devised by mountains, called up by the thunder, climbing and growing out of the bottomless stony depths into the light to a pure crystal utterly obedient to the longing of the stone itself. (p. 19)

He uses his imagination to escape from awkward situations and to impress his family and his patron Barrett with all the guile of a sorcerer; and with it he boosts his pride especially in his secret visits to Eleanor, climbing up the ivy to her room at night with all the bravado of a conventional Romeo, but cruelly set on by dogs awoken by his cries of panic when she tries to embrace him for the first time. These episodes all more or less take place in a state of trance half way between the almost dead newly-born baby he is reported to have been and the deliberately earnest young impoverished poet he will become in London. The turning-point comes in a fantastic 'prise de corps' when Eleanor literally kidnaps Chatterton with the aid of her Moor bodyguard, whisks him off to her castle somewhere in Somerset, and proceeds to try to seduce him while he is being held by the Moor. Eventually Chatterton persuades her to dismiss the Moor, and he leaves at dawn having forcefully attained his manhood. His imaginative powers as Rowley are stilled from this point on, and Penzoldt leads him relentlessly to his suicide through ever-increasing stages of disillusion. Preparing himself for death he reads through the whole of Rowley's poetry again as a final acceptance of the collapse of his imagined world. As he dies he enjoys the thought that he is entering a company of humans far greater than the living, yet his final gesture is one of despair and loneliness. The suicide is shown as unavoidable, but it is so simply told in contrast with the interpreted, imagined and often somnambulistic episodes of the rest of the novel, that it seems to be the only true experience that Chatterton has. In his postscript Penzoldt compares him with such poets as François Villon, Cyrano de Bergerac and Christian Günther:

> to those then who led a truly fabulous life, poets and poetry in one person. (p. 163)

And as Penzoldt puts it:

> In the story of 'the marvellous Boy, the sleepless Soul' (Wordsworth) I followed the historical dates superficially, most of the names and stages of his life, however binding them together in a Chatterton way—the probable with the true. (p. 164)

Hans Henny Jahnn's tragedy opens almost as a modern naturalist drama. The oppressive forces of tradition, family respect and difficulties in bringing up children in poverty to lead a correct life form a background against which Chatterton reacts with vigour and despair. It is hardly surprising he seeks a more colourful life than the morbid resignation of his mother and grandmother.

'Geist' is the attraction and object of trust for Chatterton, an idea brought to him by his meeting a stranger who offered him money and whom he refers to as Aburiel. Chatterton is forced by his mother to sign a harsh seven-year contract with Lambert the lawyer; with resignation he accepts the social order as a formal duty, but it is clear from the start that this Chatterton needs little encouragement to break out from it, so restrictive are its impositions on youth. Lambert represents Bristol business with his comment:

> Whatever seems bad or harsh is nevertheless good, for otherwise God would not suffer it. The namby-pamby is rejected. So severity is the virtue of the state, the church and of those in authority. (p. 32)

Chatterton's reply that he has heard this before points to the socio-political tension that underlines the whole play. The entry of Aburiel who declares he loves Chatterton 'in his own way' had led Hans Wolpe to see him as Chatterton's guardian angel, but Aburiel has more demonic features about him, and throughout he remains an enigmatic embodiment of Chatterton's aspirations. Aburiel is without doubt a tempter, coming as he does just when Chatterton could most make use of him. He is cynical and expresses nihilistic views about humanity; he also points out with apparent ease to Chatterton that only through documents can the past be brought to light again. It is not difficult to realise that Jahnn presents the problem of Chatterton as the problem of post-1945 German youth face to face with the immediate past. For he was almost dead when he was born and had to have life smacked into him by his uncle the gravedigger. And as Aburiel points out of the dead in Bristol:

> There is poverty and richness. There are spirit, genius and bodily beauty. There are failed lives, dullness, incompletion, cripples, self-satisfied dunderheads and wanton crawlers. The earth swallows them all indiscriminately. But they are always there. In us and by us. (pp. 42–3)

Aburiel tempts Chatterton back to the past, and in a scene woefully reminiscent of Gilbert and Sullivan's *Ruddigore* most of the fifteenth-century Bristolians in Chatterton's works including Thomas Rowley appear in full costume through the bookshelves of Lambert's office. Chatterton is not assured enough to face up to such an unexpected event, and with the clearsightedness that marks his character throughout the play he comments:

> Phantasies crowd in on me, split my consciousness. . . . Noise on the street, is that the universe? (p. 47)

Chatterton takes to sleep-walking and to creating the Rowley poems in which he is swept along and out of his own self. He finds that true freedom is one of complete withdrawal from one's personal commitments, a form of non-identity half way between life in society and death:

> One must be faithless enough so that at every hour one is ready to escape its unpleasantnesses and shoot oneself through the mouth. (p. 60)

Jahnn's Chatterton has become like a Gottfried Benn type 'Genotyp'—like Benn in Brussels he could say: 'I lived on the brink where existence falls and the self begins.'[8] Jahnn's Chatterton in many ways is similar to Benn's concept of the 'lyrisches Ich'. The apparent ease with which Chatterton can adjust his feelings when he discovers that he has mourned the wrong brother, and the supposedly dead friend walks in, seems at first sight an unnecessary piece of extra dramatic effect. Yet it is precisely in such a moment that this Chatterton triumphs, for his confidence lies in the potentiality of the human spirit and not in its socially tempered and restricted range of manoeuvre.

> Close your eyes and before you is the breadth of nature, the great landscape of all possible experiences. Our religion is the certainty that we are defended against all that the world can bring. (p. 61)

he says to Peter the brother who commits suicide, opening up the way for Chatterton himself.

Jahnn portrays through caricature and intrigue a most effective section in which Chatterton is taken to task by the Bristol businessmen—as a comment on class distinction outwitted by the lively opportunist this is closer to tragi-comedy than is perhaps suited to the play as a whole. Yet it serves well to represent the intrusion of the everyday world on to Chatterton's imaginary one, and their interdependence. Lambert releases Chatterton from his contract in order to avoid the scandal of his threatened suicide. This enables him to go to London to try and have his work published and cut off his relations with all his friends and acquaintances which have become too complex to continue. Before leaving Bristol Chatterton is confident of success and of shaking off all previous restrictions, whether in friendships or love affairs. Only Polly retains his affection, and even she he turns into the image of a goddess. Chatterton has gained knowledge of his true inner self which he describes:

> I have longing, nothing but longing. My blood wells up into my mouth when I think of my restlessness. But God has sent his creatures into the world with arms long enough to reach all that they are tempted to possess against all reason. (p. 91)

The final Act shows Chatterton's pride and hunger in London. Jahnn allows for a brief interlude of happiness in Polly's visit, and includes one of Chatterton's most simple and delightful songs: 'Away, to the Woodlands, away', before he is plunged into the final depths of despair and understands that the poet's imagination is but a form of self-pity. His death follows quickly, almost before the audience realises it, and it is left to Aburiel to ring down the curtain with the moral of the play:

> But it is the duty of man not to lay blame on all that is best. (p. 125)

Johannes Bobrowski's interest in the theme of the suicide of a young unrecognised poet is expressed in his short prose work *Epitaph für Pinnau.*[9] But Pinnau dies because of the relentless elitism of Kant's circle, which is described with irony and humour. The young poet's death is but a device to show up the heartlessness and temporary unease of the selected circle of Kant's admirers. Pinnau is but a foil to the inhuman antics of 'Geist' in a petty provincial setting. Bobrowski's interest is mainly for the effect of this unexpected suicide on the magic circle of Kant's local court. It is a study in the behaviour of cold reason temporarily checked by a fatal gesture of despair. Kant only feels qualms of conscience for a moment, and once that moment is smoothed away, once the painful episode is forgotten, he and his guests can turn to the weekly luncheon and to the Grace that they offer before it.

Bobrowski's poem on Chatterton, however, attempts to bring Chatterton's world close to us by revealing the intimate human anxieties within it. The spirit of Bristol, and in particular of St. Mary Redcliffe, is caught, and various conclusions are drawn that reach out beyond Chatterton and the poem itself. It is one of the few examples of the Sapphic ode in twentieth-century German literature, and keeps regularly to the classical form with a few minor exceptions. The opening description of St. Mary Redcliffe is in itself a poetic tour de force, unavoidably filling the landscape yet full of intricate detail—a world of unexpected contrasts and syntactical devices, protecting yet somehow awesome in its variety. The loneliness and apartness of the boy is emphasised by his being on the church parapet, part of its upward striving architecture, in contrast with the heavy downward effect of the description of the gravedigger. Chatterton, not able to call back the past, is led into more and more despair. This is turned into a more general reflection on poetic inspiration and creation expressed in the tree-image that is with its shadows parallel to the architecture of the church. Bobrowski's tree image suggests something far more realistic and complete than that of Heinrich Blau in his Chatterton play:

> . . . here is
> A tree, out of whose branches
> Truth and the love of man do spring.
> From every blossom breaks a freedom song,
> Into a roof the green leaves arch themselves
> And under them there stands the god of love,
> Offers his hand to the whole of human kind,
> Unites them through love's all-embracing power. (Blau, p. 20)

Bristol, for all Chatterton's song, carries on regardless—an elegiac strain enters the poem that is typical of much of Bobrowski's poetry. Yet the eighth and ninth strophes are held back in their flow by phrases that describe parts of the landscape almost as parts of a collage in contrast to the flowing rhythm of the descriptions of the church and even more of the tree. Some of the implacable indifference of nature that we find elsewhere in Bobrowski's poetry is felt here as a sign of Chatterton's distance from life in the town and in the surrounding landscape. The last two strophes suggest that Chatterton's time in London was but a mere extension to this loneliness, a more vivid realisation of the closeness of love and death. Bobrowski personifies death who comes—fittingly for someone who has frenziedly sought to bring back the middle ages—as a medieval bony figure. Bobrowski's Chatterton is more than a lament to Chatterton's fate—it is also a warning. Part of Chatterton's life in two worlds, that of his everyday environment and that of his poetic phantasy, is reproduced here, yet like Bobrowski himself the poet's presence is hardly emphasised at all. Town and landscape, church and tree almost submerge Chatterton as a character until all that is written in his book, all that he will be remembered for is summed up in two words: 'Rowley' and 'Aella'. Unless the reader knew beforehand of Chatterton's suicide, he would hardly realise it from this poem. It is Chatterton's lack of profile that interests Bobrowski, especially when set against the features of the church architecture and their shadows, and even more poignantly in contrast with the intricate yet for ever moving and rustling tree structure of his poetry.

Heinrich Blau's tragedy in four Acts is a strange mixture. This is due to the reasons the author confesses to in his foreword; finding Chatterton an unsympathetic character due to his pride and ambition, Blau allows himself considerable poetic licence to set up an ideal character. At times (due doubtless to extensive use of 'Knittelvers') he appears as a Faust prior to the pact with Mephistopheles in Goethe's *Faust* Part I, and is even caught in the net of his own reputation, as a philanderer, smooth-tongued trickster or hopelessly romantic victim of fate. Most striking of all in this play is Chatterton's passivity—at times he plays as it were a double role, that of the poet who is forced to deceive in order to bring attention to himself, and that of the hapless youth astounded and even horrified by his effect on other people. Chatterton is presented here both as a victim and as the key-figure to a whole circle of other people's sufferings. That these sufferings are largely due to misunderstandings about Chatterton's true motives, means that the drama has a strong element of the tragi-comedy about it. Indeed, there are times when it descends to the worst forms of over-romanticised melodrama.

The plot is centred on Chatterton's success in writing love-letters for his friend Baker to Leonore. Her identity is unknown to Chatterton at first, but when Baker discovers Chatterton has fallen in love with her, his friendship turns into hatred, and he publicly denounces Chatterton's secret that he wrote the Rowley poems. Baker, due to his poverty, has not dared ask Cathcott (Leonore's Uncle) for permission to marry her. Leonore calls Baker a coward, and having met Chatterton for the first time, is fascinated by his rhapsodic love at first sight for her. Lady Julia Heskett, niece of Sir Horace Walpole, has come to find Rowley, and saves Chatterton from almost certain murder at the hands of Baker by taking him back to London. We next see Chatterton after a year in London, ignored by Walpole, and too proud to accept Walpole's eventual invitation to come to see him. Chatterton is told of Baker's request for Leonore's hand, which is refused, and that Baker and Leonore have fled to London, where he has left her with nothing but shame ahead of her. Cathcott comes to find her, but only manages to find Baker who has been driven mad by Chatterton's curse on him before he left Bristol. Baker thinks Cathcott is Chatterton and stabs himself in Cathcott's arms. Cathcott persuades Chatterton to visit Walpole, who explains to Julia that he has acted as a father to her in accordance with her dying mother's instructions. He has deliberately kept her away from Chatterton, as he detected in her love for him, and denounces this union for reasons of class difference, which had driven her parents apart (and which the audience realises is played out as a sub-plot between Baker and Leonore). Julia, an early suffragette-type figure, refuses to accept this and in a scene in which she addresses the imagined spirit of her mother as 'erhabner Geist', she claims her heart only beats for Chatterton. Walpole decides to send him back to Bristol, tries to buy him with a yearly £100, but fails in the face of Chatterton's demand for his manuscript back of *Aella*. Walpole's motives are eventually realised by Chatterton who now reacts even more strongly against this 'Machiavelli'. Chatterton places the indissolubility of love before all else, but it is Leonore he loves, and it is Leonore whom he finds dying in the street in a more than operatic final Act. Entering just on time to save her from the reproaches of the drunken but honourable citizens, Chatterton (against a background of New Year bells and redemptive hymn) listens to her final words which contain the main love images of the play:

> Weightless I feel, a bright light I do see
> And hear sweet tones. O Chatterton
> I have loved you as a sister should,
> So kiss me now with a fraternal kiss.
> With the sun's beams the lotus blossom plays,
> Until it a tender flower fades. (p. 98)

The final scene is in Chatterton's room with Leonore's corpse behind a curtain. Julia tries to give Chatterton renewed faith in life, for she fears what has now become obvious. Throughout the play there have been partly obvious borrowings from various German plays, but Julia's advice and Chatterton's response are the most clearly reminiscent of all:

> Julia: Woe to the man who loses courage,
> He is like that lost sailor on the sea,
> From whose hand the storm has wrenched the helm,
> Who then into the dark depths has plunged,
> Too much afraid to trust his sinking bark.
> And we too travel in a boat that's weak
> Through this life's wild and turbulent sea,
> The rocky reefs and cliffs that

We call blows of fate, they are but there
To prove our value in necessity.
In shipwreck stands out clearly the true man,
In hardship is revealed the stalwart heart.
Chatterton: Yet when you but see nothing else but rocks,
And cliffs that tower out of the raging flood,
What else remains to you except the final plunge?
(p. 104)

Alas, poor Chatterton! Not for him the rock of Antonio to whom he could cling, but merely the body of his beloved to show Julia and his final manuscripts to offer her as a form of consolation prize. But Blau manages an excruciating suicide scene to follow (not without a final reminiscence, this time of Bürger's *Lenore*: 'Rufst Glocke du bereits zur Hochzeit mich?' when St. Paul's strikes two), and dies with the words:

Now with the lotus flower the sunbeam at last
Is wed. And this is the marriage night,
The bridal bed black coffin of the dead,
The funeral bell rings out the marriage song. (pp. 110–11)

Morning sun (it is just after 2 a.m.!) pours over the scene, and Julia re-enters, swooning with the cry 'Chatterton'.

For all its faults, Blau's play is uniquely full of potential conflict in Chatterton literature, has a complex if obvious construction, and does not attempt to concentrate attention all the time on Chatterton himself. It includes social, family, moral and religious problems. The fate of Chatterton and his effect on his contemporaries are used both as a romantic tragedy and as a forum for the expression of ideas which must have preoccupied the author as a young man living in London at the end of the nineteenth century. Its characters may seem types, but they present forceful and undeniably valid arguments from within their social context.

In all four works discussed, the writer has made use of the Chatterton material to produce a work of art that only partially deals with Chatterton as an historical personality. The legendary detail around his life and works has been selectively used by Penzoldt to represent the problem of the repressed individual, a child prodigy until the moment when he really experiences 'life' in the arms of Eleanor; by Jahnn as an example of almost spiritual inner emigration in the face of inhuman materialism, not that

Jahnn idealises Chatterton—he is shown as too obviously proud for that; by Bobrowski as a figure unable to establish himself because he was the true poet, a perfectionist and experimenter, hopelessly alone and oppressed by a sense of transience, a stranger in his own landscape which both protected and enveloped him; and by Blau as a swashbuckling figure of fate, mouthpiece like his real-life model for noble sentiments and lush sentimentality cribbed from former writers, a would-be Don Juan equipped with all the necessary trappings but too young to get away with it.

In the German research on Chatterton there is one outstanding contribution by Helene Richter who understands Chatterton mainly as someone with a fanatic admiration for the past and an unanswerable desire to bring it back to life. Chatterton for her was a Janus-figure, never at home in his own times and split between the past and the future. For her he appears as a typical 'Sturm und Drang' character, restless because of the more and more unbearable contrast between the great world of imagination inside him and the existence he led as a scribe. She does not equate him with Goethe's *Werther* despite her narration of the episode where he held a pistol to his head and found he did not have the courage to pull the trigger, but mainly because she points out that such gestures were commonplace among youths of his generation.

Paul Staubert offers a psychological analysis of Chatterton's Rowley complex, and claims that the psychology of puberty should be applied to his case with Goethe's description of genius as an 'extended puberty' in mind. His poetry is understood as a developed version of childhood games, and his experimentation with lettering is compared with that of the German mystic Hildegard von Ruppertsberg (1089–1179)—the one held in the thrall of puberty, the other by unknown magic powers producing a state 'closely related to puberty' (p. 82). Staubert sees the whole problem of Rowley as one of self-deceit based on a split in personality typical of a primitive attitude. Genetic inevitability, not conscious deceit lay at the root of Chatterton's personality and means of self-expression.

J. Schmidt (who styled himself Professor in Cheltenham) centres his report on the claim that deceit, pride and ambition prepared the way for Chatterton's fall. But he also adds the political events of the month of Chatterton's arrival in London as a major cause for his failure to achieve recognition. For all London was preoccupied by the triumphal exit from prison on 17 April 1770 of the notorious John Wilkes, and on the very day of Chatterton's arrival disturbing news of trouble in Boston reached London. The American problem had arrived!

Hans Wolpe has pointed out how much Penzoldt and Jahnn used Helene Richter's work for their background knowledge, and it is clear that Blau must have used either Püttmann's translations or have adapted some of the original Chatterton poems for his play. What is striking in all of the works in German on Chatterton or about him is a sense of futility.

Germans, in short, have admired the ingenuity of 'the wonder-boy', but have primarily understood him as the victim of a society that through its indifference and lack of understanding forced out of him attitudes of despair that could only lead to disaster. Chatterton's fate has become for them one example of the potential hazards that wait on the demands of rampant individualism, especially when it seeks to express itself in poetry.[10]

NOTES

1. The most recent is the booklet issued by the Bristol Branch of the Historical Association in 1963 by my colleague Basil Cottle, whom I thank for his interest and advice. Dr. Cottle in his bibliography mentions especially E. H. W. Meyerstein, *A Life of Thomas Chatterton* (1930) as an exhaustive study. He also refers to the two bibliographies by F. A. Hyett and W. Bazeley (1914) and by E. R. Norris Matthews (1916). It is interesting to note that although the 200th anniversary of Chatterton's death fell on 24 August 1970, no official ceremony had been organised to mark this in Bristol.
2. Vigny's drama is most readily available, in the *Oeuvres Complètes* in the *Bibliothèque de la Pléiade* (i, 809–903) edited by F. Baldensperger (Gallimard, Paris 1950). A new paperback edition has just been published by Garnier/Flammarion. Written to justify the existence of the poet type, this became popular as a romantic tragedy because of the disastrous love between Kitty Bell and Chatterton her lodger. Indeed, it is possible to claim that the drama is primarily concerned with the involvement and eventual death of Kitty Bell rather than with Chatterton's plight. In the chronicle *Dernière nuit de travail* Vigny points out that it is not Chatterton himself in whom he is primarily interested, but rather in 'l'homme spiritualiste étouffé par une société matérialiste, où le calculateur avare exploite sans pitié l'intelligence et le travail'. Kitty Bell, seen as a saintly figure by the Quaker, has many of the characteristics that Vigny enumerates for the 'poet type', so one feels that when Vigny wrote: 'Y a-t-il un autre moyen de toucher la société que de lui montrer la torture de ses victimes?' he could have had both Chatterton and Kitty Bell in mind (p. 823). Their plight is caused by the impossibility of finding and maintaining an ideal world within and yet apart from the twisted inhuman society in which they exist. Vigny's depiction of that inhuman society, especially in the opening scenes before Chatterton appears, has all the harshness and suppressed violence of Naturalist drama. John Bell's treatment of the workers and the young Lord's ribald mockery of Chatterton and Kitty as young and mutually attractive persons stand in acute contrast to the soothing wisdom and patience of the Quaker supposed to have

been modelled on Benjamin Franklin. Out of a social drama springs a Romantic tragedy. Out of the rough way of the world stands the hopeless idealism of an impossible love. An earlier version of this is found in Vigny's *Stello* in the same volume which also includes other material on the theme.

3. Ernst Penzoldt, *Der arme Chatterton. Geschichte eines Wunderkindes.* Suhrkamp Verlag, Berlin, 1948, 164 pp. (originally published by Insel Verlag, Leipzig 1928).
4. *Thomas Chatterton.* Eine Tragödie von Hans Henny Jahnn. Suhrkamp Verlag, Frankfurt/Main, 1955, 125 pp. After several enquiries it was found impossible to trace the essay by Jahnn, 'Zur Tragödie Thomas Chattertons' mentioned in Kosch, *Literatur-Lexikon* and other sources.
5. Johannes Bobrowski, *Das Land Sarmatien. Gedichte.* Deutscher Taschenbuch Verlag, München 1966, pp. 84–86 (originally published in Sinn und Form, Berlin 4. Heft 1955, 500–501).
6. Heinrich Blau, *Thomas Chatterton. Tragödie in 4 Akten.* London, 1887, 111 pp. (Copy in Central Library, Bristol.)
7. Helene Richter, *Thomas Chatterton.* Wiener Beiträge Band XII, Wien, 1900, 258 pp.
   Paul Staubert, *Thomas Chatterton und seine Rowley Dichtung. Untersucht auf Grund der Psychologie der Reifezeit.* Bonner Studien zur englischen Philologie Heft XXIV, Bonn, 1935, 162 pp.
   J. Schmidt: *Thomas Chatterton, eine biographische Skizze.* Archiv für das Studium der neueren Sprachen (Herrigs Archiv) 1857, Band 21.
   There are three other relevant works, which were not available to me for this article:
   Eduard Engel, Ein dichtender Wunderknabe, *Vossische Zeitung,* Berlin 22.11.1908 Nr. 549.
   Hermann Püttmann, *Chatterton,* Burman, 1840. This is in two parts, one a critical essay, the other translations of Chatterton's work.
   Helene Richter, 'Chattertons Sprache', In: *Bausteine Zeitschrift für Neuenglische Wortforschung,* Schöneberg, Berlin, pp. 29–97 (Copy in Gloucester Public Library).
   Also consulted were:
   Sigrid Hoefert, *Ode auf Thomas Chatterton* in: *West-Östliches in der Lyrik Johannes Bobrowskis,* Uni-Druck, München, 1966 pp. 44–51.
   Hans Wolpe, 'Thomas Chatterton. The marvellous boy', In: *Revue de Littérature Comparée,* XXXVII (1963), 33–49.
8. Gottfried Benn, *Gesammelte Werke. Band 4 Reden und Vorträge,* Limes Vlg., Wiesbaden, 1968 p. 1874.
9. Johannes Bobrowski, *Boehlendorff und andere.* Deutsche Verlags-Anstalt, Stuttgart, 1965 pp. 36–41.
10. An interesting example of the same conclusions in English is to be found in the Werther-type novel written in letter form: Sir Herbert Croft's *Love and Madness* (London, 1780). Half of this book is one letter on Chatterton. Its level of critical approach may be judged by the following comment on Chatterton's suicide: 'That his despair should fix on August, that it should not have staid, at least, till the gloomier months of winter, must surprise those who are sensible of the influence of such a climate as ours' (p. 197). Croft's apologia for his own interest expresses perhaps best of all why German and English writers still turn to Chatterton: 'At present, if I fall down and worship Rowley, it can only be as the golden image which Chatterton has set up' (p. 203).

10

THE 'COMEDY OF POLITICS': DÜRRENMATT'S *KING JOHN*

By A. Subiotto

In the notes to his adaptation Dürrenmatt announces that *König Johann* is a political play 'showing the machinery of politics and how its agreements and accidents are brought about'. It is a game played out among the murderers, not the victims, but its relevance for us is proved by the kind of problem we face: 'I do not deny it is a nasty play but it is borne out by our times'. At first sight it may appear that Dürrenmatt's intention was to bring up to date the content of *King John,* the first of Shakespeare's plays to introduce a sombre political theme into his work. The contemporary interest is avowedly present, but the significance of Dürrenmatt's version lies almost entirely in its structural divergence from Shakespeare, not in the similarity of material used. Indeed, Dürrenmatt's formal innovations are primary and so deeply embedded in the play that they actually alter its content. A preliminary comparison of source and adaptation gives a clue to Dürrenmatt's working method: the plot and action of Shakespeare are kept almost intact as is the essential act division and the rhythm imposed by it, yet Dürrenmatt uses well under a quarter of Shakespeare's actual lines, most of them in the early part of the play, possibly in order to launch it in an idiom expected by the audience.

Dürrenmatt took over 'the configuration of Shakespeare's play and thought it out anew':

> I set myself the task of working out more clearly the dramaturgical dialectic of the existing material, retaining Shakespeare's constant twists and arriving at a more elegant conclusion. I aimed at shortening the game so as to reach checkmate with few moves and thereby making the action obvious, in place of the laborious guerilla warfare of Shakespeare and his predecessor. Out of a dramatised chronicle I have made a parable: the comedy of politics, a particular sort of politics.

This explains in part the increasing erosion of Shakespeare's lines as the play proceeds and also throws stress on the chess-like moves that Dürrenmatt evolves in his theatrical presentation of the shifting political patterns.

Shakespeare notoriously handled the facts about King John in cavalier fashion (this 'dramatised chronicle' has been described as his most unhistorical *History*) and Dürrenmatt too juggles with events and dates to suit his rather different purpose—to create a parable. But the great discrepancy in the impact of these two plays is not to be sought in their varying factual distortions, it ensues from Dürrenmatt's determination not to allow political thinking to dominate dramaturgical thinking. Although he does have opinions about politics—and forceful, well-argued ones at that—his primary aim is aesthetic; he is intent on creating a viable theatrical experience. The key to Dürrenmatt's dramatic processes in adapting *King John* is perhaps to be found in a *Monstervortrag über Gerechtigkeit und Recht* delivered a year later, in 1969, to Mainz students and sub-titled 'Eine kleine Dramaturgie der Politik'.[1] Dürrenmatt quotes a tale from *The Arabian Nights* and justifies the fantasy of the story on aesthetic grounds (as he might do for the improbabilities he inserts in *König Johann*):

> The usefulness of this story lies in its incredibility; and we should really ask ourselves . . . whether the literary parable does not in fact demonstrate something which cannot actually be proved, only conjectured—in the frivolous terms of literature.

In *König Johann* too the formal means by which Dürrenmatt shapes his political parable are the *raison d'être* of the adaptation.

Despite the retention of most of Shakespeare's plot, *dramatis personae* and act divisions, Dürrenmatt does introduce a shift in political perspective that calls for commensurate expression through fresh ways of patterning. The political preoccupations in *King John* were those that recurred in most of Shakespeare's 'royal' plays—the place and function of the head in the state, his relationship to his people, the question of loyalty of subject to ruler, the rights and wrongs of rebellion, and above all the need to maintain or to reassert order and harmony at all costs under the threat of prospective chaos through invasion or internecine conflict. Shakespeare introduced into *King John* the central motif of usurpation of the crown, and the use of blatant force to contend this issue has led one critic to describe the play as 'the most cynical and disillusioned of the histories', 'a political jungle', and Blanch as 'just an innocent pawn in the game of power politics'.[2] The same critic goes on:

> It is a dark picture. Issues of right and wrong are debated freely, and every time the wrong prevails. Force and expediency appear in all the distorting colours of conscience, honour, patriotism, domestic piety and religious duty. Never before has Shakespeare's world been so ubiquitously and subtly evil.

The Bastard is seen as having been placed at the centre of this web of evil in order to mirror the baseness of political life; his illegitimacy (like that of his more notorious counterpart in *King Lear*) is symbolic and enables him—rootless, landless, without responsibility as he is—to adapt swiftly to an evil world and, like Edmund ('All with me's meet that I can fashion fit'), exploit situations to his advantage:

> Since kings break faith upon commodity,
> Gain, be my lord, for I will worship thee.

Shakespeare does not necessarily condemn 'commodity', nor are right and wrong rigid absolutes; in a suitable context—the re-establishment of stability in the state—evil actions may be welcomed. The murder of King John is justified because it clears the way to unity in the nation by forcing the acceptance of his son, Prince Henry, as the rightful monarch. The Bastard too is absorbed into this unity and it is he who gives voice to the common defiance of a foreign foe (a live need in the 'Armada period' of Elizabeth's reign preceding the composition of *King John*):

> Come the three corners of the world in arms,
> And we shall shock them: nought shall make us rue,
> If England to itself do rest but true.

The troubled strife of *King John* is thus resolved in tranquillity and amity at the end.

Dürrenmatt's conception is very different. He asserts that Shakespeare's ideological equations (John = England, Philip = France) are no longer tenable, the formula valid for our day is John = Philip = feudalism, and what he is depicting in the adaptation is 'the political power struggle within a system' to which not only the Plantagenets and Capets but also the Church belong. Consequently Dürrenmatt sharpens the conflict of John with Rome, which Shakespeare had toned down despite its prominence in his probable source play, the anonymous *Troublesome Reign of King John,* and also stresses the exploitation of 'das Volk' in the pitiless tussle for dominance between the king and his barons. The first long speech added by Dürrenmatt introduces the new political configuration with John's reasons for going to war against France explicitly stated:

> Durch meines Bruders Richard genial
> Verschlampte Heldenwirtschaft kam
> Das Land in Unordnung. Der Adel murrt.
> Er liebt nicht meine starke Hand. Er will
> Die Freiheit, England auszuplündern,
> Für sich allein, drum neigt er Arthur zu.
> Die Kirche sucht mich zu erpressen, pocht
> Auf ihre Pfründe, und des Himmels Gnade
> Fließt bloß für bares Geld. Das Volk ist dumpf.
> Gesund ist nur das Heer, und diese Waffe,
> Bevor sie rostet, muß ich brauchen. Krieg
> Den Lords wär Bruderkrieg, er schwächte mich,
> Doch Krieg mit Frankreich eint die Nation
> Und zwingt den Adel sich zu unterwerfen.[3]

Later John announces that his second coronation (which Shakespeare had left almost unmotivated) is expressly to demonstrate his independence of Rome and to challenge the pride of his lords. On their defection to France he calls them 'traitorous lords, leeches on the body of England', and his dying speech paints a sorry picture of the country's prospects in their hands: with no king to obstruct their rapacious will, England would be at their mercy.

The people, who are the victims of the political game played out 'among the murderers', never actually have a voice in the play (unless we think them represented by the citizens of Angers, this 'pack', these 'shopkeepers' and 'half-hearted dogs'). They are the excuse for self-seeking actions by those in power, they foot the bill in war and peace, and they are wooed or whipped according to political expediency. John's contempt for the vegetating doltishness of his people ('they bed down in the same straw to mate and to die') swiftly turns to paternalistic 'love' when the Bastard reminds him that this 'rabble' constitutes the political majority. Pandulpho greets the king's new concern for his people with scepticism: 'He wants to give the people their freedom, is getting socially-minded, if you please.' (The Erzminister in *Ein Engel kommt nach Babylon* had voiced a similar opinion of Nebukadnezar's plans for reform: 'When kings are up against it they always get democratic, your Majesty.') The final abuse in the name of the people in Dürrenmatt's version occurs with John's entrance from his sickbed where he has excogitated the Magna Charta—such a blatant inversion of the historical facts that it can only be meant ironically.

The participants in this exercise in *Realpolitik* are not only accorded opportunist motives for their policies, Dürrenmatt also gives their formulation of these motives a modern reality by recasting Shakespeare's verse with its wealth of circumlocution and baroque imagery and contradictions in a plainer, unadorned mould. Philip, for instance, summarises the military-political situation with clearminded directness:

> Wir sind im Recht, doch nicht in Übermacht,
> England in Übermacht, doch nicht im Recht.
> Bevor der Kampf beginnt, sind eingeladen
> Die feindlichen Parteien zu verhandeln.
> Vielleicht kann so der Krieg vermieden werden,
> Vielleicht sieht Johann seinen Irrtum ein,
> Vielleicht geschieht ein Wunder, hoffen wir,
> Denn dieser Krieg käm mir zu früh. Verschuldet,
> Provinzen rebellieren, schlechte Ernte,
> Viel Pech mit teuren Weibern; Österreichs Zug
> Hierher ist nur ein Vorwand, unser Land
> Zu plündern.[4]

This is the tone in which all the negotiations, tirades and philosophisings of the play are now conducted, and there is an immediate understanding on this level between the two royal heads. War between them is a business matter, a game, an amusement that need in no way really upset their friendship—both are after all kings, and related. Thus Philip quickly musters pragmatic reasons for obeying the Pope and later readily agrees to desert Arthur to match John's betrayal of Blanka, and they discuss the merits of their tactics in the battle just concluded. Indeed, Philip is astounded when John suggests they should settle their differences in an 'ungentlemanly' personal fight:

> Im Kampf? Du bist beleidigt? Nimmst persönlich,
> Was unumgänglich durch die Politik?
> Das kann dein Ernst nicht sein, mein lieber Freund,
> Im Kampfe wäre scheußlich. Doch von einem

Zum andern Feldherrnhügel grüßend, wollen
Wir sehen, welchen von uns zwein bevorzugt
Die Hure Glück.[5]

When it comes to what Konstanze describes as 'bride-bartering'—Louis to marry Blanka, John to take Isabelle—Louis protests to his first betrothed Isabelle that he will love her for ever, 'but here duty decides, not feelings'.

These and many other instances of political opportunism totally blotting out moral considerations are in themselves only an intensification of what is potential in Shakespeare, and render the play in contemporary terms. The particular quality of Dürrenmatt's vision emerges in the articulation at one point or another by almost every major character of the purposelessness of their actions. They each voice the negation of any value in their activity and so establish its absurdity, and themselves at the same time as unfree agents acting out their social roles. Philip counsels his son to ignore the adultery of Blanka with the English lords:

Du hast die Welt und nicht dein Weib zu zügeln.
Verführbar sind sie beide, lerne, Dauphin,
Die Welt zu reiten, dieser Ritt, ich meine,
Ist eines Königs würdig.[6]

And Blanka herself complains she was sold like an animal for a scrap of peace, as she earlier accuses the Bastard of throwing her at Louis 'like a hunk of meat to the first cur that comes along', this degradation of her body not having diminished the agony and bloodshed by one whit. The unfeeling disillusion expressed by Philip, Blanka, John, the Bastard and Pandulpho is most powerfully formulated by John's mother, Eleonore, as she awaits death in the dungeon of Le Mans, betrayed by her son ('I stood in the way of the flesh of my flesh') as a logical move in the tactical game with his enemies. Facing the blank wall of hopelessness Eleonore coldly exposes to her erstwhile opponent, Konstanze, the realities of power:

Wir beide haben ausgespielt, mein Kind.
Wir haßten uns, wir boten Heere auf,
Um wider uns zu streiten. Tausende
Fraß dieser Zwist um unsren Wurf. Wir liebten
Gewalt und Männer, schworen, brachen Treue,
Betrügend wurden wir betrogen. Alles
Ist nun vorbei. Macht, Ehrgeiz, Reichtum, Ruhm

Und Liebe auch. Da sitz ich alte Vettel
Dir kahlgeschoren gegenüber, stinkend,
Dem Henker zubereitet, kalt und häßlich . . .
. . . Ich sterbe gern, doch du mußt weiterleben
In dieser leeren Welt, ein Leib,
Der nur gebar, um Schlächtern Fleisch zu liefern,
Ein Opfer deiner Tat wie ich der meinen.[7]

This bleak picture of the grey uselessness of frenetic political activity is reflected at several other points and confirmed in the closing lines of the play when the Bastard has returned to the anonymity of illegitimacy and Pembroke orders :

Ihr Lords, verscharrt den König irgendwo
Wie irgendeinen. Auf zum Staatsgeschäft,
Dies Land durch unsre Zeit zu karren
Im alten Gleise, ungestört von Narren.[8]

In place of the restored stability and harmony of Shakespeare's conception Dürrenmatt offers us a return to a patched-up status quo, the strife and expended energy petering out in nothing, the reforms forgotten, the state being 'carted' through the times in a blundering, makeshift way. This has not even the optimism of Brecht's version of *Coriolanus* where at the end, though the dead hero is consigned to ignominious oblivion, the new Senate at least embarks on real measures for the material welfare of the citizens.

It is not difficult to find in this adaptation—as in most of Dürrenmatt's plays—a pessimistic philosophy of political motive and action that sees human beings enmeshed in the consequences of stupidity and chance, caged beasts lacerating each other, unable to escape the role of either aggressor or victim. When the protagonists of the gangster business world in *Frank V* are announced as 'no less big and bloody than Shakespeare's heroes', it is no surprise to find ruthlessness to the fore (with no hint of mercy) in the adaptation of *King John*. (The other compound of political action, ineffectualness, is the burden of the closing speech in *Herkules und der Stall des Augias*, when the dying Augias tells his son Phyleus that politics performs no miracles and 'is as feeble as human beings themselves, only a reflection of their fragility, and perpetually doomed to failure'.) In *König Johann* Pandulpho says they are all 'locked in a wild beasts' cage' and this reminds us of Dürrenmatt's distinction (in his *Monstervortrag*) between the 'Wolfsspiel' (the 'Wolf game'—free-for-all freedom to fight for survival in a capitalist structure) and the 'Gute-Hirte-Spiel' (the 'Good Shepherd game'—justice for all of a state-planned economy in a Marxist system), for in *König Johann* he is analysing the destructive characteristics of the former without implying that the other equally intolerable absolute is any better. Instead, each has a special quality of hell in Dürrenmatt's vision: 'Indeed both would represent a form of hell: the world of absolute freedom a jungle where man is hunted like a wild beast, the world of absolute justice a prison where man is tortured to death.' It is irrelevant that Dürrenmatt may *privately* believe one of these worlds is preferable; he makes it abundantly clear (in *Theaterprobleme*, for instance) that his concern as a *dramatist* is to create an image of the baffling monstrosity of the world and to devise 'brave individuals' as an assertion of human independence refusing to capitulate before it. The *Monstervortrag* may put an end at last to the interminable discussions about Dürrenmatt's political standpoint and dispel the misconception that it is relevant to his drama:

> ... I think in dramaturgical terms. That is to say, my technique of thinking as a dramatist consists in transforming social reality into theatre and thinking further with this transformed reality. I think out the world by playing it out. The result of this thinking process is not a new reality but a construct for the stage in which reality appears in analysed form, or more precisely, in which the spectator sees himself analysed. This analysis is governed by imagination, intellectual experiment and the joy of acting; it is not therefore strictly scientific, but in many respects frivolous and for that very reason useful. The great Wolf game and the Good Shepherd game therefore do not stand for any liberal theories or for Marxism but are equivalents for the stage of political structures in which we all live. Dramaturgical thinking investigates the inner tensions of reality. The more paradoxically reality can be presented the more suitable it is as material for the theatre. Dramaturgical thinking is dialectic, but not in any politically ideological sense.

The playwright constructs a 'komödiantisches Gebilde' as a mirroring analysis of the world, and for this reason it has no need to be naturalistic—since it is not attempting to copy the content of reality—but it must have organisation in order to reflect the structure of reality. Dürrenmatt measures the distinction between political and dramaturgical thinking in the metaphor of chess:

> Whereas dialectical thinking of a political nature tries to set up a system for white to win in a game of chess, dialectical thinking of

> a dramaturgical nature presents a description of the game in which it does not matter whether black or white wins, whether the game ends in checkmate or stalemate—only the game as such counts, the opening gambit, the dramatic structure of the final stages. Dramaturgical thinking applied to politics attempts to discover its rules, not its content...

In *König Johann* the pattern of chess becomes an integral element in the play's structure in the terms here used: there is the formal symmetry of the opposing 'players' at the negotiating table and in battle array, there is the jockeying for a better position by slight concessions that yield no true advantage (the double marriage), there is the merciless sacrificing of prize pieces (Eleonore, Arthur, Blanka) as well as countless pawns (the armies) in the effort to checkmate one's opponent.

The chess analogy is an admirable model of the workings of political action, but, though prominent in the adaptation, it is overshadowed by other factors that draw the play firmly into the ambit of Dürrenmatt's creative imagination. Chess-like rules, even allowing for changed sequences of moves deriving from altered characters, do not turn the play into a rigid 'mathematical' structure. Instead, Dürrenmatt's dramatic fantasy and theatrical gusto transform the material into a pulsating organism that is dominated by the paradoxical unpredictability familiar from his original plays. This transformation is generated by his 'dramaturgical dialectic' that opposes to the rational, logical workings of 'Vernunft' the uncontrollable chaos of existence that is constantly threatening to burst through and swamp the stage of life. In its elemental manifestations life is a matter of appetites, immediate sensuous confrontations with reality denuded of protective reason. Dürrenmatt's motifs drawn from crude bodily functions and activities, like the celebrated metaphor of 'le visqueux' in Sartre, capture in imaginative terms the 'glutinous' and amorphous aspects of existence. Sex, food, blood and violence are the evidence of life's constant abrasion and yet at the same time the only guarantors of organisation and continuity resisting the innate entropy of living organisms. In his characteristic manner Dürrenmatt uses these appetites as structural elements to undermine the illusion of men that they can control and even direct existence by reason. Shakespeare had used imagery of outrage to the body, rape, blinding and suppression to embody his perception of violence in *King John*, and Dürrenmatt translates this into the currency of his own dramatic idiom. Blood becomes a vivid visual motif. The protagonists appear smeared and encrusted with blood, sometimes wearing butchers' aprons, and even the traditional three thuds that precede the raising of the curtain are revealed as the decapitation of John's three brothers. The Bastard articulates the butchery linguistically, as when he describes how the maimed soldiers, if they survive the battle,

> Zwar lebend, aber ohne Arm und Bein,
> In Körben in die Sonne glotzen werden,
> Bloß Rümpfe noch, entstellt, verbrannt, zerhackt.[9]

And he acknowledges his shared guilt as he soliloquises over Arthur's shattered body:

> Wie jedermann, der mitbaut am Gebäude,
> Das sich Gewalt errichtet, Blut als Mörtel,
> Als Balken Habgier nutzend . . .[10]

The hunting and spilling of blood with its concomitant hangmen, torturers, victims and murderers, is a thirst recurring throughout Dürrenmatt's work. Under one aspect it represents the inescapable process of living, and is paralleled by the appetite for food that is another salient feature in Dürrenmatt. *Die Panne, Der Richter und sein Henker, Romulus der Große, Die Wiedertäufer, Die Physiker, Der Besuch der alten Dame* all introduce eating—as banquet, as gluttonous feast, as gourmet fastidiousness, nearly always as a form of excess. (Like Fontane and Thomas Mann, Dürrenmatt is well aware of the ritualistic and theatrical potential of eating as a central and usually social activity.) Thus Dürrenmatt inserts into *König Johann* the wedding banquet set up in front of the devastated cathedral in Angers, and then punctuates the renewal of the royal quarrel with the consumption of choice morsels by the Duke of Austria (whose head the Bastard later pops into the soup tureen). This relish is closely linked with the sexual appetite which pervades Dürrenmatt's adaptation both linguistically and thematically. The Bastard promised the Duke he would leap upon him in battle as his father (Richard Coeur-de-Lion) had leapt on the Duke's 'buxom spouse', and they would roll 'in a really wild bed full of turds and blood and entrails'. The whoring, fornicating, begetting and adultery of Dürrenmatt's previous work reach an intensity in *König Johann* that imparts a new feeling of naked existence to the play. John Masefield talked of the basic 'idea of treachery' in *King John*; Dürrenmatt transforms the absence of trust into the lack of 'love' determining the relationships in the play: parent to child, lover to mistress, husband to wife. He alters Shakespeare's Blanch from 'a touching, innocent creature' to a self-possessed heiress who can afford to 'buy' the Bastard, and reduces the only truly loving bond (between Constance and her son Arthur) to slender proportions, eliminating altogether the latter's famous eloquence that softened Hubert's heart. What is left is the *Realpolitik* of sexual desire, most brutally formulated by the Bastard as he consigns his wife Blanka to Louis' bed:

> ... Dazu, pickfeine Lady,
> Ist Euer Leib gemacht, die weißen Brüste,
> Der Schoß, die Schenkel, daß sich Politik
> Mit solchen Schätzen ihren Frieden schaffe.
> Drum geht zu Louis, diesem fetten Gockel,
> Halbschwul, doch geil nach Euch und Euren Ländern.[11]

Sexual directness permeates the behaviour as well as the speech of all the protagonists and serves to bring down the abstract power game to an elemental level of blood, sweat and semen. Smeared bodies are signs of birth as well as killing, and Eleonore hopes the royal matches have smothered the strife 'in the pillows of hot marriage-beds', enjoining on them to 'beget and bear for the furtherance of our houses'. When Isabelle does present John with a squalling brat (where Shakespeare goes the other way, introducing a young man who takes over the helm of state with a firm hand), he complains he has been toppled 'by the soiled nappies of my son'. In this final tirade against the Bastard for urging him to take Isabelle to wife John continues in earthy vein:

> Nun wird das kalte Brett, mit dem ich schlief,
> Der Deckel meines Sargs. Verflucht die Stunde,
> In der ich dich aus warmen Fladen kratzte
> Ans Tageslicht. Du brachtest nichts als Unglück.
> Die Welt verbessernd, machtest du sie nur
> Verdammter. Kehr zurück zu deinen Schweinen,
> Zurück in deinen Bauernmist, hinweg
> Aus meinen Augen—[12]

Farmyard imagery is in keeping with the overall tone of Dürrenmatt's version, for, in that soliloquy on 'worshipful society' following his knighting and paralleling his 'commodity' speech, the

Bastard evinces an unmitigated knowledge of the sphere he has been elevated to:

> Weiß doch mein Sinn, daß alles Hurerei.
> Was diese noble Welt in Ehren treibt...
> Erklettere mit kühnen Heldentaten
> Der Ehre Hühnerleiter voller Dreck.[13]

The arc of his career descends at the end in a mirror reflection of its inception, still conditioned by the farmyard theme and language, and with unabated expression of sexual appetite:

> Mein Land, du liegst darnieder. Tauchend in
> Dein Volk, werd ich ein Teil des Volkes wieder,
> Und sei es auch als Stallknecht meines Bruders.
> Auf deinen Adel, deine Ehren pfeifend,
> Mit jeder Kuhmagd schlafend, die ich schnappe,
> Mit jeder Wirtshausköchin, deren Hintern
> Mir diese Welt voll Finsternis erleuchtet,
> Zeug ich Bastarde, wie ich selber einer,
> Und senke in das Volk die Kraft des Löwen!
> Nur so ist diesem England noch zu helfen.[14]

Several further devices can be analysed to determine precisely how Dürrenmatt structures this 'world of power' with which the Bastard so unsuccessfully meddles. The language is colloquial and coarse, reducing the emotional level everywhere to a dispassionate coldness and producing a tension between the noble and the common, the ceremonial and the everyday. A similar result is reached by the frivolity with which these leaders of men face up to serious, epoch-making situations. The absurdity of either the reaction or the situation is cast by Dürrenmatt into a theatrically visual effect: the Bastard shaving King John; the banquet amidst the ruins; the Duke of Austria gorging himself and his severed head subsequently stuffed into the soup tureen; John sluicing himself down with water from the banqueting table while later Philip and Louis are soaped in wash-tubs as they hear Pandulpho's arguments for their leaving England; Pandulpho himself shivering in a benighted bed in Swinstead Abbey, calling for hot-water bottles and then being pursued round the room by a penitent King John, both of them on their knees; Chatillon limping off the stage and the barons drenched through in a downpour of rain so that their armour rusts and jams. All these details are calculated to make an immediate physical impact; they are the flesh of theatre, deliberately contrived to maximise the discrepancy between how men claim to act and their true behaviour, between ideal and reality. The theatrical presentation alone can achieve this refracted image of reality in which the structural principle is the bizarre and the grotesque and this is why Dürrenmatt sees in the dramaturgical thinking of the playwright a useful corrective to politics: 'It puts reality in another light, under the spotlights of the stage, in the fierce light of satire. Dramaturgical thinking points out the contradiction between the thought and action of human beings.'

In Dürrenmatt's adaptation the Bastard is the key figure in the constellation of characters. Dr. Johnson had detected in him a 'mixture of greatness and levity' and Dürrenmatt thought Shakespeare's Bastard an ideologue or visionary. Dürrenmatt's Bastard cannot justifiably be called 'a tragic figure'[15] for Dürrenmatt says he 'is neither an ideologist nor a moralist, for him kings are the wielders of power and the nations their victims. What he asks of kings is only that they rule with common sense, he tries to make John act rationally'. But reason and intelligence play no greater part than stupidity and chance, so that the course of men's actions is an uncontrolled stumbling forward that is no more meaningful than marching on the spot. The Bastard finally sums up his abortive efforts to involve himself in the sphere of power and to improve the world.

The incongruities of political intent and behaviour provide a basis for satirical comment on social structures and institutions that is valid now as always. Yet Dürrenmatt operates with the grotesque well beyond the limits of political satire and attains effects that were defined by Victor Hugo in his enthusiastic manifesto of French Romantic drama, the *Préface de Cromwell*: 'If [the grotesque] moves from the ideal world to the real world, it displays in the latter inexhaustible parodies of humanity'. Hugo had seen the drama, 'which fuses in the same breath the grotesque and the sublime, the terrible and the ludicrous, tragedy and comedy', as the true expression of the modern age and Shakespeare as the embodiment of drama. He further maintained that 'the essence of drama is the real, and this results from the completely natural combination of two types—the sublime and the grotesque—which are merged in drama, as they are in life and creation'. Contemporary drama has distanced itself more and more from the 'ideal' world of tragedy, and Dürrenmatt is groping for an aesthetic structure that will adequately capture the movement of the whole of reality as it presents itself to our consciousness now—not just reproduce a reflection in a naturalistic manner. He has always striven to render the ambiguity of life in its amalgam of human aspirations and grandeur on the one hand, and the soiled product of day-to-day appetites on the other, an ambiguity that the great 'modern' realist of the nineteenth century, Büchner, so potently sensed and expressed. The grotesque is generated wherever the ideal and the real collide and it is in this sense that Dürrenmatt can say: 'We can achieve tragedy through comedy, produce it as a terrible moment, as a yawning abyss. Thus many of Shakespeare's tragedies are comedies from which the tragic arises'.

The Life and Death of King John, woven of incident and language in Shakespeare's particular vision, is recast by Dürrenmatt into a 'Komödie der Politik' that puts the doers and the done-to on the stage of history and tells in its grotesque structures of the frustration and futility of ideals and the sensuality of living.

NOTES

1. *Mammoth Lecture on Justness and Justice. A short dramaturgy of politics*, Zürich, 1969.
2. M. M. Reese, *The Cease of Majesty*, London, 1961, p. 280 f.
3. The land fell into disorder as a result of my brother Richard's administration, a hero's brilliant chaos. The barons are grumbling, they don't care for my firm hand. They want to be the only ones free to plunder England, hence they lean towards Arthur. The Church is trying to blackmail me, insists on its benefices, and grace drops from heaven only for hard cash. The people are apathetic. Only the army is sound and I must use this weapon before it rusts. War with the barons would be war with my brothers and would weaken me, but war with France will unite the nation and force the barons to submit.
4. We have right on our side, but not might; England might, but not right. Before the battle begins the opposing sides have been invited to negotiate. Perhaps war can thus be avoided, perhaps John will see the error of his ways, perhaps a miracle will happen; let us hope so, for this war would come too soon for my liking. In debt, provinces in revolt, bad luck with expensive women, and Austria's march to our aid is just a pretext for plundering our land.
5. A fight? You are offended? You are taking personally what is forced on us by politics? You must be joking, my dear fellow, a fight would be ghastly. Rather let us wave across from one general's vantage-point to the other and see which of us is favoured by Whore Fortune.
6. Your job is to keep a firm rein on the world, not your wife. Both can be led astray. Learn, Dauphin, to ride the world—that is a truly royal occupation.
7. The game is up for us, my child. Our hatred was mutual, we summoned armies to fight against each other. Thousands perished in this quarrel over our whelps. We loved violence and men, pledged our word and broke it, betrayed and were betrayed. It's all over now: power, ambition, wealth, fame and love too. Here I sit before you, an old hag with shaven head, stinking, got ready for the executioner, cold and ugly . . . I am glad to die, but you must live on in this empty world, a body which gave birth

only to provide meat for the slaughterers, a victim of your deed as I of mine.

8. You lords, bury the king without ceremony anywhere you like. Let's get on with the business of the state and cart this land through our time along the old lines, undisturbed by fools.
9. Will sit in basket-chairs gaping at the sun, alive it's true, but without arms and legs; nothing but mutilated, scorched, hacked-about torsoes.
10. Like everyone who helps erect the building which power raises to itself, using blood for mortar, greed as the beams.
11. My fine madam, your body—the white breasts, the belly, the thighs—is there for politics to use such treasures to make its peace. So go to Louis, that fat rooster—half a queer he is, but lusting for you and your lands.
12. Now the cold plank with which I slept will be the lid of my coffin. Cursed be the hour in which I scratched you out of the warm cow-dung into the light of day. You brought nothing but bad luck. Improving the world you made it only more beastly. Get back to your pigs, back to your farm manure, out of my sight—
13. I know that what this noble world does so honestly is all just harlotry . . . and with bold heroic deeds I shall clamber up the chicken ladder of honour that is thick with droppings.
14. My country, you are sunk low. Disappearing amongst your people I will become once again part of them, even if it has to be as my brother's stable-boy. I shall snap my fingers at your nobles and your honours, sleep with every milkmaid I can catch, with every tavern cook whose backside brightens this dark world for me, and so beget a race of bastards like myself and sink a lion's strength into the people! This is the only way left to help this England.
15. Armin Arnold, *Friedrich Dürrenmatt,* Berlin, 1969, p. 87.

II

TRADITION AND NIGHTMARE SOME REFLECTIONS ON THE POSTWAR NOVEL IN ENGLAND AND GERMANY

By W. E. Yuill

The laws of historical perspective dictate that the division of literature into eras becomes progressively more blurred and arbitrary the nearer one approaches the present. It is perhaps excusable, then, to use for the purposes of retrospect somewhat fortuitous landmarks like the twenty-fifth aniversary of the end of the Second World War. There is at least some justification in political terms for regarding as a significant epoch the quarter of a century in which England and the Federal Republic have moved from hostility in the direction of a common destiny and some kind of political union. In comparing the literary output of English and German writers during these years a factor of paramount importance will clearly be the implications of the war for the two countries; this applies particularly to the novel, which perhaps more than other genres may be expected to mirror social and political conditions. Clearly there is all the difference in the world between the continuity—no matter how tenuous—vouchsafed by victory and the cataclysm entailed in defeat, and it would be surprising if this difference were not reflected in the novels of victors and vanquished respectively. There is more to it than this, however. Changes wrought by political circumstance and the fortunes of war have inevitably been superimposed on divergent views of the novel and its function in society; often enough these changes have tended to emphasise still further characteristic attitudes on the part of writers, critics and public, to force traditions and practices even further apart.

It need hardly be pointed out that the regeneration of the German novel in the eighteenth century was largely inspired by English example, by Defoe, Richardson and Fielding. It was from these models that German novelists evolved their own most characteristic variety, the 'Bildungsroman', a variety that was more self-consciously poetic than the pragmatic English novel, more orientated towards the individual than towards society at large, consequently more introspective, more philosophically reflective. It was the Romantics, however, who, by fanciful speculation and formal experiment, most clearly moved the German novel away from its erstwhile models, a trend renewed and reinforced in the early decades of the twentieth century by writers like Thomas Mann and Franz Kafka.

In comparing the novels of England and Germany, then, one must allow for the fact that novelists of the two nations proceed for the most part from different premisses and have different aims. It is undeniable that writers in English—James Joyce, Virginia Woolf, Samuel Beckett—have made quite revolutionary contributions to experimentation in the novel, but they are outside the main stream. English novelists have shown themselves to be remarkably conservative and may even be said to have become more so during the last thirty or forty years. The English novel since 1945 is a rich tapestry but it has been worked in a variety of patterns which, although they may be on a smaller scale than they once were, are mainly traditional. This may well be because, for historical and political reasons, the social fabric on which these patterns are imposed has not radically changed. There is a continuing adherence, for one thing, to E. M. Forster's dictum that the first task of the novelist is to tell a story. The preference for the 'pure novel', concentrating, as Robert Liddell writes in his *Treatise on the Novel*, 'on human beings and their mutual reactions' is explicable in the light of technical resources accumulated during two centuries and a half. The sheer competence of even relatively inexperienced authors bred in this tradition is enviable. The aspiring English novelist is workmanlike without being either over-ambitious or meretricious. So pervasive is this expertise that English fiction appears as a broad continuum embracing works of high intellectual distinction at one extreme and ephemeral detective stories at the other. The stories of Graham Greene, although they deal with man's search for self and God, are justly designated 'entertainments' and can be read as such.

In Germany writers, critics and public have promoted a rift in the literary firmament by distinguishing sharply between poetic literature and literature of entertainment, a distinction contingent on the concept of 'Dichter' and its associated mystique. The German critic appears to detect a difference of essence and not just of degree between the novels of, say, Georg Simmel, and those of Siegfried Lenz. Even a writer as serious and influential as Heinrich Böll is rarely promoted beyond the rank of 'Schriftsteller'. For the English critic, on the other hand, it is precisely in the novel that the poetic and the non-poetic may coalesce: as Elizabeth Bowen defines it, the novel is 'a non-poetic statement of a poetic truth'.

For the German novelist technical competence rarely seems to have been the starting-point for literary enterprise. A philosophical thesis rather than the impulse to represent social behaviour for its own sake has tended to be his point of departure. One feels that the eminent German novelist, so often schooled in the philosophy of idealism, hopes to embody in each work an ultimate statement about the national destiny or even about the human condition as such. Massive as the resultant opus may be, it is at least designed to be complete, coherent and self-contained. The English novel of the typical social kind is inevitably lacking in synthesis, open-ended, its scale disguised by division into separate publications—and capable of almost infinite extension, should the television public demand it. Thomas Mann's *Buddenbrooks* and Galsworthy's *Forsyte Saga* illustrate, precisely because of their similar themes, something of this essential difference.

The heritage of Romanticism joined to historically determined physical limitations has tended to drive the German novelist in on himself: his emigration is an inner emigration, his dimensions are those of the mind—historical perspectives, patterns of myth and cosmic design. The possibilities of oblique or symbolic representation have been more thoroughly explored than they have been by most English novelists. The world-wide dissemination of English culture as well as the far-flung political and commercial interests of the English race provide even in post-colonial days an amplitude of background and a diversity of theme in comparison with which the German novel may seem claustrophobic. Even after the war the remnants of Empire provided enough frontiers to satisfy the Conradian quest for self and Kiplingesque initiation to the white man's burden that one still finds, for example, in P. H. Newby's *Journey into the Interior* and Gerald Hanley's *Consul at Sunset*. Indeed, the processes of de-colonisation themselves have offered possibilities for satire exploited by Denis Enright in works like *Academic Year*. It is not without significance that English novelists have access through traditional links to landscapes and cultures which are exotic but not entirely alien and which they can use to amplify and reinforce their themes. Lawrence Durrell's Alexandria is the properly pungent and poetic setting of an amoral sensuality, Doris Lessing's Rhodesia, the Nigeria of Joyce Cary and Graham Greene are arenas of race conflict or cultural confrontation, George Orwell's Burma epitomises problems of imperialism. With a few exceptions like Hans Henny Jahn German novelists have had little access to the literally outlandish.

Even those varieties of the English novel that could be described as 'home' rather than 'colonial' are, culturally speaking, narrowly localised. English society as reflected in the contemporary novel has the appearance of a complex of semi-autonomous sub-cultures, each of them linked with a symbolic locality: Whitehall, Oxbridge, Mayfair, Bloomsbury, Redbrick. It may be that the relative stability of English society stems from this system of counter-balancing elements that allows inter-communication and personal mobility. In Germany, on the other hand, the Romantic quest for transcendental unity has produced in the past a monolithic ideological edifice, massive but unstable. Amongst English novelists there are those who specialise in one or more of the sub-cultures. C. P. Snow and William Cooper explore in quasi-autobiographical fashion the worlds of Whitehall, Oxbridge and the provincial universities; Evelyn Waugh, Anthony Powell and Nancy Mitford are most at home in Mayfair; Angus Wilson and Iris Murdoch circulate in Whitehall and Bloomsbury; the angry young men, Kingsley Amis, John Wain, John Braine, Malcolm Bradbury, belong to a generation associated with provincial towns and colleges. A number of other writers operate still within that most rudimentary but increasingly outmoded sub-culture, the family, particularly the large Victorian or Edwardian family which offers ideal opportunities for the study of complex emotional relationships in a stable society. The purest exponent of this kind of family chronicle is Ivy Compton-Burnett, whose stories are all set in the years before 1910. There is nothing nostalgic, however, in her account of what might aptly be called strained relations in a family jungle teeming with tyrannies, where only the mental toughness of adults and children and a steely adherence to rational self-interest guarantee survival. The motto of these novels might well be, 'The family that preys together stays together'. In the case of L. P. Hartley the family climate is milder although there is something pathological in the mutual dependence of brother and sister in the *Eustace and Hilda* trilogy. An effective note of melodrama is struck in Hartley's *Go-Between*, remarkable alike for its representation of tensions in Edwardian society and the almost mythical transformation of a clandestine love-affair through the imagination of a twelve-year-old boy. Joyce Cary's two trilogies (*Herself Surprised*, *To be a Pilgrim, The Horse's Mouth* and the Chester Nimmo stories) also hark back to Edwardian days and many of his characters also share something of the supineness of Hartley's. The world of these novels is rationally ordered in a way that now seems oddly outdated: even the Bohemian Gully Jimson is a rational Romantic whose ideas are derived from Rousseau and Blake; his idiosyncratic aims are pursued with logical rather than daemonic determination. The social relevance of Cary's work is broader than Hartley's, however. The Chester Nimmo series hinges on the interaction of political expediency and private morality and gives a realistic account of the reform fever bred in England before the First World War by the Noncomformist conscience. Jim Wilcher in *To be a Pilgrim* registers his morose observations on the younger generation between the wars; Tolbrook, the ancestral home where he waits for death while his niece's husband operates a threshing machine in the eighteenth-century drawing-room, itself epitomises the changing social and economic face of England. Cary's world is less private than Hartley's.

An element of burlesque is introduced into the family chronicle as evidence of social history by Angus Wilson in his novel *No Laughing Matter*. The children of 'Billy Pop' Matthews and 'Countess' Clara, diverse as they all are in talent and personality, combine to mock the hypocritical gentility of their parents in periodic ritual games. Wilson is one of the most versatile and inventive as well as the most deadly social commentators. His novels display an unusual diversity of theme and a range of characters extending from Bloomsbury intellectuals to Mrs. Salad in *Anglo-Saxon Attitudes* and Stoker, the Matthews' cook-general, creations of Dickensian egregiousness. In nearly all his stories Wilson displays a morbid fondness for humiliating and embarrassing social situations as well as a kind of angry compassion for the victims of social change. Iris Murdoch is equally inventive and her ironic sense of the bizarre is even more fully developed than Wilson's. She enjoys the counterpoint of respectability and Bohemianism and a precise play of emotional forces that expresses itself in symmetrical exchanges of sexual partners And yet there remains in character, situation and motivation a residue of the inscrutable that may or may not be construed as symbolic.

Other writers have graver pre-occupations: C. P. Snow, for instance, the most unromantic, the most prosaic, the most conservative of contemporary novelists. Snow concerns himself with the administrators and scientists who run our society, with the moral implications of a quest for power that is pursued at every level and in every sector of society, with the impact of the 'new men', the scientists and careerist scholarship boys, on traditional centres of power. Anthony Powell regards his 'new men', Widmerpool and Quiggin, sardonically as effective bounders, but Snow takes a more sympathetic view of them. His hero, like Snow himself, is a 'new man': throughout the *Strangers and Brothers* cycle Lewis Eliot shows himself as a reasonable and adaptable man, a stoic and moral agnostic who prefers to understand rather than to condemn, an observer of trusted judgment quietly watching the conflict of ambition and conscience and counting the cost in disillusion and lost integrity. Snow's great assets are his insight into problems and processes of government and the strong sense of authenticity of his stories, especially where he is dealing with a closed community like the Cambridge college in *The Masters.* His greatest failings are lack of irony and humour and seemingly an inability to represent either the emotional processes of women or the daemonic forces in men: his George Passant and Roy Calvert epitomise very imperfectly the 'sleep of reason'. The humour that is lacking in Snow is a feature of the earlier novels of William Cooper but Cooper's later works, especially *Memoirs of a New Man*, are little more than inept and rather meretricious replicas of Snow's works.

The difference between Snow and Collins on the one hand and the 'angry young men' on the other is to some extent simply a difference of generation. The scholarship boys of the pre-war era were willing to join the Establishment; the post-war generation, more numerous and with scholarships perhaps more easily acquired, regarded the Establishment, in the words of Professor Karl, as 'the hated hierarchy of institutionalised hypocrisy'. They were rebels without any well-defined cause and sufferers from an ill-defined sense of grievance. Their protest was self-centred and largely unpolitical, for the political ideas of these anti-heroes are of the most rudimentary. Edgar Banks in *Living in the Present* has no sympathy for 'the people' or 'the working-class' and Charles Lumley in *Hurry on Down* deliberately dissociates himself from the idealistic intellectual Left of the 1930's. What they are seeking is 'neutrality' and if they are lucky they find it in peripheral occupations of doubtful utility as comic scriptwriter or secretary to a millionaire. Charles Lumley, in assuming the motley, has very different motives from the hero of Heinrich Böll's *Ansichten eines Clowns*, Hans Schnier, who goes on the stage because he is sickened by a hypocrisy more abominable than anything Lumley has known. Where the 'angry young man' does pursue social ambitions in spite of his contempt for bourgeois values he makes his way, like Joe Lampton in *Room at the Top*, by methods that are brutally unscrupulous—only to lay the blame for his success by implication on a society that compels him to use such methods.

The novels of the 'angry young men' do not form a glorious chapter in the annals of the novel : they are of sociological rather than of literary interest. And they belong to a distinctive era that is past. The erstwhile 'young men' are now of an age to have adolescent sons and daughters of their own—and the representatives of this youngest generation, as we meet them in recent novels like B. S. Johnston's *Travelling People* and the works of Miss Edna O'Brien, are much cooler, less full of class-prejudice than their elders of the 1950's. Their ethos and ambience is that of the Chelsea discotheque rather than the provincial pub. They are, in a word, 'hip'.

All these writers, however diverse in pre-occupation and style, seem to depend on the massive English tradition of plain narrative and social observation. In the case of the older writers it may be that recourse to the urbane domestic tradition of the great Victorian novelists was an unspoken response to the implied authoritarianism and ominous irrationalism of D. H. Lawrence, Pound, Yeats or Wyndham Lewis as well as to the alien experimentation of Joyce and Virginia Woolf. Even the 'angry young men' could be regarded, however, as rather debilitated descendants of Fielding.

In Germany, under the portentous shadow of Oswald Spengler and through the example of works like Mann's *Zauberberg* and Kafka's *Prozess* and *Schloss* the novel acquired an eschatological function. It became the vehicle of recondite philosophies and cultural analysis, cryptically symbolic in its idiom and often pervaded by a nightmarish sense of fatality. According to Hermann Broch the novel can no longer make a significant contribution to particular fields of human knowledge; its new function must be to take over from the sciences, which have grown too specialised, the task of presenting an integrated picture of society and man's experience:

> Nowadays, in an age so expressly radical, there can be no pseudo-science of a belletristic sort, and the knowledge of this kind conveyed by means of the novel consists at best of popularised platitude. On the other hand, science is incapable of giving us an integrated whole, this is exactly what it must leave to the novel.

In consequence the novel has had to develop in Broch's view a complexity and comprehensiveness it did not previously aim at.

The advent of National Socialism and the catastrophes of the Second World War—referred to characteristically by Hermann Kasack as a 'Schicksalszäsur' (caesura of destiny)—were interpreted by German novelists not so much as the consequences of economic crisis or political miscalculation but seen rather within a wider context as the apocalyptic realisation of nightmarish forebodings. The ambitious attempts to comprehend these events transcended the social and even the political level and penetrated into metaphysical or theological spheres, for the phenomena of the Third Reich and the war seemed like a direct irruption of absolute evil into human civilisation. Where Orwell and William Golding had to conjure up the future, find remote settings or have recourse to extended fable in order to represent evil, German writers were in a position to observe it at first hand. Their task became, as Hermann Broch put it: 'Konkrete Kampfansage an das apokalyptische Hier und Jetzt des Untiers.' The nightmare reality of Nazism was analysed in different terms and with different methods by various writers: in quasi-theological terms and with the help of historical parallels by Heinrich Mann in his Henri IV novels, in legendary and cultural historical terms by Thomas Mann in *Dr. Faustus*, in Christian theological terms by Elisabeth Langgässer in *Das Unauslöschliche Siegel* and

Märkische Argonautenfahrt, in terms of Oriental mysticism and in an Expressionistic idiom by Hermann Kasack in *Die Stadt hinter dem Strom*, in Spenglerian terms of cultural disintegration and with a somewhat incongruous mixture of narrative and philosophical discourse by Hermann Broch in *Die Schuldlosen*.

The most memorable of these monumental works is undoubtedly *Faustus*, in which Mann interweaves time levels, creates complex symbolic figures from legend and historical tradition, evokes the decadent intellectual atmosphere in which National Socialism was able to grow. In his Andreas Leverkühn he epitomises both the pathological nature of genius and the power of music to enrapture and enslave. Leverkühn embodies the equivocal spiritual qualities of his nation and his agonising death parallels the moral and military collapse of Germany. *Faustus*, for all its historical perspectives and symbolic patterns is a direct commentary on the nightmare of the Third Reich. *Die Schuldlosen* and *Das Unauslöschliche Siegel* are more oblique statements. Broch remarks of his own work:

> The novel describes German conditions and types of the pre-Hitler period. The figures chosen for this purpose are absolutely 'unpolitical'; in so far as they have any political ideas at all they hover in a vague and nebulous void. None of them is directly 'guilty' in regard to the catastrophe of Hitler.... Nevertheless this is precisely the intellectual and psychological condition from which—and it did happen like that—Nazism drew its actual strength.... The politically guiltless are generally pretty deeply involved in ethical guilt.

Broch attributes the catastrophe to an epidemic moral disease which destroyed the traditional values of the West and precipitated Germany into political delirium. The earlier stages of this disease are described in *Die Schlafwandler*. Germany was particularly prone to the infection because it was the domain of the 'Spiesser', the characterless bourgeois, whose dissemination through all the levels of German society spread the disease throughout the body politic. In Germany there were no effective sub-cultures to provide immunity against the virus.

Elisabeth Langgässer sees the German crisis in a far wider context, ultimately *sub specie aeternitatis*, but more immediately as a phase in the age of rationalism which began in the eighteenth century and achieved a disastrous climax in our own time. The action of the novel covers the years since the outbreak of the First World War, but the events and characters are peripheral, set in small provincial towns remote from Armageddon. The literal scale of the events is immaterial since they are simply symbolic of the conflict between God and Satan that is conducted in the soul of everyman. Langgässer's theological views—too Manichaean for some of her Catholic co-religionists—entail departure from such conventions as chronological narrative, the single identity of characters, and psychological motivation. The novel revolves round timeless concepts of damnation and salvation by divine grace, forces of good and evil are embodied in duplicate or triplicate characters who are moved not by logic or psychology but by transcendental forces. Langgässer writes of the work:

> If in fact the causally integrated world view with its upstart claim on all the domains of the mind is shattered, then the novel which proceeds on psychological lines, that is, operates with causal determinism has lost its credibility, and the self-evident plausibility of its characters and destinies is no longer based on measurable psychological qualities but on purely providential and non-causal factors which remain in the background and operate from the background ... Imaginative literature ... has become existential.

Kasack's message is less orthodox than Langgässer's and also more indeterminate. What Robert Lindhoff perceives in the 'Schrecksekunde des Todes' as represented by his visit to the Dantesque limbo of the city beyond the river is little more than an assurance that the evil in the world, in spite of man's rationalised stupidity, will never outbalance the good. The individual is exhorted to forsake the trivial routine of life and prepare himself for a mystic assimilation into the cosmos.

Such ambitious works represent the response of the older generation of German novelists to the nightmare. Younger writers, who had in some cases been directly involved, produced grimly realistic chronicles of battle and disaster. Of this kind are the earlier works of Heinrich Böll, *Der Zug war pünktlich* and *Wo warst du, Adam*, for example. The idiom of these younger writers was sober, astringent, unsentimental—in line with the purgation of the German language undertaken under the slogan 'Kahlschlag' by the association of liberal writers known as Gruppe 47. In the years 1951–53, however, at about the time the 'angry young men' raised their plaintive voices in England, German writers began to find new themes and a more ironic and satirical tone. With the advent of the economic miracle and the first symptoms of the affluent society the younger German novelists began to see that their function was to be, in the words of Günter Eich, 'not oil but sand in the works of society'. The early novels of social protest—for example, Wolfgang Koeppen's *Treibhaus* and *Tauben im Gras* and Martin Walser's *Ehen in Philippsburg* —are certainly abrasive enough. Their authors are more serious-minded, less self-centred and politically better informed than the 'angry young men'. The later novels of Böll, Siegfried Lenz and Walser have become more sophisticated (in Walser's case perhaps all too whimsically ingenious) but they have retained and even deepened the ideological commitment of their authors. Böll's family chronicle, *Billard um halb zehn*, has much more obvious political and religious relevance than its English counterparts; Lenz's *Deutschstunde* shares the theme of Cary's *Horse's Mouth* but transposes it into a political key; Anselm Kristlein, the hero of Walser's *Halbzeit* and *Einhorn*, is the kind of outsider figure who reminds us superficially of the Jim Dixon fraternity, but he and his creator are politically aware. Walser comments satirically on the complex situation in the Federal Republic, where old and new, Teutonic and Anglo-Saxon attitudes are oddly mingled, and where vestiges of National Socialist ideology coalesce with the ethos of international big business. The works of Heinrich Böll express a humane Catholicism which is much more than the mark of social and intellectual distinction which it tends to be with Evelyn Waugh's low-spirited Guy Crouchback. Böll has something of Greene's fondness for material squalor and human inadequacy coupled with the mystery of consecration (a liking for 'Beta minus priests' he calls it somewhere). Where Greene remains for the most part on a realistic level, however, and realises Catholic doctrine in terms of human conscience and ethical choice Böll uses a bolder technique and does not hesitate to introduce symbolic 'angelic' messengers like Schrella in *Billard um halb zehn* and to divide his characters into apocalyptic categories of 'Büffel' and 'Lämmer'. In *Entfernung von der Truppe* Böll himself comments ironically on this practice: 'Engel(bert) is not a symbol for an angel, although this is his name and he is described as looking like one.'

The most impressive achievement of the younger generation of novelists in Western Germany is undoubtedly represented by Günter Grass's *Blechtrommel* and *Hundejahre*. In scale and complexity these works return to the monumentality of the older generation, but they are more autonomously inventive than the earlier works with their dependence on patterns of myth, dogma and historical tradition. Grass creates a satirical mythology with its own bizarre gods and demons—Oskar Matzerath and Eddi Amsel, for instance. Oskar is not a 'character' in the ordinary sense, he is a literary construct, the organ of the author in a satirical account of the rise and fall of National Socialism. *Die Blechtrommel* is at the same time a bizarre parody of the 'Bildungsroman' or 'Künstlerroman'. Oskar manifestly fails to develop in either physical or moral stature, and his obsessive tuneless drumming is a travesty of artistic expression. Where Thomas Mann, Langgässer and Kasack see the nightmare of Nazism through a philosophical or religious magnifying glass, Grass views it through a poetic prism that distorts, refracts and diminishes but somehow presents an image that is essentially true.

The fantasticality of Grass's imagination and the baroque mannered virtuosity of his style are linked with the sharpest observation of detail, and this concern, even obsession, with the texture of physical reality which is equally characteristic of Böll, Walser, Gerd Gaiser, Siegfried Lenz, Günter Herburger and a number of other young novelists is one feature at least that brings the German novel closer to its English counterpart. There are signs, too, of a rapprochement from the other side. Although most English novelists adhere to tradition in scale and technique certain of them have since the war evolved works which, although they are fundamentally realistic, possess the ideological implications and symbolic patterns that so often characterise the German novel. George Orwell's political fable *Animal Farm* and his futuristic fantasy *1984* were signs of a new departure, while the remarkable and little regarded novel of Malcolm Lowry, *Under the Volcano*, suggests religious and political meanings in the despairing life and violent death of a dipsomaniac diplomat. The novels of Henry Green and Rex Warner might also be regarded as evidence of a trend towards a more symbolist idiom in the novel, while the works of Iris Murdoch contain germs of symbolism which may yet flourish into a coherent pattern. The trend is most marked, however, in the stories of William Golding.

Few writers combine more economically plain narrative and theological import. His *Inheritors* is an imaginative *tour de force*, and the situation in *Pincher Martin* is a more forceful and succinct version of that in Kasack's *Stadt hinter dem Strom*. In Golding the search for ulterior meaning that is typical of German novelists is impressively combined with the realistic narrative tradition that represents the mainstream of the English novel. The finest product of this combination is Golding's *Lord of the Flies*.

With the growth of cultural links between England and the Federal Republic and the fading in memory of the German nightmare the novelistic traditions of the two literatures may well come even closer together. Grass's latest novel, *Örtlich betäubt*, although much less distinguished in a purely literary sense than his earlier works, is also less nightmarish. It shows that pragmatic concern for moral issues within a distinctive social framework that has long been a feature of the English tradition. If this is a sign that German novelists are liberating themselves from an arcane interpretation of life and an undue dependence on cultural myth then perhaps it should be welcomed. No one knows what bizarre turns the development of the novel may yet take in England and Germany—but one thing is fairly clear: our fate is increasingly a common one and any future nightmare is unlikely to be confined to one or the other nation. And by the time it is dreamed out there will be precious little left in the way of tradition. It is precisely towards the forging of common traditions and the exorcising of nightmare that men like Oswald Wolff have worked. We may only hope that their work will continue.

BIBLIOGRAPHICAL NOTE

The following books and articles are relevant to writers and movements mentioned in this essay. Some of them include bibliographies.

W. Allen, *Tradition and Dream. A critical survey of British and American fiction from the 1920's to the present day*, London, Pelican Books, 1965.
F. R. Karl, *A Reader's guide to the Contemporary English Novel*, London, Thames and Hudson, 1963.
H. W. Richter, *Almanach der Gruppe 47*, Hamburg, Rowohlt, 1962.
R. Hinton Thomas and W. van der Will, *The German Novel and the Affluent Society*, Manchester, Manchester Univ. Press, 1968.
H. M. Waidson, *The Modern German Novel*, London, Oxford Univ. Press, 1959.
W. E. Yuill, *Malice in Wonderland, Contemporary Satire in Western Germany*, Inaugural Lecture, University of Nottingham, 1967.

E. Heller, *The Ironic German. A study of Thomas Mann*, London, Secker and Warburg, 1958.

I. Hilton, 'Gerd Gaiser', in: *Essays in Contemporary German Literature*, ed. B. Keith-Smith, London, Wolff, 1966.

W. F. Mainland, 'Hermann Kasack', ibid.

A. V. Subiotto, 'Günter Grass', ibid.

W. E. Yuill, 'Heinrich Böll', ibid.

W. E. Yuill, 'Heinrich Mann', *German Men of Letters II*, ed. A. Natan, London, Wolff, 1963.

H. C. ARTMANN AND THE ENGLISH NONSENSE TRADITION

By J. C. Alldridge

Hans Carl Artmann, or hans carl artmann, as he prefers to write his name, is one of the most remarkable poets writing today. In spite of a very large body of published works, he remains one of the least known of contemporaries. He has translated from English, French and Spanish literature into German and from his earliest days has pioneered experimental forms in verse. It is largely due to him that Vienna, the place of his birth, has changed its former extremely conservative status in the literary world to one of an avant-garde of literary progress. Experiment in writing does not always produce art; for this vision is needed, and this Artmann has in great measure.

Even today his reputation is greater outside Austria than inside it. His best-known works there are still his two early works, one of which is written in Viennese dialect (*Med Ana Schwoazzn Dintn*) and the other a collection of droll stories in imitation of the seventeenth-century 'Schwänke' (*Von denen Husaren und anderen Seil-Tänzern*). Membership of the Wiener Gruppe, which he helped to found in 1952, and of which he was the leading member, brought him some renown in his homeland; but the Gruppe has disbanded, and Artmann writes now independently of any group.

He was born in Vienna in 1921, where he remained, with brief intervals, until 1960. In that year he left it finally and has since moved continuously, to Sweden, to Berlin, back to Sweden and on to Berlin again, via Graz. Since 1967 he has been constantly travelling and has not even a permanent address. This restlessness is a manifestation of that inability to settle anywhere, to which he has given such a touching expression in his short autobiographical sketch (*Verfehltes unterfangen sich einer geographie zu erinnern*) and which is characteristic of so much of his writing.

His contention that poetry is for him not merely an aim in life but life itself is a little startling when we realise what a large amount of his work is of a surrealist and nonsense nature. He leaves his editors and publishers to follow him, almost literally step by step, to snap up his regardlessly tossed-aside manuscripts; they have even had to sit beside the radio and make shorthand transcripts of his broadcast readings, in order to obtain a working text at all. It is miraculous that so many of his writings have survived.

Artmann has himself always emphasised the necessity of animation and freedom of expression in poetry. His earliest serious expression of this view is set out in an 'Eight Point Programme', issued in 1953, of which the 'Leitgedanke' is 'der poetische Act'. The main contentions of this programme, to some extent repetitive, can be reduced to four points: (1) the rejection of second-hand versions and the emphasis on poetry for the sake of pure poetry; (2) poetry must be free from all ambition and desire for official recognition, praise or even criticism; (3) pure poetry is transmitted by chance and it is so pure and clear that it cannot become public and be shared commonly; (4) pure poetry is a pose free of vanity and full of humility, it has no material value and is essentially noble. Comforted by the thought of 'Don Quixote', Artmann thus feels justified, if any justification is necessary, to indulge in nonsense writing. From his letters and scattered sayings there emerges the impression that his 'defence' is akin to Edward Lear's: a defence mechanism against a world in which he feels so disoriented. Both are adrift and interested in 'fringe' characters, some indeed of their own creation. They may be 'ohne tiefere Bedeutung'; Artmann's may be, as one recent critic has said, his 'literarisches Schnorrertum' (Ernst Nef in *Die Zeit*, 11 July 1969), which echoes faithfully Artmann's own words 'ich bin schnorrhabardian'. More than once Artmann has quoted approvingly Nestroy: 'einen Jux will er sich machen'.

It is possible to detect two significant origins of nonsense writing (much of which is in verse, in any language). These are: relief of one's own insufficiencies, whether physical or social; and anger and dissatisfaction with some condition, organisation or persons. In English Literature Edward Lear is an example of the first. His acute sense of physical idiosyncracies (we recall the frequency, especially in the limericks, of reference to persons with grotesque noses, and are reminded thus of his own unshapely one) and of his resulting social uneasiness, provided him with an inexhaustible source of fun to hide his malaise. His was, in general and apart from temporary irritabilities, a gentle and kind nature; in consequence his nonsense writings ridicule without rancour.

A trenchant and bitter exponent of the second form of nonsense writing in English is Jonathan Swift. His satires clothed in nonsense form were expressly intended to hurt. The jumbling of names and 'monkeying with words', as Archbishop Tait said of Edward Lear's verse, was Swift's intention and aimed at intensifying the satire.

Lewis Carroll seems to partake of the nature of both Lear and Swift. His nonsense writings sprang from his frustration at realising that he was continually on the verge of madness; hence the horrific in much of his writing. Lear's distress at his unshapely nose and his weak feet ('the Pobble without any toes') remains somehow a matter of concern which the reader can understand and share. There are such things, but there are no such things as Jabberwocky or Bandersnatch; there is no such quality as brillig, but, hearing brillig in connection with slithy toves, we need no explanation to render the poems in which they occur vividly memorable and in some way disturbing. These last two characteristics are the epitome of Carroll's verse, and are not confined to one author or age. They appear also in the work of one of Artmann's fellow-countrymen and contemporaries, Ernst Jandl, who, like Artmann, eschews capital letters. The following lines by Jandl (born, also in Vienna, in 1925) are an amusing view of 'standard authors':

zwei bräute: ein deutsches denkmal

goethe:

komm und stirne mich mein kind
denn ich habe viele stellen
unter denen keine sind
die nicht aus dem herzen quellen

schiller:

komm und herze mich mein kind
denn ich habe viele stellen
unter denen keine sind
die nicht aus der stirne quellen

('sprechblasen', Neuwied, 1968)[1]

The border between nonsense and humour is hard to define; a working hypothesis may perhaps be found in thinking of humour as expressing in ordinary language some of our every-day experiences, and of nonsense as expressing possible experiences in language hitherto unencountered. Lear found a succinct version of this when he wrote:

GER/man
GER/women
GER/children.

Here the border is reached where ordinary words gradually give way to invented ones, many of them portmanteau words. Their invention requires skill in the application to the object of the satire. Here Swift excelled. His word 'biffmarklub' does not, of course, exist in the standard language, but in his *Voyage to Laputa* its application to the Lord High Chamberlain is delightful for its suitability and memorable for its very scurrility.

The roll of similarities of this kind between earlier nonsense writers and Artmann is too long for detailed reference here. Artmann has his own linguistic peculiarities, in addition to those he has borrowed from his predecessors. An outstanding one is his refusal to use capital letters, a habit more disconcerting in German than in any other language since the tracts and broadsides of the seventeenth century, particularly those of Commonwealth England. Artmann's usage has the effect of 'Gleichschaltung'—whether this is a levelling down or up is debatable. It is part protest and part throwing words to and fro, the intermingling of innovations and inventions with established canons of language, until the original is hardly recognisable. Whatever the plan or reason, its effect is one of continual youthful vigour and movement.

Juxtaposition, enjambement, double-talk, puns, spoonerisms, non sequiturs—all these and others seems to be some of the means by which writers of nonsense achieve their effects. Often nonsense is merely an extreme form, or an extension of, rational possibility (for example, Lear's reference to a 'coachman's cushion stuffed with muffins'). Reflections on the mind and oeuvre of such writers bring to us a ready awareness that they are also remarkably prolific. As the Artmann principle quoted already above indicates, verse for them is more than an aim in life: it is life itself. Their sheer inventiveness is astounding, otherwise how came Artmann to translate Lear's limericks so well? And yet—there is something more to them. They all have marked intellectual qualities, a fact to which L. W. Forster has drawn attention (*Poetry of Significant Nonsense*, Cambridge, 1962, p. 8).

But German nonsense verse is entirely, or almost entirely, a sub-genre. Artmann has gone beyond even Morgenstern in creating nonsense, since he does not bring existing or known metaphors to life, but creates already distorted ones, ones whose very first breath is taken in an Artmann piece of verse. In his small group of poems entitled 'lieder zu einem gutgestimmten hackbrett' he has these lines:

o du mei augenzahn
bist a scheans bleamal

verwundet ist der lachs
im tulpenfeld
mit warmer röte
der waldmond zieht
die holde kreiselbahn
mit einem wehlaut
falscher leitgedanken
entdacht der spröde auerhahn
die sommernacht
die sterne schwirren ab
von ihrer pfeilschnur
stumm und scharf

(*ein lilienweißer brief aus lincolnshire*)[2]

With Morgenstern we feel that the poet has a belief of some kind, even if it may be one which points away from the conventional God of our civilisation. But Artmann seems to know and to allow only absurdity *per se*. Nonsense, for him, is faith, but not necessarily orthodox faith, as Chesterton said (Forster, op. cit., p. 42), parody and satire denote aggression but nonsense does not.

Artmann's models for his nonsense writing are largely English, and three writers seem to merit special attention for their influence on him. They are: Swift, Lewis Carroll and Edward Lear.

The Swiftian influence is seen preeminently in Artmann's satirical use of word distortions and inventions, and partly also in the bizarre rearrangement of words. This is evident already in 1954, in which year he began his satirical poem on Punch and Judy, completed in 1961:

...und der caspar
mit seinen sieben freundinnen
hört
johann
sebastian
bach
und sie trinken
den guten cinzano
aus nagelneuen gläsern . . .
milch und
cinzano,
bosheit und
unschuld,
caspar und
maorifrau,
johann und
sebastian,
nixon und
kennedy,
moskau und
peking,
rolles und
roycelach. . . .
('anselm, antonia und der böse caspar'
in *ein lilienweißer brief aus lincolnshire*)[3]

Not very far below the surface of this 'toy-train' of words can be discerned a protest against Austria's political involvements at the time, especially in affairs outside Europe. The formation of a 'Bundesheer' (Artmann: 'das makarbre Kasperltheater'), alignment with the U.S.A. and even the diplomatic victory over Russia in 1955 are seen by the poet as a Punch and Judy Show. It is a determined, though unusually expressed 'ohne mich'.

Other poems written by Artmann at about this time liken political manoeuvring to 'Neanderthal behaviour' and legalised cannibalism. In his call to his country he appeals to it to be unique in leaving such unspeakable folly to others, if indeed such folly is to be committed at all. Artmann summarised these political views in his 'Coole Manifest', which he drew up and issued on 17 May 1955 in Vienna. It was signed by twenty-five people, most of them members of the Wiener Gruppe. Artmann concludes his manifesto with the warning that if Austria's voice is raised later, it will resemble nothing more than a croaking of frogs, which will sound even more hollow than that heard in the last decade of the Empire which disintegrated in 1918.

Equally bizarre and satirical, this time of German accidence, is the little poem, without a title, like most of Artmann's, in which he merely declines the proposition 'a new penknife'; the satirical note is contained in the irritating insistence on the 'new penknife' being *always* 'sharp'. Thc comparative mildness of this satire is uncharacteristic of Artmann while he still lived in Austria. The tone of the verse in his large collection *ein lilienweißer brief aus lincolnshire* which has been published as his collected verse to date (1945–66), is mainly one of growing anxiety of mind and a corresponding sharpness of tone. The bitterness and the deliberate rearrangement of word-order, as well as enjambement, all so typical of Swift, is much more effectively expressed in an untranslatable poem Artmann wrote in 1960, just about the time of his departure from Austria, and published in the *lilienweißer brief aus lincolnshire*

> ... ich bin ein schamloser ... ein
> johann sebastian orth am örthersee auf rollschuhen ...
> in döbling im dehmelschokoladentortenstil von dipl. arch
> und stadtbaumeister woswasdardeiföwiarahastdeadschuschdea ...
> ('liebe verehrte orchideengrüne primaballerina')

In another important aspect, Artmann follows Swift, whose satires were also strictures on some of the shoddy literature published in his age. The most conveniently arranged examples of this kind of satire in Artmann are found in his prose work 'Die Anfangsbuchstaben der Flagge' ('Flag initials'—it is interesting to observe, in passing, how his use of capital letters becomes more readily acceptable to him when he is writing with an entirely Anglo-Saxon concept and background in mind). This collection of short 'stories', published in 1969, has James Bond themes and a mock James Bond style. The mockery is only thinly disguised. In spite of the nautical background suggested by the general title, not all the scenes are laid at sea. Other settings are the Italian Alps, country houses in Kent, the streets of Kilburn, Hornsey and other London suburbs, as well as the fairy world of Tolkien. Nearly all the names have a strong English sound and appearance. Some echo the 1930's, like Jane Hislop, Millicent

Naish, Jarvis, Sir Percival Davenport, all of which seem to be figures out of Warwick Deeping, Somerset Maugham or John Betjeman. Others, like Ochuyo Gowin and Isbister Tregallas, could well have been taken from any recent English newspapers. Nevertheless, the language throughout is a constant reminder of Swift.

Two examples will show an almost photographic imitation of Swift, both in theme and in language. In one story ('Der Tänzer') in this collection, an Italian frontier guard is perplexed by the approach in the mountain mist of a headless and trunkless pair of legs; both wander about the mountainside separately. The headless part is fired at by a guard, but is not deterred by this shot. The guard receives little comfort from a voice in the region of the legs telling him to 'tremel schnan driar urrechtvar n snern'. A hurriedly summoned N.C.O., addressing the space from which the voice appears to come, is told by it that he is a 'coindl' and advised to 'asnurc n hart'. The mystified appeal of a third guard is dismissed with a harsh 'snarca', as the pair of legs disappears from view in the thickening mountain mist.

Likewise, in another story somewhere near the Southern Cross, Millicent Naish, aimlessly wandering, and described by Artmann as an 'armer LSD-Schlucker', finds herself experiencing James Bond and Tarzan-like encounters, during which she loses most of her scanty tropical clothing, and consoles herself with pondering the meaning of the words of the 'teufelsschamane' who has pursued her: 'oarrngh mmmflullwl ahrhkpp nn-nschnl', all of which is not one jot removed from words in Swift's *Voyage to Laputa* (1726): 'Inckpling gloffthrobbsquw tserumm blhiop mlashnalt zwin tnodbalkuff hstiophad kurdlubhasht.'

It is impossible to avoid the conclusion that there is also in this prose of Artmann a strong element of melodrama and the grotesque, especially in his latest writings. It has long been accepted that the grotesque has some relation to comedy, humour, caricature and satire. The question is whether in Artmann this grotesque is akin to the earlier grotesque of Raphael and Ghiberti, who saw it as ornamentation for its own sake, or to later conceptions, which saw in the grotesque something of the sinister and 'fratzenhaft' which Heine saw in much of E. T. A. Hoffman's writings. It seems, on balance, that Artmann's nature is too mild a one for his element of the grotesque to be more than ornamentation for its own sake.

The closeness between Artmann and Carroll is even more remarkable, as much in spirit as in language and theme. It may be most conveniently studied in Artmann's *Frankenstein in Sussex*. This short work consists of 32 scenes, in which Alice, bearing a strong resemblance to Carroll's creation, experiences some terrifying adventures in her eventual escape from pursuit by the monster Wilbur von Frankenstein. As in *Alice in Wonderland* so here Alice is overcome with curiosity; she peeps into a chimney stack projecting from the ground and falls in. Artmann's Frankenstein is cast very much in the mould of Mary Shelley's fiction, but it is not certain that Artmann was aware of the fact Mary Shelley drew largely on a German version for her Gothic novel *Frankenstein*, published in 1818, written as a wager between her, Shelley and Byron. (It is amusing to reflect that she alone of the three fulfilled her part of the bargain, and that neither Shelley nor Byron even started their promised volume.)

Alice's adventures in Artmann's version occur with the breathless speed we are accustomed to in Carroll. The Artmann Alice has less time and inclination for reflections, partly because the Artmann Frankenstein has at his command more modern methods of pursuit and of terrorising Alice or any intended victims. Alice is, however, still partly a demure little Victorian girl. When asked by Frankenstein if she can play the organ, she replies: 'ich vermag nicht bis an das register und die tasten zu langen.'[4]

Reflection is provided by Mary Shelley herself, who sits, accompanied by Frau Holle, at the TV set, watching the show set in a wonderland where Frankenstein is a hippie. Opinions exchanged by Mary Shelley and Frau Holle are in fact Artmann's own satirical views on much of contemporary life and on much of the melodramatic literature and entertainment offered. On their TV screen Mary Shelley and Frau Holle have just observed Frankenstein in a scene where he puts to Alice the question quoted above. Upon receiving her answer, he moves towards her in the conventional manner of a 'tückisches monster' ('deceitful ogre'), with more than a 'desire for music in his synthetic mind'. Frau Holle is incensed at the possibility of this horrid ogre doing something dastardly to Alice. Appeals to Mary Shelley are disregarded; she merely asks if anyone can think her so naïve.

Artmann's problem in recreating this Frankenstein monster was not so difficult as Mary Shelley's. For him there is none of the anxiety at the enormity of his creation that takes up so much of the early chapters of the original; nor has Artmann had to suffer any of the tortures Carroll suffered in taking his heroine through her frantic evasions attendant on the oppressive feeling of relentless pursuit. Modern melodrama has cleared all conscience away from pursuing evildoers and their creators perish with them. Frau Holle sets off in an atomic submarine to rescue Alice from Wilbur von Frankenstein; she succeeds, but Mary Shelley, who rushes after her to assist, is snapped up by her creation Wilbur, with whom she disappears down a noisy plug-hole into a 'stalaktitenhimmelüberdachten' ('stalactic-roofed') river.

The familiar Freudian symbols of sudden descents, pursuits, frights, horrors and visions of imaginary monsters are in Artmann as vivid as they are in Carroll. The political, academic and social undertones of meaning of which *Alice in Wonderland* is so full are in Artmann toned down to a level which makes them almost inaudible. The general reader today is not so fixed on such themes; his interests are wider and he finds the satirical outlet more on the stage or, maybe, in public demonstrations. Much more than his fellow spirits of the late nineteenth century, he finds this outlet in cartoons and caricature drawings.

Artmann's debt to Edward Lear pays homage to all the latter's range of expression, save that of his pencil and paintbrush. In person and in way of life there is much common ground, from which one can in part explain their poetical idiosyncracies. Perhaps Lear's skill with the paintbrush finds a counterpart in Artmann's disregard of capital letters and normal punctuation, leaving his verse as a design, a visual pattern on the page. Lear's joking suggestion in a letter to a friend that he should be appointed Lord High Bosh and Nonsense Producer is perhaps not so light-hearted as may at first appear. Artmann's reference to himself as 'der unartmann' echoes Lear's Grand Peripatetic Ass. Waggishness sometimes arises out of a depressive condition and writing may well be a compensation. For Lear it was a compensation for chronic illness, for uneasiness in society (although he craved for company) and the distress of recurrent impecuniousness. Artmann has for much of his creative life been a self-imposed wanderer, facing continually the strains of restlessness and never feeling at home anywhere. An expression of this in the verse of both writers appears as 'double-talk', within which several currents of emotion run side by side, and the preoccupation with nonsense is for both a means of surviving, and even enjoying, well-nigh intolerable situations. It is but a short step to include curious spelling, used as a deliberate rampart to protect inner feelings, to insulate the sensitive inner self against a rough outside world. It has been suggested that one reason for this curiousness in spelling and punctuation, as well as in the imaginary situations, is an extremity of a pathological nervousness, too primitive, or perhaps too scurrilous, for committal to the language of ordinary rationality.

It is impossible to say with certainty, but it is likely that both Lear and Artmann have found ordinary human attachments difficult. Both have minds well-stocked with disordered and miscellaneous information, which is poured out with little regard to selection. Lear's phonetic spellings (for example, 'rox', 'ski') are a commonplace in Artmann. The effect in verse is mysterious, almost uncanny. Artmann's verses:

ein iblis
ist ein ding
das lieber
dort bleiben
sollte
wo es
hingehört

—or:

rab und räbin
schnee zu schnee
verlorne kohle
alle wege
gehn nach rom . . .
(*ein lilienweißer brief aus lincolnshire*)[5]

are not a whit less mysterious and defy interpretation just as much as Lear's:

The Dolomphious Duck,
who caught Spotted Frogs for her dinner
with a Runcible Spoon.

The oddness of Artmann's writings has burst upon the world with something of the same effect as Lear's oblong-shaped book of rhymes-without-reason. Yet a slight difference is discernible:

this was not Lear's living or at least not his main work; we can only assume that Artmann must be living from his writing. Noteworthy is also the fact that their excursions into nonsense were at first occasional but became more frequent. In his collected verse Artmann has included some poems of a sensitive nature. 'o tod du dunkler meister' ('o death thou dark master'), for example, stems directly from the spirit of Donne and the Caroline poets; it could well be set alongside Dylan Thomas: 'Death, thou shalt have no dominion.'

The supreme example of Lear's influence on Artmann is seen in his translation into German of fifty-five of Lear's limericks. Although this is no more than a quarter of the total, it represents a stupendous achievement of intuition, sympathy and skill. The range of Artmann's ability makes him a worthy follower and pupil of Lear, even though he has not yet published any limericks of his own. This is not to say that none have appeared in recent years in German. One German newspaper (*Die Zeit*) has published limericks in its regular issues for the past three years. No attempt is made here to assess their quality; the reference is to the mere fact of their existence, and may serve as a reminder that limericks are possible reading matter now for at least a part of the general German public.

In his published translations of Lear's limericks, Artmann has shown a deep understanding of three underlying subtleties of his originals. These are: a sensitiveness to rhythm and rhyme; an insight into the surreality of the themes; a sense of Lear's natural sympathy for any and all creatures. Proper nouns constitute the main obstacle for the translator of limericks. Artmann faced not only the difficulty of English proper nouns, but also foreign ones. Both inevitably clash with German ones. Artmann's skill is soon apparent. From some of the best-known Lear limericks, his 'Cromer/Homer' becomes in Artmann 'Meer/Homer', 'Nepaul/fall' becomes 'Matrei/entzwei', and 'Madras/ass' reads in Artmann: 'Wesel/Esel'. One could list dozens of this kind. But it will be observed that the sense is retained. Even where proper nouns offer no obstacle or do not even exist, other line-endings may well prove troublesome to the translator. Such a translator may rejoice at being confronted with 'There was an old man of Peru', knowing that the sound and syllable coincides exactly with the German. But what of the continuation?: 'Who watched his wife making a stew.' Thus Artmann: 'Sah öfters der Bäckerin zu.' The limerick continues:

Lear: But once by mistake,
In a stove she did bake,
That unfortunate man of Peru.

Artmann has: Doch weil er sie neckte,
Nahm sie ihn und steckte
zu den Kuchen den Herrn aus Peru.

But this is a comparatively straightforward one. Even English place-names in the Lear original are retained with consummate ease by Artmann. Thus, for example:

There was an old person of Pinner,
as thin as a lath, if not thinner;
they dressed him in white,
and roll'd him up tight,
that elastic old person of Pinner.

Ein lustiger Alter aus Pinner
war dünn wie ein Draht, wenn nicht dünner;
man hat ihn vernickelt,
zusammengewickelt,
den elastischen Alten aus Pinner

where the translator's slight liberty with the internal phrasing has not diminished either the meaning or the enjoyment of the original.

The substitution of new names dictated by considerations of rhythm and rhyme seems to offer Artmann no special difficulty. Lear's 'old person of Sheen' is rendered by Artmann as 'einen jüngeren Herrn aus Siegen' (we note a frequent interchange in Artmann between Lear's old/young); the Lear-given qualities 'calm and serene' become in translation 'äußerst gediegen'. The limerick continues:

he sat in the water,
and drank bottled porter

for which Artmann finds the happy version:

jeden Tag um halb vier
trank er fröhlich sein Bier.

The last line—'that placid old person of Sheen'—one might almost find improved in Artmann's words—'auf 'nem Stühlchen im Fischteich von Siegen'.

With his felicity in the manipulation of place-names, it seems strange that Artmann has not included in his collection a translation of Lear's limerick about the 'Old Man of Coblenz'. A last example, taking a Lear limerick without any proper nouns, must serve as a summary of this brief survey of this aspect of Artmann's talent.

> There was an old man with a beard,
> who said : 'tis just as I feared—
> two owls and a hen,
> four larks and a wren,
> have all built their nests in my beard'.
>
> Ein Herr ohn Brille mit Bart
> rief : 'Teufel ! mir bleibt nichts erspart,
> ein Nachteulenpärchen,
> ein Huhn und fünf Lerchen
> benisten ganz frech meinen Bart.

(Would the retention of Lear's 'four'—'vier' have made any difference?) One's only wish is that Artmann had Lear's, or even Thurber's, skill with pen and brush to illustrate all his work.

There are in Artmann more connections with English writing : Edith Sitwell, Moby Dick, James Joyce, even Bulldog Drummond and Donald Duck, Samuel Butler, the author of *Erewhon*, Barham of the 'Ingoldsby Legends' and the Border Ballads all are embedded in the work of this remarkable Austrian contemporary. He is the Robinson Crusoe of contemporary literature. Has he a Man Friday, and, if so, where and when will he ever find him?

BIBLIOGRAPHICAL NOTES

med ana schwoazzn dintn (Poems in Viennese dialect), Otto Müller Verlag, Salzburg, 1958.

Von denen Husaren und andern Seil-Tänzern (Concerning hussars and other acrobats), R. Pier Verlag, München, 1959.

Edward Lear's Nonsense Verse (A translation of 55 of Lear's Limericks), Insel Verlag, Frankfurt/M, 1964.

Verfehltes unterfangen sich einer geographie zu erinnern (Unsuccessful attempt to remember one's whereabouts), Atlas, von deuschen Autoren zusammengestellt. pp. 297–303, Klaus Wagenbach, Berlin, 1965.

Dracula Dracula (Illustrated), Rainer Verlag, Berlin, 1966.
Verbarium (Poems), Walter Verlag, Olten & Freiburg, 1966.
Fleiß und Industrie (Diligence and Industry—30 short sketches on various occupations), Suhrkamp, Frankfurt/M, 1967.
Grünverschlossene Botschaft (Green-enclosed tidings—An interpretation of 90 dreams), Residenz Verlag, Salzburg, 1967.
ein lilienweißer brief aus lincolnshire (A lilywhite letter from Lincolnshire—Collected Poems to date), Suhrkamp, Frankfurt/M, 1969.
Frankenstein in Sussex (Alice's underground adventures with the monster), Suhrkamp, Frankfurt/M, 1969.
Die Anfangsbuchstaben der Flagge (Flag initials—Short stories), Residenz Verlag, Salzburg, 1969.
die fahrt zur insel nantucket (the trip to Nantucket Island—Dramatic sketches), Luchterhand Verlag, Neuwied, 1969.

NOTES

1. (The reference is to the statue in Weimar, depicting Goethe and Schiller standing side by side and holding hands)

the two betrothed: a German monument

Goethe: come and stroke my forehead, child/for I have many parts/ amongst which there are none/that do not spring from my heart
Schiller: come and hearten me, child/for I have many parts/amongst which there are none/that do not spring from my head

('dialogue bubbles')

2. (Songs for accompaniment by a well-tuned chopping-board)

Oh, my eyetooth
what a sight you are

the salmon lies wounded
in the field of tulips
with its warm glow
the forest moon tows
the winsome scenic railway
with a pained cry
of flashing basic thoughts
the prudish capercailzie uncovers
the summer night
the stars shoot off
from their bowstring
sharp and silent

(*a lilywhite letter from Lincolnshire*)

3. . . . and Punch
with his seven girl friends
listens to
Johann
Sebastian
Bach
and they drink
good Cinzano
from brand-new glasses. . . .
milk and
Cinzano,
wickedness and
innocence.

Punch and
the Maori woman,
Johann and
Sebastian,
Nixon and
Kennedy,
Moscow and
Peking,
Rolls and
Royce. . . .
(anselm, antonia and naughty Punch)

4. 'it is not within my power to reach up to the stops and the keyboard'

5. an iblis
is a thing
that would do better
to stay
where
it belongs

male and female raven
snow to snow
lost coals
all roads
lead to Rome. . . .

PART TWO

German Themes

LAVATER, MENDELSSOHN, LICHTENBERG

By E. J. Engel

> Ich möchte zum Zeichen für Aufklärung das bekannte Zeichen des Feuers (△) vorschlagen. Es gibt Licht und Wärme, es [ist] zum Wachstum alles dessen, was lebt unentbehrlich, allein—unvorsichtig behandelt, brennt es auch und zerstört auch.
>
> Lichtenberg[1]

I

Almost two centuries ago, Lavater (1741–1801), Moses Mendelssohn (1729–86) and Lichtenberg (1742–99) found themselves swept into an intellectual conflict that put all three men to the test as thinkers as well as human beings. What was really being called into question, however, was not the integrity of personal faith and belief but the viability of the Enlightenment in the Germany of the 1770's. The one person unable to perceive the nature of the problem was Lavater, the young and as yet unknown theologian, the author of an ill-conceived challenge to Moses Mendelssohn, the philosopher. Mendelssohn, for his part, throughout the debate gives a masterly example of clarity of thought and form, as also of the courage and perception postulated in Kant's subsequent definition of Aufklärung (Enlightenment):

> Aufklärung ist der Ausgang des Menschen aus seiner selbst verschuldeten Unmündigkeit. Unmündigkeit ist das Unvermögen, sich seines Verstandes ohne Leitung eines anderen zu bedienen. Selbstverschuldet ist diese Unmündigkeit, wenn die Ursache derselben nicht am Mangel des Verstandes sondern der Entschliessung und des Muthes liegt, sich seiner ohne Leitung eines andern zu bedienen. Sapere aude! Habe Muth dich deines eigenen Verstandes zu bedienen! ist also der Wahlspruch der Aufklärung.[2]

In 1769 and 1770, 'all Berlin' as well as the educated men of many professions and classes of society in Germany and Switzerland provided the critical audience for all the phases of this exchange of statements. Dramatic tension, guilt, peripeteia, turned debate into drama complete with exposition, tying of the knot, solution. It was left to Lichtenberg to provide the satyr play. The discussion between Mendelssohn and Lavater has been minutely described, commented and analysed; Lichtenberg's satire still awaits proper recognition.

In March 1763, J. C. Lavater arrived in Berlin for a stay of just over five weeks. He was on a study tour during which he hoped to meet men of note. One of these was Mendelssohn. In a letter (18 April 1763) to J. J. Breitinger, critic of literature and scholar of Greek and Hebrew, he reported of this visit:

> The Jew Moses, the author of the Philosophical conversations and of the Letters on perception, we came upon in his office ... a man of keen discernment, refined taste and extensive knowledge. Frank and trusting in his talk, more modest in conversation than in print and unaffected by praise, at ease, a stranger to all base vainglorious tricks, generous and obliging. A brother to his brethren, the Jews, reverent and kind towards them and by them beloved and revered.

Diary entries by Lavater, as well as F. Nicolai's notes to Lessing, give evidence of further meetings with the philosopher. Clearly, the impression of the contact with Mendelssohn was a deep, lasting and perplexing one. Compelling to Lavater, too, though for different reasons, was Charles Bonnet's *Palingénésie philosophique ou Idées sur l'Etat passé et sur l'Etat futur des êtres vivants.* A few months after its appearance in 1769, Lavater immediately translated chapters 16 to 22 of this work, together with part of Bonnet's preface. This fragmentary translation he published in Zürich under the title of

> *Herrn Carl Bonnets, verschiedener Akademieen Mitglieds, philosophische Untersuchung der Beweise für das Christentum.* Samt desselben Ideen von der künftigen Glückseligkeit des Menschen.

Lavater added a preface of his own and a dedication ('Zuschrift'). This dedication bore Mendelssohn's name. Lavater sent an unbound copy of the work to Mendelssohn on 4 September 1769, together with a handwritten letter stressing Lavater's respect for the Berlin philosopher and hoping to see 'believed or belied' ('geglaubt oder beurteilt') by him what to Lavatar appears as 'the most important truth'. And so he presents the following 'invitation' in his dedication of Bonnet's *Palingenesis*:

Most venerable Sir.
I know of no better way to express my esteem towards you, an *Israelite, in whom there is no guile*, inspired as it is by your excellent writings and your even more excellent disposition and by the delight I enjoyed in your amiable company a few years hence, than by dedicating to you the best *philosophical* inquiry into the arguments for *Christianity* known to me.

I am acquainted with your profound insights, your steadfast love of verity, your incorruptible impartiality, your tender regard for philosophy in general and for *Bonnet's* writings in particular. I cannot forego the remembrance of that gentle modesty with which you viewed Christianity, remote though you may be from it, and the *philosopher's* esteem for the moral nature of its founder which you gave expression to in one of gladdest hours of my existence. This remains so ever memorable and so important withal that I can venture to beg and beseech you in the presence of the God of truth, your father and creator, and mine too, not to read this treatise with a philosopher's impartial mind, for truly you will do that even without my pleading. What I beg of you is to refute it publicly should you find fault with the *fundamental* arguments supporting the facts of Christianity. Should you, however find the arguments sound, do what wisdom, love of truth, probity bid you do—and what *Socrates* would have done, had he read this treatise and found it irrefutable.

May God yet divulge much truth and virtue through you; may He let you experience all that is good and all that my heart wishes upon you.

Zürich
25 August 1769 Johann Caspar Lavater

A number of factors becomes self-evident from this Dedication and helps us to understand the naïveté and the perplexities of the man who wrote it. Lavater used the terms but not really the language of Enlightenment, he shared the contemporary admiration for Socrates as defender of truth, even as personification of truth itself, but Lavater's real language is that of Emotionalism and the centre of his universe is Christ. We know from the evidence of his early autobiographical material 'Gott war mir Bedürfnis', 'Gott kennen ist die größe Glückseligkeit'.[3] The evidence of this Dedication of 1769 reflects the subsequent development of Lavater's intense religiosity into fanaticist casuistry.

Lavater, moreover, was no longer arguing for the divine nature of religion, he used his conviction on this score to proclaim 'the divine nature of my religion' as being 'the shortest way to the utmost virtue and blessedness. . . . According to my notion of Christian religion, the Christian can reach the highest degree of this moral quality the most easily and most swiftly' (to M. Mendelssohn 14 February 1770).

Such an extreme of language and conviction on Lavater's part, however, aroused almost compassion among his contemporaries. Lessing spoke of him as 'enthusiastischer Narr', and even Lichtenberg, his fierce opponent on the grounds of Lavater's intolerance, sentimentality and lack of scientific exactitude, attributed these foibles to a dearth of intellectually exacting company rather than to intellectual and moral dishonesty. However, the discrepancy between Lavater's avowed intention, and the methods used to attain them, remains. So does the discrepancy in the verdict on Lavater's character. J. J. Spalding in his autobiography refers to the 'so noteworthy Lavater', his 'purity of soul' his 'vivid and active moral sense', 'his candid flow of innermost feelings'. This was the Lavater, a young man of twenty-two, on his Grand Tour in search of the great figures of his time. His travels (8 February 1763–26 March 1764) took him from Bodmer's and Breitinger's Zürich, to St. Gall, to Augsburg, to Nürnberg, to Gellert in Leipzig, to Gleim in Magdeburg, to Moses Mendelssohn (and the Crown Prince Friedrich Wilhelm) in Berlin, to the theologian Spalding in Barth, and on the return journey to Klopstock in Quedlinburg, to the philosopher T. Abbt in Braunschweig, to J. D. Michaelis, orientalist and biblical scholar, in Göttingen, to Frankfurt, Strassburg and Basel. In Göttingen he might have met Lichtenberg who had come to study there in 1763 but it was not till 1786 that the two so vastly different men met face to face. To this visit we owe two amusing and revealing vignettes. In a letter to J. D. Ramberg (3 July 1786) Lichtenberg gives a racy summary of his own impassioned speech on the lines that further millennia of the study of nature would lead to Spinozism. 'Do you know what Lavater said—having listened to me with incredible attention : *That he believed this too.* He merely made a few objections which he himself didn't put much store by and which—sketchy the whole lot of them, were all derived from the Christian system.'

By a freak of circumstance there is yet another eye-witness

account of this visit. Lavater's host, Lichtenberg, had remained standing throughout, but for no other reason than, very literally, to cover up the fact that he had used a recently bestowed author's copy to prop up a chiming clock. Lavater interpreted the situation as follows: 'that Lichtenberg had borne the avowal of the injustice done to Lavater in letters of fire on his forehead, that he had stood there so contritely before Lavater as to have lost use of his limbs and unable to move from the spot'.[4] This self-centred self-righteousness which expresses itself here so drastically, is clearly discernible long before 1786. It speaks to us already from the Dedication. Lavater's notion of religion could therefore not possibly coincide with the philosophical approach to religion professed by those men who represent German Enlightenment. Lavater's God is a biblical, personal, passionate God, a God who lets miracles come to pass. And such a 'miracle', the conversion of the outstanding Jew of the time, Lavater apparently sought to bring about. Lavater at twenty-eight is still thoughtlessly impetuous and clearly incapable of gauging the mind and the integrity of the Berlin philosopher with whom he had talked six years before he embarrassed him publicly by expecting him, the philosopher, to apply personal judgment to questions of religious dogma and doctrine. Lavater's choice of means and venue for such an emotional and provocative step remain unclear, not for want of his stating them, but for their successive and diverse plurality. But whereas the means remains in doubt, the motivation is clear: to Lavater only a Christian may truly be termed a human being, and only Christian belief is true, eternal and absolute.

To Mendelssohn, Christianity is but one of several forms of religion. He, and the German Aufklärer in general, were striving for a universal and rational deism. But up to 1769, it is not religious but metaphysical and aesthetic problems that claim his interest. Mendelssohn's *Phaedon* (1767) with its arguments for the immortality of the human soul presents a case in point. The main figure of this treatise is Socrates, and Mendelssohn shares his dignity, his steadfast self-discipline, his inquiring mind. In one of his conversations with the young religious enthusiast, Mendelssohn in his open-minded, concilliatory way must have made one remark or even several which gave Lavater rise to hope to convert not only Rousseau, Ramler and Goethe[5] to Christianity but also Mendelssohn in whom he saw not the Aufklärer or the sage, but the Jew.

The publicity of his appeal and its challenging nature emphasise that Lavater palpably was not interested in saving souls. To Mendelssohn, whether as Jew or as Aufklärer, religious controversy of any sort seemed destructive and was therefore to be avoided. But neither as Jew nor as Aufklärer could he bypass this challenge. As a Jew, he had to justify Judaism, and his loyalty to it, in the eyes of his fellow Jews, as an Aufklärer he had to come to grips with Bonnet's arguments.

The details of the controversy that inevitably developed need not concern us except in brief outline. It is, however, important to remember that Lavater had issued his challenge publicly. To serve its purpose, the whole matter had now to be argued out in public. Argument and counter-argument developed into a drama in which Lavater played a part of questionable integrity.

In his reply (*Schreiben an den Herrn Diaconus Lavater zu Zürich*, 12 December 1769) Mendelssohn expressed his being taken aback at having Lavater issue a *public* challenge, particularly since the challenge as such had been the outcome of a conversation provoked by Lavater and his friends, not only against Mendelssohn's will, but also after a promise had been given *never* to make public use of any part of their talk together. From this defensive opening, Mendelssohn moves into attack, but on rational grounds. The concept of proselytising other believers and, therefore, the insistent missionary zeal are incomprehensible to him as a Jew. It follows that, as far as he is concerned, the religious challenge is non-existent. Philosophically too, the challenge is as unacceptable as the arguments which support Bonnet's thesis are faulty. Only 'prejudice and upbringing' could read more into them. Here Mendelssohn permitted himself the only sentence which betrays the edginess of personal feelings; for the rest, the *Schreiben* presents an admirably controlled, 'enlightened' sequence of argumentation.

By now the educated public was aroused. Bonnet hastened to indicate that he disapproved of the tenor as much as of the content of the Dedication; the Berliners took specific interest in the case, many of them espousing Mendelssohn's side, and even Lavater's Berlin friend, pastor F. G. Lüdke, using pragmatic arguments, sought to help without taking Lavater's side. Mendelssohn did not need wise counsel, nor care for it; in fact he dealt sharply with any who offered it in print. 'For the time being, we have bidden the public to sit in as spectators, not as judges. If reviewers wish to provide the seconds in our duel (*Kampfspiele*) may I ask them not to intervene too soon.'[6] To minimise further misunderstandings, a kind of committee was set up in Berlin at Lavater's suggestion to scan future statements by either party and to prepare them for joint publication. The four men involved in this strange team are Mendelssohn and his friend and publisher Nicolai, and on Lavater's behalf the theologians Spalding and Lüdke. Their aim, a peaceful and definite termination of the controversy, was achieved with difficulty due to Lavater's many 'second thoughts'. (*Antwort an den Herrn Moses Mendelssohn zu Berlin von Johann Caspar Lavater.* [14 February 1770] *Nebst einer Nacherinnerung von Moses Mendelssohn.* [6 April 1770] Berlin, Nicolai)

Unfortunately the story still does not end there. With skill and patience, with firmness and integrity Mendelssohn had stated his views without betraying his conscience and without becoming involved in an irksome, acrimonious discussion on the relative virtues of Judaism and Christianity. Barely had the attention died down when *Jenaische Zeitung von gelehrten Sachen* (92. Stück, 1770), apparently without Lavater's knowledge, published an excerpt from his Latin report to the consistory in Zürich. Such an account was expected from each theological student on his return from his travels. The passage chosen and printed, concerned Lavater's visit to Mendelssohn in 1763, the writer's impression of the philosopher, and extracts from their conversation revolving around Mendelssohn's stance towards Christianity and Christ. Taxed by Mendelssohn as to the provenance of this diary extract, Lavater confirms the genuineness of the entries but, unconvincingly, attributed their authorship to a deceased friend.

II

We come to the prolegomena of the satyr play. As the only outcome of the publicity aroused by the Mendelssohn-Lavater conflict, there were the two Jewish students C. P. Sachs from Breslau and B. E. Fränkel from Fürth who travelled from Berlin to Zürich and after their arrival there appealed in writing to Lavater on 18 November 1770 asking to be baptised. Since such conversions were extremely rare in Switzerland, the sensation was great. Lavater undertook their religious instruction, and reported on it to Bonnet (31 January 1771). He added

> they tell me that if Moses [Mendelssohn] would convert to Christianity, some thousand Jews would follow suit; but there is little hope; yet to God and to him who believes, all things are possible.

Before the baptism was carried out with great solemnity (12 March 1771) Lavater gave an exceedingly lengthy sermon and subsequently published it together with a preface as *Predigt bey der Taufe zweyer Israeliten samt einem kurzen Vorbericht.*

It was not to Lavater, however, that the last word, as it were, or the summing up was given. Mendelssohn's contemporaries and friends could easily beat Lavater in argument and comment. For the main part, this finds expression in aphorisms and letters[7] and, subsequently in Goethe's comment in *Dichtung und Wahrheit*:

> [Lavater's] concept of mankind, grown as it had within him and in his own human image, was so closely related to his personal and living vision of Christ that it seemed incomprehensible to him that any human being could live and breathe without also being a Christian. . . . Irritating to me was thus this clever, sentimental man's vehement importuning which he directed at me, at Mendelssohn and others, asserting that either like him, one ought to be a Christian, a Christian of his brand, or there was the obligation of traducing him over to one's own side and likewise convince him of those matters that proffered appeasement and reassurance to oneself. (loc. cit.)

Goethe's irritation was with Lavater's character; the more immediate and productive concern of the other writers and thinkers was with Lavater's irrationalism. His lack of stylistic elegance, his confused arguments, his extraordinary syllogisms and emotional deductions were a negation of Enlightenment. A serious but also a ludicrous situation of 'nothing new under the sun' had thus come about. And when Lavater's *Taufpredigt* roused Lichtenberg to write a parody of it, his satire has all the appearance of an eighteenth century sequel to the *Epistolae virorum obscurorum* of Hutten (*et. al.*).

The parallel suggests itself on a number of counts. The *Epistolae*, in making a laughing stock of the scholastic pseudo-learning of the Cologne clergy around the year 1500, its hollow pretentiousness, its clumsy handling of style and language, hit out in 1515 and again in 1517 at the denigrators of Humanism in order to defend Humanism as such. Similarly, and with the same end in view, Lichtenberg's 'Gegenschrift' *Timorus* caricatures the denigrators of Enlightenment. The parallel continues to the central figures under attack: the outstanding representative of Humanism, J. Reuchlin, had suffered under a vindicative campaign, similar to that directed at Mendelssohn some two hundred and fifty years later. Again, both men stated and restated their point of view, hoping to see rational argument prevail and bitterly disappointed that the intellectual movement they had helped to initiate had to fight for survival against anti-rational opponents. As final parallels, just as the authors of *Epistolae* attempted to remain anonymous, so did the author of *Timorus*. In both works, the fictitious accuser-attackers seem to defend what in reality is being caricatured: sanctimoniousness, intellectual dishonesty and pettiness. In the case of both texts, the authors have good reason to try to remain anonymous; in both cases, the resultant texts are satirical parodies of genuine documents, in both works the language is alive with drama, rhetoric and passionate concern.

In content, Lichtenberg's *Timorus* is a parody of Lavater's emotionally charged, rabulistic style, as well as a satire on Lavater's 'Situationsethik'. The very name of this 'Gegenschrift', the 'Defender', recalls the need for such action; its publication under a pseudonym ('Photorin') highlights the reluctance of even such an independent mind as Lichtenberg's to acknowledge publicly Mendelssohn's leading part in bringing about the renaissance of German philosophy, literature and history of ideas. Twentieth century critics believe that Lavater acted out of nationalistic pique and religious bigotry, that he wanted to bring home to Mendelssohn

> that the growing new Germano-European civilisation was a Christian one, that this new civilisation could only prosper on Christian soil, so that only he who had his feet firmly rooted in this soil, could be the guide to this new German intellectual existence.[8]

The Enlightenment, however, with its postulates and ideals happened to have been the cause to which Mendelssohn had given all his energy. Lichtenberg as scientist, critic, philosopher, shared these goals; as a human being, he linked a capacity for 'mathematical' thought to an extraordinary perceptivity for 'Bilderschrift der Ohren', delighted in methodical experimenting and experienced the heights and depths of life to the full. He was thus a man of high hopes but few illusions, of shrewd analytical insight, of wit and literary skill:

> They talk a lot about Enlightenment and long for more light. Good God, to what purpose, if people either have no eyes, or shut those that they do have very deliberately.[9]

The opening of his own eyes, Lichtenberg attributed to his first long journey from Göttingen through Holland to London, a journey that took sixteen days, an immersion into a new world that lasted only a few weeks. There was such a tremendous inrush of impressions that no time remained for diary entries. Three letters, however, convey the whirlpool of images, and the nucleus of thoughts they gave rise to, of sights and sightseeing, of scientific talks, of direct contact with a nation of people who 'live and let live' and who, in various walks of life, enjoy freedom of speech.[10] In retrospect, it seemed to him 'I went to England to learn to write': such had been the fullness of impressions that he was consumed by eagerness to use them constructively.

But apart from some scientific communications, in the months after his return from England, his first years as professor (*extra ordinem*) of pure and applied mathematics in Göttingen, Lichtenberg's writing during this period is restricted to personal entries in diary and note book. These give us an account of literary plans, of growing disappointment with matters German, of his personal struggle for greater insight and knowledge. There is a growing flood of self-analytical entries towards the end of 1770 when he underwent some inner crisis. From this period dates his fragmentary 'Essay on Man', which consists solely of numerous short entries. Personal doubts and uncertainties are formulated and examined and eventually reformulated in what amounts to ethical postulates. The concept of originality troubled him sorely but when eventually Lichtenberg felt assured that he was capable of original thought, he laid down this maxim:

> Ich muß in mir selbst eine Freiheit zu denken einführen . . . ich muß sehen und hören, vergleichen, aber nur ein Richter muß in mir sein, niemals zwei: The whole man must move together. (*Versuch über den Menschen*)

(Within myself I must set up the freedom to think . . . I must see and hear, compare, but there should be only one judge within me, never two.)

The year 1771 offered many an opportunity to use this freedom to think, and this judge to appeal to. However, we know exceptionally little of Lichtenberg during the period that may have been crucial for the gestation of *Timorus*, i.e. the period since Lavater's sermon of 12 March 1771. There are no entries in his 'Gedankenbuch' before 1 June and few afterwards. Our main source of information are diary entries (in English) and these reflect the extremes of anguish experienced over a love affair that led to a breakdown of his faith in God. Twelve months subsequently Lichtenberg adds to the poignant diary entry for 21 August 1771

Exactly a year after. Thank God my heart is perfectly well after a fundamental cure. Yes there is a God. I can swear to it. I know it. I was never easier in my Life than this year and very seldom happier, for I can be happy and uneasy in the same time. I never doubted more than in this year. I do not know whether it is weak or sharpsightedness that makes me see things different from what they appear to other people.

(original entry in English)

The year that passed between August 1771 and 1772, Lichtenberg spent mostly away from Göttingen, since he was having an observatory built for him in Hanover. It was a year of warmth and welcome, of new contacts, of ripening friendships and of a growing interest in the pictorial arts.

On either side of these two months of August with their climax and solution of a crisis of conscience lie the only two sources of information that we have of Lichtenberg's concern with the Enlightenment in connection with the Lavater-Mendelssohn debate.

The Preface to *Timorus* carries the wording 'written in August 1771', and the final sentence of the main text ends with 'written in G . . . in August 1771'. We have no means of confirming whether this dating is correct. The first mention of *Timorus* and its publication by Nicolai occurs on 20 July 1773. It seems more than likely that Lichtenberg wrote the satire while away from his close friends in Göttingen. This would put the date of composition between December 1771 and early August 1772.

Between the date suggested in the Preface for the completing of the manuscript and its publication nearly two years later, there occurs the first, and, at the time, the only negative comment of Lichtenberg's on Lavater under the date of September 1772;[11] this may have, but does not have to have succeeded the completion of the satire:

> In reading the early part of Lavater's reply to Mr. Mendelssohn's Letter, I felt an indescribable indignation ... Go to, fearful prattler, I wanted to say to him ... Do not vex those who are better men than you. What kind of a fellow must this Johann Caspar Lavater be, who in reading a fine sentiment by Mendelssohn, could belch out: if only he were a Christian.

If we believe the Preface of the Editor, and we have no reason to doubt its truthfulness, the editor 'had firmly intended not to use his quill till duty and conscience bid him. But when they do, he'll not put down his pen till an eyesore has been uncovered or disgrace covered up.' To us, the question remains to guess at what point in time 'duty and conscience bad him'.

Clearly, Lichtenberg enjoyed writing *Timorus* but equally clearly he shrank from being taxed with its authorship. We know that he went out of his way to keep his great friend, the publisher Dieterich in Göttingen, in the dark as late as July 1773 and his own brother Friedrich Christian till August of that year. In fact he teased Dieterich that the friend is not the only one to charge him with being the author of *Timorus*, that he had even received a letter from 'a noted author' (Nicolai)

> who congratulated me on it, and even Germany, who has high hopes of me. ... Could anyone dream up anything more foolish and crazed than this tale. But, upon my honour, when I find out who the author is, let him be who he may, perhaps I'll confront him in such a way that he'll be sorry. For such a booklet as this Timorus I expect I'd trust myself to write. Now, do me the favour and write to Hartknoch in Riga. He is supposed to have printed it, he must know who the author is. You publishers surely confide your secrets to one another. ... I'd like to know what on earth possessed that first denouncer to proclaim me as the author. Have I ever spoken mockingly about anything in Göttingen? or written similar treatises. ... I am also told that the convert himself takes me for the author. Try to get reliable information on this score so that it can be used in court, for surely I shan't write any satires against him but bring suit against him forthwith. I'll

formulate the charge myself and then he can see for himself who writes more powerfully, I or Photorin.

(18 July 1773)

Since Dieterich knew Lichtenberg very well, and also his epistolary style, his letter may have been a clear case of admitting 'I am the author, but please keep quiet about it'.

Events succeeded each other rather rapidly at this stage. On 20 July 1773 Lichtenberg sent his thanks to Nicolai, 'the noted author' who had moreover, also invited him to become a contributor to his *Allgemeine Deutsche Bibliothek*:

> The approbation of such a connoisseur and master in the field will be my greatest encouragement. Various matters that displeased you and which just passed muster in the manuscript, struck even me as abominable once I saw them in print.

At the end of July, and too flustered to date the letter properly, Lichtenberg appealed to Dieterich and advised him what to do about a convert's 'Gegenschrift' to *Timorus*. He begged him

> not to fling back the manuscript at the man as you threaten to. Tell him you'd get it printed elsewhere since you didn't think the censor would pass it on account of its indecent words. I'll get it printed myself, and with a preface and with notes—just put him off with promises. It will make us laugh. But silence, thousandfold silence; however, should the Jew say that I am the author, he must be talked out of it most seriously for I shall never, never admit it and rather would do anything.... Should you however, have returned the manuscript already, find out where he sent it so that his book shan't come out before mine. I won't alter a word in the entire book... If I had the time, I'd make an even better satire out of it, but I have a great deal to do....
>
> That you got me a copy of the stuff is truly a masterstroke of yours... If I really consider the matter, it does seem too vulgar to have anything to do with the fellow, particularly since I do not believe that he wants to get it printed but merely brought it to you so that you would get in touch with me. Should he hint, that I wrote it, take him to task, severely, for he can't prove any of it. You must say at all social gatherings that I am taking it very much amiss to be taken for the author. That I didn't deny having uttered remarks about Jews and that these had presumably given rise to surmising me to be the culprit. And that it was for this reason that the author had assumed the name Photorin.

The treatise in question never seems to have found a publisher, so that scare died a natural death. However, as the letter to his brother shows on 13 August 1773, Lichtenberg was clearly not very happy about the uncovering of his pseudonym.

> At the bookfair a small piece of writing of five sheets has been published in Berlin under the title Timorus, or Defence of two Israelites etc. It has created a big stir in Göttingen. In the beginning Kästner was held to be its author, later Michaelis—though it wasn't written in the style of either. And now I am supposed to have written it merely because the author called himself Photorin and Professor Dieze was the first to discover that this meant Lichtenberg in German. I have no idea what caused the author to give himself this name, however, I am not the author, though I must admit that I would not have to feel ashamed of the greater part of the book.... The piece of writing is crude and does go too far but nevertheless it does contain parts which display humour and originality ['Laune und Genie'], and no one of any sense will deny it. And yet, I have not read them, the reviewers in Frankfurt are supposed to have made fun of it. Do tell me who these reviewers are...

There were other reviewers in other journals too, one of them presumably Matthias Claudius, the other Hamann: Lichtenberg reports on these and others in a letter (3 April 1774) to Nicolai

> As you put it in your kind letter, you were the midwife officiating at the birth of Timorus, and so I consider it my paternal duty to give you some news of the fate of the poor wretch.
>
> The Frankfurters have maltreated him very badly because he found fault with Lavater who at this time began to become all the fashion out there in Boetia. If Timorus had battered the face of sound Reason ['gesunde Vernunft'] with both his fists, no one in Frankfurt would have cared.
>
> ....
>
> If circumstances should permit it, I should like Timorus to be reviewed in your [Allgemeine] Bibliothek. If he were given just treatment in those parts where I am not as blameworthy, then I shall most gladly put up with the appropriate critique in those parts where—let me admit it—in a joking mood I wrote down all sorts of things that I would never have let stand if only I had seen the galley proofs....

III

It is appropriate at this point, to turn back to Lavater's *Taufpredigt* and to compare it with Lichtenberg's *Timorus*. Lavater gave the sermon in the Frauenkirche in Zürich on 12 March 1771, as part of the baptismal church service for the two young men who had come to him from Berlin in mid-November 1770, asking to be admitted as converts. A printed version of the sermon based on *Acts of the Apostles,* II, 22–39, appeared subsequently as *Predigt bey der Taufe zweyer Israeliten.* There is a 'Vorbericht'[12] (op. cit., 107–110) which recounts the incidents leading up to the church service; the youths' desire 'to study at leisure the Christian religion in a place where they enjoyed complete freedom and feared no persecution', how the many Christian sects 'had proved no mean stumbling block to them' until the moment they were handed the New Testament 'without the slightest reference to any factions'.

The New Testament text is quoted in full, it is followed by an injunction to the congregation to listen attentively: no unnecessary plea if we consider the length of the sermon to follow. Its first part is addressed to the two 'Israelites on the day of their baptism (pp. 118–156), a second, shorter part to the congregation (pp. 157–162).

Lavater proceeds by systematic exegesis of the text, verse by verse, phrase by phrase, with a great deal of pathos and mixed metaphor. (op. cit., 128: 'Here now, dear friends, stop still with your thoughts', p. 130: 'His strength is withered like a flower pot,' p. 133: 'wash off your estwhile prejudices as thought and intentions which tarnish the soul,' p. 145 'by baptism you have clad yourself in Christ', p. 148 'a thousand eyes and arrows are directed at you'.) The baptised youths are addressed as 'Friends of truth, childlishly simple disciples of Christ' (p. 144). The tone to the congregation and the two youths alike is that of a teacher dealing with illiterate and reprehensibly recalcitrant children. The God whom Lavater held out to them is hardly the God of love, the preacher even included the threat: if you should ever turn away from Him, 'may blood be upon your head'. With holy wroth, Lavater worked up to the 'Repent, and be baptised' (*Acts* II, 38). He turned fiercely on the two youths, charging them with views they had once held. 'Distance yourself from

all ideas and notions that run counter to truth as you turn to Christ' ("in Absicht auf diesen Jesum"). 'Be baptised in his name' and then, very abruptly, Lavater launched into a diatribe (*Taufpredigt*, 135):

> No human being on earth, no sage, no teacher of philosophy ['Weltweisheit'] or divinity, as learned, as judicious, as famous he might be, as excellent and engaging his written and spoken word, no one has the right to press upon you any doctrine, any opinion, or even any single word, any expression that he has not learned from Jesus, that he has not heard through the Holy Ghost. Only one is your master, the Messiah, only one your teacher, Christ!

This bigoted interpretation that does not even refrain from a personal attack in the pulpit is hardly the natural religion common to all men that the Enlightenment envisaged, nor the language in which it would choose to communicate ideas. It is easy to see why it would enrage Lichtenberg to the point where he would be driven to write a 'Gegenschrift' and with spirit and verve succeed in doing justice to the dialectic and the style of his self-appointed task. It is customary to refer to Lichtenberg's abundance of felicitously worded ideas, to the range and depth of his knowledge but to remark on the existence of only a small number of really structured works of any length. *Timorus* is an exception.

It is as if Lichtenberg set out to illustrate and to outdo his own dictum: 'The most handsome kind of irony consists in defending an indefensible cause by bitterly satirical arguments, to provide a wealth of quotations together with their exegesis.'[13] The very title of *Timorus* is an indication of the double part he set himself to play: Timorus/das ist/Verteidigung zweier Israeliten/die/durch die Kräftigkeit/der/Lavaterischen Beweisgründe/und der/Göttingischen Mettwürste/bewogen/den wahren Glauben angenommen haben/von/Conrad Photorin/Der Theologie und Belles Lettres Candidaten.[14]

Like Lavater's translation of Bonnet's *Palingenesis*, like most books in the eighteenth century, the satire opens with a Dedication in the shape of an open letter. Photorin addressed himself to her majesty Oblivion, 'since this little treatise would sooner or later reach you anyhow' and because 'there is little doubt that you would receive it graciously since it concerns a religious dispute and your majesty, as is well known, is wont to extend her especial protection to this kind of work. And do they not merit it by their import, their moderation, their certainty and customary clarity.'

There follows another open letter in which the editor invites the reader to 'take off a few prejudices at the door, they'll be as little use to you as a fencing foil in a picture gallery or at Vauxhall!'. The first prejudice concerns the author's motive ('duty and conscience in uncovering an eyesore or covering up disgrace'), the second the author's attitude towards his public ('if he is zealous, it is religious zeal, if he curses, they are benedictory curses').

The key is thus set for an attack on theological sophistry. It takes place under the guise of a public defence, in exegetical manner, of an indefensible premise. Two Jews of ill repute are persuaded to accept baptism. Were they 'persuaded' by material blackmail, or by argument? If the latter, were the converts in fact not wise to get themselves locked up? How else could they have found or afforded the necessary leisure to consider the arguments? And is imprisonment itself proof of crime? Inversely, since many an honest or patriotic man had to suffer it, could not imprisonment be taken as a definition of honesty? In short, Lichtenberg fashioned his parody, his satire by using the sophistry and captiousness he appears to attack, and by Socratic irony.[15] He goes out of his way to invent impossible 'red herrings' and then proceeds to debate and defend them with dexterous and paradox logic. In all good faith he appears to seek definitions of fundamental concepts (stealing: 'to take your neighbour's property without using force') and then to apply them logically but paradoxically (the rich 'who borrow and do not pay'). Thus the scene is set for the ultimate syllogism: conversion is brought about by argument. If sausages prove an acceptable reason, why not Lavater's sophistry? Lichtenberg's road towards this conclusion meanders and makes several detours. The main argument, however, is: Is it true that diseases of the body can only be healed by physical means? If the answer is in the affirmative, does one not heal certain diseases by applying the remedy to the opposite part to that affected? Thus, since the soul is the opposite extreme to the body, the soul is solaced by application of the remedy to the body. (The stating of the converse brings out the paradox even more forcefully: in England you cure men of their errors by applying physical therapy, i.e. punishment). If the inverse procedure holds good, it is valid to effect conversion of the spirit by the partaking of sausage.

It is at this point where the facetious argumentation is pushed aside, and the decisive purpose of Lichtenberg's treatise becomes apparent. Photorin's statement on the nature of religiosity reflects the view held by other supporters of the Enlightenment, by Mendelssohn, by Lessing, by Lichtenberg himself. The universality of true religion manifests itself in the indivisible, 'identical ring'-like nature of its fundamental precepts and ideas. Conversions can therefore only be achieved by 'recruitment', and recruitment depends on canvassing and the promise of reward.

At this point of the treatise, Lichtenberg assumed the diction and fervour of Lavater, the representative of an avenging God, in the passage of his sermon that led up to 'Repent, be baptised'. However, Lichtenberg used Photorin as devil's advocate (thus 'twisting the tail' of the paradox and the syllogism) by letting Photorin paraphrase current 'repulsive blasphemies', i.e. the views held by Mendelssohn: 'Let there be no more proselytising, let each honest man stand fast by his religion, or, if he change it, let him do so before God, in privacy and without pomp.' Lavater had betrayed his lack of judgment and philosopher's *savoir faire* by toying with Mendelssohn and the philosopher's calm of mind, unbidden, and as if he owned him. He, Lavater, had wanted to have his hand in this sage's conversion. And presently the slogan in religious matters was no longer 'Quake and worship' but 'Think, and examine'.

In this decisive and outspoken manner, the simpleton Photorin countered Lavater's oblique reference to Mendelssohn and Lavater's misplaced criticism of him in the *Taufpredigt* as well as in the writings that had led up to it. Lichtenberg, using a more sophisticated method of truth, pun and irony made open reference to Lavater, adducing pseudo-compassionate interpretations of Lavater's motives for his attack on the philosopher. He gave a scintillating 'Bilderschrift für die Ohren' (auditory verbal picture) of Lavater's style and thought. His summing-up judgment is frankly mocking and accusing:

> er habe sich durch sein langes Gucken in die Ewigkeit die Augen ganz für den zeitlichen Horizont verdorben.[16]

Almost to the end of their lives Lichtenberg was to cross swords with Lavater over other issues and fight him fiercely. Never again, however, did he best Lavater in such a brilliantly enlightening way.

NOTES

1. A. Leitzmann (ed.), *Lichtenbergs Aphorismen*, Berlin 1902–8, J 948. 'As emblem for the Enlightenment I should like to propose the well-known symbol for fire. Fire gives light and warmth, it is essential for the growth of all organisms. However, treated carelessly, fire can also burn and destroy.'
2. 'Beantwortung der Frage: was ist Aufklärung,' *Berlinische Monatsschrift*, December 1783, p. 516. 'Enlightenment is the only way by which man can escape from his self-inflicted minority. Minority is the inability to use one's intelligence without guidance from without. This minority is self-inflicted whenever it is brought about not by lack of intelligence but in the lack of determination and the courage to use it without external guidance. Dare to know! Have the courage to make use of your very own intelligence: this then is the motto of Enlightenment.'
3. E. Staehelin (ed.), Johann Caspar Lavater, *Ausgewählte Werke*, Zürich 1943, 3 vols. vol. I Die neue Kreatur in Christo, p. 2: 'I had need of God.' 'To know God is the greatest bliss.' The *Jubiläumsausgabe*, vol. 7 has 'können', not 'kennen' in this quotation.
4. G. Chr. Lichtenberg *Vermischte Schriften*, Göttingen 1844–54, vol. 4, 107 f. The ancedote is told by F. von Matthisson in 1794, quoting Lichtenberg verbatim.
5. *Dichtung und Wahrheit, Jub.* xxiv, 93.
6. Moses Mendelssohn *Gesammelte Schriften* (*Jubiläumsausgabe*) Berlin, 1930, vol. 7, 22 f 'Erwiderung Mendelssohns auf eine Rezension seines Schreibens', 10 January 1770.
7. G. E. Lessing and his brother Karl, Nicolai, Bonnet, Spalding; from Göttingen the orientalist J. D. Michaelis, the classicist C. G. Heyne and the scientist G. C. Lichtenberg.
8. S. Rawidowicz in Mendelssohn, op. cit., LXXIX.
9. A. Leitzmann, op. cit., L 469.
10. 17 April 1770 to C. G. Heyne, the Göttingen classicist.
11. A. Leitzmann, op. cit., C 37.
12. J. C. Lavater *Sämtliche kleinere Prosaische Schriften vom Jahr 1763–83*, Stein, Winterthur, 1784. In vol. 2 *Gelegenheits-Predigten* the sermon referred to is on pp. 107–62.
13. A. Leitzmann, op. cit., KA 12.
14. Published by Hartknoch, Königsberg, 1773. 'Timorus, i.e. the defence of two Israelites who by virtue of the vigour of Lavater's argumentation and the Göttingen sausages were moved to accept the true faith.'
15. In *Lichtenberg. Geschichte seines Geistes*, Berlin 1968, F. H. Mautner draws attention (p. 86, footnote 100 and p. 54) to an earlier, unpublished article in which the technique of irony was explored: 'Zwo Schriften, die Beurteilung betreffend, welche die theologische Fakultät zu Göttingen über eine Schrift des Herrn Senior Götze gefällt und dem Druck übergeben hat.'
16. A punning reference to Lavater's *Aussichten in die Ewigkeit* (1768–78). 'By gazing too long at eternity he had ruined his eyes for the temporal world.'

2

GOETHE'S *UNTERHALTUNGEN DEUTSCHER AUSGEWANDERTEN*

By H. Popper

The earliest reference to the *Unterhaltungen deutscher Ausgewanderten* (*Conversations between German Refugees*) occurs in Schiller's reply to Goethe's question concerning 'what further contribution you might wish me to make to the *Horen* and when you would need it . . .'[1]

> May I remind you [Schiller replies] of your idea to produce a new version of Boccaccio's story of the high-minded lawyer [Prokurator] . . .[2]

Schiller's mistake—the *Prokurator* story is in fact the last piece in the *Cent Nouvelles Nouvelles*—indicates that the two friends must have discussed the *novella*-form at some time in the past; Boccaccio was Goethe's obvious model for the use of a framework which the *Cent Nouvelles Nouvelles* lacks.[3] But when? Was Goethe at that time planning the earlier works concerned with the French Revolution, notably *Der Bürgergeneral* and *Die Aufgeregten*, which he later associates in his mind with the *Unterhaltungen*? Occasionally he even dates the composition of the latter a year too early.[4]

Progress must now have been rapid,[5] for the framework and the first six narratives had been sent off by 27 June 1795.[6] The last part, *Das Märchen*, is complete by 23 September and on 2 October Schiller writes that it 'has given us much pleasure and it will certainly have a very wide appeal'.[7]

Indeed, the vivid imagery contrasts strongly with the cool restraint, bordering on irony, prevalent in the earlier parts of the work. Contemporary readers often felt that they were moving from one anticlimax to the next.[8] But this is deceptive. The framework, the earlier stories and *Das Märchen* are all of one piece:

> *Das Märchen*. I would make this the concluding piece of the *Unterhaltungen*, and perhaps it might not be a bad thing if,

through a product of the imagination, [the *Unterhaltungen*] finished up, so to speak, in infinity.[9]

This 'infinite' potential is thus present in the whole of the work. For its structure develops according to the principles of 'morphology' which underlie his poetic writing as well as his views on all forms of existence.

Denn man wird mir gerne zugeben, daß alle natürlichen Dinge *in einem genauen Zusammenhange stehen,* . . .[10]

He means both the interconnectedness of all things, and that the same general principles hold in every sphere of existence. Thus, in *Metamorphose der Pflanzen* he shows how, through phases of gradual development and radical change, the basic form of the leaf is repeated in ever changed, heightened, intensified form, from the seed to the petal, until the finished plant uses its fragrance to bring about the union of opposites in love—

Hymen schwebet herbei, und herrliche Düfte, gewaltig,
Strömen süßen Geruch, alles belebend, umher.[11]

This, according to the principle of *stirb und werde* ('die and evolve'—that is, death and regeneration: the poem *Selige Sehnsucht*), is sacrificial. In *Faust II* it leads to the birth of Euphorion (hermaphroditic, like the 'rebis', or Philosopher's Stone[12]), and after Helen's departure, to Faust's life of action on a new plane; after his collapse, followed by the victory of grace over Mephistopheles, angels bear him upward through new phases of growth by gradual development and radical change.

On the purely biological plane the death of the plant, the eventual liberation of the seeds and their return into the earth, constitute the cycle of life, a chain of interlocking *rings of nature's eternal forces*, where the quality of life is expressed by each individual as well as by the whole community of beings.[13]

But man is endowed with the powers of conscious thought and feeling, so that he can transform his evolving experience from the mere chain of rings into meaningful destiny:

Bildsam ändre der Mensch selbst die bestimmte Gestalt.[14]

And within this destiny the combination of insight and energy will lead, through ever heightened stages of love, to discovering 'the higher world'.[15] This is now exemplified in the growing union between the poet and his wife, to whom the poem is addressed.

Now, if sacrifices and losses are not compensated for by corresponding gains elsewhere,[16] inner contradictions and outward conflicts will turn such a union into a nightmare. That is the situation in the poem *Urworte. Orphisch.* The alliance of *Daimōn* (structure inherent in organic growth)[17] and Tychē (playful chance activity) is transformed on the plane of *Erōs*, whose expansiveness only fulfils itself when it confines its devotion to the one unique object. The aberrations of *Tychē* are then dammed in by a *heightened and intensified* (*gesteigert*) form of *Daimōn* : *Anankē.*[18] But this one-sided progress issues in slavery. There is no way out unless the wings of *Erōs* are reactivated as the wings of *Elpis* (hope).

We must now apply these principles of existence, first to the composition of the *Unterhaltungen*, then to the action. *Novellas* and shorter narratives with a similar content had, of course, been written and translated in great abundance, certainly between the twelfth and sixteenth centuries. In the eighteenth century they were no longer a living tradition in German prose writing; and the convention of a framework had never been a principle of composition among German writers.[19] By adapting this convention from the Romance tradition, Goethe thus broke new ground and he was followed by many writers, from Wieland (*Das Hexameron von Rosenhayn*, a pastiche) down to the present day.

But Goethe did not produce a *novella*-collection of the orthodox kind. Instead he fused types of short narrative in vogue at the time with the *novella* and developed them according to his own principles of organisation. Thus the first two stories (*Antonelli; the knocking ghost*)[20] are a combination of ghost story and documentary (that is, the true, or true-to-life story, satisfying the taste for psychological study, moral reflection and preaching, often found in eighteenth-century literary journals).[21] The third story, taken from the mémoirs of Marshal Bassompierre,[22] uses the mould of a *chronique scandaleuse*[23] converted into a tale of terror. The fourth and last story in this group, also taken from Bassompierre, concerns a legendary tradition regarding one of his ancestors and has many parallels in the tradition of fairy tale and legend; it also comes close to the story of *Melusina* which is itself part of a far-flung tradition.[24]

The second group consists of two pieces, both of them *novellas*.[25] The first of these, the *Prokurator*, from the *Cent*

Nouvelles Nouvelles, is derived from much older material.[26] It stands in sharp contrast to the air of mystery which thrills and horrifies the audience in the first group. The moral element predominates, so that it represents a fusion of the *novella*-form with that of the moral tale. The second, *Ferdinand and Ottilie*, is freely invented and said to be the earlier life of one of the narrator's friends, so that the fusion of the *novella* with the moral tale is now extended to include the documentary. As a pair of moral tales illustrating the same theme—here called 'parallel stories'—they exemplify a principle of composition which Goethe came to use on an increasingly large scale.[27]

The last story in the work, *Das Märchen*, is again freely invented. Its blend of reflection, symbol and allegory is an extension of the eighteenth-century philosophical *conte*, more especially as practised by Voltaire and Charles Perrault.[28]

Goethe's organisation is thus open-ended in two respects. Firstly, the live episode, the ghost story, the tale of mystery, grow into the *novella*. Thence, through the stories which were originally thought of as a possible second part to the *Unterhaltungen*,[29] but were eventually included in the last of Goethe's novels, *Wilhelm Meisters Wanderjahre*, they develop further, until *Der Mann von fünfzig Jahren* is almost a full-scale novel. And *Die Wahlverwandschaften*, originally conceived as an inset piece for the *Wanderjahre*, is, in fact, a novel in its own right. And secondly, the matter-of-fact is transcended by the symbolic-legendary (here: Bassompierre's ancestor; later: e.g. *Die neue Melusine*)[30] the supernatural (here: Ferdinand praying; later: e.g. the character of Makarie)[31] and the symbolic-prophetic (here: *Das Märchen*; later: e.g. in *Die Novelle*: the transmutation of the whole human and natural situation into ecstatic song).[32]

The action in the *Unterhaltungen* is patterned according to the same principles of dynamic morphology.

It is conceived, true to the spirit of Schiller's announcement to the public of *Die Horen*,[33] as a conversation between the narrator and the reader in the guise of conversations between German refugees; these extend into stories whose relevance to the revolutionary age arises from the narrator's humane attitude, not from topicality. Thus he opens the work[34] by branding 'those unhappy days' as *harmful*; the French are called, after their savage forebears, the *Franks*, because for them the virtue of respecting their ancestors and making provision for later generations is a crime.

This is not a defence of the *sans-culottes*. The narrator's impartiality[35] reflects, in point of fact, the author's attitude, whose play *Die natürliche Tochter* is one example of a severe indictment of the aristocracy and its court intrigues.[36] A much deeper principle is at stake; it is the need for being rooted in a tradition. Without such roots society drifts and the individual loses all bearings.[37]

The narrator's attitude already shows itself in the syntax. The whole paragraph, one single tortuous sentence, is a bare résumé of the situation. There is only one metaphor, the 'badly guarded leak'; but it transforms the military situation into a symbol of man's ramshackle defences against macrocosmic and psychological forces (fire, plague; war, passions, instincts). The narrator, then, regards his task as a painful one. Schiller emphasises the *closeness* of the war, invading even *the most intimate circles*; he starts with 'At a time when . . .', followed by verbs in the present tense. Goethe's narrator puts every verb in the past historic and starts with 'In *those* unhappy days . . .', as if he were referring to the *remote past*. This attempt at keeping the crisis at arm's length may be one cause of Goethe's ante-dating the composition of this work.[38]

Author, reader and narrator thus share with the party of refugees—the characters in the framework—the feeling of anxiety that naturally spills over into the stories. The widowed baroness von C., who heads the party, keeps the same tight rein on the practical situation as on the demonic passions. But she has her share of sheer passive suffering.[39] Her eldest daughter Luise alternates between eccentricity, pertness and terror when she cannot be gay and affectionate.[40] Friedrich, her elder son, has some of his mother's circumspectness,[41] while her nephew Karl resembles Luise in her impulsiveness.[42] An old priest, friend of the family, is far-sighted like the baroness, but more detached and philosophical.[43] A younger son, his tutor, two relatives and some domestics remain in the background.

This dialectic of character traits—the impulsiveness of *Erōs* and *Tychē* (Kirl, Luise) as against the self-containment of *Daimōn* and *Anankē* (the baroness, the old priest, Friedrich) is then reflected in the arrangement of characters and issues in the stories. Conflict situations have this same structure; they arise due to the threat from two sets of forces: those coming from outside (nature, war) which are beyond the individual's control, and those inherent in the human character, where insight and the moral will hold out some hope. We must consider each in turn.

The threats of nature and war evoke terror, but also a curiosity which softens the impact of what has to be faced. Thus, a discussion of what reports and rumours are to be believed, leading on to occult phenomena,[44] prepares the ground for the first group of stories. The war is hardly mentioned again, although the rumble of heavy artillery is in constant evidence.[45] Later, two events divert attention from the terrifying impact of the second story: the outbreak of a fire on a family estate at the same time that a bureau in the room where the company is sitting is cracked. Its twin, standing in a building on the estate, is destroyed by the fire.[46] The shock caused by this double encroachment of nature on human civilisation[47] is softened, however, by Fritz' curious suggestion of an occult relationship existing between the two pieces of furniture. Indeed, after returning on the following day from an inspection of the extent of the damage, he appears to be *serene* ('heiter')[48] and the others follow suit, expressing credence or scepticism regarding his theory.

Threats within the human situation. The renewal of the political battle 'in nearly every intimate circle',[49] is exemplified by a heated argument between Karl, who sides with the revolutionaries, and the Geheimerat von S., who favours the royalists. He has brought his family on a visit, but this quarrel leads to their sudden departure. His wife's close friendship with the baroness and a promising relationship between the two daughters is thus cut short. The baroness is left desolate. She charges Karl with the consequences of his quarrel and he pleads leniency.[50] But the baroness takes the opposite view.[51] To face the truth regarding one's fears and one's aggressiveness is not easy but must not be shirked. On this is based the truce which the baroness now calls, and her principles of *polite sociability*[52] which make coexistence possible. Avoidance of arguments about conflicting ideologies and regard for the vulnerable spots of the other person are no more than common politeness. Conversation should be instructive and entertaining. The company now disperses, only Luise stays with the baroness. The old priest enters and is told what has happened. He offers to tell stories which fulfil the baroness' requirements, and when Luise suggests that such stories can only be *chroniques scandaleuses* he characterises his stories as studies of *the inner conflict of a good man on a small scale*, 'where chance has its sport with human weakness and inadequacy'[53]—in other words, human attitudes are to be the central concern; the accent is, for the present, on entertainment. But by the penultimate framework (between the two *novellas*)[54] the discussion, based on Kantian ethics, fulfils Schiller's programme for *Die Horen*, that is, non-trivial, non-ideological, human discourse.

The discussion about occult phenomena occurs after dinner, when the baroness has gone to bed. It gives rise to the priest telling the story of the famous Italian singer Antonelli,[55] an intelligent, successful, pleasure-loving woman, who longs for a deep personal relationship, yet fears losing her freedom. She engages a young Genoese merchant in a friendship-pact,[56] but he ends up by pressing a lover's suit. She gives way, but this spells ruin to their friendship, as she had feared. After a series of crises—due to the disordered state of his finances—his health is broken and eventually he dies. In spite of the old priest's pleadings she refuses to see him on his deathbed. Very soon after she begins to be pursued by a series of ghostly noises—at first terrifying, eventually trivial. It turns out that, on his deathbed, her former friend has vowed not to leave her in peace. The conversation concentrates on the phenomena themselves. Antonelli's motives in refusing her friend's summons from his deathbed are suppressed by the old priest. This is curious, for he had been one of her trusted friends and his account of her character at the beginning of the story shows a thorough grasp of her motivation. The human problematic thus remains an unexplored substratum.[57] The priest senses the state of anxiety among members of the circle and he saves them for the moment from facing the human predicament by stimulating their curiosity.[58]

The next story,[59] told by Fritz, concerns a girl who is plagued by a knocking ghost, until the father of the family with whom she is staying threatens to use the horsewhip on her unless the ghost desists. The manoeuvre is successful, which elicits the comment from Luise that the girl must have been playing a joke on the family. The grotesque incongruity of her remark is a measure of her anxious state of mind. Fritz answers her by telling the rest of the story. The ghost disappears, but she is reduced to a mere shadow of her former self. Human destiny thus breaks through the preoccupation with the occult—but only for a moment, because this is when the bureau is cracked and the fire breaks out. Karl's joking allusion to Antonelli's ghost frightens Luise, because she is reminded of her fiancé serving in the war. Again human destiny has broken through.

Karl now relates the erotic adventure of Bassompierre, which contrasts the love of the woman Bassompierre has picked up with his own lasciviousness and emotional insensitivity. Two amendments are significant. Where Bassompierre's text quotes the woman as consenting to become his lover 'de bon coeur',[60] our text has 'freiwillig'; the emphasis is thus on the woman's *deliberate choice.* This points forward to the moral perspective in the *novellas.* Secondly: Bassompierre concludes that the woman had been 'so lovely that I have regretted her and would have desired a great deal to have had a chance to see her again'. But Karl makes him recall that perhaps she was one of the corpses, victims of the plague, that he encountered when he went to their second assignation; for he says that this would have been one of the most charming adventures, *but for the disagreeable outcome.*[61] Destiny has reared its ugly head and Karl's Bassompierre is shaken. The sense of crisis reminds the audience of their present circumstances and prepares the ground for the serious tone in the second *novella* and in *Das Märchen.* And while the dialectic tension between Antonelli's self-containment and her partner's inordinate passion is transcended by the ghostly noises, nature now overwhelms, first the victim of the knocking ghost, then the woman who loves Bassompierre *beyond measure.* Bassompierre is shaken, Luise is terrified; curiosity regarding the occult has itself been instrumental in bringing the human problematic to the fore. To calm her down Karl tells the story of the love affair of one of Bassompierre's ancestors which reminds Luise of *Melusina*; the gifts which the woman leaves behind remind Fritz of a similar tradition in his own family which he does not discuss further. Like restraint, the basis for the baroness' sociability, discretion[62] enhances the status of the human person; symbols—here, as in *Das Märchen* at the end of the work—canalise psychic forces so that they are harmless without losing their creative energy; and the reference to family tradition, here as in the narrator's opening sentence, reminds us of the only way in which man can evolve without losing his bearings.

The two *novellas*, which the old priest tells on the following morning after breakfast, are prefaced by the baroness' explanation of what kind of story meets with her approval. The combination of realism of content and economy in form propounded by her is now taken up by the priest when he fuses the moral tale with the *novella* and the documentary. The combination of entertainment and serious thought reflects the baroness' criteria for sociable discourse and the priest's own criteria for story-telling and it points forward to the discussion based on Kantian ethics.

The first is the *Prokurator* story which concerns an old merchant who goes on a voyage to Alexandria. At his departure he tells his young wife that, if she were to take a lover, she should choose a man of discretion. The young lawyer whom she finally chooses pretends to be under obligation of a vow of fasting and abstinence and gets her to share it with her. In the older versions she simply ends up by being too weak and too ill for a love affair. In the Goethe text suffering opens her eyes to the recognition that man possesses the power to exercise self-control and to realise his better nature.

Ziolkowski maintains that this moral does not ring true.[63] On the positive side one may say that its 'untruth' is, in fact, a judgment on a world in which such catharsis is most unlikely to happen —the world of such men as Bassompierre, whose interest is really confined to *chroniques scandaleuses*. On the negative side, we note that the moral remains unconvincing because the motivation is not studied in sufficient depth. To achieve this it is necessary to widen the scope of story telling as propounded hitherto.[64]

Using as our model Goethe's view of evolving plant structure, the stories may be grouped as follows:

(i) *lower forms of leaf* (root to calyx)—
  (*a*) on the lower level: (1) *Antonelli*, (2) *knocking ghost*, (3) *Bassompierre*;
  (*b*) on the higher level: (5) *Prokurator* and (6) *Ferdinand and Ottilie*—i.e. two *novellas* as "parallel" (moral) stories.

(ii) *the highest form of leaf* (the petal), OR *the blossom as a whole*—
  (*a*) on the lower level: (4) *Bassompierre's ancestor*, i.e. legend (the gifts) and implicit fairy tale (Melusina);
  (*b*) on the higher level: (7) *Das Märchen*, after a major break inaugurating *the second epoch, that of the blossom.*[65]

The two *novellas* are further differentiated. For the moral reflection at the end of the *Prokurator* story gives Luise and the priest their cue for arguing over the conflict between duty and inclination along Kantian lines. The baroness' view of inclination guided by reason and conscience[66] makes more explicit what the merchant's wife in the *Prokurator* story means by the 'something . . . the capacity for moral excellence'[67] which can hold inclination in check and save man from guilt and confusion over material possessions. Now in *Ferdinand and Ottilie* the difficulty of understanding and developing this capacity becomes the central moral and psychological issue. The story is a *family portrait*,[68] so that Ferdinand is described as one of the *rings of nature's eternal forces*[69] in a chain spanning three generations and linking the family milieu with that of society. As with Antonelli's partner, the symptom for emotional disorder is the mismanagement of money.[70] The impulsiveness and prodigality of Ferdinand's father is only partially kept in check by his mother; the resulting emotional instability and moral disorientation in Ferdinand's attitude lead to extravagant spending, finally to stealing from his father's bureau.[71] In terms of *Urworte. Orphisch*: an excess of *Erōs* and *Tychē* perverts the *devotion to the one unique object* of *Anankē*, making Ferdinand a slave to the continued necessity of stealing. Resentment of his father gradually gives way to remorse. He is sent to another part of the country where an old business friend is to help him start a new branch of the family business. As he succeeds, his dream of restoring the stolen money becomes a palpable hope. But his mother discovers the theft about the same time that his father is missing a much larger sum. Ferdinand, in despair, resorts to prayer. His growing determination to retrieve his moral status, coupled with his mother's mediating role and divine aid,[72] bring about a resolution of the predicament. Ferdinand's recognition 'that man has the capacity to will what is good and right'[73] may be more explicit than the 'capacity for moral excellence'[74] recognised by the merchant's wife at the end of the *Prokurator* story. It also shows up the problematic nature of the 'inclination guided by reason and the conscience' propounded by the baroness;[75] for reason is morally neutral and conscience requires a minimum inclination to be active.[76] In other words, inclination has to be divided against itself; moral awareness must end up in disgust with inclination when it is immoral, because it is seen as violation of one's true self—one's *Daimōn*. The crisis of *Anankē* must therefore be a *moral* one. Ferdinand had inherited his mother's moral sense and his father's impulsiveness,[77] so that the basic terms of his moral crisis are there from childhood. In his determination to mend his ways we should note that he replaces mere pleasant dreams by definite hope—which contrasts sharply with his father's violent impulsiveness[78]—and its expression, first in constructive action, then in the belief that, built into man's moral potential, there is the possibility of divine aid.[79]

After his reinstatement Ferdinand is faced with the typically Goethean choice between his erstwhile partner, the pleasure-loving, frivolous Ottilie and the more modest, unsophisticated niece of the business friend who had helped him in his commercial venture. The countryside, where Ferdinand now settles for carrying on his business, repels Ottilie. They both recognise their mutual incompatibility and Ferdinand marries his friend's niece. The priest concludes with an account of Ferdinand's family life and his educational views, which combine a large amount of freedom with occasional acts of self-denial.

> He would refer half-jokingly to my vows as a Catholic priest, maintaining that every person ought really to vow denial of self and in the same way obedience towards others, not in order to exercise these all the time, but to do so at the right moment.[80]

We should note the subjunctive of the modal verb: 'ought really to vow' ('eigentlich . . . geloben sollte'), the implication being that this is not the case. In the one sphere where man has some control over the forces of existence, his own self, it is only rarely that he even attempts to exercise it. And in the framework immediately following this story, the baroness compares this with the organs of government in a state. Without the executive, she says, even the most prudent legislative organ would be powerless.[81]

This reminder of political problems is followed by Friedrich's return from the fire, which reintroduces the seemingly arbitrary and mysterious workings of the macrocosmic forces. The area of concern is thus once again wide open to all the difficulties that oppress these refugees. But the area of hope is correspondingly enlarged, because all spheres of life are interlinked and the promise of divine aid is a first intimation that the forces which build and destroy are at the same time organs of a universal order. If, therefore, the last story in the work, *Das Märchen*, is again a comment on life, it would apply to all areas, so that the second half of the framework which follows *Ferdinand and*

Ottilie and introduces *Das Märchen* would only tell us the way in which it is conceived by its narrator, the old priest.

Luise, cheered by good news from her fiancé, now fortifies her morale further by falling in with Friedrich's theory of correspondences, and the whole company follows suit by giving free rein to the *power of the imagination* ('Einbildungskraft'). But Karl would prefer to see the *power of the imagination* employed in its own proper sphere, untrammelled by actual objects. Tied to 'understanding' and 'reason' (i.e. Kant's 'Verstand', 'Vernunft') it produces 'monstrosities' ('Ungeheuer');

> [die Einbildungskraft] soll, wenn sie Kunstwerke hervorbringt, nur wie eine Musik auf uns selbst spielen, uns in uns selbst bewegen, und zwar so, daß wir vergessen, daß etwas außer uns sei, das diese Bewegung hervorbringt.[82]

Like music a fairy tale is to stimulate movement in us, and we can follow the patterns of a purely internal experience, oblivious to what had caused them. The word 'spielen' ('play') is ambiguous: (i) like the bow of a violin its texture and its movement cause movement in the strings it touches; their texture and their movement are different, yet they correspond and they interact. (ii) The music produced is aesthetically autonomous, although it obeys a law of its own which is as necessary to its existence as the rationality of Kant's Practical Reason is to its freedom. The priest answers that we must make no demands on it. Like *Erōs and Elpis* it has wings, and its course, seemingly erratic like *Tychē*, follows 'die wunderlichsten Bahnen', that is paths which are—the word 'wunderlich' is ambiguous—'odd' or 'strange', and at the same time 'miraculous'. It is, the priest says, a gift, simply to be enjoyed; using our analogy: the response to such a fairy tale must be as passive and as co-operative as that of the violin string to the bow—*or*, going back to the last *novella*, of Ferdinand to divine aid when praying. Accordingly, the priest will go for his usual walk and allow 'the strange pictures to come to life again in my soul which would often entertain me in years gone by. This evening I promise you a fairy tale which will remind you'—that is, like the *playing* of the bow on the strings—'of nothing and of everything'.[83] Like music, then, *Das Märchen* will present a constantly moving panorama. Its elements will be symbolic and in one instance allegorical;[84] but we must never interpret any one of them in isolation. Understanding of the story can only be gained by seeing any one motif as the focus of interacting forces in a whole series of events. Schiller's allusion to Goethe's own remark—'. . . die Idee, deren Sie einmal erwähnten, "das gegenseitige Hilfleisten der Kräfte und das Zurückweisen aufeinander" '[85]—is perhaps our most valuable clue. His wife, Schiller continues, considers it to be 'im Voltairischen Geschmack' ('in the manner of Voltaire'); it is, in other words, a philosophical *conte*,[86] a unique blend of sheer inspiration and deliberate construction. It reflects the organically structured experience of life that we find, plant-like, in the whole of this work. It will, the priest says, remind the audience of *everything* and of *nothing*. They will, therefore, see themselves reflected in it and yet the reflection will be quite unlike themselves. For the story unfolds entirely in terms of alchemistic, masonic and 'Orphic' symbolism.[87] Its texture is thus dynamic and we will consider it from two angles. We will be following out motifs as moving threads of action; and we will recognise them as the motifs that have pervaded the whole of the previous work—as similar and as different as leaf and petal in Goethe's conception of the flower.

A similar distinction (on the analogy leaf and petal) can be made within the *Märchen* itself: motifs grow *until the time is ripe*,[88] and when this has been said three times a radical change, a rebirth takes place, and the landscape and its inhabitants are transformed.

We will start with the landscape. On one side of a river there are a mountain formation with underground passages and a large cave, and a swamp; it is the home of the snake, the giant and the old man with the lamp, his wife and their pug. On the other side the beautiful princess Lily lives in a park (with a lake) and garden. On the same side a little lower down stands the ferryman's hut, counterpart of the old man's hut by the mountain side, just as the ferryman's oar[89] is the counterpart of the old man's lamp. For the former *initiates* (and, like his orphic and masonic counterparts, operates in one direction only),[90] the latter *transmutes* (and, like his fellow-alchemists, he is also a priestly and prophetic figure). *When the time is ripe* the snake achieves the union of opposites (the alchemistic Opus)[91] by forming a bridge between the rugged country on the one side and the parkland on the other side of the river. At the beginning of the story the ferryman is woken by two will-o'-the-wisps who want to be taken across the river; without knowing it they start a circular movement, for the story begins and ends at the ferryman's hut (the alchemistic symbol for the circular nature of the Opus is the snake biting its own tail).[92] As the will-o'-the-wisps really want to get to Lily, their crossing the river is a mistake. But there are only two means of recrossing:[93] the snake forms a temporary bridge at noon and the giant's shadow at sunset.

The giant is a weird menacing character. To understand him we must first note the sharp distinction between living organisms acceptable to water (the element of growth *par excellence*), and human artefacts which are rejected. Thus the ferryman demands a fare,[94] on behalf of the river, of three artichokes, three cabbages and three onions. The coins which the will-o'-the wisps toss into the boat he throws down a mountain crevice. They are saddled with the burden of their debt until it is taken over by the old woman, wife of the man with the lamp.[95] (The number three is thus tied up with organic life and its transactions, turned into the stranglehold of inescapable debt, redeemed through the threefold announcement that *the time is ripe*. It is an instance of a motif realised in a moving thread of action, transformed in regeneration.)

The giant[96] bathes daily in the river, he therefore belongs within the elemental sphere. Completely powerless in himself, he exerts great strength indirectly, through his shadow. As with other macrocosmic phenomena (fire, plague) his true nature remains remote, while the outer effects are sometimes dependable, sometimes erratic and terrifying. After regeneration he becomes a monumental pillar which acts as a sundial, so that in this case the inorganic and the organic, nature and man, are brought together in the union of opposites. The elemental forces become part of human life, they are seen as a rational order which can be harnessed by man in the same measure that man acknowledges the order of the Universe and submits to it. And just as the arbitrary is now banned from the impact of the elements, so the erratic display of vital energy displayed by the will-o'-the-wisps[97] disappears under the new order.

Such mature coming to terms with the macrocosm overcomes the stark terror aroused, for instance, by the plague in Bassompierre's adventure, or the mixture of reason and escapist dreaming (a *monstrosity*, according to Karl) in Fritz' theory of correspondences. Its foundation is faith in the active hand of Providence—called on by Ferdinand, dynamic but anonymous in *Das*

Märchen, where only the stars[98] indicate that the regenerative process, *through the interaction of forces as they co-operate with each other*,[85] expresses the divine and cosmic order. This co-operation is the new factor in the situation. It distinguishes the regenerative process and the new era from the previous state of dissociation.

Thus the friendship pacts of Antonelli and the Prokurator are, each in its way, designed to prevent the two sexes from uniting; for them passion does not embody love, and coitus implies the loss of personality rather than one of its supreme fulfilments; again, the wife and the lover of Bassompierre's ancestor have to remain dissociated, just as Melusina's union with a human lover is only temporary; however, the three gifts which the lover (or Melusina) leaves behind point forward to the realisation of a higher synthesis. The plot of *Das Märchen* revolves round the overcoming of dissociation.

We have already seen that the river will not accept the gold coins of the will-o'-the-wisps. Similarly, when they visit the wife of the man with the lamp, her pug eats some of the coins and dies.[99] She takes the required *triadic* arrangements of vegetables to the river but is caught unawares by the giant's shadow who eats one each of the vegetables. On the advice of the ferryman she pays what she has, and as a pledge that she will pay the rest within twenty-four hours[100] she puts her hand in the water; immediately it turns black and diminishes in size. The use of the hand is unaffected, only its appearance suffers; but she wishes it were the other way round: the muscular force of the hand is thus separate from its appearance. Association with the watery element has given the hand an appearance which is at odds with human notions of what a hand should look like—regardless of what it really does. And as the power of the element becomes stronger, outward appearance may cease altogether.[101] The old woman, who takes pleasure in the beautiful shape of her hands,[102] and who had been attracted[103] by the extravert behaviour of the will-o'-the-wisps (adepts at mere outer appearance),[104] is worried by this. The disparity between gay talk and social refinement on the one hand, and the reality of natural (macrocosmic and psychological) forces on the other, causes her anxiety (as it does Luise). At the end she casts off her terrestial appearance, her concern for it and her debt, through a regenerative bath in the river. She comes out rejuvenated.

But the outstanding example of dissociation appears in Lily herself. When the pug had died, the old man's lamp, with its power of transmuting stone into gold, wood into silver and dead creatures into jewels,[105] has turned the pug into an onyx.[106] The old man had advised his wife to put the onyx in the same basket as the vegetables and to carry it across to Lily as a gift.[107] She can, by her touch, revive the dead and kill the living.[108] She sings of her plight—for through this fatal power she must remain separated from all living creatures, worst of all from the young prince who loves her. Her song is as beautiful as her appearance and is in direct proportion to her impotence when it comes to exercising her emotions in actual life. Hers is a power that forces whomever she touches to exchange one mode of being for another, the two being as hermetically sealed off from each other as death is from life. Accordingly, she touches the onyx who becomes a dog again; she accidentally touches—and kills—her canary whom she tries to shield from the hawk, because she is frightened of him; this is not surprising, for the hawk turns out to be a messenger of the new dawn, for which she longs—but which she also fears, because of her dissociated state.[109] She also kills the young prince when he approaches and unwittingly touches her. The revival of the latter is part and parcel of the redemptive action;[110] for the canary she suggests a similar process of double transmutation to that of the pug: if the old man's lamp can turn the dead animal into a jewel she can bring the jewel back to life.[111]

Lily's transmuting power, therefore, establishes the life/death dissociation, yet at the same time it can also break its stranglehold by linking its power with that of the lamp. This brings us to the overcoming of dissociation. It happens through the appropriately-timed mediating action, guided by insight, of two characters, the old man with the lamp and the snake. Furthermore, they know how to communicate with each other and with other characters, so that they all act as a team of forces co-operating with each other[85] according to the time schedule of the redemptive plan. If the old man is more of a seer, the snake is more of a mediator and a sufferer. In these two respects they are in the redemptive plot of *Das Märchen* what the old priest and the baroness are in the plot of the framework; in other respects, however, the baroness carries out much of the *executive*[81] function of the man with the lamp, while the ferryman (called in one passage[112] 'der Alte'—'the old man'—just like the man with the lamp) has the initiator's role of the priest, who grades his stories, from Antonelli to Ferdinand's catharsis, thence to the new era at the end of *Das Märchen*. Coupled with the *executive function*[81] there is the value of *conversation*, the sociability of the framework, which consists in knowing when to speak out and when to be silent. In *Das Märchen* the old man with the lamp takes on the prophet's prerogative issuing his instructions and announcing the closeness of the crucial hour.[88]

Providence, then, expresses its decree through the prophetic wisdom and authoritative leadership of the man with the lamp on the one hand, and the mediating, sacrificial actions of the snake on the other. But each of the characters must play his or her part as well. The redemption, in true Goethean 'semi-Pelegian' style, is (as with God, Ferdinand and his mother) a *corporate* effort.[85] Furthermore, their awareness of the plan of salvation must lead to responsible decision-making. The snake takes the initiative,[113] and the other characters follow suit. It is the reversal of arbitrary behaviour (in nature: the fire, the plague, the knocking ghost/death; the giant and his shadow; in man: Karl's quarrel with the Geheimerat von S., Luise's eccentricities, Ferdinand's father, Ottilie; the will-o'-the-wisps), first given explicit formulation in the baroness' principles of sociability, then in Karl's amendment of Bassompierre's text, where 'de bon coeur' was replaced by 'freiwillig'.[114] Each person is thus challenged by the divine will, its moral (rational—i.e. the Kantian Practical Reason) laws, to avoid psychological and moral confusion and to work for the divine-natural-human order (the stars: *Daimōn*). Practical life, the baroness' executive organ,[81] is at stake; responsible decisions are tested through the very tools man uses for carrying them out: his natural vitality and his physical and economic power—*fire* and *gold*. These two symbols run through the entire work. Antonelli's partner and Ferdinand are both in financial difficulties; fire troubles the refugees both, in the form of heavy artillery and when it breaks out on the family estate. In *Das Märchen* they join forces with silver and precious stones and with light. For the transmuting power of the old man's lamp shows us that they are really cross-breeds of mineral, vegetable and animal matter (stones to gold, wood to silver, dead animals to precious stones) and of the rays of light and energy issuing from the flame[115] of the lamp. They are therefore powerful and significant organisms, products of the union of opposites, small-scale anticipations of the universal regeneration, in which the cave travels, under the river, to the ferryman's (wooden) hut, to enclose it as a great temple, the hut becoming a smaller temple or altar. The lamp has turned it into silver.[116] Water from the river has sprayed the cave, or temple, during the subterranean journey; at the climax, when the snake has already become the permanent bridge and a large crowd has entered the new sanctuary, the hawk catches the light of the risen sun in a mirror and throws it on to the prince and Lily, now king and queen, and on to their rejuvenated companions, the ferryman, the man with the lamp and his wife, who are standing by the altar. They had entered the cave in the first instance and initiated the transformation under the direction of the old man with the lamp. The heavenly aura causes the crowd to fall down in ecstatic worship.[117] The sun and the human sanctuary thus join to inaugurate the new era for the royal couple, their friends and subjects.

The dynamism of the sunlight should also be considered in connection with the giant: The co-operation of light with a friend of the watery element produces the powerful shadow; in the forecourt of the new sanctuary he is transmuted into the monumental pillar, made of a red stone, which serves as a sundial.[118] Its stone is as lasting as the cosmic order, its redness relates it to the hawk, whose red plumage had caught the last rays of the previous sunset,[119] thence to gold (red gold is the climax of the Opus)[120] and its planet, the sun, which it now also serves as a sun dial. The restoration of order in Ferdinand's financial affairs here acquires a cosmic perspective. But while Ferdinand had quite explicitly received divine aid, no explanation is here given of the giant's transmutation.

Gold first comes into the story in the form of the coins thrown by the two will-o'-the-wisps into the ferryman's boat. But this is not its origin. The will-o'-the-wisps are opportunists who pick up the raw metal where they can to feed their fiery bodies;[121] their function is to mint it and scatter it as fancy takes them. Its true origin may only be inferred from the old woman's account, to her husband, of the visit the will-o'-the-wisps had paid her in their hut at the foot of the mountain.

> Und sieh dich nur um, wie die Wände aussehen; sieh nur die alten Steine, die ich seit hundert Jahren nicht mehr gesehen habe: alles Gold haben sie heruntergeleckt, . . .[122]

If the 'hundred years' is to be taken literally, then we may perhaps assume that the rock, macrocosmic parent,[123] had received the gold through the transmuting agency of the lamp. That is, indeed, what happens afterwards.[124] The rock, as the Neptunists taught,[126] would have been gradually shaped under the influence of water; the lamp contains a flame. The alternative would be to regard the 'hundred years' as foreshortening, in line with the naïve, this-worldly outlook of the old woman.[125] In that case the origin of the gold would go back much further, perhaps to the time of volcanic eruptions, as taught by the Plutonists.[126] In either case it is the result of the union of water and fire and of the co-operation between gradual development and radical change.

The minted gold produced by the will-o'-the-wisps can be trivial, e.g. in the new era, when the crowd at first fights for, but eventually tires of it,[127] or highly significant, for example, when it is thrown to the ferryman. In either case it could be dangerous; in the former instance, it might still have seduced the crowd, just as financial troubles had nearly ruined Ferdinand's character; in the latter case, the river might have overturned the boat and its passengers.[128] Such a disaster is avoided when the ferryman pours it into a crevice. There the snake finds it. The snake eats both, these coins, and the coins which the will-o'-the-wisps throw down to her when they meet soon after.[129] Unacceptable to the river and the pug, the snake eats the coins and, mediator that she is, transmutes their glitter into transparency and light. This enables her to explore the cave,[130] while the light of the sun transfigures her into a majestically glowing temporary bridge made of precious stones.[131] At the height of Lily's crisis she forms a 'magic circle' (or the alchemistic 'ouroboros')[132] round the dead prince, and the light coming from her body together with the light from the lamp produce the effect of dawn in the gathering darkness.[133] The ouroboros is thus not only protective, but also an earnest of the regenerative dawn. She now forms another temporary bridge of precious stones glowing in the darkness, so that Lily with the pug and her attendants, the old man with the lamp, his wife, the two will-o'-the-wisps (temporarily transformed into solemn flames) and the basket containing the dead prince and the dead canary, can cross the river and enter the cave. But first Lily must touch the snake and the dead prince simultaneously.[134] This is the moment of the snake's supreme sacrifice. Her life goes over into that of the prince and the canary, while she becomes a circle of precious stones which the old man throws in the river, there to become the piers of the permanent bridge.[135]

In the dissociated age, the mirror had only reflected Lily's sterile beauty; in the age of synthesis, the mirror catches the light from the sun and, throwing it on the supreme union, that of the prince and Lily, evokes ecstatic worship. Similarly in the dissociated age, the river had found the glittering gold coins unacceptable. But at the hour of sacrifice, the mineral texture and the glitter of gold and precious stones are transmuted into the prophetic light of her transparent body, and in that form the water promotes the growth of the bridge, at once the fulfilment of the snake's mediating function and a monument to her self-sacrifice.[136]

But there is a further dimension which demands our attention. After the snake has eaten the gold coins she goes to explore the cave; she discovers that the parts untouched by human hand run imperceptibly over into the part that has been modified by the skill of the craftsman, just as the hut belonging to the man with the lamp leans against the side of the mountain as if it had always been part of the landscape; similarly its counterpart, the ferryman's hut, is in complete harmony with the river. The cave and the ferryman's hut thus realise from the beginning the harmony between natural growth and artefact that pervades the whole of the regenerated community, from the sun, the hawk and the mirror down to the piers of the bridge and the river itself. As for the inhabitants, the snake eats money; the man with the lamp is 'dressed like a peasant'.[137] And in the previous story Ferdinand does not marry Ottilie but settles in the country. The conflict between man and nature (e.g. Bassompierre's lover—the plague; the old woman—the giant's shadow) is thus overcome.

Now, the whole of this drama of regeneration is prefigured and watched over by four allegorical (therefore also didactic) statues of kings which stand in four niches of the cave, or temple, that eventually becomes the outer shell of the new sanctuary. The snake encounters them during her first exploration of the cave, when she also meets the old man with the lamp for the first time. In this way the four kings, who guard the old and prepare the ground for the new dispensation, can examine the two principal initiators of the regenerative process; they use the Orphic-

Masonic device of question and answer. But we must first consider the kings. The first is made of gold, the second of silver, the third of brass, and the fourth of a mixture of the previous three metals, only in the casting they had not fused properly,[138] so that this king becomes a figure of dissociation. At the end of the story the will-o'-the-wisps lick all the golden veins clean, so that the whole figure caves in on itself. This grotesque sight is covered over by a splendid carpet.[139]

Soon after the arrival of the cave at the ferryman's hut[140] and their union as the new outer temple and the inner temple or altar, the old man with the lamp identifies the golden king as wisdom, the silver king as outer appearance[141] and the king made of brass as force, or power ('Gewalt'). A little later, each of the kings confers on the young prince, about to become a powerful ruler, a precept; these are at the same time mottoes indicating their own qualities which they are conferring on him.[142] There follows the union of Lily and the young prince, who addresses the old man:

> '... O! mein Freund,' fuhr er fort, indem er sich zu dem Alten wendete und die drei heiligen Bildsäulen ansah, 'herrlich und sicher ist das Reich unserer Väter, aber du hast die vierte Kraft vergessen, die noch früher, allgemeiner, gewisser die Welt beherrscht: die Kraft der Liebe.'...
>
> Hierauf sagte der Alte lächelnd: 'Die Liebe herrscht nicht, aber sie bildet, und das ist mehr.'[143]

We note the identification of the kings and their three functions or powers, with the glory and stability of the kingdom of the ancestors; tradition must not be absent even in complete transformation, so that the motif raised by the narrator of the whole work in his very first sentence here finds its place in the priest's last narrative, which ends with 'down to the present day',[144] —but in the manner of legends or fairy tales, that is, it is completely open-ended. But human tradition is not enough. Something more fundamental is needed, the fourth function, or power, the very antithesis of the fourth king, the figure of dissociation: love. But love is on a different plane, being the function, or power which 'bildet'—by which, in Goethe's language, is meant the initial forming of an organism (and everything is really organic!), together with its subsequent shaping and articulating, as well as the shaping of its destiny according to the principles of: growth;—heightening, intensification and elaboration;—creative death and regeneration through the union of opposites.

The close connection of this dialogue with the redness that appears on Lily's cheeks as the sun rises (the redness of dawn had not been noticed!)[145] shows that, what was previously hidden, enveloped in the night, has now, with the new era, come into the light of day; the prophecy is fulfilled, the secret is revealed. Love, as Camilla Lucerna shows,[146] as the forming and shaping power, is also the fourth secret, the three previous secrets having been wisdom, outer appearance and force. These occur in the first dialogues of initiation, when the golden king examines the snake and the old man with the lamp.[147] The latter knows the first three secrets, the *manifest* secret ('Das offenbare') being the most important. He will reveal it when he knows the fourth—which the snake now whispers in his ear. The old man reacts by proclaiming that 'the time is ripe'![148]

According to this passage, the third secret is the fact that *the time is ripe*. How are we to identify this with the 'manifest' secret and with the force of the king of brass?

The answer is twofold. First of all we must note that, since existence is organic, being the product of *forming and shaping love* ('Die Liebe . . . bildet'), all these forces, powers, functions, qualities, are interwoven; strict separation of categories is out of place.

For the second part of the answer we must go back to the first of these dialogues of initiation in which the snake calls light 'more glorious' than gold and conversation 'more quickening' ('erquicklicher') than light.[149]

Gold—wisdom, the highest secret, the inmost truth, must have outer appearance (silver); a community cannot exist without laws, customs, norms, and organs of government to enforce them. In that sense the manifest secret is already that of silver. But this must be extended to the foundation of truth manifest: force, or power/brass—the sword; and *at the same time*: the breadth of vision which can shape policy—moral and political conduct in general, the ability to go forward into regeneration and to accept the consequences of such a course: 'the right hand free'. The third secret is thus the baroness' executive function, which she also sees realised in Ferdinand's will to put his affairs in order and to invoke divine aid. But it is arid without constant interchange of units of manifested truth: words. *Conversation* makes the patterned progression of human destiny at once a living reality and something enjoyable: the double connotation of 'erquicklich'—'quickening'. The conversation with its inset pieces, leading up to *Das Märchen*, is at once deeply significant and enjoyable.

But there is a close interdependence between the third and the fourth secret. The snake knows the fourth secret: the forming and shaping process of love involves the sacrificial moment as the foundation for the new life. The snake loses its identity in order to become the permanent bridge. Ferdinand prays, using the spoken word ('conversation'), later sheds his previous love, Ottilie, and thereafter continues to train himself in *doing without*. And the baroness *suffers*.

NOTES

The Translations are my own.

H. = The Hamburg edition of Goethe's works.
H.Br. = Goethes Briefe (Hamburg edition).
W.A. = The Weimar edition of Goethe's works.

All other abbreviations are listed in alphabetical order in the Bibliography.

1. Goethe's letter to Schiller, Weimar, 26.10.1794, postscript.—A great deal of this background material is collected together in *Graef I.*, 316–61.
2. Jena, 28.10.1794.
3. Later, Goethe's library contained Boccaccio's *Decameron* (Ital. 1725; German 1830), *Les Cent Nouvelles Nouvelles* (1786) and La Fontaine's *Contes et Nouvelles en Vers* (1696; 1806): cf. *Ruppert.*, pp. 236, 228, 220, 227.—Goethe's reading of the *Decameron*: letter to Cornelia Goethe, Leipzig, 6.12.1765 (H.Br. I, 23, 30–31; 533); he acquired his father's copy in 1794: cf. *Götting.*, pp. 27, 32, 55.—cf. further his letters to Charlotte v. Stein, Ilmenau, 8.8. and 12.8.1776 (W.A. IV. Abt., III, 94 and 96); diary entries, 10 and 11 August 1776 (W.A. III. Abt., I, 19).—His reading of the *Novelas Ejemplares*: letters to Charlotte v. Stein (Weimar, 9.8.1782) and to Schiller (Weimar, 17.12.1795): This seems to be the same French translation that he borrowed from the Weimar Library (H.Br. II, 568;—*Keudell.*, p. 52).—His reading of the *Contes et Nouvelles en Vers*: versions of Venetian Epigram 65 and *Zahme Xenie* 96 (W.A. I, 464; V[2], 381 No. 65. 6 and 7), 402 (No. 96, 5 and 6), 403, 16 and 20.—His reading of Marguerite de Navarre's *Heptaméron*: *Die guten Weiber* (1801), *Tag- und Jahreshefte 1807, Paralipomena*: W.A. XVIII, 291, 22–25; XXXVI, 388, 4; LIII, 16, 162 and 163; LIII 439, 13.—On the bearing of the *Decameron* on the *Unterhaltungen* cf. *Graef I.*, p. 317, footnote 2; *Fambach.*, p. 10; cf. further: *Kunz.*, p. 15; *Polheim.*, pp. 244*–58*.
4. Instances of this antedating: Previews of works in the editions of the *Works*, published by Cotta, 1808 and 1828 ("aus letzter Hand"); the chronological list of his works (written spring 1819); *Tag- und Jahres-Hefte 1793* (written mainly 1822–25).—On this and on this group of works as a whole cf. *Graef I.*, pp. 357–9 (where further references are given).—cf. also *Conversations with Eckermann* 4.1.1824; 27.4.1825.—

Inner relationships between these works would merit more detailed study; one particularly striking example is the similarity between the baroness and the countess in *Die Aufgeregten*; this latter work is yet another instance of Goethe's refusal to take sides in this conflict.

5. Goethe's covering letter to the first instalment (which also mentions other contributions he was making to the early issues of *Die Horen*, as well as his work on *Wilhelm Meisters Lehrjahre*), dated Weimar, 27.11.1794. Judging by Schiller's reply (Jena, 29.11.1794), this seems to have been the introductory framework. He returns the revised manuscript and makes his first enquiry regarding the mystery of Hyppolite Clairon's ghost: letter to Schiller, Weimar, 5.12.1794.
6. Goethe first announces the 'ghost stories' as a group: letter to Schiller, Weimar, 3.1.1795; he sends them off (together with the relevant portions of the framework): letter to Schiller, Weimar, 10.1.1795. He completes and sends off the *Prokurator* story with the introductory framework: letters to Schiller, Weimar, 11, 18, 19, 21 March 1795. His other main project, the *Lehrjahre*, is also completed in instalments in that period. The framework following the *Prokurator* and *Ferdinand and Ottilie*, but excluding the concluding framework (which also comprises the sequel to the story) is sent off with the covering letter, Weimar, 27.6.1795. The sequel to *Ferdinand and Ottilie*, together with the last framework, is sent off with the covering letter, Weimar, 21.8.1795. But Goethe has already started planning *Das Märchen*: cf. letters to Schiller, Karlsbad, 8.7.1795 and Weimar, 17.8. and 18.8.1795.
7. Schiller's letter to Goethe, Jena, 2.10.1795.—Goethe's rhythm of writing and despatching instalments corresponds to the size and sequence of instalments as published in *Die Horen*; cf. *Graef I.*, pp. 316–36.
8. Cf. *Graef I.*, esp. pp. 327–28, 333 ff;—also *Fambach.*, pp. 10–16.—On the history of the genesis and reception of the work cf. *Duentzer/E.*, pp. 37–141 and *Duentzer/W (D.N.L.)*, pp. 3–29. Comments by recent critics: *Ziolkowski*, pp. 57–58, *Fricke*, p. 273.
9. Goethe's letter to Schiller, Weimar, 17.8.1795.—Goethe's conception of the living structure of a piece of poetic creation, as of all organisms, is very flexible. Even if the reception of the *Unterhaltungen* had been more favourable, he might still have transplanted stories originally thought of as belonging to a Part II of the present work into the *Wanderjahre*, simply because the two parts of *Wilhelm Meister*, together with *Die Wahlverwandtschaften*, which grew up side by side with the *Unterhaltungen*, exerted such a strong pull. We do not have to be too rigid about interpreting the word 'schließen' ('concluding') as meaning *either* the whole work, *or* Part I only. Ziolkowski's assertion that this work 'remained a fragment and must be regarded as such' (p. 58) is, therefore, an exaggeration; on the other hand it draws our attention to the fact that it belongs within one continuous series of creative endeavour, in which various types of narrative crystallised in a number of prose works (and, indeed, ballads—cf., for instance, the use of the motif of debt in the ballad *Ritter Kurts Brautfahrt*) which culminated in *Die Wahlverwandtschaften*, a full-length novel, very elaborate in its motifs, yet taut and single-tracked in its composition, holding the balance between the *Wanderjahre*, an epic of vast proportions, and *Die Novelle*, a concise narrative, where the turning-point is intensified until it is a metamorphosis from the down-to-earth to the musical-ecstatic.—The other series of which the *Unterhaltungen* forms a part revolves round the French Revolution.
10. '. . . For everybody will readily agree with me that all things existing in nature are *linked with one another according to an exact pattern*, . . . ('*Über den Granit*'; H. XIII, 255, 12–14; the whole essay: 253, 33–258, 4. The italics are my own.)—cf. *Wachsmuth.*, esp. pp. 25–27, 34–42; further: *Zur Farbenlehre. Didaktischer Teil. Vorwort*: H. XIII, 315–22.—cf. also *Müller.*, esp. pp. 17 ff; pp. 32 ff: natural and artistic necessity (i.e. rationality) embodied in God,

articulated according to the principles of morphology; on the unity of Goethe's thought and creative activity cf. *Wilkinson-Willoughby.*, esp. nos. X (pp. 167–84), XI (pp. 185–213), XII (pp. 214–28).—cf. further: *Spranger.*, esp. pp. 43–47, 54–87, *Milfull.*, p. 53.—For the relevance of these principles to the structure of the *Unterhaltungen* cf. *Jürgens*, p. 336.

11. 'Hymen [god of marriage] approaches on his wings and clouds of vapour, pregnant with glory and power, spread around sweet fragrance, giving life to all things.' (*Metamorphose der Pflanzen*, ll. 55–56: H. I, 200; the whole poem: 199–201; the notes: 505–9.)
12. Cf. *Pernety/Dict.*, arts. *Rebis* and *Androgine ou Hermaphrodite.*—Also *Read.*, pp. 196–211, 236–46.
13. *Metamorphose der Pflanzen*, ll. 59–62.
14. 'With his capacity to reflect and impart shape and pattern, man is himself to change the rigid defined form (or structure).' (ibid., 1.70) On man's task to rule over the constellations of forces in his own being (his 'stars') cf. note 17.
15. Concluding lines (77–80) of *Metamorphose der Pflanzen.*
16. Cf. *Metamorphose der Tiere*, especially ll. 40–42.
17. 'Geprägte Form, die lebend sich entwickelt.' ('Organic structure, its character clearly defined, developing according to its own living dynamic.'—*Urworte. Orphisch*, l. 8; H. I, 359; the whole poem: 359–60; Goethe's commentary: 403–7; notes: 566–67.) The expression 'geprägte Form' refers not only to the character of the organism, potentially present already in the seedling (so that the leaf and its modifications will have quite definite shape, colour and texture), but also to the symbolism used by Paracelsus in expounding the doctrine of *signatures*. There are the outward manifestation of inner essence, or character, given to each being by the stars; like a coin which is minted, or a piece of wax which gets a seal stamped on it, the creature receives its character (the way its own inner forces will mould themselves: the 'inner firmament', acc. to Paracelsus) from the constellations of macrocosmic forces,, the stars and planets (hence ll. 1–4 of this poem). In certain respects man must rule his stars; otherwise he degenerates into behaving 'like the beasts in the field' ('viehisch'). It is worth pointing out that Paracelsus only reformulated traditional ideas. (In Paracelsus esp.:—*De natura rerum neun bücher, Liber nonus, De signatura rerum naturalium* (*Paracelsus/S.*, XI, 373–403, but esp. 377–81, 400–3); *Philosophia Sagax*, cf. esp. Bk. I, ch. 4, sec. *Was signatum und was signator sei* . . . (ibid., XII, 91–93); Bk. II, ch. 7 (ibid., 382–95); *Erklärung der ganzen Astronomei*: *Probatio in scientiam signatam.*—Cf. also *Paracelsus/J.*, pp. 112–119, 152, 195–96.—For traditional formulations cf. the *Centiloquium*, ascribed to Ptolemy, with Pontanus' Commentary; esp. Sent. VII–IX, XIII (*Pontanus III.*, pp. 2626–36, 2643–46). The *Daimōn-Tychē* dialectic receives further significant formulation in *Faust*, the Prologne in Heaven; cf. esp. ll. 344–49 (H. III, 18–19; and cf. the further refs. in the notes: 494–95).
18. Goethe's commentary on *Erōs* and *Anankē* (esp. H. I, 405, 31–407, 26) highlights the nightmarish conflicts which seem to be the necessary result of confusion.—On 'Steigerung' ('heightening', 'intensification') cf. note 16.
19. It was, of course, known. An example is the 'Volksbuch', *Die sieben weisen Meister*, which goes back to oriental, Greek and Latin models; many versions throughout Europe and the Near and Middle East are extant: cf. *Klapper.* and *Campbell.* For a good modernised text cf. *Benz* (*Volksbücher*)., pp. 9–96, 664, 667.—For an example of the diffusion of Italian *novella* material in Germany cf. *Strauch II.*—For a brief historical survey of the *novella* and its ancestry cf. *Wiese.*, pp. 34 ff.—Goethe took up the *novella* structure (framework and inset narrative) while he was also developing the full-length novel, using the traditional plan of inset pieces (an eighteenth-century example: J. G.

Schnabel's *Die Insel Felsenburg*; original title: *Wunderliche Fata einiger See-Fahrer...*, Nordhausen, 1732; a recent reprint of the 1828 text: publ. Reclam, Stuttgart, 1959). *Wilhelm Meisters Wanderjahre* really represents a fusion of these two principles of composition. Cf. *Lockemann.*, esp. pp. 208–11.

20. Both these stories seem to have acquired a certain notoriety in the society gossip of that period: cf. Charlotte von Stein's letter to Charlotte von Schiller, 19.2.1795 (*Urlichs II.*, 299). When Goethe first intends to use the tragédienne Hyppolite Clairon as a model for the Italian singer Antonelli he asks Schiller (Weimar, 5.12.1794) whether he had heard anything about her ghost. Schiller's reply (Jena, 9.12.1794) is negative. But his enquiry with Prince August von Gotha seems to have been more successful. In a letter to him (24.10.1796; cf. W.A. IV. Abt., XI, 241–42, No. 3419) Goethe refers to a manuscript, which had been circulating 'more than a year ago', copied, he thinks, by the prince, which related 'a strange episode that had been experienced by Clairon'. We may guess that Goethe had read this and got further facts and views (written? oral?), for his grasp of what had allegedly occurred *and* of what her character must have been like at that time is uncannily accurate. Clairon published her memoirs four years later. The incident in question is related by her in a 'Lettre à M. Meis[ter], qui desirait avoir l'Anecdote suivante par ecrit'. It is here published for the first time: cf. *Clairon.*, pp. 167–88. Perhaps the prince's 'manuscript' is this letter, or a report closely related to it, as the versions in the letter and in the Goethe text are at times very close to each other; cf. also *Ziolkowski.*, pp. 65–66. One of the most crucial differences, however, between the priest's narrative and Clairon's letter concerns her reasons for refusing to go to her friend when he is on the point of dying. The priest (H. VI, 151, 29–39) neither quotes her as giving any reasons nor puts forward any himself. However, where the priest asks her in all charity not to refuse, Clairon first states that 'mes entours m'empêchèrent de faire cette démarche' (p. 170), but then explains herself in a conversation with the woman in whose house her friend had died (pp. 184–5): She had herself refused to see him on his deathbed, 'parce que ce spectacle aurait déchiré mon coeur; parce que j'ai craint de me montrer trop barbare, en refusant ce qu'on pouvait me demander, et trop malheureuse, si je l'accordais: voilà, madame, les motifs de ma conduite: j'ose me flatter qu'elle ne m'attirera le blâme de qui que ce soit'.—This contradicts her own earlier statement, but it is consistent with her behaviour as described by the priest ('. . . sie ward bewegt und vertraute mir ihre Verlegenheit . . . sie schien unentschlossen, aber nach einigem Nachdenken nahm sie sich zusammen'.—'. . . she was excited and told me in confidence about her feeling of embarrassment . . . she seemed undecided but after thinking about it for a while she pulled herself together'.) Regarding her character, cf. earlier in the letter (pp. 168–9, when he presses his suit: '. . . Cela me déplut . . . Je pouvois consentir qu'on m'arrêtât avec des fleurs, et non qu'on me retînt avec des chaînes . . .'); also elsewhere: pp. 21–22 (*Agenda*: end of *Neuvième Réflexion*); p. 197 (*Réflexions sur les mariages d'inclination, ou Pourquoi j'ai refusé de me marier*); but esp. her juxtaposition of 'L'amitié, l'amour et la galanterie', pp. 217–18 (*Conseils à ma jeune amie*).

21. *Merck.* teaches the country life unadorned by corrupting urban refinements; *Anekdote.* purports to be the translation of a 'Tale of Woe', which had appeared in *The Craftsman*, London, 1781 (I have not found it in the British Museum); it is addressed 'to the readers who only take pleasure in what is true' (in the framework introducing the story: pp. 140–1).

22. *Bassompierre I.*, pp. 158–62.—Goethe borrowed the work from the Weimar Library between Dec. 1794 and early Jan. 1795: *Keudell.*, p. 10.

23. The eighteenth-century *chronique scandaleuse* is really an offshoot of the *fabliel* ('Schwank') and *novella* tradition. One important link in the chain of development is La Fontaine's *Contes et Nouvelles en Vers*, which Goethe knew: cf. note 3.
24. *Bassompierre I.*, pp. 4–6.—On the fairytale and legend traditions of which this story is a part cf. *Waldeck/Bass.*, pp. 254–55; *Grimm.*, esp. I, 16–19, 51–54, 61–96; II, 249–319; *Simrock.*, pts. III and VI.—The continuity in Goethe's own activity of writing fairy tales (new versions of old material and original compositions): cf. *Waldeck/ März.*—cf. also *Kunz.*, p. 17.
25. Our use here of the term *novella* is entirely as of a series of works within a literary tradition; if taken as a type of composition, over and above historical criteria, it could be defined so narrowly that none of the stories in the *Unterhaltungen* would qualify (cf. *Kraft.*, pp. 702–9), or so widely that they could all be said to be *novellas*, or at least to conform to the most significant norms of *novella*-writing (*Kunz.*, pp. 18–20). The term 'private Geschichten' brings out an important aspect of the narrator's point of view (i.e. answering the baroness' 'sociability'): cf. *Klein*, p. 63 (H. VI, 142, 38–39). Cf. also *Marache.*, p. 155.
26. It seems likely that the original version was Italian and that the extant Latin (*Marina*; for a German fifteenth-century version cf. *Strauch I.*) and French (in the *Cent Nouvelles Nouvelles*) versions were based on it: cf. *Herrmann.*
27. 'Parallelgeschichten': H. VI, 187, 15; cf. Trunz' notes on this passage, ibid., p. 612. Goethe seems to have coined this term, but it arises naturally from the technique of telling stories within a framework, i.e. as extensions of a conversation; an instance in didactic literature would be the parables in Mt. 13, 44–46, and in the *novella* tradition the *Heptaméron* where all the stories exemplify various types of conjugal fidelity and infidelity. On the level of aesthetic organisation it is, of course, the common practice of poets to put analogous or contrasting symbols or character-types alongside each other; sometimes they are symmetrical, sometimes they appear in an ascending order. Thus the motif of intrigue is exemplified by a male (Antonio) and a female (Leonore) character in Goethe's *Tasso*; while in *Faust II* the union of opposites occurs in the ascending order, Homunculus-Galatea and Faust-Helen.—According to the *Conversations with Eckermann*, 6.6.1831, Goethe saw the *Philemon and Baucis* episode in *Faust II* as a parallel theme to the Ovidian archetype.
28. Schiller to Goethe, Jena, 29.8.1795: the letter quoted below; cf. notes 85 and 86.
29. Cf. note 9.—It seems likely that the chain of creative activity which gave rise to *Das Märchen* and to the later fairy tales goes back to the projected *Reise der Söhne Megaprazons*; but this attempt at writing a predominantly allegorical work foundered as much as 'that second fairy tale' mentioned in his letter to Schiller, Weimar, 15.12.1795 (cf. *Waldeck/Märch.*, pp. 14–18, 170–1); for an action—whether imaginative or *vraisemblable*—must be a living organism in its own right, communicating its meaning by the very fact that its characters and events are shaped in one particular way—i.e. it is, *in principle*, a metaphor and not a simile (although similes can be used within the metaphorical texture.
30. H. VI, 165, 15–38. The fact that this is really a Melusina version is not mentioned in the story itself, but its recognition grows out of the very action of being narrated. The further recognition is now implicit that it revolves round three motifs: (1) The dissociation of the world of human sensibility and the world of the elemental forces; (2) Melusina's giving up of her love is something she has to do; (3) she rises above the law of her existence by *choosing* to leave gifts.—In *Das Märchen* the snake gives up her life before she is forced to do so (cf. note 113), thus raising her fate to the status of the baroness' and

Ferdinand's self-discipline; giving up thus becomes *self-sacrifice.* If the Melusina-type episode in the life of Bassompierre's ancestor, therefore, makes itself memorable by conferring gifts, the snake's self-sacrifice has further depth (cf. note 135), in that it is her counterpart to Melusina's gifts and, being a bridge, it overcomes Melusina's dissociated state; it also confers a prophetic dimension (*the growth into infinity* of Goethe's letter to Schiller, Weimar, 17.8.1795) on the importance of family tradition stressed in the very first sentence of the whole work.

31. Makarie's first appearance: *Wanderjahre* Bk. I, ch. 10: H. VIII, 115–16; the stars: ibid., p. 126; she plays the part of Divine Providence: *Der Mann von f–nfzig Jahren* (Kk. II, ch. 5, H. VIII, 222–4).
32. H. VI, 506, 33 to the end.—For a stylistic analysis cf. *Jessen.*
33. Introduction to the first vol. (1795) of *Die Horen*: *Jena,* 10.12.1794 (p. [III]; cf. *Horen/R. I.*, p. [7]).
34. H. VI, 125, 3–13.
35. In the dispute between Karl and the Geheimerat von S. it is the conflict as such which stands condemned: H. VI, 130, 25–136, 5.
36. In *Die Aufgeregten* the Countess stands between the advocates of keeping the peasants in subjection (the Amtmann) and the supporters of the Revolution (the Magister): cf. the first three scenes of Act II. —Goethe's own comments on the French Revolution: *Conversations with Eckermann*, 4.1.1824; 27.4.1825.
37. This motif recurs again and again in Goethe's works; cf. for instance the poem *Der Sänger* (H. I, 155–56); a number of instances in *Wilhelm Meister* (Mignon and the Harfner; *Die pilgernde Törin*; etc.); *Tasso*, I, 1, Leonore's speech, ll. 56–82 (H. V, 75); etc.
38. Cf. note 4.
39. H. VI, 125, 14–17. The German word order ('erwies sich . . . zum Troste'/'erwies sich . . . entschlossen und tätig') suggests that *she proved herself a comfort* . . . although, according to the syntax, the fact that *she proved herself a determined and active person* is a source of comfort to those around her. The suffering of the baroness: cf. ibid., 134, 26–135, 19.
40. H. VI, 126, 12–25; 130, 22–24; 140, 15–29; 141, 37–9; 142, 11–13, 21–9; 143, 28–145, 6; 145, 21–3, 32–4; 146, 8–9; 158, 27–30; 159, 24–6; 165, 9–11, 37–9; 185, 33–188, 2; 208, 12–14, 28–32.
41. Ibid., 126, 26–9; 157, 11–159, 5; 159, 27–37; 160, 24–161, 10; 165, 1–4; 166, 1–10; 208, 14–25.
42. Ibid., 126, 31–2; 127, 11–128, 11; 131, 21–136, 5; 138, 36–139, 2; 159, 6–26, 39–9; 161, 19–36; 208, 33–209, 8.
43. Ibid., 126, 32–3; 140, 10–15; 140, 30–146, 11; 146, 34–157, 10; 159, 12–19; 160, 8–10; 166, 13–185, 21; 185, 29–186, 9; 187, 18–208, 5; 209, 9–241, 30.
    The discussion with Luise and the baroness on Kantian ethics: 186, 10–187, 17, in which he does not, however, argue according to the rules of logic!
44. Ibid., 146, 12–33; cf. also *Lepinte.*, pp. 100–1, 163.
45. H. VI, 130, 25–8.
46. Ibid., 159, 20–161, 10; 208, 14–32.—cf. *Lepinte.*, pp. 67–71, 122–3.
47. Notice the interruption of the intellectual discussion: ibid., 159, 20–6, where Karl's joke distracts from the noise but frightens Luise. Further, perhaps partly ironical considerations are again interrupted by a servant who reports a fire, which startles the already susceptible company.
48. Ibid., 208, 14.—Luise 'took it into her head' (the idea of *pleasure* is also suggested) to combine the two incidents (i.e. according to the theory of an occult correspondence between the two bureaux), 'especially since she had had news that her fiancé was *well and happy*; and so once again imagination was given free rein'.—ll. 28–32.
49. Cf. Schiller's Introduction to *Die Horen*, 1795.
50. H. VI, 134, 34–7 and 135, 20–2.

51. Ibid., ll. 23–5.
52. Ibid., 137, 3–139, 39; notice the expression 'gesellige Bildung' (137, 36) which denotes the shaping (both, the process and the finished product) of intellect and sensibility so that the whole man should be adapted to the pressures and the needs of other persons, ultimately of society (as a collective term).—A few examples of Goethe's use of this term: *Geschichte der Farbenlehre, 16. Jahrhundert, Alchymisten* (H. XIV, 78, 21–79, 2); *Wanderjahre* I, 4 (ibid., VIII, 35–41) and II, 11 (ibid., 268–69); *Zur Morphologie 1817: Die Absicht eingeleitet* (ibid., XIII, 55, 30–36).
53. Ibid., 144, 27—145, 6.—The priest makes no distinction between a report based on first-hand experience and a reconstruction of people and events based on (written and oral) source-material.
54. Ibid., 185, 22–188, 2.
55. Ibid., 146, 36–157, 21.
56. Cf. note 20.
57. Karl's emphasis on *facts* as against *explanations* (H. VI, 161, 19–31; cf. *Fricke*, pp. 282–83) highlights the contrast between the first three stories, where the company's interest centres on sensational events, and the two moral *novellas* which concern moral decisions made in the light of the meaning each character sees in his/her life. But this is only a shift in attention; the morally explicable is not excluded from the earlier stories, only it is kept at arm's length. Similarly, the favourable or unfavourable chance event (i.e. not morally or psychologically motivated) is always liable to occur; notice the word 'Zufall' (chance event') used in connection with Ferdinand's discovery that he can open his father's bureau without key (H. VI, 193, 10) and with Ottilie's discovery that Ferdinand had been the anonymous donor of the jewellery (ibid., 194, 24); also 'unglücklicherweise' ('by a stroke of misfortune') in connection with Ferdinand's father discovering that money is missing from his bureau (ibid., 199, 19–20). (Ferdinand's opposition to his father is also tied up with the word 'Zufall': ibid., 192, 19.)—Chance events also occur frequently in the later *novellas*. For Goethe, man's moral responsibility arises only within the unfolding of an existence shaped by forces which have nothing to do with moral scruples or intelligible purpose (cf. already such poems as *Grenzen der Menschheit*, or *Das Göttliche*). In the present work this is anticipated in the introductory framework, ibid., 145, 2 referred to above; cf. note 53).—cf. further note 72.
58. In *Fricke*, p. 277, the priest's irony in the face of the company's interest in sensational events is only tempered by his didactic purpose of gently guiding his listeners towards greater moral seriousness in their literary tastes (as the counterpart to *sociability* in their conduct). This takes insufficient account of the acute state of anxiety; the *therapeutic* element seems to me far more important: cf. *Raabe*., p. 31: 'Die Gefahr, daß das "Ungeheure" erneut von den Seelen der jungen Menschen *Besitz ergreife* . . .'—'The danger that the "Uncanny-Demonic" might once again *take possession of* the souls of these young people . . .'—italics mine).
59. H. VI, 157, 22–159, 5.
60. Ibid., 163, 22; *Bassompierre I*., p. 160, l. 18.
61. *Bassompierre I*., p. 162, ll. 13–15: '. . . mais elle estoit si jolie, que je l'ay regrettée, & eusse desiré pour beaucoup de la pouvoir revoir.'—H. VI, 164, 35–6: '. . . daß ohne den unangenehmen Ausgang es eins der reizendsten gewesen wäre . . .'
62. H. VI, 166, 9–10.—cf. *Wolf*., esp. pp. 97 ff, 142 ff, 134–35.—The connection between silence, discretion, sociability and awe ('Ehrfurcht') is the substratum of so much of Goethe's work. It is frequently understated—as when the old man with the lamp, towards the end of *Das Märchen*, keeps well within the action (and therefore its symbolism),

as he exhorts the prince: 'Gedenke der Schlange in Ehren!' ('Honour the memory of the snake!'—H. VI, 238, 30).—cf. further note 72.

63. *Ziolkowski.*, p. 69.

64. When the priest first learns about the quarrel and the imposition of the principles of *sociability* he starts the conversation from this principle and people's interest in 'the new' (i.e. the sensational), which stimulates the imagination, barely touches ('nur leicht berührst'—H. VI, 141, 28–29) the emotions and never reaches the intellect; he then steers it towards his collection of stories (ibid., 142–5) which entertain by *revealing for a moment human nature and its hidden depths and amuse us with its strange follies* (ibid., 143, 5–8); but the conflicts (144, 33: 'in leichtem Widerspruch'—cf. note 53) are still on a small scale, so that they do not engage the emotions very much more than the 'new' episodes; but the intellect is now given a great deal of scope. The priest does not 'climb down' completely when he offers to tell *romantic and uncanny tales* ('vom Romanhaften, vom Geisterhaften': ibid., 146, 26–7), for the *Antonelli* adventure reveals *human nature and its hidden depths* if properly listened to. On the following morning (ibid., 166, 23–167, 13) the baroness only adds unity of form to the criteria already laid down by the priest; but the *Prokurator* story centres on the conflict between emotional confusion and *man's capacity for moral excellence* (ibid., 185, 15 and 18), so that the conversation between the two *novellas* reaches the intellectual level of Kantian ethics. The progress in moral insight is seen clearly when Luise (notice the word 'bilden': ibid., 187, 29) demands, not merely an entertaining story, but a 'Familiengemälde' (l. 30: 'family portrait'—i.e. a serious moral and psychological study, albeit in fictitious form). If *Ferdinand and Ottilie* is in any sense the second of a pair of 'parallel stories', it is within an ascending order.

65. Cf. Goethe's essay, *Die Metamorphose der Pflanzen*, end of section II: H. XIII, 72, 12–19; in the *Conversations with Eckermann*, 18.1.1827, Goethe himself compared *Die Novelle* with the growing plant.—The stories under (i) (*a*) in the table can be further differentiated: Antonelli's predicament is only temporary and she fails to rise to the moral challenge; the knocking ghost is blackmailed and responds by undermining the girl's personality, so that the mystery of a completely amoral force is preserved; Bassompierre faces the challenge of love and the hand of destiny (the plague), and while his lover creates destiny on the level of love and falls a victim to the destiny imposed by nature, he on his side remains insensitive to the first and is barely ruffled by the second. (3) thus draws together the themes of (1) and (2) but there is (in (3)) only the beginnings of comprehension in the committal to the love of which Antonelli (in (1)) is frightened.

66. H. VI, 187, 10–15.

67. Ibid., 185, 3–6, 17–19: '. . . etwas . . .' (l. 3)—'. . . die Kraft der Tugend . . .' (l. 18).

68. Ibid., 187, 30.

69. Cf. note 13.

70. H. VI, 150, 1 and 18; 193, 1 and 12–13; 194, 16–20 are particularly telling passages. The function of different kinds of gold then plays a crucial part in *Das Märchen*.—This importance of money can be traced throughout the tradition of *fabliaux* and *Schwänke* in the medieval and sixteenth-century tradition, where worldly wealth and power is of central importance; similarly, in picaresque novels, or e.g. in *The Merchant of Venice*, where it is tied up with the adventurer as a character type, it may even come into conflict with spiritual qualities: love, forgiveness. It is this dilemma that Tellheim inherits, in Lessing's *Minna von Barnhelm*; but Lessing also inherits the moral problem of money and social responsibility from the ballad *George Barnwell* (later included by Percy in the *Reliques of Ancient English Poetry* 1765), dramatised in Lillo's *The London Merchant* (1730) which

had an immediate influence on his *Miss Sara Sampson* and the German tradition of domestic tragedy ('bürgerliches Trauerspiel'). But elsewhere (e.g. in Diderot's *Père de Famille*) the basic themes are the same. And this also applies to the prose fiction of the period. For Goethe it is also important that Lessing extended the use of gold to symbolise a responsible attitude towards the search for and the dissemination of truth: cf. *Nathan der Weise*, in Nathan's monologue, III, 6.

71. H. VI, 193, 19–29.

72. Ibid., 199, 34–200, 8; 202, 7–203, 18.—For a semi-Pelagian formulation of the co-operation between divine grace and human effort cf. the commentary on the chorus of angels in the final scene of *Faust II* (Act V: *Bergschluchten*, ll. 11934–41) in the *Conversations with Eckermann*, 6.6.1831, with the suggested amendment in *Witkowski II.*, p. 408.—Goethe rejected both, the over-optimistic rationalism of his period, which glorified human intellectual and moral effort at the expense of divine grace, and, on the other hand, the dogmatic, rather mechanical and superficial formulations of theologians regarding the monopoly of divine forgiveness through the Crucifixion, which deprived Christ's suffering of all mystery and depth and made the worshipper's attitude exoteric and shallow; he also opposed the doctrine of total human depravity (cf. esp. *Dichtung und Wahrheit*, the opening passage of III, 15, more esp. H. X, 34–45;—*Paulsen.*, pp. 9*–13*; *Obenauer.*, pp. 143–45). Man, by virtue of his intellectual and creative gifts, and his moral consciousness and will, had both an active and a passive role to play. The latter consisted in accepting the impact of superior forces in a resigned, reverent manner, but also to rise above this to a trust in the overall rationality of divine government and then to co-operate with it, by adaptation, sociability and constructive action within the total constellation of events; the transition to the active role is thus natural, and the bridge-quality, so to speak, is active and passive (suffering) love. The active, *masculine*, principle reaches out in faith and hope to what is potential, unrealised; the passive, *feminine*, principle draws the former upward to its loving vision of what is—what *she is*, by virtue of her self-giving, sacrificial love, refined by insight and suffering. Goethe created such feminine types in, e.g. the princess in *Tasso*, or Ottilie in *Die Wahlverwandtschaften*, Gretchen and 'das Weibliche' in *Faust*, but supremely Makarie in the *Wanderjahre*—adumbrated in the present work by the baroness and the snake. The suffering Christ embodies this feminine principle in his saving act and it is embodied again in the Virgin Mary. cf. *Obenauer.*, esp. pp. 140–3, 175–88, 187–99, 222–6; *Spranger.*, esp. pp. 73–9, 184–206. Two important literary predecessors: Beatrice (preceded by Matilda!) in Dante's *Divine Comedy* and the Virgin Sophia in Boehme (e.g. *Three Principles*, chs. 12 ff) and taken up by Gottfried Arnold, Gichtel, Oetinger and thence the pietist tradition (cf. the satire in Act IV, scene 6 of *Die Pietisterei* by Gottsched's wife Luise Adelgunde, *Gottschedin.*, esp. pp. 193, 195). Goethe would have known about the Sophia-tradition, not only through Arnold (cf. esp. *Arnold/1729*, Th. I, B. II, C. IV, §7: vol. I, p. 68; Th. II, B. XVII, C. XVII, §27: vol. I, pp. 1101–2; ibid., C. XIX, §30: vol. I, p. 1144; cf. further vol. II, pp. 333–48, 1216–35, 1457–61.—cf. further *Götting.*, p. 37), Gichtel and Oetinger (cf. *Lepinte.*, p. 14; *Benz, E.* (*Sources Mystiques*), p. 65), but also through his contacts with pietism, more particularly through Susanna v. Klettenberg (cf. *Lepinte.*, pp. 24–28, 44–45, 74–80). According to *Besset.*, p. 34, the direct Neo-platonic influence on the final scene of *Faust II* is very strong.

73. H. VI, 204, 7–11.

74. Cf. note 67.

75. Cf. note 66.

76. *Kritik der praktischen Vernunft*, I. Teil, 1. Buch, 2. Hauptstück, opening para.: *Kant V*, pp. 57–8; *Kant/Abbott.*, p. 148.
77. H. VI, 188, 11–21.
78. Notice the gradation:—ibid., 188, 29–30; 191, 19–192, 22; 192, 38–193, 9; 199, 15–200, 8; 201, 21–25; 202, 24–5 and 32–3;—203, 30–8.
79. Cf. notes 72–75.
80. H. VI, 208, 1–5.
81. The last framework in the work:—following on from the above quotation: the baroness' comment on the organs of state: ibid., 208, 6–11; Friedrich's return and report, Luise's imagination (the occult correspondences): 208, 12–32; Karl to the priest (on fairy tales): 208, 33–209, 8; the priest's reply: 209, 9–26. There follows, after the only break in the whole work, and without any more framework, *Das Märchen* (209, 27–241, 30), the only story which is given a title in the text.
82. '. . . [the power of the imagination] ought to play on us like pure music when it is to produce works of art [i.e. we are, so to speak, the instruments on which *the music itself plays* and thereby creates itself, the music and the power of the imagination having become one substance]; it is to induce movement/feeling ['bewegen' is ambiguous] in our being, and that in such a way as to make us forget that there is anything outside us that produces this movement/feeling.'—ibid., 209, 5–8.
83. Ibid., ll. 18–23.
84. The allegory is explained in the text itself: the four kings. Older interpretations tended to treat the whole story as an allegory—cf. esp. the table of nineteenth-century interpretations at the end of *Waldeck/Märch.* This limits the perspective too much so that only very partial insights are gained. Our method of keeping well within the drama of the very dynamic images at work in this drama (cf. *Emrich.* and *Lucerna.*) gives us much greater freedom of movement and provides a vantage-point from which all the (cosmic, psychological, aesthetic, spiritual, political) fields of action can be kept in view.
85. '. . . the idea which you once mentioned, of "forces co-operating and helping each other and the one constantly referring back to the other" . . .'—Schiller's letter to Goethe, Jena, 29.8.1795.—cf. H. VI, 230, 28.—cf. also note 72.
86. Cf. also Goethe's reply, Weimar, 7.9.1795.—All the same, Goethe's composition has developed well beyond the form of its predecessors.
87. Cf. Trunz' notes on *Urworte. Orphisch*: H. I, 566.
88. H. VI, 216, 32–33; 224, 9; 226, 24; 235, 4–5; 231, 28–32.—Cf. in this connection Hos. 10, 12; Jn. 4, 23; Rom. 13, 11.
89. H. VI, 236, 12.
90. Ibid., 213, 20–23.
91. Cf. *Read.*, e.g. pp. 108, 117; other snakes: e.g. Plate 38 (i) (facing p. 153), Fig. 13 (p. 207).
92. The second frontispiece of the *Aurea Catena Homeri* (reproduced as the frontispiece in *Gray.*) has *two* snakes circling round an arrangement of the seven planets, biting one another's tails (comments: esp. *Gray.*, pp. 14, 172–73); their circular movement thus encompasses the cosmic process, and its type, the Opus, in their totality; one snake belongs to the 'Abyssus Superior', 'Volatile', the other to the 'Abyssus Inferior', 'Fixum'; this duality is not, as such, taken over in *Das Märchen*; but there are analogous dualities (e.g. the two contrasting landscapes on either side of the river) which are united by the circular nature of the plot as well as through the sacrificial action of the serpent (who is first green, then transparent).
93. H. VI, 213, 25–214, 5.
94. vegetables only: ibid., 210, 33–8, 219, esp. 28–31; gold rejected: ibid., 210, 19–20; the gold buried by the ferryman: ibid., 211, 6–11.
95. Ibid., 218, 1–3.
96. the giant bathing in the river: ibid., 213, 30–8; he snatches the

vegetables from the old woman's basket: ibid., 218, 39–219, 11; his last appearance on the bridge and transformation into a sundial: ibid., 239, 26–240, 34.

97. Their erratic behaviour (e.g. ibid., 210, 4–14; 217, 15–218, 10; etc.) is seen many times over. But they have a sense of graver matters in hand—hence the importance of wanting to get to Lily. I take it, that this is what they want to discuss with the ferryman, but which they had previously forgotten: ibid., 211, 6.—When the *happy/propitious hour* arrives, they become solemn young men, 'the most serious-minded flames' (ibid., 231, 23-232, 21); at the end of the procession they have the office of unlocking the sanctuary (ibid., 233, 38–234, 24). But at the end of the story they revert to type (ibid., 241, 18–25).
98. Ibid., 231, 27; cf. note 17.
99. Ibid., 217, 38–9.
100. Ibid., 219, 38.
101. Ibid., 220, 11–15.
102. Ibid., 220, 5–6.
103. —although she also finds them somewhat overwhelming! (ibid., 217, 13–20; 218, 2).
104. Ibid., 212, 11–20.—This vital energy, sometimes usefully active, sometimes unharnessed, wasting its resources and effort, can also appear in such youthful (near-hermaphroditic) genius-types as Mignon, Homunculus, Knabe Lenker or Euphorion: cf. *Emrich.*, pp. 42–46.
105. cf. note 116.
106. Ibid., 218, 15–16.
107. Ibid., 218, 19–24.—Notice that the old woman finds carrying the onyx no problem, while anything living (vegetables, or a small living animal) a terrible burden (ibid., ll. 34–38); she thus shares with the will-o'-the-wisps the same this-worldly outlook, one-sided in a state of dissociation.
108. Ibid., ll. 24–25; we note the limits of her power, in that it assumes the Either/Or of life/death in the present dissociated state. She is, however, anxious to complete a circle by joining her powers to that of the lamp: ibid., 226, 7–9. But the true way is only found at the right moment, when, by her touch, she *forms a bridge* between the snake and the prince; it is held together by the old man's *word*, then broken again by the snake turning into thousands of jewels (ibid., 233, 7–24) which, for a time, form a *circle* (ibid., l. 27). They shine *like stars* in the river (ibid., l. 35) in order, eventually, to become the piers of the permanent bridge (ibid., 238, 30–37). The major *circle* is formed by the route of the party, led by the old man, first to the cave, then back to the transformed ferryman's hut.
109. death of the canary and Lily's fear: ibid., 223, 27–224, 3; she hates the hawk (as he detests the pug!): ibid., 227, 23–228, 14; the hawk as messenger of the new era: ibid., 230, 11–17.
110. death of the prince: ibid., 228, 21–2; his resurrection: ibid., 233, 11–20.
111. Ibid., 226, 7–10.
112. Ibid., 219, 20–220, 19.
113. Ibid., 233, 2–5.
114. Cf. note 60.
115. H. VI, 215, 36. (In the days before electricity was generally used, *all* sources of light—more especially the seven planets and the fixed stars —were simply regarded as flames.)
116. Ibid., 236, 1; cf. ibid., 216; 39–217, 3. The power of destroying other metals does not come up in the story; but it is a necessary part of the alchemistic Opus that all baser metals must first die (i.e. be reduced to the black 'prima materia') before they can be regenerated in nobler form. For everything must return to the existence from which it sprang (*Kirchweger/Aurea Catena.*, p. 46; Goethe does not here follow the cycle of cosmic ascent and descent, *diastolé* and *systolé*, of

which, according to Kirchweger, the Opus forms an integral part; cf. *Lepinte.*, pp. 51–58). According to *Kirchweger/Microscopium.*, pp. 31–3, this death is also a kind of judgment.

117. H. VI, 240, 35–241, 1; cf. ibid., 232, 4–6.
118. Ibid., 240, 19–23.
119. Ibid., 230, 10–13; notice the juxtaposition of putrefaction and redness ('rubedo' as the highest stage in the Opus).
120. Lily's fiery red veil: ibid., 229, 1; the light of dawn on her pale cheeks: ibid., 231, 2; redness (the cloak, his face exposed to the sun: ibid., 220, 24–29) is associated with the prince from the start; the sun is traditionally the planet associated with gold, and the most precious kind of gold is red; cf. *Read.*, pp. 55, 73, 102; *Gray.*, p. 17.
121. H. VI, 217, 26–9; 234, 30–235, 1; 237, 1–6.
122. '... But have a look round; have a look at these old stones which I have not seen these hundred years: they have licked away all the gold ...'—ibid., 217, 26–9.
123. Cf. *Über den Granit*: H. XIII, 254, 24–31; 255, 11–12, 25–33; 256, 4–12, 24–35, 39.
124. H. VI, 218, 13–15.
125. Ibid., 217, 24–6; 218, 32–9; 220, 1–9, 32–3; 224, 31–8; 226, 4–5; 235, 35–9; 236, 23–5. Her rejuvenation: 239, 3–20.
126. Cf. esp. *Der Kammerberg bei Eger*: H. XIII, 267, 13–269, 12; and Dorothea Kuhn's note, p. 593. Goethe, following Werner, did not take sides in the controversy between Neptunists and Plutonists; cf. *Faust II*, Act II (*Klassische Walpurgisnacht: Am obern Peneios*), ll. 7495 ff and notes thereto in H. III, 570–72; *Witkowski II.*, pp. 344–5.
127. H. VI, 241, 22–8.
128. Ibid., 210, 17–22.
129. Ibid., 211, 10–213, 9.
130. Ibid., 214, 30–215, 1.
131. Ibid., 222, 6–20; this temporary structure prefigures the permanent structure, where jewels also play an important role (ibid., 238, 34); their connection with the stars (ibid., 233, 27–37) constitute the prophetic dimension; hence the expressions 'mit Ehrfurcht ... schweigend' ('with awe ... in silence'—ibid., 222, 19–20) and 'Gedenke der Schlange in Ehren' ('Honour the memory of the snake'—ibid., 238, 30).
132. Ibid., 228, 30–6; 230, 8–11; cf. notes 91 and 108. The two functions of the circle—that of a protective barrier (magic) and that of the wholeness, the perfection, the eternity of the Opus (alchemy)—are here fused.
133. H. VI, 230, 37–231, 3.
134. Cf. note 108.
135. H. VI, 238, 30–37; the purpose of the protective circle is to guard the prince against the *natural* process of putrefaction; his regeneration must come about through the voluntary self-sacrifice of the snake which raises his rebirth on to the plane of *moral* action.
136. Cf. note 131.
137. H. VI, 215, 34–35; this gives depth to the contemporary arcadianism (e.g. *Merck*), because nature is not simply an ideal state, free from urban corruption, but because it constitutes man's antecedents; uncultivated and cultivated nature (on either bank of the river) must grow together, just as man must harmonise past and present, physical environment and civilisation.
138. Ibid., 216, 20.
139. Ibid., 237, 4–15; 241, 7–12.
140. Ibid., 235, 25–236, 7.
141. Ibid., 236, 30–35. 'Schein' ('outer appearance') here has the force of Paracelsus' term 'signature' (cf. note 17), more particularly one of its forms, the tinctures of metals as used in alchemy. In the era of dissociation, appearance and inner essence are out of step with each other, so that the old woman is concerned with the appearance of her hand

but neglects its function (cf. note 125; no wonder, therefore, that its appearance degenerates even further in the presence of such a powerful transmuting agent as Lily (she does not attend to what Lily says about *her* hand!): H. VI, 224, 26–34). But the snake's power of mediation can transmute the mere glitter of gold coins into true light.

142. Ibid., 237, 16–27: gold, silver, brass—thus:—*gold*:—'Learn to know the highest'; *silver*: 'Feed the sheep' (alienated version of Jn. 21, 16 b); *brass*: 'The sword girt on the left, the right hand free.'

143. ' "O my friend," he continued as he turned to the old man and looked at the three sacred memorial pillars, "how glorious is the kingdom of our fathers and its foundations secure. But you have forgotten the fourth power whose ruling of the world is still more ancient, universal and sure: the power of love . . ."—The old man smiled as he answered: "Love does not rule, but creates and shapes and that is far more." ',—ibid., 238, 3–12.

144. 'bis auf den heutigen Tag'—ibid., 241, 28.

145. Ibid., 238, 9–10, 13–14.

146. Cf. *Lucerna.*, pp. 54–5.

147. H. VI, 216, 24–33.

148. Ibid., 216, 31–3.—Note that previously the golden king had spoken to the snake and to the old man separately. But with the snake revealing the fourth secret to the old man their state of dissociation ends. And the snake's *hidden* communication causes the old man's *proclamation* that 'the time is ripe'.

149. Ibid., 215, 10–15.

SELECT BIBLIOGRAPHY

Anekdote

Eine Anekdote für Leser von Gefühl. An den Herausgeber des teutschen Merkurs. [signed: B. im Nov. 1782. R.]—in: *Der Tuetsche Merkur vom Jahr 1782*. Weimar. November; pp. 140–5.

*Arnold/*1729

Gottfried Arnold, *Unpartheyische Kirchen—und Ketzer—Historie, Vom Anfang des Neuen Testaments biß auf das Jahr Christi 1688* . . . 2 vols., Franckfurt am Mayn, 1729. [First edn.: 1699–1700; suppl. vol.: 1703. The second (1700–15) and third (1729) edns. contain all material, 1699–1703. The fourth edn. (1740–42) also includes editorial revisions and further additions.]

Bassompierre I

Memoires du Mareschal de Bassompierre contenant l'Histoire de sa Vie et de ce Qui s'est fait de plus remarquable à la Cour de France pendant quelques années. Reveus et Corrigés en cette nouvelle edition. (2 vols. Cologne, 1666.) *Volume I.*

Benz, E. (Sources Mystiques)

Ernst Benz, *Les Sources Mystiques de la Philosophie Romantique Allemande.* Vrin, Paris, 1968.

Benz (Volksbücher)

Richard Benz (ed.), *Deutsche Volksbücher.* Lambert Schneider, Heidelberg, [1956].

Besset

Maurice Besset, *Novalis et la Pensée Mystique.* Aubier, Paris, 1947.

Campbell

Killis Campbell, *A study of the Romance of the Seven Sages with special reference to the Middle English Versions.*—in: P.M.L.A., vol. XIV, 1; New Series, vol. VII, 1; 1899; I, pp. 1–107.

Clairon

Mémoires d'Hyppolite Clairon, et Réflexions sur la Déclamation Théatrale; publés par elle-même. Seconde Edition, revuee, corrigée et augmentée . . . A Paris. . . . An VII de la République. [i.e. 1799].

Duentzer/E

Heinrich Duentzer, *Goethes Reise der Söhne Megaprazons und Unterhaltungen deutscher Ausgewanderten.*—in: *Erläuterungen zu den deutschen Klassikern.* Erste Abteilung: *Erläuterungen zu Goethes Werken*; XV: *Erzählungen*; 1.

Duentzer/W (D.N.L.)

Heinrich Duentzer (ed.), *Goethes Werke XIV.*—in: J. Kürschner (ed.), *Deutsche National-Litteratur*, 95.

Emrich

Wilhelm Emrich, *Symbolinterpretation und Mythenforschung. Möglichkeiten und Grenzen eines neuen Goetheverständnisses.*—in: Euphorion 47, 1953; pp. 38–67.

Fambach

Oscar Fambach, *Goethe und seine Kritiker. Die wesentlichen Rezensionen aus der periodischen Literatur seiner Zeit, begleitet von Goethes eigenen und seiner Freunde Äußerungen zu deren Gehalt. In Einzeldarstellungen, mit einem Anhang: Bibliographie der Goethe-Kritik bis zu Goethes Tod.* Düsseldorf, 1953.

Fricke

Gerhard Fricke, *Zu Sinn und Form von Goethes Unterhaltungen Deutscher Ausgewanderten.*—in: *Formenwandel. Festschrift zum 65. Geburtstag von Paul Böckmann.* Herausgegeben von Walter Müller-Seidel und Wolfgang Preisendanz. Hoffmann und Campe Verlag, Hamburg, 1964; pp. 273–93.

Fürst/Erz

Rudolf Fürst (ed.), *Deutsche Erzähler des Achtzehnten Jahrhunderts.* Leipzig, 1897.—in: Deutsche Litteraturdenkmale des 18. und 19. Jahrhunderts. No. 66/9. Neue Folge No. 16/19.

Götting

Franz Götting, *Die Bibliothek von Goethes Vater.*—in: *Nassanische Annalen*, Bd. 64, Wiesbaden, 1953; pp. 23–69.

Goncourt

Edmond de Goncourt, *Mademoiselle Clairon d'après ses correspondances et les rapports de police du temps.* G. Charpentier, Paris, 1890.

Gottschedin

Luise Adelgunde Viktorie Gottschedin, *Die Pietisterei im Fischbein-Rocke oder Die doktormäßige Frau. Ein Lustspiel aus dem Jahre 1737.*—in: *Deutsche Literatur . . . in Entwicklungsreihen* (gen. editor: Heinz Kindermann), *Reihe Aufklärung* (ed. F. Brüggemann), Band 3: *Gottscheds Lebens-und Kunstreform in den zwanziger und dreißiger Jahren, Gottsched, Breitinger, die Gottschedin, die Neuberin.* Reclam, Leipzig, 1935; pp. 137–215.

Graef I

Hans Gerhard Graef, *Goethe ueber seine Dichtungen. Versuch einer Sammlung aller Aeusserungen des Dichters ueber seine poetischen Werke. Erster Theil: die epischen Dichtungen.* Erster Band. Frankfurt a.M., 1901.

Gray

Ronald D. Gray, *Goethe the Alchemist. A Study of Alchemical Symbolism in Goethe's Literary and Scientific Works.* C.U.P., 1952.

Grimm

Brüder Grimm (ed.), *Deutsche Sagen.* 2 pts. Berlin, 1816–18.

Herrmann

Max Herrman, *Die lateinische 'Marina'.* in: Vierteljahrsschrift für Litteraturgeschichte, III, 1890; pp. 1–27.

Horen/R. I.

Die Horen, eine Monatsschrift herausgegeben von Schiller, Cotta, Tübingen, 1795–97. 12. vols. Facsimile reprint in 6 vols. and a supplementary vol. (introd. and commentaries), ed. Paul Raabe. Cotta Nachf., Stuttgart, 1959.—Vol. I.

Jessen

Myra R. Jessen, *Spannungsgefüge und Stilisierung in den Goetheschen Novellen.*—in: P.M.L.A. LV, 1940; pp. 445–71.

Jürgens

Ilse Jürgens, *Die Stufen der sittlichen Entwicklung in Goethes 'Unterhaltungen deutscher Ausgewanderten.'*—in: Wirkendes Wort, vol. VI, 1955–56; pp. 336–40.

Kant V

Kant's gesammelte Schriften, Herausgegeben von der preußischen Akademie der Wissenschaften. Berlin, 1902–38
I. Abt., V. Band: *Kritik der praktischen Vernunft. Kritik der Urtheilskraft.*

Kant/Abbott

Kant's Critique of Practical Reason and Other Works on the Theory of Ethics. Translated by Thomas Kingsmill Abbott. 6th edition, new impression. Longmans, Green. London, 1923.

Keudell

Elise von Keudell, *Goethe als Benutzer der Weimarer Bibliothek. Ein Verzeichnis der von ihm entliehenen Werke.* Weimar, 1931.

Kirchweger/Aurea Catena

[A. J. Kirchweger], *Aurea Catena Homeri. Oder: Eine Beschreibung von dem Ursprung der Natur und natürlichen Dingen....* Franckfurt und Leipzig, 1723.

Kirchweger/Microscopium

A. J. Kirchweger, *Microscopium Basilii Valentini, sive Commentariolum et Cribrellum über den großen Kreuzapfel der Welt*...Berlin, 1790.

Klapper

Jos. Klapper: art.: *Meister, Sieben weise (Septem sapientes).*—in: W. Stammler and K. Langosch (ed.), *Die deutsche Literatur des Mittelalters. Verfasserlexikon.* 5 vols. Berlin & Leipzig, 1933–55; III, 338–44; V, 155, 676.

Klein

Johannes Klein, *Geschichte der deutschen Novelle von Goethe bis zur Gegenwart.* Wiesbaden, 4th edn., 1960.

Kraft

Werner Kraft, *Von Bassompierre zu Hoffmannstal. Zur Geschichte eines Novellenmotivs.*—in: Revue de Littérature Comparée. 15, 1935; pp. 481–90, 694–725.

Kunz

Josef Kunz, *Die deutsche Novelle zwischen Klassik und Romantik.* Erich Schmidt, Berlin, 1966.—in: Grundlagen der Germanistik, 2.

Lange

Victor Lange, *Goethe's Craft of Fiction.*—in: *Goethe. A Collection of Critical Essays.* ed. Victor Lange. A Spectrum Book (Series: Twentieth Century Views. ed. Maynard Mack). Prentice Hall, Englewood Cliffs, N.J., 1968; pp. 65–85.

Laroche/Capr

[Sophie von Laroche], *Les Caprices de l'Amour et de l'Amitié. Anecdote Angloise; suivie d'une petite Anecdote Allemande.* Zuric . . . 1772.

Laroche/Mor

Sopie von La Roche, *Moralische Erzählungen. Dritte verbesserte und vermehrte Auflage.* 2 Bändchen, Mannheim, 1850.

Laroche/St.

[Marie Sopie von Laroche], *Geschichte des Fräuleins von Sternheim. Herausgegeben von C. M. Wieland.* 2. Th. Leipzig, 1771. [An English translation, by J. Collyer, appeared in London, 1776.]

Lepinte

Christian Lepinte, *Goethe et l'Occultisme.* Paris, 1957.—in: Publications de la Faculté des Lettres de l'Université de Strasbourg; Fascicule 134.

Lockemann

Fritz Lockemann, *Die Bedeutung des Rahmens in der deutschen Novellendichtung.*—in: Wirkendes Wort, 6, 1955–56; pp. 208–17.

Lucerna

Camilla Lucerna, *Goethes Rätselmärchen Eine Betrachtung.*—in: Euphorion, 53, 1959; pp. 41–60.

Marache

Maurice Marache, *Le Symbolisme dans la Pensée et l'Oeuvre de Goethe.* Nizet, Paris, 1960.

Merck

Johann Heinrich Merck, *Geschichte des Herrn Oheims.*—in: *Der Tuetsche Merkur vom Jahr 1778.* Weimar; January II, pp. 30–48; February V, pp. 151–72; April III, pp. 51–65; June II, pp. 212–27; October II, pp. 27–37.

Milfull

John Milfull, *The Symbolism of Goethe's 'Das Märchen'.*—in: A.U.M.L.A., 29, May 1968; pp. 52–60.

Müller

Günther Müller, *Die Gestaltfrage in der Literaturwissenschaft und Goethes Morphologie.*—in: *Die Gestalt. Abhandlungen zu einer allgemeinen*

Morphologie. Begründet und herausgegeben von Wilhelm Pinder, Wilhelm Troll, Lothar Wolf. Heft 13. Max Niemeyer Verlag, Halle (Saale), 1944.

Obenauer

Karl Justus Obenauer, *Goethe in seinem Verhältnis zur Religion*. Diederichs, Jena, 1923.

Paracelsus/J

Paracelsus. Selected Writings. Edited with an introduction by Yolande Jacobi. Translated by Norbert Guterman. Routledge & Kegan Paul, London, 1951 (German: 1942).

Paracelsus/S

Karl Sudhoff and Wilhelm Matthiessen (ed.), *Paracelsus. Sämtliche Werke. Erste Abteilung: Medizinische, naturwissenschaftliche und philosophische Schriften*. München, Berlin, Oldenburg, 1922–33. 14 vols.

Paulsen

Friedrich Paulsen, *Goethes ethische Anschauungen. Festvortrag gehalten in der 17. Generalversammlung der Goethe-Gesellschaft in Weimar am 24. Mai 1902*.—in: Goethe-Jahrbuch, XXIII, 1902; pp. 1*-32*.

Pernety/Dict

Antoine-Joseph Pernety, *Dictionnaire Mytho- Hermétique* ... Paris, 1787.

Pernety/Fables

Antoine-Joseph Pernety, *Les Fables Egyptiennes et Grecques Dévoilées & réduites au même principe, avec une Explication des Hiéroglyphes et de la Guerre de Troye*. 2 vols., Paris 1758; repr. 1786.

Polheim

Karl Konrad Polheim, *Novellentheorie und Novellenforschung* (1945–63.—in: D. Vjs. 38, 1964, Sonderheft (October); pp. 208*–316*.

Pontanus III

Ioannis Ioviani Pontani ... Opera ... Basileae, Anno MDLXVI ... [4 vols] —Tomus III: *De rebus coelestibus Libri XIIII. De Luna fragmentum. Commentariorum in Centum Claudii Ptolemaei sententias, libri duo.*

Raabe

August Raabe, *Der Begriff des Ungeheuren in den 'Unterhaltungen deutscher Ausgewanderten'*.—in: Goethe. Viertelmonatsschrift der Goethe-Gesellschaft. Neue Folge des Jahrbuchs. Verlag der Goethe-Gesellschaft, Weimar. Vierter Band. 1939; pp. 23–39.

Read

John Read, *Prelude to Chemistry. An Outline of Alchemy. Its Literature and Relationships*. Reprinted 2nd edition, Oldbourne, London, 1961.

Ruppert

Hans Ruppert, *Goethes Bibliothek. Katalog*. Arion Verlag, Weimar, 1958.

Simrock

Karl Simrock (ed.), *Die deutschen Volksbücher* ... 13 pts. Frankfurt a.M., 1845–67.

Spranger

Eduard Spranger, *Goethes Weltanschauung. Reden und Aufsätze*. Insel Verlag, Wiesbaden, 1949.

Staël

Mme. de Staël, *Essai sur les fictions*.—in: *Oeuvres Complètes de Mme. la*

Baronne de Staël, publiées par son fils; ... 17 vols. Paris, 1820–21; tone II, pp. 175–216 [written in 1795].

Staël/G

[Mme. de Staël, transl. Goethe], *Versuch über die Dichtungen.*—in: *Die Horen*, Fünfter Band, 1796, Zweytes Stück, II; pp. 20–55.

Strauch I

Philipp Straunch, *Deutsche Prosanovellen des fünfzehnten Jahrhunderts.: I. Marina.*—in: Zeitschrift für Deutsches Alterthum, 29 (Neue Folge: 17), 1885; pp. 325–42.

Strauch II

Philipp Strauch, *Deutsche Prosanovellen des fünfzehnten Jahrhunderts.: II. Grisardis von Albrecht von Eyb.*—in: Zeitschrift für Deutsches Altertum, 29 (Neue Folge: 17), 1885; pp. 373–443.

Urlichs II

Ludwig Urlichs (ed.), *Charlotte von Schiller und ihre Freunde.* (3 vols.)—Zweiter Band: Cotta, Stuttgart, 1862.

Wachsmuth

Andreas B. Wachsmuth, *Goethes naturwissenschaftliches Denken im Spiegel seiner Dichtungen seit 1790.*—in: Sinn und Form, 11. Jahr, Berlin, 1959; pp. 20–42.

Waldeck/Bass

Friedrich Meyer von Waldeck, *Die Memoiren des Marschalls von Bassompierre und Goethes Unterhaltungen der Ausgewanderten.*—in: Herrigs Archiv für das Studium der neueren Sprachen und Litteraturen, XLV, 87, 1891: Kleine Mitteilungen; pp. 252–55.

Waldeck/Märch

Friedrich Meyer von Waldeck, *Goethes Märchendichtungen.* Heidelberg, 1879.

Wiese

Benno von Wiese, *Novelle.* (3. Aufl.) Stuttgart, 1967.—in: Sammlung Metzler, No. 27.

Wilkinson–Willoughby

Elizabeth M. Wilkinson and L. A. Willoughby, *Goethe Poet and Thinker. Essays.* Edward Arnold, London, 1962.

Witkowski II

Georg Witkowski (ed.), *Goethes Faust.* 10. unveränderte Auflage, 2 vols. Brill, Leiden, 1949–50.—Zweiter Band: *Kommentar und Erläuterungen/Literatur/Bilderanhang/Faust-Wörterbuch.*

Wolf

Eugen Wolf, *Über die Selbstbewahrung. Zur Frage der Distanz in Goethes Dasein.* Cotta Nachf., Stuttgart, 1957.

Ziolkowski

Theodore Ziolkowski, *Goethe's 'Unterhaltungen Deutscher Ausgewanderten': A Reappraisal.*—in: Monatshefte, vol. L, January 1958, No. 2; pp. 57–74.

3

MÖRIKE AND HÖLTY

By R. B. Farrell

A German poet at the beginning of the nineteenth century (Mörike: 1804–75) and coming quickly to maturity in the early 'twenties, as far as his reading of German poetry is concerned, would turn, after Goethe, Schiller, and possibly Hölderlin, to Klopstock and the poets of the 'Empfindsamkeit', the Göttinger Hain. Mörike in his letters has given us no extended piece of literary criticism, but he occasionally does make reference to Goethe, Schiller, several times to Hölderlin without much recognition of his genius, and twice to Hölty. The first of these is the more important and bears an early date (11 November 1821), written to his friend Wilhelm Waiblinger, and reveals how close he felt to Hölty. 'Das sind gewiß selige Augenblicke, wenn ich draußen an einem Lieblingsplatze den Hölty auf dem Schoß habe, seinem echten, frommen Liede zuhöre, mit ihm weinen muß und bei dem Gedanken an Jenseits vorstelle, daß ich einmal mich dort dem lieben blassen Getrösteten zutraulich nahen darf, und ihm ins freundliche Auge blicken.' And in the same letter he calls him a poet 'der sicher trefflich in seiner Art ist. Was ihn besonders liebenswürdig macht, ist wohl auch seine Persönlich keit, wie sie in der Biographie durch Voss geschildert ist.'

More revealing than the references in the letters to poets (and musicians) are the few poems in which by means of an image Mörike conveys what he saw as the most important characteristics of the poet (or musician) in question. Of the poets of classical antiquity he has conjured up in this way the image of Theocritus and of Tibullus, some of whose poems he translated, and from amongst the German poets of the eighteenth century Brockes and Hölty. The way Mörike saw the latter is presented in a poem bearing the title 'An eine Lieblingsbuche meines Gartens', beneath which by way of more precise explanation stand the words: 'on whose trunk I carved Hölty's name'.

Holdeste Dryas, halte nur still! es schmerzet nur wenig:
  Mit wollüstigem Reiz schließt sich die Wunde geschwind.
Eines Dichters Namen zu tragen bist du gewürdigt,
  Keinen lieberen hat Wiese noch Wald mir genannt.
Sei du künftig von allen deinen Geschwistern die erste,
  Welche der kommende Lenz weckt und reichlich belaubt.
Und ein liebendes Mädchen, von deinem Dunkel umduftet,
  Sehe den Namen, der, halb nur verborgen, ihr winkt.
Leise drückt sie, gedankenvoll, die Lippen auf diese
  Lettern, es dringt ihr Kuß dir an das Innerste Mark.
Wehe der Hand, die dich zu schädigen wagt! Ihr glücke
  Nimmer in Feld und Haus, nimmer ein friedliches Werk.

The poem is typical of the playfully tender element in Mörike's work or at least in a part of it (the so-called Biedermeier part). It expresses not only a feeling of closeness to Hölty's poetry but characterises the latter's poetical world as Mörike saw it. The central image is that of a girl in a springtime garden who, surrounded by the mystery of the tree and aware of the significance of the name Hölty, gently presses a kiss on to the letters of the name. The image of the girl in the garden occurs again and again in Hölty's poems so that we may assume that Mörike thought this central in Hölty or at least in that aspect of the latter's work which appealed to him most. *Auf Henriettens Geburtstag* may serve as a typical example.

Rosen und Nelkenblumen, glänzet lichter,
Wann das beste der Mädchen euch besuchet,
Dank gen Himmel lächelt und Wonnetränen
  Auf euch herabweint.

Tränen des Danks, daß ihre Jugendtage
Gleich dem Säuseln des Mains vorüberfließen,
Und ein frohes Reigen ein neues ihrer
  Jahre begonnen.

Schönstes der Mädchen! Spiel auf Veilchenauen,
Tanz im Nachtigallwäldchen sie dein Leben,
Gleich dem Lorbeer blühend, der deine finstre
  Locke beschattet.

Rosen und Nelkenblumen, glänzet lichter,
Gleicht Elysium's Blumen, wann sie meiner
Denkt; dann komm' ein Lüftchen und flüstr' ihr tausend
  Seufzer entgegen.

The two poems do not correspond in all details and Hölty uses certain conventional motifs (for example, nightingales, Elysium, flowers) which do not reappear anywhere in Mörike, just as little as do the moonlight and roses. But the central image, the girl in the garden, occurs often in Hölty, at times of course varied (das Beben der Brust unter einem Blumenstrauss). It is sufficient to mention a few titles: 'Laura'; 'An ein Veilchen'; 'An einen Blumengarten'; 'Der Anger'; 'Der Bach'; 'Das Traumbild'. In another Mörike poem, which was not intended as a characterisation of Hölty's Muse, we find the same image, so that we are tempted to assume a direct or at least a semi-conscious borrowing. This poem, which is entitled 'Im Weinberg' and is idyllic in character, relates how the poet is sitting in a vineyard gazing at a dainty butterfly and, moved by its beauty, calls to it:

Jetzt eile hinunter zum Garten,
Welchen das beste der Mädchen besucht am frühen Morgen,
Eile zur Lilie du—alsbald wird die Knospe sich öffnen
Unter dir; dann küße sie tief in den Busen: von Stund an
Göttlich befruchtet, atmet sie Geist und himmlisches Leben.
Wenn die Gute nun kommt, vor den hohen Stengel getreten,
Steht sie befangen, entzückt von paradiesicher Nähe,
Ahnungsvoll in den Kelch die liebliche Seele versenkend.

Here there is a verbal correspondence in the phrase 'das beste der Mädchen', which Hölty uses in more than one poem. With Mörike the figure of the girl is subordinated to the theme of delight felt by the beholder at the beauty of the butterfly and it serves to emphasise the gracefulness of the little creature and its significance for the human spirit. For the rest there are not unimportant differences: the Mörike poem is incomparably more complex in its feeling, much more vivid in the presentation of objects and reveals a more intimate relationship with nature. How much more effective is Mörike's 'paradiesischer Nähe' than Hölty's 'Elysiums Blumen'. If Hölty shows traces of graceful play these are much more developed with Mörike. Further, the Hölty poem reminds one of the many birthday greetings and pretty compliments in the Biedermeier section of Mörike's work, less, it is true, in the subject matter and imagery than in the tenderness of tone.

Are we entitled to assume an influence of the older on the younger poet in view of the strong attraction which Hölty had for Mörike? There are no substantial correspondences in subject matter and imagery beyond those already pointed out, even though there are remote echoes in the type of imagery and in subsidiary motifs in Mörike's work, mainly, in fact, in poems whose themes have nothing in common. It may be said, however, that Hölty helped Mörike to realise himself and that an affinity is certainly observable even if this is limited to certain aspects of the work of both poets. Hölty's voice is thin though genuine when heard against the thematical and musical richness of Mörike, but the inner kinship remains.

In his typewritten dissertation *Die Eigenart der Lyrik Mörike's* (Göttingen, 1949) Helmut Schnabel treats Mörike's relationship to other German poets, among them Hölty. He compares two Hölty with two Mörike poems ('Trauerlied' with 'An eine Äolsharfe', 'Mailied' with 'Er ist's'), but basically he works out only a contrast. Yet this contrast, while undoubtedly a fact, should not be exaggerated and blind us to the affinities. The themes Hölty treats are mostly love and spring (often linked), death, whose presence, like Mörike, he constantly felt, friendship, particularly with members of the Hain, in a number of poems the *Deutschtümelei* of the time, simple and honest wisdom, and Trinklieder. In the *Deutschtümelei* Mörike, who later remained unmoved by the unification of Germany under Bismarck, would have found little to interest him, though he also treats wisdom and virtue, if not in the manner of the eighteenth century. Mörike's poems of friendship go incomparably deeper than Hölty's and reveal as in 'An Hermann' an awareness of the friend erupting from the subconscious mind, just as his love poems, unlike Hölty's, dispense with conventions and, apart from the more playful Biedermeier group, express intense passion, a filling of the self with the image of the beloved and at times the conflicts and an anguish arising from this passion. Both have humour (witness Hölty's 'An eine Tobakspfeife' in case it should be thought that his work is all 'Empfindsamkeit'), although Mörike's poems in this vein are admittedly much more numerous and betray a wider range of humour. Both knew an intense delight in the world and its beauty and are often penetrated by a tender melancholy which reveals their knowledge of the end of all things and springs from their awareness of the omnipresence of death. But if Hölty sees the beauty of the world more often than not at night in a moonlit grove, the position with Mörike is much more complex: he experiences it just before or at dawn when the world is full of promise and not sullied by the ageing day; his spirit senses the beginnings of things in their pristine beauty and knows the Edenic mood. His work contrasts sharply with that of the Romantics as well as of Hölty in its absence of evening poems. The work of both reveals the influence of the Volkslied, with Mörike, admittedly, linked with greater passion than in case of Hölty. The latter practised a number of forms characteristic of his time: from antiquity the ode, the idyll, and the elegy and the Germanic ballad and Lied. Mörike was less bound by fixed forms except in his epigrams, where the style is consciously that of the Greek Anthology. If the great 'Wintermorgen' poem has something of the manner of the ode about it by virtue of its apostrophisation of nature, the feeling is much more inward than is usual with this genre, and in general the ode was little suited to Mörike's passivity and his way of letting himself be absorbed by the object and of allowing it to pour into him through all his senses (often synesthetically). A comparison of the 'Wintermorgen' poem with Hölty's 'Hymnus an die Morgensonne' clearly demonstrates the difference in the feeling of the two poets for nature. The centre of Mörike's poem lies in the perception of the creative process of nature (the coming of dawn) which is paralleled by an awareness of the creative process in the human self, so that the two coalesce, whereas with Hölty sunrise, though presented as a process in time, remains basically a painted picture, this feature being emphasised by the verb 'bemalen' ('Sie [i.e. the nymph] bemalt den Ost'). Both poems use personification, in both the rising sun opens an eye, but how different the effect is! Hölty does not succeed in transcending the conventional mythology of his time (which appears again and again in his work), while nature in the 'Wintermorgen' poem retains its mysterious otherness and is not reduced to the level of the familiarly human. The revelant Hölty lines run:

Jetzt zerreißt sie den Schleir, der ihr Auge verhüllt,
Zeigt die blitzende Stirn, hebt ihr funkelndes Haupt,
Welches die goldenen Locken umfliegen, empor,
  Blickt Munterkeit über die Flur.

As against this Mörike's

Dort sieh! am Horizont lüpft sich der Vorhang schon!
Es träumt der Tag, nun sei die Nacht entflohn,
Die Purpurlippe, die geschlossen lag,
Haucht, halb geöffnet, süße Atemzüge:
Auf einmal blitzt das Aug; und, wie ein Gott, der Tag
Beginnt im Sprung die königlichen Flüge.

Mörike has obviously travelled much further along the road to the inner soul of nature than Hölty, whose description remains external, but it is difficult to resist the thought that Mörike when he wrote these lines was thoroughly familiar with the Hölty picture. A number of Mörike's greatest poems reveal an awareness of the sources of life, the hour of birth, the freshness of the new-born beauty of the world, over which however the shadow of death is perceived so that a sense of loss, a feeling of wistfulness overwhelms the self. Such feeling and vision penetrate into the remote and hidden corners of the cosmos, even in the spring poems, which are much more than the simple, uncomplicated joy in the green garment of spring, which is the substance of Hölty's May poems. In contrast, Hölty's nature appears essentially as a garden in which little flowers and bushes unfold their colourful splendour. In it a stream murmurs, or more frequently the nightingale sings like a flute ('flötet') and the whole is bathed in gentle moonlight. Nature with Hölty does not exist as a power in her own right, as an independent theme, but merely as a background to human experience. Thus, through the figure of the girl, the garden is linked with the motif of love, which remains quite uncomplicated. But despite colours ('rot' and 'röter' constantly recur) the image, even when the sun and gold are woven into it, has the effect of silver ('silbern' is a frequent adjective). Hölty's world then, compared with that of Mörike, appears shadowy and lacking in substance. In the whole range of German poetry, not excepting Goethe, the earth and what grows on it have not been conjured up with such sensuous power as Mörike has demonstrated, experiencing them, so to speak, through all the pores of the body (for example, in 'Besuch in Urach') nor have distant things—the sky, the spaces of the cosmos—been brought so sensuously close (for example, in the 'Nacht' poems). The impression of plenitude so characteristic of Mörike's world is absent from Hölty's. The latter's closeness to Christianity despite occasional statements which seem to point in the opposite direction, may well have been for him the reason why nature was not for him the great power it was for Mörike. The difference in the age to which each respectively belonged becomes clear in every aspect of their work. Between them was not only Goethe but also the Romantics with their developed sense of the complex and differentiated life of the soul and their partial discovery of the appropriate techniques for the expression of this. Mörike, who has features of the late-born artist, is here the heir of the Romantics, and he further develops this heritage, however much his sense for solid objects and his fondness for the idyllic in the common pursuits of everyday life link him with certain sides of Biedermeier! (Both poets, moreover, translated from Greek bucolic poetry, Mörike from Theocritus and Hölty from Moschus and Bion.)

It would, however, be a mistake to see in Hölty only gardens and girls that dissolve in the moonlight and to deny him a sense for objects and for the doings of people in everyday life. First, there are his idylls (which admittedly lack the enchantment of Mörike's), then poems such as 'Erntelied' and 'Trinklied im Mai' and also such humorous fancies as the already mentioned 'An eine Tobakspfeife'. This side of him links him with Mörike's Biedermeier world, with his loving but humorous of the portrayals of the everyday life and situations of people in a rustic setting. Mörike's humour, as already pointed out, has a wider range—from the good natured whimsical to the grotesque—his imagination frequently weaving round the object playful arabesques which none the less often transfigure it. All this is lacking in Hölty in his realistic moments. But both have a love of small things and, as witness Hölty's and Mörike's greetings and the like, a love for simple and unaffected human beings. As an example from Hölty suffice it to mention 'Das Landleben' and in particular the first two lines of the following stanza:

> Sein bestrohetes Dach, wo sich das Taubenvolk
> sonnt und spielt und hüpft winkt ihm süßre Rast
> Als dem Städter der Goldsaal,
> Als der Polster der Städterin.

We may now characterise more fully the tone of the two poets. To begin with, the ode, which constitutes a considerable part of Hölty's work and which strongly, if not exclusively, betrays the influence of Klopstock, was foreign to Mörike's manner. The grand gesture, the lofty and the strained feeling so characteristic of Klopstock's muse, which dwelt in supersensuous regions are at the opposite pole to Mörike's strongly sensuous style, his quiet meditative manner, his passivity and openness to the things about him. It would be unfair to say that he rejected Klopstock, but that he was aware of a comical side to his grandeur and sublimity is attested by the poem 'Waldplage'. This is a description of the poet sitting in the forest under his favourite pinetree and reading Klopstock, 'den ich jahrelang vergaß', while winged insects torment him. When one of these stings him he addresses it with the Klopstock verse: 'Du fliehst—o bleibe nicht, Gedankenfreund!', and adds in brackets: 'Dem hohen Mond rief jener Dichter zu dies Wort'. But 'sinnend still auf Grausamtat' he shuts the book so that the 'Ungeziefer' is crushed flat. Finally he reflects:

> So mag es kommen, daß ein künft'ger Leser wohl
> Einmal in Klopstock's Oden, nicht ohn' einiges
> Verwundern, auch etwelcher Schnaken sich erfreut.

The grotesque humour lies in the mingling of the sublime and the trivial and of course in the double meaning of 'Schnaken'.

If Hölty in some of his odes betrays the influence of Klopstock, it is equally true that others have something of the character of the Lied. Both here and in most of the Lieder is revealed a tender, sensitive spirit, whose contact with things, especially small ones, is gentle, humble and loving (note, for example, the expressions 'Liebster der Gärten' in 'An einen Blumengarten'). This tone is also audible in Mörike, though much more inward and complex (sometimes due to the changes of mood). Typical of both is a quivering awareness and the echo in the soul. Examples from Hölty:

> Sie starb—Stets blieb im Innern meiner Seele
> Des Mädchens Bild zurück. ('An Minnas Geist')
> Sie, deren Ton mir in der Seele hallte... ('Auf den Tod einer Nachtigall')

That is the Mörike tone, connected with the poet's way of experiencing sensuous beauty in memory and therefore inwardly. The last stanza of 'Josephine', a poem which does not treat the motif of loss, where one might expect such a tone, may be considered typical:

> O dieser Ton,—ich fühlt' es nur zu bald—
> Schlich sich ins Herz und macht es tief erkranken;
> Ich stehe wie ein Träumer in Gedanken,
> Indes die Orgel nun verhallt,
> Die Sängerin vorüberwallt,
> Die Kirche aufbricht und die Kerzen wanken.

It is characteristic of both poets that the self of the poem is penetrated by quiverings—feelings, in the case of Mörike often arising from the subconscious. The verbal correspondence in the following examples suggest that Mörike had the Hölty line in his ear.

Hölty: Ein süßes Zittern zittert durch mein Gebein . . . ('Die Künftige Geliebte')

Mörike: Eine süßes Schrecken geht durch mein Gebein . . . ('Neue Liebe')

A favourite word of both poets which points to the same sensitivity is 'plötzlich', which with Mörike expresses a sudden emotion and is occasionally used of happenings in the external world which at the same time causes inner vibrations.

Hölty: Sie entwand sich dem Arm ihrer Gespielin, flog
Mir entgegen und goß unter der grünen Nacht
Einer flüsternden Myrte
Sich urplötzlich an meine Brust . . . ('Der Traum')

Mörike: Aber auf einmal,
Wie der Wind heftiger herstößt,
Ein holder Schrei der Harfe
Wiederholt mir zu süßem Erschrecken,
Meiner Seele plötzliche Regung;
Und hier' die volle Rose streut geschüttelt . . .

Such lines reveal an essential attitude of Mörike's: the sensitive soul open like the Aeolian harp to the slightest stirring, exposed at every moment to sudden changes of feeling, which the rhythm and construction of the poem perfectly reflect. By contrast, Hölty adheres to strict and regular forms, which do not allow the expression of a changing course of feeling and of an awareness of time which accompanies such changes.

If Mörike went much further than Hölty in the revelation of the complexity and changeability of inner states, both resemble each other in the basic colour of the soul: in the subdued, wistful tone, which springs, however, in each case from a different source. Hölty's graveyard imagery, his wreaths for the dead, which are often linked with the love motif, may well be associated with his ravaged health, with the certainty of an early death. With the hypochondriac Mörike, who was so sensitively responsive to the beauty of the world, this tone, in which the awareness of transience and of death is audible, springs in large part from a distaste for his own age and a feeling that his true home was in an earlier time to which he looks back longingly. We may assume that Mörike was attracted to the Hölty tone precisely because it was subdued and free from the loud posturings of his contemporary Weltschmerzler.

In one further point there is an affinity. However frequent the direct expression of feelings may be by naming them, characteristic of both is a love of the visual image through which feelings are suggested rather than named, for example, the 'Aufbeben des Straußes am Busen des Mädchens' in Hölty's 'Die künftige Geliebte'. The playfulness in this type of expression which nevertheless reveals deep feeling, the delight in weaving images together is an essential element in Mörike's art, so that a poem like Hölty's 'Vermächtnis' with its tender and subdued tone, its avoidance of all loud expression of suffering, its art of suggesting feeling through images must have made a strong appeal to him. The central image is of the little harp which he wishes to be hung after his death behind the altar, where the 'Totenkränze verstorbener Mädchen schimmern' and on which a red ribbon is 'festgeschlungen'. The last stanza runs:

> Der Küster zeigt dann freundlich dem Reisenden
> Die kleine Harfe, rauscht mit dem roten Band,
> Das an der Harfe festgeschlungen,
> Unter den goldenen Saiten flattert.

The work of both poets shows numerous such tender and graceful fancies that nevertheless convey deep feeling.

One final detail may be mentioned: the love of both poets for compound substantives consisting of three parts. Hölty uses 'Maienhimmelbläue' ('Elegie auf ein Landmädchen'), 'Lebensblütengeruch' ('Die Liebe'), 'Kirschenblütenzweige' ('Mailied'); Mörike has 'Liebesschauerlust' ('Mein Fluß'), 'Ackerblumenkranz' ('Ach nur einmal noch im Leben'), 'Felsentrümmersaat' ('Göttliche Reminiszenz').

One must guard against overstating the affinities; after all, much had happened in German poetry since Hölty's day. But the degree of kinship I have pointed to does suggest that Hölty not only appealed to Mörike, but that the latter saw clearly certain aspects of his art and was in some measure influenced by them.

4

HERDER AND NIETZSCHE

By D. Williams

It is a commonplace of literary criticism that the main contribution of the Germans to the world of European letters is basically and in many different ways connected with the concept of Romanticism. Admittedly the term has in recent years come in for a great deal of criticism, alike because of its impreciseness and because it attempts to include such various and heterogeneous manifestations in all the arts, and even in philosophy and sociology too, as to be in danger of losing any recognisable reference it might once have possessed. Nevertheless there is substance in the general contention that the particular German contribution, in the last two centuries at any rate, has been in essence Romantic. That German music plays such a large part in our tradition, and that the historical methods which are so dominant today owe so much of their persuasiveness to the work of Germans—these are only two of the corollaries of the essential Romanticism of the German mind. It is this too which explains perhaps the fact that it is only in the sphere of lyrical poetry that German literature, with our own, may be said to have surpassed its European rivals.[1] There is something therefore to be said for considering two of the most important figures in German writing, who stand also in a more specifically Romantic tradition, one at the beginning of it and the other perhaps heralding its end. Herder and Nietzsche, it may be said, show in greater degree than any other figures in the German tradition the fundamentally Romantic qualities so characteristic of their nation.

The two men were born, of course, exactly a hundred years apart; Herder in 1744, coming from East Prussia, and educated at Riga and Königsberg, Nietzsche in 1844 in Saxony, and educated at the universities of Bonn and Leipzig. Their social inheritance and environment could hardly be more different, yet the similarities in the cast of their minds and their personalities are, as we shall see, most marked.

But a preliminary point must be made at the outset. With both of these men it is very difficult to make up one's mind what one is dealing with. Are these thinkers or essayists, or philosophers, or poets, or moralists? Each of them can be regarded as most of these things, but each resists any precise classification. This will become clearer as we proceed. Herder for instance shows this quality in extreme form. His starting-point is fundamentally an interest in poetry—all his other studies, in history, in theology, in anthropology, in philosophy, revolve round this essential axis, his questions are designed continually to illuminate the nature of poetry, and his theory of poetry goes very much deeper than either his immediate disciples, the German *Sturm und Drang*, or his real heirs, the Romantics, realised. Indeed, translated into the appropriate psychological jargon, it is frequently propounded in our day as something new.[2] But Herder was not a poet. He collected folk-songs, and he did write a certain amount of poetry of his own, but not, most readers would agree, of the highest significance. But nor on the other hand can he be called an aesthetician, or even a philosopher. He wrote a good deal of metaphysics, and engaged in a famous polemic with Kant, who had been one of his teachers at the university. But no system emerges from his works, no ordered coherent theory of the universe, only fragments, brilliant *aperçus,* from which no doubt a system could be built but was not by him. Even his religious thinking bears this fragmentary character, and it is this as much as his pantheistic leanings which aroused bitter doubts of his orthodoxy and of his fitness for the high ecclesiastical office he held at Weimar. Similarly he cannot be called a historian—his major work, the *Ideen zur Philosophie der Geschichte der Menschheit,* is just what its title states, ideas for a philosophy of history. It has earned him honourable mention in some recent books on the philosophy of history,[3] but in general has, perhaps rightly, been ignored by historians. And one could go on in this way considering his theories of education, his scattered comments on politics, and so on. What is the upshot of all this? That his mind moves, in what may be thought a typically German way, on the borderland between the various fields of study. He is concerned above all things with the interconnectedness of the various activities of the human mind and personality, so that he operates *between* poetry and philosophy, between history and metaphysics, ultimately between analysis and prophecy. He is a mystic in some ways, like his revered teacher Hamann, but it is a great mistake to interpret him as an irrationalist, as has sometimes been done. He is much more, like Pascal, concerned to investigate the connection between thought and feeling, to study the 'raisons du cœur', to react to the world as a man and not as a logical machine. He has, of course, been criticised as self-contradictory and illogical, and often his phrasing is so. But the various contradictions which one can point to in his work seem to me to be the marks of a mind entirely concerned to think out the deliverances of his intuition and attempt to reconcile them with each other—and in this attempt he more often succeeded than failed.

Consider some of these contradictions. His main interest throughout is poetry, and literature generally in so far as it approximates to poetry. And his major contribution to literary insight is, I suppose, his recognition that the application of criteria appropriate to one literary context is unjustified in another, different, one. You must not judge Shakespeare by the same standards you apply to or derive from the analysis of Sophocles or Racine. This is by now a platitude, and even in his own day, just before the French Revolution, it was not such a striking insight as has been made out. Herder himself pays tribute to some of the English writers, like Young and Shaftesbury, who pointed the way here. But, one may well ask, how is this to end? It may come finally to the dangerous position that there are no general standards or rules in literary criticism, so that no two works can be compared and nothing can be evaluated, since there is nothing to evaluate it by. This looks like pure relativism, pure subjectivism. Herder is often reproached with holding just this attitude, with holding that the critic's function is to describe only, not to evaluate or to discriminate. And yet he himself regarded Homer and the early books of the Old Testament and Ossian (he was persuaded of the authenticity of Macpherson's compilations, but his argument remains unimpaired if this is denied) and such folk poetry as the Border ballads, and Shakespeare, and various others, as the prime exemplars of poetry, and he regarded the productions of the eighteenth century, say Voltaire's plays or the German literature of his day (before the advent of Goethe) as essentially decadent, artificial, dead, inartistic. But on his own showing apparently this preference of his is of the same category as a preference of boiled eggs to poached, and carries as little weight. Or he is applying criteria appropriate to primitive poetry (in a real sense he regarded Shakespeare as primitive, as are the Border ballads) to his own century, which his own theory brands as unjustified. This is a frequent reproach brought against him, but to my mind wholly unfairly. He is not in fact a relativist in this sense at all, he does not hold that there are no criteria of literary value, only that the criteria change and develop. And they do not change arbitrarily, for then they would still exist only in name. They are, says Herder, all of the same kind, which can be summed up in the word *Natur,* naturalness, only they develop historically and are a function of the racial, social, national, environmental conditions of a given time and place. Now I suppose that most, if not all, literary revolutions have been carried on under the slogan 'Back to nature', and the whole crux of the matter is in what is meant by 'nature'. Herder fights his battle against the artificiality of the salon culture of the eighteenth century in the name of nature, but he goes out of his way to make clear what he means by the word. It is connected, he thinks, with the *Volksseele,* the unconscious spirit of the race or people, it is a compound of environment and tradition, it is moulded essentially by historical factors, and as far as literature is concerned by linguistic factors. Hence his immense interest in what we should call primitive anthropology, and in the history of language. His essay on the origin of language was designed to answer the question: was human language a divine gift to man or was it created by man for himself? A typically eighteenth-century question; and in this essay it receives an answer thoroughly characteristic of the age. Yet the investigation of this apparently academic matter leads Herder to what is in effect a theory of poetry and poetic utterance as revealing the most primitive and most immediate central aspect of human communication, with language as a whole seen not as a mechanical operation of arbitrary symbols, but as the most characteristic self-expression of the mind, not in essence intellectual at all, but as Herder calls it 'sinnlich', that is, immediately expressive of sensation. And this in turn is productive of what in the end we must recognise as a theory of the unconscious, with poetry seen as the most immediate revelation of our human nature—not, let us emphasise again, because it is irrational or unaccountable, but because it expresses a realm of being which is more absolute, more 'natural', in Herder's sense of the word, than the operation of the intellect alone can be.

On this showing, the primitive poets and Shakespeare are natural, not because they use natural everyday language, which they plainly do not, but because their works express most intensely the spirit of their culture, the fundamental spiritual experience of their time and place. And this has relevance to all times and places because in expressing the human spirit thus immediately they are giving form to the most fundamental quality in man, which is his birthright, his defining characteristic, and thus ultimately one and unchanging—whereas Voltaire, say, is unnatural because his works express ideas and feelings and sensations divorced from those which are the basis of his culture, fortuitous ephemeral things with relevance only to the contemporary fashions. This last proposition may of course be questioned, but Herder's theory, involving both the recognition that a literature grows and changes with the historical and environmental changes of the people concerned, and yet also that poetry springs from a level of consciousness which underlies all human awareness and is thus unchanging in essence—this theory cannot, I think, be rejected.

The essence of the matter is his double conception of the nature of the poet. On the one hand he is an individual, he is an original genius, he goes his way independently of all around him, inspired by his personal muse. But on the other hand he is the mouthpiece of all those qualities which make the civilisation he inhabits what it is. If either side of this paradox is emphasised unduly, the truth is distorted, and Herder is concerned throughout to keep both in balance in his thinking. This *organic* conception of literature, which he repeatedly compares to a flower, growing from seed to full bloom and then dying, but in its decay passing on fresh seeds for new growth, is an immensely fruitful one. Marxists have claimed Herder as a forerunner of the Marxist idea of literature and culture generally as a sort of epiphenomenon of the development and change in the various economic relations which they see as determinative in human history. But it can be seen that Herder's doctrine is very much more persuasive than any such over-simplification.

And his doctrine can be generalised. When he turns to the examination of the whole of human history, as he must to explain the emergence and morphology of poetry, he applies the organic concept in exactly the same way. That is to say, he sees historical processes as essentially teleological and thus expressing a divine purpose—for like Kant he sees that logically if the argument from design for the existence of God applies in nature, then it must in history, too, if God has fashioned the universe, then its development too cannot be haphazard—and yet he is quite clear that the idea of progress, as an automatic march onwards and upwards, is a myth. Just as Shakespeare is not to be regarded as an advance on Sophocles, each of them being a supreme expression of his own culture and people, so one historical age, or one civilisation, is not to be regarded as an advance on previous ones. It is true that Herder holds the great age of classical Greece to be the most perfect flowering of the human spirit to date, and sees in his own time an age of barbarism and soullessness, but each age and each civilisation he thinks contributes its particular piece to the great unfolding pageant of history, and no period is ever in any real sense dead, for like the flower it passes its seed to succeeding ages. Even the Dark Ages, he holds, find a place in the pattern of the whole since during these centuries the Arabs, to take one example, kept alive much of the traditions of the Ancient world, which were to bloom once more at the Renaissance.

It is important to see the originality, if not of conception, at least of application, of this historical genetic idea of Herder's. Nothing can be understood, he argues, without going back to its origins. All things are in a continual flux and movement, and that movement is organic, not a mere pushing of levers to turn a wheel. All things are in growth. And all are impelled by a system of forces. *Kraft* is a word which continually spatters his pages.[4]

Poetry is a form of this ultimate force. God himself is seen as essentially a force. At the level of consciousness this force is a striving to achieve full self-realisation. This is an essentially vitalistic and dynamic view of the world. Herder has studied Montesquieu and applies his ideas about the effects of environment on legal systems to life as a whole. But he has not stopped there. He stands squarely in the tradition of Rousseau, with all the latter's distrust of intellectualism, his equation of conscience with instinct, his belief in the logic of the heart and the cramping and throttling effects of the monster 'civilisation'. But he has not stopped there. He has generalised this too and built his whole world view upon it, and he has extended it in two directions. First he has applied it to literature, believing that the heart of man beats most clearly in his songs. And second, he has added to it this historical view of things, and this in effect radically transfers it. This is the point of greatest consequence. For in doing this Herder steps outside his century. The eighteenth-century mentality is an extremely complicated thing. It is far too simple to call this the Age of Enlightenment and think of it simply as a time which paid homage to reason, which saw all problems as soluble by the intellect, which allowed no dogma or privilege to go unchallenged by the intellect. This is the attitude of the French *philosophes*. But it represents only one side of the climate of the time. Alongside this brilliant and forceful intellectual critical activity there is a very strong current in the opposite direction—the cultivation of feeling and intuition, to which many eighteenth-century novels and plays bear witness, and of which such a movement as the pietism which was so strong in Germany is evidence. And above all, Rousseau embodies just this force, which in him, soon after the middle of the century, seems to explode and send off reverberations which have not ceased today. Herder is interesting because he attempted to combine these opposites, and could do so only by mingling them with a third current, the historical. For it is broadly true that eighteenth-century thinking is, or tends to be, unhistorical, at any rate as compared with that of the nineteenth century. And Herder parts company with his time at this point. This is not to say that he is a historian of note. Voltaire and Gibbon were certainly both of them better historians. For Herder's effort is not designed, as theirs, despite all their prejudices, mainly was, to find out 'wie es eigentlich gewesen ist', in Ranke's famous phrase. Herder as a historian is weak, and often laughable. He has not the critical sense in weighing evidence and assessing probabilities. But in all that he touches he shows a much deeper awareness than the other thinkers of his century of the fact that all things carry their pasts with them, and are what they are not because they were made thus but because they grew, and grew in certain soil, under certain conditions, and in growing are striving to achieve certain purposes.

All his thinking plainly points to a philosophy of ends, and it is natural that his vitalistic conception of human development, mirrored for him most completely in the development of language and literature, should culminate in the doctrine that human perfection, in the sense of complete realisation of human potentialities, is the goal of human striving, a sort of totality of being which is the light leading men onwards, a blessed state of total self-fulfilment. This goal he called *Humanität*. It is a cultural ideal, beckoning us on through the centuries. At first, in common with many others, he thought it was brought nearer by the French Revolution, but the upshot of this cataclysm soon disillusioned him. The more positivistic of his critics blamed him then, and at times still do, for erecting what seems like a will-of-the-wisp, a mystical ideal set in the far future, or even in the next world, which can have no real relevance to human problems. But this is again plainly a misinterpretation of his thought. *Humanität* is the goal of all human striving, but Herder does not see it as a future goal, rather as a perennial or eternal one. Indeed he gives a list of great men in the past who have come near to it, of whom it is interesting to note that Benjamin Franklin is one. And his historical and genetic approach to things does not carry with it any doctrine of progress, rather indeed the reverse. Herder criticises Rousseau for setting up the imperative 'back to nature'—rather, he asserts, we should set as our watchword 'onwards to nature'. But in fact this quibbling obscures the real issue. The *Humanität*-doctrine is essentially Rousseauistic in its basis, and is the necessary complement to the historical viewpoint, without which the latter degenerates into a superficial and untenable meliorism.

Now it is no accident that this very same criticism of Rousseau, in almost the same words,[5] was levelled by Nietzsche, a hundred years later. Indeed, much of what has been said of Herder could be asserted of Nietzsche too. It is unfortunate in a way that we stand so near to Nietzsche, so much in his shadow, so that his often very difficult thought has been interpreted and re-interpreted and often in the process simplified to the point of becoming a series of catchwords with which we frighten each other. We tend to think of such phrases as the 'blond beast', the 'will to power', the 'eternal recurrence' as giving us real insight into his thought, which they do not. He has been called the most brilliant mind Germany ever produced,[6] and one need not quarrel with this evaluation. He ended in madness, and it is a matter of opinion exactly when his mental faculties began to be clouded, so that some of his later works, and the more savage ones, particularly the notorious *Antichrist,* his most sustained attack on Christianity, and *Ecce Homo,* his very strange autobiographical sketch, are often to greater or less degree disregarded as the products of a mind already deranged. His thinking appears also to evolve during his life by successive radical transformations, so that what he asserts in one book he is likely flatly to contradict in another a few years later. Nevertheless, there is far more unity in his work than is generally admitted, his whole life is a search, carried out with ruthless honesty and extreme precision of mind, for a faith which ultimately has to be religious. If Herder's two main interests are poetry and history, Nietzsche's are culture and religion. But, as with Herder, we have the same difficulty in coming to grips with his work. Is it philosophy, or psychology, or literary criticism, or *Geistesgeschichte,* or even poetry? Again we are dealing with a man whose mind moves always on the border between the different fields of study. But a man now much more concerned than Herder to sharpen his thought continually to paradox, to shock his readers out of what he felt to be their complacency, and a man therefore whose intellectual daring invites most dangerous misinterpretation, so that he can for instance devote his whole effort to attempting to set forth a particularly stern and rigorous morality while labelling himself an 'immoralist'. The famous 'beyond good and evil' has misled a great many of his most fervent admirers, with results like the flabby epicureanism of Gide's early works. The 'transvaluation of all values', which he urges so strongly, is not a mere sweeping-away of accepted values, and is not to be taken as a declaration of positivism or pragmatism. He is concerned all the time to bring men back to an awareness of their personal responsibility as moral agents, which he sees threatened by ready-made moralities and especially by the machine-mindedness of what he already analyses as the Welfare State. Even the famous Eternal Recurrence is not to be regarded primarily as a doctrine of the cyclical nature of historical development, but rather as a most telling poetic symbol of the eternal significance of all moments in life. 'Denn ich liebe dich, o Ewigkeit' is the constant refrain of Zarathustra.

Nietzsche's morality is often regarded as pure relativism and subjectivism—'I make my good and evil, which is not yours'—just as we saw Herder's ideas on poetry were so regarded, and with just as little justification. His doctrine of the will to power, which he sees as the mainspring of all life, indeed of all existence, and not simply as a basis for human psychology, is not an invitation to ruthlessness and cruelty and the licence of the jungle. He says at one point that when he uses the word *Macht* he has in mind a quality of which a mouse can show just as high a degree as an elephant. Just as Herder speaks continually of *Kraft* as the whole principle of life, so Nietzsche analyses life in terms of power, and the two are here not far separated. And in each case what is being proposed is a vitalistic doctrine of personality. 'Do what you will', says Nietzsche, echoing Rabelais rather than St. Augustine, and then goes on 'but first be a person that *can* will'. In all this it can be seen that Nietzsche and Herder had similar visions of the sovereign independence and even divinity of the human mind and spirit. One can even, perhaps, go on to say that the Superman, the supreme goal of Nietzsche's yearning, which is an essentially mystical ideal of perfect pure humanity and not an extrapolation from past history, is not in essence different from the ideal state which Herder called *Humanität*. When Nietzsche divides humanity into lords and slaves, those who have the courage and power to set their own goals and follow their own path, as against those who are sheep and do no more than obey the prescribed moral rules, he is not claiming any innate superiority of certain races and certain classes. Each of us, in his view, is a unique miracle, each of us can choose himself, become what he is, in the phrase he takes over from Pindar, each of us can obey the superman in him, or fail, shirk the task and the responsibility and relapse into the automatic functioning of the slave.

In this Nietzsche is plainly reacting violently against his age, against the comfortable nineteenth-century reliance on technological advance to save us the trouble of decision and living, against the view that culture and study and the arts and so on are a sort of cushion to absorb the shocks of life. Real culture, he urges, is like virtue, a continual creating, and not a feeding on the spiritual capital of the past. And it cannot be spread widely without becoming thin, like jam on a piece of bread and butter. Mass education, mass culture he regarded as a contradiction in terms.[7] And Herder's views are here again not dissimilar. Both men react against what they see as essentially unnatural in their age, against the squeezing out of human values by the artificial, the second-hand, the second-rate. Both see the history of recent European civilisation as a tale of decadence. Both urge a respect for quality and a disdain for mere numbers. Both are essentially aristocratic. Neither would be at home in the 'century of the common man'. Herder's high regard for the primitive quality in the peasant and the tiller of the soil need not mislead us here. He sees the peasant as the real aristocrat because his humanity has not been overlaid by the artificial trappings of mechanical civilisation. And Nietzsche similarly reveres the unspoilt genuineness of the primitive.

Yet we started by implying that Herder in a real sense killed the eighteenth century and brought the nineteenth to birth, and it is increasingly clear that Nietzsche can truly be said to have killed the nineteenth century and in many ways heralded the twentieth. And this conclusion, in view of their similarity of mind, plainly contains a paradox. This brings us to the most profound difference between them. There are, of course, obvious points of divergence —Nietzsche has all the armoury of nineteenth-century psychology behind him, all the insight into life given by the researches of Darwin, he has imbibed to the full the logical criticism of Kant,[8] he has followed in the footsteps of Schopenhauer, and these things are quite foreign to Herder. Nietzsche is a trained philosopher and classical philologist, which Herder never was. He wrote that when yearning and scepticism are united, the result is mysticism; and his own mysticism is indeed of this sort, whereas Herder's has not the sceptical quality at all. These are important differences, and the fact that Nietzsche is the product of the disillusionment and desperation and fading faith of the nineteenth century has left its mark on his work, which could not have appeared in the more leisurely and if not more settled at least more devout time of Herder. And of course Herder speaks throughout as a convinced Christian, even if he was accused not entirely unjustly of being a Spinozist, whereas Nietzsche's attack on Christianity, a much more telling and radical criticism than say the sharpshooting of Voltaire, runs through all his works and seems to place him on the opposite side to Herder.

But even this final divergence is, I think, less radical than it seems. Herder's brand of transcendental pantheism is not fundamentally unlike Nietzsche's cult of Dionysos. When Nietzsche opposes Christianity on the one hand, the religion of the slaves, which inculcates the mean virtues, pity and patience and renunciation and selflessness and meekness and so on, and thus, in his view, breeds a stunted race of half-men, to the heroic and tragic view of life which he finds expressed in the pre-socratic philosophers and the earliest Greek tragedy, and which he feels Socrates and Euripides between them destroyed, the view whose supreme expression is the ecstasy and triumph of Dionysos—when Nietzsche opposes these two things, he is seeking to find his own religious attitude which shall give full weight to both of them, to all the impulses he feels to be sacred in man and in life. There was only one Christian and he died on the Cross, he asserts, and in his descriptions of the personality of Jesus there is a tenderness rarely found in his works. Saint Paul, not Jesus, is for him the real villain, whose motives he stigmatises as resentment and envy, and the whole Christian tradition, he feels, has been twisted and distorted by him and his followers. No, the fundamental difference between Herder and Nietzsche is not here, as I see it, but in the simple fact that Herder has the historical genetic approach to all his problems, and in Nietzsche it is almost entirely absent. For Herder all things grow and develop and the mind must rehearse their history to come at them. For Nietzsche all things are eternal and timeless. Nietzsche's famous essay on history bears this out, 'only from the highest power of the present may you interpret the past', he cries, and in speaking of the Eternal Recurrence he urges as one of the merits of the doctrine that it allows the will to will backwards in time, that is to say that the past is never truly past, but always amenable to the willing of the thinker. Or rather that the will can transcend time altogether and in the spirit place us in the realm of eternity, where past and present and future are as a single instant. We are here on the edge of difficult thinking, in essence mystical, and the 'perspectivist' position which Nietzsche finally elaborated is susceptible of a variety of interpretations.[9] It is sufficient for the present purpose to urge that his thinking is at bottom unhistorical throughout, and this marks him off sharply from Herder. The fact that he fills his pages with analyses of the history of our culture, tracing its decline and decadence from the glory of the ancient world, should not obscure this, to my mind, cardinal truth. His mind moves in the realm of the eternal, like Plato's, whom he so much despised as an escapist.

But where have we now got to? Herder, the product of the predominantly unhistorical eighteenth century, makes the historical view the cornerstone of his work. Nietzsche, the product of the most historically-minded century we have ever known, the nineteenth, reacts violently in precisely the opposite direction. Each the product of his time in so many ways, each violently rejecting and reversing the tendency of his time in this. Each forming a pivot, ending his century, swinging the culture of Germany in a new direction. And yet each, as we have seen, sharing so many of the qualities of the other.

This brings us to the final term of the discussion. It has been suggested that Herder's thinking is fundamentally rooted in Rousseau. And the same thing can be said of Nietzsche. In his case, his dependence on the reading of French literature goes very much farther than this, and one will find in his work traces of his reading of almost every important French author from the sixteenth century onwards.[10] But at present we are considering only the fundamental similarity of mind of these three, the prophet of Geneva, the parson from East Prussia, and the Saxon Dionysiac.

All three have been accused of irrationalism. Neither of them, I think, with any justice. But all certainly make central in their thinking the emotional impulsive unconscious forceful individual part of the personality. All of them see man essentially as a force, operating below the level of rational thought, striving for an innocence and purity which is truly beyond good and evil. All of them to some degree deify the personality, all of them embrace what is fundamentally a tragic view of life, together with the doctrine of individual personal life, morality as the creation of the agent, salvation as the fruit of 'willing overself'. Rousseau's 'homme naturel' is not as far as one might think from Nietzsche's Superman.

We started by singling out Herder and Nietzsche as typical examples of the peculiarly German contribution to our culture. It is not without significance that we find them both thus dependent on a non-German thinker. There may here be something profoundly characteristic of the German mind, namely the regularity with which its greatest representatives, at least in literature, seek out and follow foreign guides, sometimes with their eyes open, sometimes unconsciously. Goethe is here no exception, only his eyes are continually open. And in the case of Nietzsche we have a good example of the often unconscious following of the foreigner, since almost every time he speaks of Rousseau, or of Pascal, the two Frenchmen most akin to him in spirit, he does so in terms of violent and vituperative rejection. And yet his debt is incontestable, as is Herder's. One of Nietzsche's most mysterious sayings is a sentence which goes 'gut deutsch sein heißt sich entdeutschen'.[11] It seems to me that this is very true, not only of Nietzsche himself, but of the German spirit in general, and he and Herder are both good examples of it.

NOTES

1. A striking formulation of the point is made by Fritz Strich: 'Wo der deutsche Geist sich selber folgt, ist er Geist der Romantik. Sein klassisches Ideal vermag er nur mit fremder Hilfe zu verwirklichen.' (Whenever the German spirit remains true to itself, it is Romantic. It can only realise its Classical ideal with foreign help.)
2. Such a recent pronouncement, for instance, as Professor Day Lewis's Clark Lectures of 1946 owe a great deal, perhaps unwittingly, and almost certainly indirectly, to Herder.
3. Cf. for instance, the treatment of Herder in R. G. Collingwood, *The Idea of History*.
4. Cf. for instance in the opening paragraphs of the *Ideen*: Die Kraft, die in mir denkt und wirkt, ist ihrer Natur nach eine so ewige Kraft wie jene, die Sonne und Sterne zusammenhält . . . Denn alles Dasein ist sich gleich, ein unteilbarer Begriff; im Größten sowohl als im Kleinsten auf einerlei

Gesetze gegründet. Der Bau des Weltgebäudes sichert also den Kern meines Daseins, mein inneres Leben, auf Ewigkeiten hin. Wo und wer ich sein werde, werde ich sein, der ich jetzt bin, eine Kraft im System aller Kräfte, ein Wesen in der unabsehlichen Harmonie einer Welt Gottes. (Suphan ed., vol. XIII, 16.) (The power which is thinking and operating in me is by nature just as eternal as that which holds the Sun and stars together. . . . For all being is a unity, an indivisible concept, in its greatest, as in its smallest, spheres based on a single set of rules. The structure of the Universe is therefore the guarantee of the core of my being, my inner life, for eternity. Wherever I exist and whoever I am, I will be that which I am, a power in the system comprised by all powers, a being in the illimitable harmony of a world in the hands of God.)

5. Nietzsche puts the point thus: 'Auch ich rede von "Rückkehr zur Natur", obwohl es eigentlich nicht ein Zurückgehen, sondern ein *Hinaufkommen* ist—hinauf in die hohe, freie, selbst furchtbare Natur und Natürlichkeit, eine solche, die mit großen Aufgaben spielt, spielen *darf*. . . .' (*Götzendämmerung. Streifzuge eines Unzeitgemäßen*, Section 48) (I too speak of a 'Return to Nature' although it is in fact not a going back but a moving upwards—upwards into the high, free and even terrifying nature and naturalness. A moving which plays, and is permitted to play, with large tasks. . . .)
6. By E. M. Butler, *The tyranny of Greece over Germany.*
7. We shall know perhaps in the next half-century whether he was right in this, but the indications are already pointing towards the correctness of his view!
8. Both Darwin and Kant are repeatedly and explicitly rejected by him, but without them his own position is unthinkable.
9. One may cautiously suggest that Schlechta's reduction of Nietzsche's mature thinking to a basic nihilism is unduly limited and does less than justice to it (F. N. *Werke in drei Bänden*. iii, 1433 ff).
10. For details see my *Nietzsche and the French*. Oxford, 1952.
11. 'To be German means to un-Germanise oneself.'

5

'MARIA STUART': AN INDICATION OF AGNES MIEGEL'S ORIGINALITY AS A BALLAD-WRITER

By G. Rodger

It seems fashionable, these days, to suggest that the traditional *Kunstballade*, as originated by Bürger and developed by subsequent generations of ballad-writers is now dead and that it was already moribund by the end of the nineteenth century. The ballad genre itself, it is argued by such present-day scholars as Kurt Bräutigam, Walter Hinck, Heinz Piontek and Karl Riha, is still alive in our modern world, but only in the renewed form of the vigorous, harsh Brechtian ballad with its echoes of Villon, the *Bänkelsang* and the *Moritat*. To these critics the degeneration of the 'classical' *Kunstballade* shows itself in a variety of signs and symptoms. Riha, for example, finds that the *Kunstballade* 'sich im Lauf ihrer Entwicklung immer mehr ins Pathetische, ins Gehoben-Feierliche stilisiert und auf geschichtliche Inhalte und altertümelnde Techniken festgelegt hatte'.[1] And he sees further evidence of the literary ballad's decline, evidence more fundamental than either the remoteness of its subject-matter from the realities of life or the increasing stylisation of its presentation, in the growing emphasis of its narrative at the expense of its lyric and dramatic values. In fact Riha largely attributes the decay of the conservative *Kunstballade* to the gradual devaluation of the old Goethean conception of the 'Ur-Ei'; he deplores the nineteenth-century developments which have led to the disturbance of the traditional equilibrium of the genre and points to its 'Episierung', to the consequent loss of 'innere Spannkraft' suffered by its lyric and dramatic elements and to their survival only in external features of form and style.[2]

Not surprisingly, the heroic historical ballad is the type most often singled out as exemplifying, in such respects, the degeneration of the genre and it is understandable that Börries von Münchhausen, the champion of this form at the turn of the century, should be recurrently represented as its most reactionary exponent. Riha voices a widely-held view when he applies to Münchhausen the epithet 'epigonal'. He applies it also, however, to Lulu von Strauß und Torney and, with even less obvious reason, to Agnes Miegel, attributing to them, as to Münchhausen, the 'antiquierte Balladendichtung' which he finds so regrettable.[3] Not that he is the only critic to have reservations about Miegel's contribution to the history of the literary ballad. Walter Hinck, too, insists that she clings with Münchhausen to the traditional ballad taboos of the nineteenth century, but he differentiates tentatively between the two poets to Miegel's advantage: her ballads, he finds, show a commendable lack of the mannerisms which embellish Münchhausen's work and he acknowledges: 'Gewiß . . . hat die Dichterin die Ausdrucksmöglichkeiten überlieferter Balladenkunst erweitert.'[4] Kurt Bräutigam goes so far as to admit her originality, but he recognises it in a somewhat restricted aspect of her work, namely her exploitation of mythical and supernatural rather than heroic historical subject-matter.[5] Hans Fromm, on the other hand, is positively, though superficially, aware of Miegel's achievement—she represents for him 'den bisherigen Höhepunkt unseres Jahrhunderts'.[6]

Even among the modern ballad-scholars, then, while there is no unanimity in condemning Agnes Miegel unreservedly as 'epigonal', there is little certainty as to the extent and nature of her originality. In view of such critical vagueness it is a profitable exercise to examine one of her poems which might be expected to show recognisable symptoms of degeneracy. *Maria Stuart* suggests itself: it makes no claim to individuality on the grounds of its subject-matter, since it is uncompromisingly historical in content; and it dates, together with Agnes Miegel's other 'English' ballads *Anna Bullen, Graf Bothwell* and *Junge Mary,* from her earliest collection, being published in 1901, at a time when she had already been brought to public notice by Münchhausen's *Göttinger Almanach* and so stood clearly within his sphere of influence.

At first sight, the poem appears to confirm Riha's unfavourable judgment. Here is sixteenth-century regal subject-matter, remote from the actuality of 1901; here too are the familiar features of ballad style and form—archaisms of vocabulary and syntax, conventional epithets, incremental arrangement, parallelism, abrupt dialogue, metrical patterns and verbal echoes—such as have been cultivated by innumerable ballad-writers since Bürger. Here, one might well think, are the stereotyped content and outworn techniques of presentation which to Riha would indicate exhausted inspiration and insincerity :

MARIA STUART

I

Das war ein lustiges Leben
Im Königsschloß der Touraine,
Auf weißen Marmorstufen
Ein ewiges Kommen und Gehn.

Im Park bei den Platanen
Ging lachend die Dauphine,
Alle Vögel sangen lauter,
Wo die schöne Marie erschien.

Ihre jungen vier Marien
Gingen der Fürstin zur Seit,
Sie trugen die Purpurschleppe
An ihrem Sammetkleid.

Sie hatten so weiße Hände,
So schmale, die vier Marien,
Doch weißer waren und schmäler
Die Hände der Dauphine.

Es lachten die vier Marien
Hell in den Frühlingswind,
Heller lachte und süßer
Schottlands Königskind.

Die Lippen der vier Marien
Waren zum Küssen gut,
Der Stuart stolze Lippen
Brannten so rot wie Blut.

Die Büsche und die Bäume
Im Schloßpark der Touraine
Gedenken jener Tage,
Wenn die Frühlingswinde wehn.

Die Marmorfliesen sprechen,
Wenn die Wolken vorüberfliehn :
'Hier wiegte sich einst im Tanze
Der schmale Fuß der Dauphine.'

2

Lady Stuart, es geht in den bitteren Tod,
Mylady, was brennt euer Mund so rot?

"Wohl seh ich den schwarz verhangenen Saal,
Meine Stirn und Wangen sind weiß und fahl,

Doch mein Mund glüht rot, wie zu jener Zeit,
Da ich den schönen Bothwell gefreit.

Noch einmal an meines Lebens Rand
Wie von heimlichen Küssen bebt meine Hand.

Im Ohre liegt mir der Laute Schlag,
Die Rizzio spielte vor manchem Tag.

Ich weiß, daß der Herr meine Sünden vergibt,
Denn ich liebte, wie nur eine Stuart liebt!"

And yet a second glance at this early example suggests that Agnes Miegel's ballad-writing involves a more subtle process than the mere reproduction or, worse, caricature, of certain distinctive features and that she does not conform in blind obedience to the canons of her nineteenth-century predecessors. If, for example, she handles the familiar devices of ballad style and form, she does so with a light touch—she indulges only once in a dramatic question: 'Mylady, was brennt euer Mund so rot?', only twice does she use a formalised or alliterative phrase: 'Kommen und Gehn', 'Die Büsche und die Bäume', and the incremental pattern which she establishes in stanzas 4, 5 and 6 is flexible enough to admit of variation. It is evident that, far from parodying the features of the traditional genre, she employs them with restraint to evoke impressionistically the age-old ballad atmosphere.

Agnes Miegel's independent attitude to the *Kunstballade* is demonstrated more significantly, however, by the narrative aspect of *Maria Stuart* in general. As far as its actual content is concerned, this poem is completely lacking in event or action. And yet, paradoxically, the final impression which, like all good ballads, it leaves in the mind is that it 'tells a story'. Of course it is obvious even visually that this 'story' is not presented in orthodox fashion, as a straightforward, consequent and explicit narrative, but that it is divided into two apparently self-contained structural parts. The first is concerned with Mary in Touraine, young, gay, beautiful, in her role of Dauphine and in her setting of royal palace and park, the central figure in her group of Maries, supreme among them in rank and in quality; the second shows her facing death at the scaffold, in an attitude of reflection and tragic self-appraisal. Clearly, Agnes Miegel does not give a complete and ordered account of Mary's fortunes but rather illuminates two distinct settings and moments, first presenting a picture of Mary in her youth and beauty and then juxtaposing it structurally against a second picture of her older tragic self. This is in fact a poem in which the material is selected and arranged in the analytical terms of drama rather than in discursive epic development: the two sections approximate in miniature to Acts I and V of a hypothetical drama on the life and death of Mary Stuart and the intervening acts are suggested by allusions to the familiar historical background, as for instance the references to Rizzio and Bothwell. The fragmentary nature of this ballad-tragedy both intensifies its narrative effect and increases its poignancy; the transition from France to Fotheringhay, youth to middle-age, promise to its ironic fulfilment, life to death is the more vividly conveyed, and the more bitter, for its lack of intermediate stages.

If the narrative content of *Maria Stuart* is not explicitly stated, it is thus implicit in the dramatic contrast of its structure and this contrast is heightened by comparable contrasts at other levels. Stanzas 4, 5 and 6 are themselves based on a repetitive structure of contrast, the four Maries and Mary Stuart being differentiated in terms of parallel verbal comparison—hands that are 'weiß' and 'schmal' contrasting with those that are 'weißer' and 'schmäler', a laugh that is 'hell' with one that is 'heller', lips 'zum Küssen gut' with those 'so rot wie Blut'. Moreover, Part I as a whole is descriptive and contemplative in character, while Part II is presented contrastingly in the form of a dramatic dialogue. And, in consequence, the material is exposed implicitly by two forms of lyric 'Ich' and from two dramatically contrasting angles. *Maria Stuart* is not presented personally by Agnes Miegel, nor is it a simple *Rollengedicht*; Part I is seen from the point of view of an anonymous, impersonal and omniscient observer and Part II from the position of the dramatic characters involved, Mary herself and a nameless servant-confidant (indeed the servant's more detached viewpoint seems to be given precedence since, while Mary's words are enclosed in inverted commas, his are not). The two structural sections with their distinct modes of presentation are further emphasised in their contrast by the change of rhythm and metre which accompanies them, the cheerful, triple-stressed, rhyming quatrains of the first part, with their traditional effect, giving way in the second to the longer sadder line and the intimate tone of the dialogue couplets. In addition, the stylisation of the vocabulary of Part I contrasts with the precision of epithet and verb in Part II. And it is not without significance that the abrupt, fragmentary, dramatic contrasts which thus convey objectively, by implication and suggestion, so much of Mary's life-story represent a method of narration akin to the 'Sprunghaftigkeit' of the folk-ballad and recall by their very function the techniques of oral transmission.

The narrative background of Mary Stuart's life which shines in this way through a pattern of structural contrasts is further revealed and clarified by Agnes Miegel's use of tenses. Here again contrast serves to express the essence of the content. Within Part I, for example, by the change of tense from the past to the present, Miegel discloses that, since the moment of gaiety and promise recorded early in the poem, time has passed. The spring of the opening suddenly appears in the conclusion of the section to be a past, lost moment, remembered from a present spring-time. The effect of this contrast of tenses, a contrast accentuated paradoxically by the verbal echo which accompanies it, as well as by the coincidence of seasons, is to introduce into the initially happy atmosphere of the ballad a note of doubt, unease and melancholy: what seems at the outset to be a promising and tranquil situation is, it is subsequently hinted, the prelude to tragedy. Moreover, to be aware of this change of tense is to recognise that the first section of the ballad is concerned not with the actuality of past events but with their recollection and that the nature of its content is neither explicitly narrative nor yet directly descriptive of historical happenings but meditative, reminiscent, imaginative and therefore lyrical.

The tense of Part II has additional implications for the content of the whole. Situated in the present time of dramatic dialogue, this section purports to express immediate reality. It is worth noting that, while in Part I Agnes Miegel acknowledges the fantasy of attributing words to 'Marmorfliesen' by enclosing them in single inverted commas, she uses double quotation marks to indicate Mary's 'actual' speech. Despite its present tenses this section is, however, not concerned with the present moment of the dialogue; its interest is directed, rather, forward in time in anticipation of Mary's death and backwards, in remembrance of her life and the lives of her Stuart forebears. And the present tense of Part II is already ambiguous since, being historical and familiar in content, the whole section falls automatically into the context of past reality. If only for this reason, the lyric present of Part I can scarcely be understood as contemporaneous with the dramatic present of Part II. Even if one should conceivably identify the reminiscent observer of Part I with one of the four Maries and, further, with the servant of Part II, one finds no evident chronological link between the two sections. Three isolated stages of narrative development seem to be implicit in the pattern of the tenses—the period in Touraine, the subsequent moment of its recall, the actuality of tragedy which is also related by allusion to the 'future' following upon it and to a sequence of intervening past events. All three stages are, however, disconnected from each other, the first and last being, for different reasons, distanced in time. There is only one genuine present moment of lyric reality in the poem—the meditation of stanzas 7 and 8. Seen from this point of view the section of 'actual' dramatic dialogue appears as the imaginative re-enactment of a historical moment, as a hypothetical conversation touching, on the one hand, the future of life after death and, on the other, memories of the past. As such it fulfils a lyric purpose.

In this way the interrelationship of the tenses both enhances the ballad's narrative effect and illuminates its wholly lyrical conception. And the tenses in their fluidity serve also to convey the significance of its content. The external structural pattern, with its dramatic juxtapositions of scene and moment, with its changing rhythm and its contrast of description and dialogue, would seem initially to reflect, as the main aspect of Mary's life, the abrupt reversal of human fortunes and the sudden destruction of happiness. The shifting chronology, however, together with the changing viewpoint, suggests rather the gradual transitions, overlaps, developments and progressions in human life. The last two lines of the poem, with their complex of tenses—'weiß', present; 'vergibt', present with future implications; 'liebte', past; 'liebt', timeless present with past connotations, and all past in the context of history—themselves embody the interaction of past, present and future. This conception is implicit in the unifying interplay not only of the tenses, but also of memory, fantasy, actuality and history, of imagination and reality. And it is expressed in explicit form too: a clear pointer to the inner continuity of Mary's life story is to be seen in the motif of her burning red lips, a motif which occurs in both parts of the ballad. With this symbol of love Agnes Miegel binds the two structural sections together—in Part I the descriptive phrase 'so rot wie Blut' contains the motivation of Part II—and, in so doing, indicates the consistency and the quality of Mary's life.

It is evident from such observations that this ballad is not a narrative restatement of historical events, but is more a philosophical comment on a recorded life and a celebrated human frailty. Far from presenting merely the facts of history, Agnes Miegel contemplates against their background the intangible values of youth, love, life and death. And moreover she contemplates these values in a characteristic way. If only with the forceful 'Doch' of Part II:

> "Wohl seh ich den schwarz verhangenen Saal,
> Meine Stirn und Wangen sind weiß und fahl,
>
> Doch mein Mund glüht rot, wie zu jener Zeit,
> Da ich den schönen Bothwell gefreit"

she points, as she does in so many of her works, to the distinction between 'Sein' and 'Schein'. Just as Schiller allows his individual philosophical thought to shine through the historical content of his drama of Mary Stuart, so in Miegel's ballad—despite the objectivity of its presentation—events are endowed with spiritual significance personal to her. Indeed:

> Ich bin viel
> Gehasset worden, doch auch viel geliebt!

might be said also by Miegel's Mary in positive vindication of her tragic life of love.

Clearly, the emphasis of this ballad is lyrical rather than narrative. In it subjective content is given appropriate form, for Agnes Miegel communicates her own view of Mary Stuart using the oblique, introspective terms of description, remembrance and imagination which one associates with lyric expression. Indirect allusion, symbolism and suggestion by structure and syntax are the vehicles which she employs both to convey the sequence of events leading to Mary's death and to express her own belief in the real value of a life destroyed by love. But of course to dismiss *Maria Stuart* simply as a meditation on a familiar historical story or as a subjective poem with narrative overtones is to ignore its third dimension, the strikingly dramatic and objective aspect of its presentation.

If, then, one recalls Karl Riha's criticism of the nineteenth-century *Kunstballade* in its degeneracy, one discovers that this criticism simply does not apply to *Maria Stuart*. Its subject may be historical, but it is not remote in significance from modern issues; it does not ally itself to the hackneyed chivalrous traditions of the literary ballad; nor does it display the familiar clichés of ballad character and action. On the contrary, in it Agnes Miegel seeks, with the sincerity of personal conviction, to expose the timeless human, psychological and spiritual values latent in her subject; in so doing she endows her ballad of Mary Stuart with a layer of philosophical significance comparable to that which enriches such celebrated examples of the genre as *Der König in Thule* or *Die Vergeltung*. And surely no one can condemn as 'pathetisch' any ballad in which subjective preoccupation is presented with dramatic objectivity and in which tragedy is expressed with the matter-of-fact simplicity and the calm confidence of *Maria Stuart*'s closing lines:

> "Ich weiß, daß der Herr meine Sünden vergibt,
> Denn ich liebte, wie nur eine Stuart liebt!"

Nor indeed can Agnes Miegel's ballad-manner be denounced as 'gehoben-feierlich' when she so scrupulously avoids tasteless extravagance in her use of conventional stylistic and formal devices. And, while it is true that her ballad displays the 'Sprunghaftigkeit' of ancient tradition, this technique cannot be described, derogatorily, as 'altertümelnd' since its characteristic effect is produced by original structural arrangement and not by the mechanical imitation of outworn external formulae. But least of all can this poem be thought to demonstrate any degenerative tendency towards 'Episierung'. It is unmistakably composed of that blend of epic, lyric and dramatic elements which is the essential characteristic of true ballad-poetry as symbolised by the 'Ur-Ei'. And this blend does not reveal itself only in such surface features as dialogue and rhythm. There can be no lack of lyric or dramatic dynamism—or 'innere Spannkraft', in Riha's phrase—in a ballad whose narrative effect is actually created by lyric and dramatic means. Admittedly Agnes Miegel does not blend the three basic elements in the traditional proportions, but she clearly does not allow the epic ingredient to outweigh the others. On the contrary, although lacking in musical lyricism, in 'Liedhaftigkeit', *Maria Stuart* with its philosophical content and its allusive presentation appears as a modern, but no less convincing example of that elusive literary form, the lyrical ballad.

Surely, then, Agnes Miegel's little-known and early poem of Mary Stuart indicates even more effectively than do the famous and more obviously original *Schöne Agnete* and *Die Mär vom Ritter Manuel* that she may be freed, as a ballad-writer, from the suspicion of 'Epigonentum'. *Maria Stuart* may be conservative in comparison with Brecht's ballads; it may not be derived, refreshingly, from *Bänkelsang* or *Moritat*; but it can scarcely be called decadent. Agnes Miegel's fidelity, as *Maria Stuart* demonstrates, is not to the established or degenerate traditions of the *Kunstballade* but directly to the ancient form of the *Volksballade* itself. Her achievement is to have revalued its qualities and characteristics in such a way that they have fresh significance and genuine appeal for her sophisticated and introspective contemporaries of the twentieth century. It is by reason of her profound understanding of the folk-ballad's qualities, her mastery of its techniques and her lively re-creation of its effects in the modern and personal terms of allusive lyricism that she must undoubtedly be allowed to stand as an original contributor to the genre of the literary ballad at the time of its disrepute.

NOTES

1. *Moritat. Song. Bänkelsang. Zur Geschichte der Modernen Ballade*, Göttingen, 1965, p. 8.
2. Ibid., pp. 12–14.
3. Ibid., pp. 7, 11.
4. *Die deutsche Ballade von Bürger bis Brecht. Kritik und Versuch einer Neuorientierung*, Göttingen, 1968, p. 110.
5. *Moderne deutsche Balladen ('Erzählgedichte'). Versuche zu ihrer Deutung*, Frankfurt a.M., 1968, p. 7.
6. Über Geschichte und Wesen der deutschen Ballade' in: H. Fromm (ed.), *Deutsche Balladen*, Munich, 1961, p. 441.

6

THE 'TWENTIES AND BERLIN

By Alex Natan

To write about the 'twenties in Berlin serves as a reminder that Berlin was then not only the capital of Germany but also the centre of Germany's cultural life. First nights in theatres and cinemas, outstanding art exhibitions, daring opera premières and concerts with ultra-modern programmes, architectural experiments, were initiated in Berlin, and were later repeated, modified, or transformed in the provinces. This fact is of crucial importance to an understanding of Berlin in the 'twenties and an appreciation of the parochial character of the cultural life in the Federal Republic deprived of the focal point that once was Berlin.

The 'twenties in Berlin did not start on the first day of the decade nor did they end with its last day. They blossomed for a far shorter period, perhaps from the autumn of 1923 onwards, when inflation reached its end, to a hot summer night in August 1928. These few years, now so sentimentally steeped in a rosy afterglow, were rightly described as 'the time between two twilights', between the collapse of Imperial Germany and the suicide of the Weimar Republic. But why try to resuscitate what by rights ought to be dead but still lives on as the 'Golden 'twenties'?

When, in Spring 1968, at the end of the impressive production of Seneca's *Oedipus* in London's National Theatre a tremendous phallus was carried on to the stage and the Bacchantes began their dance in honour of the God of Thebes who had cleansed their town from archetypal sin, the music accompanied this ritual with a popular hit-song of the 'twenties: 'Yes, We Have No Bananas.' At this moment a friend of mine whispered to me: 'Isn't it breath-taking? To you it must be like an emotive revival of Berlin in the 'twenties . . .'

Most of the documentary evidence about the 'twenties in Berlin are records written by those who had then lived in the metropolis and had been personally involved in its important events. It is therefore necessary to understand that these diaries and notes are identical with a personal recollection or confession. However, one should be on one's guard when discussing the literary and artistic aspects of this period with young people today who seem to be dazzled by their image of what Berlin once represented. To a rather vociferous section of the contemporary intellectual world Berlin seems to have been turned into a myth, to have emerged as a fabulous city of sheer make-believe anticipating a permissive society to a degree which even London has failed to achieve.

In probing deeper into this myth of a city which hardly any of its present admirers had actually known forty or fifty years ago, one often finds that admiration stems from Christopher Isherwood's brilliant novels of Berlin. *Mr. Norris changes trains* (1935) and *Goodbye to Berlin* (1939) display a most engaging but hardly impartial or analytical panorama of the alleged corruption of Berlin and of the insecure moral position of the bourgeois intellectuals. I am the last to deny that both novels offer a suggestive and often compassionate guide to the more lurid aspects of metropolitan nightlife and its dubious denizens. However, one should not overlook the fact that Isherwood actually arrived in Berlin in 1932, when the 'twenties were over and Hitler's lust for power already cast deep shadows over things to come. Isherwood only knew Berlin at the height of the political and economic crisis. What he reports about the 'twenties stems from hearsay.

I have already touched upon the misleading fact that the 'Golden 'twenties' hardly filled the decade but can easily be encompassed between the end of the inflation in the autumn of 1923 and the climactic last day of August 1928, when Bert Brecht's *Dreigroschenoper* with music by Kurt Weill was staged for the first time. I attended this première, which became one of the most meaningful experiences of my life. In the theatre Berlin's sophisticated bourgeoisie, pampered and complacent during those five 'fat' years following the revolution that never took place applauded not only a biting satire of its own brittle existence but also—if unwittingly—the menacing approach of a political extremism which was to turn its superficial security into perilous quicksand. Shortly after the Brecht first night came bank crashes, economic depression, ever-increasing unemployment, and ultimately the short-lived triumph of those reactionary forces which had retained their influence from that decisive milestone in November 1918 when the German Social Democrats committed the act of historical treason by strangulating the incipient social revolt through their pact with those powers which had only the day before been the stalwart pillar of throne and altar.

Fifty years of counter-revolution have passed. A real revolution never took place in Germany. Only the army and the navy went on strike. No great landowner was dispossessed, no factory was ever nationalised and in no industrial enterprise were the workers allowed a right of co-management. And which revolution would have ever been so magnanimous as the November revolution in Germany which granted full freedom of the press to its arch-enemies? Only very few revolutionary minds, dreaming of an age for a new man, the coming of which had been proclaimed by the Expressionists, intended a genuine reconstruction of the social fabric. They could not tolerate the thought that nothing would be altered and everything revert to the shallowest materialism after a war which had destroyed the happiness of millions of people. The kings had indeed departed but the generals remained. They were taken on the pay-roll of the Social-Democrats. Their 'Freicorps' drenched Germany in blood and trampled the 'Neue Zeit' of which the young generation sang into the mud and mire with their jackboots. All this happened primarily in Berlin. It is all too easy to forget that Berlin's 'twenties began with disappointed hopes, with blood and tears, with political and social disenchantment. The dreams of a new and possibly egalitarian society and the faith in a new man had been nipped in the bud violently and decisively. Yet the glamorous attraction of Berlin in the 'twenties still continues to fascinate a generation born after the Second World War. We who were then young and very much alive can only shrug our shoulders and quote François Villon: 'Où sont les neiges d'antan?'.

One of the fundamental misconceptions of the Berlin myth is that this short period had indeed given birth to all those movements in the arts and sciences which are all too readily associated with Berlin in the 'twenties. Talking to young people of today one is taken aback to hear them telescoping Expressionism in literature and painting, the science of psychoanalysis, the science of the psychology of the subconscious, the adventures in architecture, music and the applied arts, the provocative trends in philosophy and sociology, as if all had occurred almost simultaneously in Berlin.

In fact, a glittering kaleidoscope of talents and creative forces was concentrated in and around Berlin and provided the source for the legend of the 'twenties. Four years of the carnage of war had severely inhibited these talents. When the war ended, the flood-gates opened and the creative forces gushed forth, uninhibited everywhere, not only in Berlin, not only in imitative Germany, but all over Europe. They exercised a tremendous impact on the cultural revolution of the Western world. For man neither remained the measure of all things nor the centre of the world. The epoch of the Renaissance was finally over. The 'twenties signified, however, the end and a new beginning of what Robert Musil described as 'the disintegration of anthropocentric behaviour'. Berlin offered a particularly good vantage point for observing this transformation.

For this cultural revolution was to be witnessed everywhere: in the Cubist paintings of Picasso, Braque and Gris, in the abstract compositions of Archipenko and Kandinsky, in the Futurist theories of Marinetti, in the Surrealism of Aragon, Breton and Elouard. Dadaism was born and propagated in the Cabaret Voltaire in Zürich. Stravinsky and Schönberg had already shocked the concert-going public before the war. Most of the poets and writers who came into their own during the 'twenties had already made their mark before the outbreak of the war. All these trends could be observed in Paris as well as in New York, even in staid London and in frivolous Vienna, simply because all these new ideas and new impulses no longer remained the privilege of a small minority but became the property of a changing society, of what the German sociologist Max Weber called 'Massendemokratie'.

Berlin stood at the receiving end of this cultural turbulence but it was not its creative birthplace. Admittedly Berlin's theatre and cinema productions had achieved a remarkably high standard. But a closer scrutiny will readily reveal that Berlin's famous first nights belonged to the period before rather than after 1923. It is too easily forgotten, for instance, that the explosion of Expressionist drama had already spent its main force when the 'twenties dawned. Wedekind had died in 1918 and the plays of his last years had proved second-rate. Sternheim, the caustic satirist, wrote his cycle of mordant comedies against middle-class morality all before 1914. From this time dated also the anti-war poems of Werfel, Stadler and Heym. The significant reviews and periodicals of Expressionism, such as *Die Aktion*, *Der Sturm* and *Die weißen Blätter* all flourished in the pre-war years. The younger generation of Expressionists, such as Barlach, Kornfeld, Hasenclever, Bronnen, Unruh, Goering and Sorge had also written their dramatic manifestos before and during the war. Even Toller's famous *Die Wandlung* was finished in 1917. What all Expressionist writers had in common was a determination to kindle a new outlook on life in the midst of a solid world of bourgeois prejudice. Hence the Imperial censorship was determined not to give them a public hearing. But a way was discovered to circumvent the censor. Matinées to which only club members were admitted were formed and already produced daring novelties during the war. When the censor disappeared in 1918 a flood of new plays and new productions could be seen all over the country, foremost in Berlin. It was the time when inventive producers like Jessner, Fehling, K. H. Martin and Piscator dominated the Berlin stage and made it a focus of new experiments in style and interpretation. It was equally significant that the great magician Max Reinhardt chose just this moment to exchange the turbulent waters of Berlin for the safer pastures of Vienna because the foundations of the German bourgeoisie seemed to be dangerously underminded, at least for the time being. In short, what was exciting in the Berlin theatre took place mainly between 1918 and 1920. When conservative forces were back in the saddle, Jessner, the director of the State Theatre, was criticised and censured in the Prussian parliament, and Schnitzler's charming dialogue *Der Reigen* prosecuted because it allegedly undermined morale and public order. The great experimental phase of Berlin's stage petered out with the end of inflation when the forces of yesterday relentlessly returned to power.

The same phenomenon can be observed in the development of Expressionist art. The 'Blaue Reiter' group lasted for only three years (1911–14). Afterwards Klee returned to his native Switzerland. So did Kirchner. Macke and Marc were killed during the war and the sculptor Lehmbruck died soon after in 1919. Since the arts had ceased to be the privilege of those who used to be their patrons their works could now be exhibited to a greater public.

And yet Berlin possessed some justification to be proud of its position as a leading avant-gardist centre between 1923 and

1928. It was then that a new style was developed which became significant for the whole period and which really put its stamp on the Berlin of the 'twenties. This was 'Neue Sachlichkeit', an attitude of mind which recognised the supremacy of material facts and worshipped materialism as an ideology. It produced the 'Zeitstück', a kind of dramatic documentation which regained popularity in the German drama of recent years (viz. Dorst's *Toller*). These plays dealt with contemporary issues, seen in retrospect and reflecting very sharply the social and spiritual currents and problems of recent and present German history. One remembers those 'Zeitstücke' which came to grips with the moral and spiritual difficulties of German adolescence, such as Klaus Mann's *Anja und Esther*, Peter Martin Lampel's *Revolte im Erziehungshaus*, Christa Winsloe's *Mädchen in Uniform* and Ferdinand Bruckner's great success *Krankheit der Jugend.* Theodor Plivier and Friedrich Wolff dramatised contemporary political events and presented them in Berlin, thus provoking much discussion and partisanship. But what used to set Berlin on fire is now completely forgotten because all these dramatic efforts were time-bound and did not possess what the Germans so admire, namely, 'Ewigkeitswert'. And then Bert Brecht, who made Germany's outstanding contribution to the post-war European theatre, appeared. Although a native of the Bavarian provinces he spent his formative years in the capital. It is hardly an exaggeration to say that Berlin made Brecht. The proposition has been advanced that the five 'fat' years of Berlin culminated with the first night of Brecht's *Dreigroschenoper*, whose philosophy is expressed by Brecht's famous dictum: 'The world is poor; man is evil', a telling obituary of the 'twenties. Brecht reversed the basic creed of Expressionism that 'man is good'. In him social cynicism identifies itself with a revolutionary challenge, directed at the 'rich' and demanding social upheaval: 'Erst kommt das Fressen, dann kommt die Moral'. First the poor, too, must be allowed to cut themselves their share from the large loaf. During that August evening in 1928 the bourgeois audience relished the antics of Macheath and his gang of cut-throats. Brecht intended them 'to represent bourgeois types, and their exploits to reflect bourgeois morality' (H. F. Garten). The poet wrote: 'The robber Macheath must be represented by the actor as a bourgeois character. The partiality of the bourgeoisie for robbers can be explained from the fallacy that a robber is not a bourgeois. This fallacy derives from another fallacy: a bourgeois is not a robber.' Berlin had not long to wait to discover the correctness of Brecht's forecast: there was no difference between bourgeois and robber, for both became ardent Nazis.

This vogue of 'Neue Sachlichkeit' manifested itself also in the visual arts. Georg Grosz, stimulated by the Dadaist technique of photo-montage, became the outstanding representative of the trend to express a grim realism in his paintings by choosing the terrible and repulsive side of war as the main theme of his work. He became the centre of a significant controversy when a reactionary judge sent him to prison for having depicted Christ on the cross with a gas-mask in his famous 'Ecce Homo'. Those in power allowed those out of power a certain amount of leeway in Berlin. However, as soon as a member of the cultural minority dared to criticise the hollow mentality of the ruling class it clamped down on him ruthlessly. And indeed, George Grosz, tried mercilessly to caricature and thus to dissect the real 'Gesicht der herrschenden Klasse' ('face of the ruling class'). In vain—he realised the truth behind the deceptive veneer of the Weimar Republic and left for the United States before the 'twenties were ended.

It has been said that Berlin was less a centre of productive and creative forces than a successful catalyst for the dissemination of new values, new ideas, new forms and shapes in the usual arts, music and so on, and there was evidence enough for such a belief. Berlin could boast three opera houses and an annual concert programme which was certainly the envy of other European capitals. At the beginning of the 'twenties the repertoire of the opera houses was still traditional: Richard Wagner, Richard Strauss, plenty of 'verismo', interspersed with the minor figures of German romanticism. Like lightning Igor Stravinsky's *Soldier's tale*, produced for the first time at the end of the war in Lausanne, heralded a new era which reached its climax with Arnold Schönberg and his dodecatonal system. Schönberg's experiments encouraged Alban Berg to compose his Büchner opera *Wozzeck* whose production under Erich Kleiber on 14 December 1925 proved probably the highlight of the feverish musical life of Berlin which also welcomed annually conductors like Bruno Walter, Toscanini, Stokowski, R. Strauss, Furtwängler, Fritz Busch, Klemperer, Mengelberg and many others.

Berlin was also the centre of Germany's budding film industry.

Siegfried Krakauer in his fascinating book *From Caligari to Hitler* has drawn attention to a sinister pattern which he finds in all German films of importance. As a reflection of the miscarried attempt of a revolution such films as *Dr. Caligari*, *Der müde Tod*, or *Dr. Mabuse* portrayed the individual soul faced with the unavoidable alternative of tyranny and chaos. *Die Nibelungen*, shot in 1922, already stressed the inexorability of fate and destiny, patterns which were resumed in the film pageantry of the Nazis. The great days of the German experimental film, usually shot in the suburb of Babelsberg, were significantly over, when the five 'fat' years set in and produced films which were primarily aimed at the entertainment of the bourgeoisie.

All these new trends, of which only very few actually originated in Berlin itself, polarised, nevertheless, in the capital of the Weimar Republic. The town acquired the reputation of a focal spectrum which knew how to attract the most divergent forces and, in return, granted them unlimited scope to play out their dynamism. Yet there were millions of people who still went regularly to church, who read Agnes Günther or Vicki Baum, if not Stefan George and the new heralds of the post-war youth movements. Many, many people longed for the 'Golden Age' of Wilhelminian vainglory or helped to get the new craze for sport started. They all remained totally immune to the glittering panorama Berlin's West End had to offer or were determined to bring it to an abrupt and even bloody end. Yet the question remains why the artistic and intellectual life represented such an exciting force for such a short time and that so many forces blazed the path into this new and uncharted world of 'Neue Sachlichkeit'. While Paris remained hide-bound to tradition and hampered by much plush and self-adulation Berlin enjoyed the advantage of not possessing any past. The town was singularly devoid of buildings of architectural interest, partly because Berlin became very late a capital, partly because the Hohenzollerns preferred Potsdam as their near-by residence.

Lacking tradition, which London, Rome or Vienna possessed Berlin found it easier to become the centre of forces which were hardly rooted on the banks of the Spree. Berlin was an ideal point of departure for the experiments of an avant-garde. They have now assumed the proportions of a nostalgic age for people who did not experience them. One should never forget that a social revolution did not take place in 1918. After some months of unrest the policeman was back in his place and guarded the bourgeois's peace, security and order. As long as these guardians of the state remained undisturbed the writer and the artist could spread their wings unclipped, certainly more undisturbed in Berlin than in the provinces. All that really happened in the 'twenties was that 'the more realistic saxophone replaced the coachman's romantic bugle'. Anyone who wishes to understand the brittleness and the hectic mostly self-deceptive fever of Berlin's 'twenties should read once more any of four books which all appeared significantly at the end of this period. Their authors had all welcomed the Expressionist dawn of an epoch which promised a new age of green pastures for a free man. They all had lost every ounce of their illusions by 1930. These are the books: Alfred Döblin's *Berlin Alexanderplatz*, Robert Musil's *The Man without Qualities*, Ortega y Gasset's *The Revolt of the Masses,* and Karl Jasper's *The Spiritual Situation of our Times.* All four books express the deep resignation of their writers. Hitler was already knocking at the gates!

Who thinks today of Berlin only as an exciting and sparkling dream, as a perpetual 'happening' of mental and physical high-powered 'trips' misses the under-current of the revolution that never was. Anyone who was born in Berlin and sang in 1918 'Mit uns zieht die neue Zeit' perceived the pulse-beat of the disillusions and frustrations of the restored 'good old days' underneath the glittering, alluring but so deceptive façade in the 'twenties. Nobody can deny that life then in Berlin was exciting and a breath-taking merry-go-round. But all who knew the ironical attitude of the Berliner towards the events of life, witnessed the interment of the man who once saw a vision of a new age which was now shattered by the harsh reality of the old establishment. Georg Kaiser's most telling drama is probably *From Morn to Midnight*. It is the story of a bank clerk who embezzles a large sum of money and strives, within the compass of a single day, to make up for a lifetime of frustration. Finally he is thoroughly disillusioned and shoots himself. Georg Kaiser's last stage direction which, to me, is synonymous with the real significance of Berlin in the 'twenties runs like this: 'His groaning rattles like an Ecce . . . his breathing hums like Homo.'

To have spent one's formative years in the Berlin of the 'twenties was certainly an education in itself which supplied unlimited stimulation for the rest of one's life. Until Hitler, the history of Berlin was the history of Germany; afterwards it became, for a time, the history of the world. It has always been the most un-German of Germany's cities, otherwise President Kennedy could never have said, 'I am a Berliner'. Imagine saying this of Bielefeld or Weilheim! The Berliner would be the first to draw a sharp dividing-line. For he, as a big-city character, is tough and cynical, and has always been somewhat unpopular with his own countryman. The satire and irony have set him aside from the rest of the Germans. How he copes with life and thus also digested the manifold attractions of the 'twenties is better told through a little anecdote. In 1848 a street urchin stops whistling as Field Marshal Wrangel approaches. 'Because of my uniform?' asks the flattered Wrangel. 'No,' shouts back the irreverent boy, 'when I see you I want to laugh, and when I laugh I can't whistle!'

7

A LETTER FROM BARLACH TO KOKOSCHKA

By L. Forster

On 12 June 1933 Ernst Barlach wrote round to a number of artists about a puzzling semi-political event in which he had involuntarily become involved. His letter to Oskar Kokoschka on this subject is in my possession. It runs as follows:

Güstrow i. Mecklbg.
Heidberg 12.6.33

Sehr geehrter Herr Kollege
Sie werden unter den Mitgliedern einer Ausstellungsgemeinschaft 'Ring deutscher Künstler' aufgeführt, deren Präsident ich werden soll. Motto: 'gegen französisches Ästhetentum—für bodenständige deutsche Kunst'. Auch ein 'Vorstand' wird genannt: Degner, Heckel, Marcks, Rohlfs, Otto Andreas Schreiber.
Ich weiß von der Sache seit gestern, soll mich möglichst bald entscheiden, weiß sonst von nichts, nichts davon wer den 'Vorstand' wählte, wer diese Mitglieder bestimmte. Die Anregung giebt der 'Nationalsozialistische deutsche Studentenbund Berlin'.
Ich bitte Sie dringend um ein Wort was Sie von der Sache wissen, setze voraus, daß Sie länger als ich im Bilde sind, nämlich 1 Tag.
Mit bestem Gruß
Ihr E Barlach

(Dear Colleague, You are listed among the members of an exhibition group, 'Ring of German Artists', of which I am to be the President. Motto: Against French aestheticism, for indigenous German art. And a 'committee' has been nominated too: Degner, Heckel, Marcks, Rohlfs, Otto Andreas Schreiber. I only heard about it yesterday and am expected to decide as soon as possible, otherwise I know nothing about it, nothing about who elected the committee, or who determined who these members should be. The impulse comes from the National Socialist German Students Association, Berlin. I most earnestly ask you to let me have a word about what you know of the matter; I assume that you have been in the picture longer than I, which is one day.)

On the same day he wrote a similar letter to Alfred Kubin, pub-

Güstrow i Mecklbg
Heidberg
12. 6. 33.

Sehr geehrter Herr Kollege,

Sie werden unter den Mitgliedern einer Ausstellungsgemeinschaft: „Bund deutscher Künstler“ aufgeführt, deren Präsident ich werden soll. Motto: „gegen französisches Ästhetentum – für bodenständige deutsche Kunst.“ Auch im „Vorstand“ wird genannt: [illegible], Heckel, Marcks, Rohlfs, Otto Andreas Schreiber.

Ich weiss von der Sache seit gestern, soll mich möglichst bald entscheiden, weiss sonst von nichts, nichts davon, wer den „Vorstand“ wählte, wer die Mitglieder bestimmte. Die Anregung gab der „Nationalsozialistische deutsche Studentenbund, Berlin.“

Ich bitte Sie dringend um ein Wort, was Sie von der Sache wissen, setze ~~voraus~~ [illegible], daß Sie ebenso wie ich im Bilde sind, [illegible] / [illegible].

Mit bestem Gruß
Ihr E Barlach

lished as no. 1049 of his collected letters,[1] in which many of the same phrases recur.

Barlach had been the object of intensive attack by the National Socialist Kampfbund für deutsche Kultur, led by Alfred Rosenberg, for some years before. The activities of this organisation were centred on Thuringia, and on 1 December 1930 Barlach had written to Richard Engelmann reporting the exclusion of his work from the Weimar Museum, together with that of Otto Dix and Kokoschka (letter no. 895); the phrase used to designate his work was 'minderrassiges Untermenschentum' (racially inferior subhumanity). This action did not stand alone; right-wing groups like the Stahlhelm had agitated against him long before the National Socialist seizure of power. The approach by a National Socialist organisation, nominating him president of an 'Ausstellungsgemeinschaft', must have bewildered him, especially as the Committee of this group was composed of people whose work he knew and respected and who were known to be no more in sympathy with the movement than he was himself.

I have been unable to establish the membership of the Ring deutscher Künstler, but two of the names we have, Kubin and Kokoschka, are in themselves significant.

There are no replies extant from either Kubin or Kokoschka to Barlach's enquiry; this is because Barlach in later years was careful to destroy all letters addressed to him in order not to compromise his correspondents in the event of his house being searched by the Gestapo.[2] He had expressed his admiration for the work of Kubin as early as 19 April 1921 in a letter to Reinhard Piper (no. 480): 'Ich schätze Kubin eigentlich immer höher, er geht unbeirrt und stetig seinen eigenen Weg und will eben nichts, als was er muß' (My opinion of Kubin grows steadily, he goes his own way undisturbed and consistently and simply wants to do what he has to do). This too was what he himself was doing and continued to do. Kubin has recorded that he did not know Barlach personally but admired his work (editor's note to letter no. 1049). There seems to be no recorded utterance by Barlach about Kokoschka, but the letter to him is rather less formal in tone than that to Kubin, and it is clear that the Kampfbund für deutsche Kultur regarded them both with equal disapproval. There was moreover another factor which united Kubin, Kokoschka and Barlach, quite apart from the political situation in which they found themselves. It was the circumstance that they were all three writers as well as artists, whose lack of sympathy with National Socialism emerges even more clearly from their writings than from their work in the plastic arts.

The background to the approach by the National-Sozialistischer Deutscher Studentenbund Berlin must have been largely hidden from Barlach in his country retreat in Güstrow. It has been illuminated by Hildegard Brenner and Robert A. Pois.[3] In 1933 the art policy of the National Socialist Party was not yet fixed. Alfred Rosenberg and his Kampfbund represented the right wing, but there was some opposition to their views within the party. Many sincere National Socialists saw ideals which they respected embodied more effectively in the work of German expressionist artists (e.g. Artur Degner, Erich Heckel, Gerhard Marcks and Christian Rohlfs) than in the sort of art praised by Rosenberg (e.g. Franz Stassen; cp. Barlach's letter to Professor Fritz Schumacher of 3 August 1936). What they sought were certain spiritual values which they felt to be peculiarly German, hence the motto 'gegen französisches Ästhetentum, für bodenständige deutsche Kunst'. This indigenous German art was to communicate the mysterious and the infinite, a certain 'Unendlichkeitsgefühl' which they felt for instance in the writings of Meister Eckhart (whom Rosenberg praised as a reincarnation of Odin) and which is undoubtedly present in the work of Barlach. 'Französisches Ästhetentum' for them meant 'l'art pour l'art', but they were also opposed to the new realism which Rosenberg favoured and which seemed to them to preach material rather than spiritual values. They might even have found ammunition in the writings of Rosenberg himself, for example 'Es gilt somit das tiefste Gesetz jeder echten Kultur zu erkennen: sie ist Bewußtseinsgestaltung des Vegetativ-Vitalen einer Rasse' (The important thing is to recognise the fundamental law of every true culture; it is the fashioning of the consciousness of the vegetative-vital component of a race.)[4] This may not now seem to mean very much, but in the language of the 1930's it could apply perfectly well to Expressionist art. The leader of this liberal wing in opposition to Rosenberg was Otto Andreas Schreiber, then aged twenty-six, a prominent figure of the National-Sozialistischer Deutscher Studentenbund Berlin which aimed at integrating the older Expressionists into the movement. Hence the plan to organise an exhibition.

The plan seems to have been very hastily conceived and carried out with a characteristically Nazi disregard for those concerned. Barlach seems not to have been consulted but simply nominated as President of the Ring deutscher Künstler; the other persons named seem either to have known as little about it as he did, or to have been alarmed by what they did know. Barlach evidently suspected that his name was being used for political purposes of which he understood little, and as the answers to his letters of enquiry came in he was confirmed in his suspicions. A fortnight later, on 26 June, he wrote a polite letter to an unidentified correspondent (no. 1051), declining to exhibit work as invited by the addressee and Otto Andreas Schreiber. Considerably earlier he had expressed his distrust of manifestoes and organisations in a letter to his cousin Karl on 30 September 1931 (no. 947):

> Bünde, Verbände, Gruppen, Orden, geraten furchtbar leicht unter Führung von Persönlichkeiten, deren furiöse Auslegung den Dingen, die man guthieß, ein Gesicht geben, das man nicht weidererkennt. Jede Woche kommen einige Aufforderungen von rechts oder links, mitzumachen, und ich tue es nie. Der bloße Unterschriftsleister gibt Vollmacht, und der Mann am Steuer legt ein 100 km-Tempo vor. Über das Genaue der Meinung gibts keine genaue Auskunft.
>
> (Societies, associations, groups, orders, get terribly easily under the control of people whose wild interpretations render the things that one had approved unrecognisable. I get invitations to participate every week from the right or the left and I never accept. The man who writes his signature gives authority, and the man at the wheel goes ahead at 60 mph. There is no means of finding out the [subscriber's] exact opinion.)

Less than two months later it was all over; the exhibition had taken place under the auspices of the art dealer and critic Ferdinand Möller (who had been the secretary of the Berliner Sezession) and it had been a political failure. Barlach wrote to the literary historian Artur Eloesser[5] on 8 August 1933 (no. 1063):

> Die Ausstellung der 30 deutschen Künstler bei Möller hat eine Vorgeschichte, man wollte mich als 'Präsidenten', nachdem ein Vorstand bereits vollzählig vorhanden war. Ich schrieb an einige der aufgezählten Genossen und konstatierte, daß sie zum Teil von dem ganzen Arrangement nichts wußten, teils schwere Bedenken hatten. Natürlich war ich von vornherein entschlossen, keinen Popanz abzugeben, weigerte mich auch, die Anstalt zu beschicken,

schließlich haben sie sich von Flechtheim zwei Bronzen geholt. Das Ganze war vom Bund national-sozialistischer Studenten unternommen. Immerhin muß ich zugeben, daß die Auswahl der Künstler nicht schlecht war.

(There is a prehistory to the exhibition of the 30 German artists at Möller's gallery: when a full committee was already in being I was approached to be 'president'. I wrote to some of the colleagues named and found that some of them knew nothing of the whole business, while others had serious objections. Of course I was determined from the start not to be an Aunt Sally, refused to send anything to the exhibition, finally they got two bronzes from Flechtheim. The whole thing was run by the Association of National Socialist Students. But I must confess that the choice of artists was not at all bad.)

The power struggle within the National Socialist Party was taking a different turn; neither Otto Andreas Schreiber's liberals nor Rosenberg's right-wingers, both of whom, in their different ways, were really concerned with art, were winning it; it was being won by Josef Goebbels, who assumed control of a much larger and more powerful machine than Rosenberg had at his disposal, namely the Ministry of Propaganda, which was not interested in art as art at all. It forced Rosenberg to toe the line and brought about the conversion of Otto Andreas Schreiber in 1935. It gradually isolated and then finally crushed Ernst Barlach and many like him, who could not or would not leave Germany. Kokoschka eventually found refuge in England.

NOTES

1. References throughout are to Ernst Barlach, *Die Briefe*, 2 vols., Munich 1969. The only important factual difference between the two letters is that Barlach mentions in the letter to Kubin that the committee consisted of twenty-five members. The names mentioned are the same, but the editors have misread Heckel as Jeckel.
2. Friedrich Dross in the introduction to *Ernst Barlach, Leben und Werk in seinen Briefen*, Munich 1952. p. 6.
3. Hildegard Brenner, 'Die Kunst im politischen Machtkampf 1933/34', *Vierteljahreshefte für Zeitgeschichte* X (1962); Robert A. Pois, 'German Expressionism in the Plastic Arts and Nazism: a Confrontation of Idealists', *German Life and Letters, New Series* XXI (1967–68). See also Paul Ortwin Rave, *Kunstdiktatur im 3. Reich*, Hamburg, 1949.
4. Alfred Rosenberg, *Der Mythos des 20. Jahrhunderts*, Munich, 1930, p. 140. For Rosenberg on Expressionism see p. 301.
5. Eloesser had praised Barlach's work in his *Die deutsche Literatur von der Romantik bis zur Gegenwart* (Berlin, 1931) pp. 603–4, where he wrote of *Der arme Vetter*: 'Es begegnet uns, auch ohne romantische

Leihgabe aus dem Symbolschatz des Märchens, als unser Widerspiel und zweites Gesicht, es bringt auch von der Rasse, der Erdhaftigkeit des Künstlers mit, ein besinnliches, eigensinniges Niederdeutschtum, obgleich seine Figuren hochdeutsch reden.' In other words he was praising Barlach for possessing just those qualities expected of National Socialist art! But his book, published by the Jewish firm of Bruno Cassirer, carried no weight in Party circles.

6. An art dealer who had taken 'about 20' of Barlach's bronzes in the autumn of 1930.

8

GERMAN MEN OF LETTERS

By B. E. Schatzky

'A title,' Lessing said roundly, 'is no bill of fare.' Schopenhauer, on the other hand, wrote:

> What the address is to a letter that should its title be to a book; its primary object should be to attract into it that section of the reading public which may find the contents interesting. Hence the title should be meaningful, concise, laconic, pregnant and, where possible, a monogram of the contents.

A tall order, indeed, and if we try to render the title of Schopenhauer's essay from which this quotation is taken—'Schriftstellerei und Stil'—'meaningfully' into English ('Style and the Profession of Letters'?), we can more than guess at the brainracking and heartsearching which must have gone into the choosing of a blanket title for Oswald Wolff's series *German Men of Letters*. To bring the poet(ess) Annette von Droste-Hülshoff at one end of the literary scale and the polymath Leibnitz (in a forthcoming volume) at the other under one common denominator, to accommodate within it such disparate writers as Herder, Morgenstern and Kokoschka, cannot have been easy.

In finally deciding upon *German Men of Letters* as the title, Oswald Wolff and his general editor, Alex Natan, may well have been guided by a precedent: a series of books about poets, playwrights and novelists, edited in England by J. C. Squire, which appeared after the end of World War I under the general title of *English Men of Letters*. The term has, to be sure, the advantage of unspecificness, of elasticity, and although, or rather because it has undergone subtle changes in connotation which are difficult to define, it tends to mean all things to all men. In his recently published book on this very subject, *The Rise and Fall of the Man of Letters*, John Gross writes:

> Originally the term denoted a scholar, then it gradually came to be applied to authors in general; in time, however, the man of letters came to denote a writer of the second rank, a critic, someone

> who aimed higher than journalism, but made no pretence of being primarily an artist.

Finally, Gross asserts, a note of pomposity or absurdity crept into the term : it deteriorated into 'a literary journalist, a commentator on other men's books'. Yet Oswald Wolff was in good company. As recently as 1942 T. S. Eliot took 'The Classics and the Man of Letters' as the title of a lecture and expressly included in the term 'the poet, the novelist, the dramatist or the critic'. Exactly a century earlier, in 1841, Thomas Carlyle had eulogised 'The Hero as Man of Letters' in his famous essay of the same name, claiming that he 'must be regarded as our most important modern person', 'a product of these new ages' :

> He is in various respects a very singular phenomenon . . . endeavouring to speak forth the inspiration that was in him by Printed Books and find place and subsistence by what the world would please to give him for doing that.

The German equivalent of the man of letters in the nineteenth century would appear to have been 'Gelehrter' (scholar) or 'Schriftsteller' (writer). Carlyle himself, in defining the man of letters, invokes Fichte's treatise *Über die Bestimmung des Gelehrten* (*On the Function of the Scholar*) in which the German philosopher speaks of him as Priest or Prophet. Schopenhauer, in the essay quoted at the beginning, defines 'Schriftsteller' as those who take their subject matter 'directly out of their own heads', combining 'inexorable integrity with unusual knowledge and even more unusual powers of judgment'—mostly professors and *literati*, but also imaginative writers : all, in fact, who have 'something to communicate'. There was, it seems, nothing paradoxical in the combination of scholarship or criticism and inspiration, the most striking proof being provided by Carlyle, who singled out Goethe as 'by far the notablest of all Literary Men', and put him on an equal pedestal with such poets and thinkers as Rousseau, Johnson and Burns. The great Olympian of Weimar would not have objected to the appellation, since he himself was wont to use the term 'Literator' in the best sense of the word; on one occasion, shortly before his death, he even envisaged a vast salon in which all the lively and striving *literati* of different tongues would feel the urge to 'act socially' ('gesellschaftlich zu wirken')—thereby giving to the word a social dimension which is of the greatest significance. For when Thomas Mann points to the preeminently metaphysical, introspective, and 'musical' characteristics of the German mind, it is worth remembering that it is precisely the opposite qualities of criticism and social concern in the widest sense for which the German man of letters *par excellence* used to be admired by fellow English writers. For Matthew Arnold, Goethe was the greatest writer of modern times,

> not because he is one of the half dozen of human beings who in the history of our race have shown the most signal gift for poetry, but because . . . he was at the same time, in the width, depth and richness of his criticism of life by far the greatest modern man.

Similarly, he spoke of Lessing and Herder as 'great men of culture who broadened the basis of life and intelligence'. Again, it was an Englishman, Bulwer Lord Lytton, author of *The Last Days of Pompeii,* who dedicated one of his lesser known works, *Ernest Maltravers* (1837), to the Germans as 'The nation of poets and critics'—an interesting variation on Mme. de Staël's more famous *aperçu* about the 'peuple des poètes et penseurs'. No wonder that these tributes to German Classicism found a ready echo in the hearts of the Germans themselves, who, by a happy stroke of alliteration, quickly made the 'Volk der Dichter und Denker' one of the *bons mots* of the language.

So far so good. If 'men of letters' could be equated with 'poets and thinkers' then, on the face of it, 'men of letters' quite simply corresponds almost exactly to 'Dichter und Denker'. But only on the face of it. What is relatively straightforward and innocuous in English, is in German ambiguous and problematic. The *bon mot* turns out to be a *mauvais mot,* flattery changes into self-irony. The medal pinned on the chest of the 'Volk der Dichter und Denker' has a reverse side : it was a consolation prize for being, in an era of revolution and political activity, nothing *more* than a people of thinkers and poets. ('Les Allemands s'ils ne savent pas jouer des grands instruments de la Liberté, savent jouer naturellement de tous les instruments de la musique'—Balzac.) Above all, there is irony in the little word 'and', since the bold coupling of poets and thinkers has in reality often implied a *separation* of the two—of poetry from thought, of 'creativity' from criticism, of 'dichten' from 'denken'.

From this fundamental dichotomy it is but a short step to an implicit overrating of the former function, and it is only natural that the Germans, as many of their dictionaries are proud to point out, should have a word for it. The sense of lofty flights of the imagination implicit in 'dichten' is subconsciously reinforced by the fact that, in general parlance, the word can mean 'to invent', 'to daydream' or 'indulge in fancies'. Goethe obviously had this at the back of his mind when he gave his autobiography the title *Dichtung und Wahrheit* ('Fiction and Truth'). At the same time it is close to words like 'verdichten' (condense, concentrate)—which is what Kafka reflects in his dictum: 'Dichtung ist Verdichtung, eine Essenz'.

Certainly, as already Carlyle pointed out, the Germans have a peculiar obsession with the concept:

> On this point many things have been written, especially by the German critics, some of which are not very intelligible at first. They say, for example, that the Poet has an *infinitude* in him.

The conception of the *Dichter* as a being apart, concerned with external values rather than 'mere' social problems—the 'All' rather than the 'Alltag'—a dreamer, a prophet, a 'Genie' (like 'Dichter', the latter has an almost mystical quality in German and, significantly, first entered the language in a literary context)—all this was of course primarily a speciality of German Romanticism. But there has never been a scarcity of German poets (notably lyric poets) to provide grist to the critics' *Dichtung* mill—from Hölderlin, whose exceptional poetic gifts coupled with his own idealisation of the 'still and mighty priesthood' earned him the title of 'Dichter der Dichter' (Heidegger), to the cult of the poet by the exclusive George circle in our own century. Modern critics, such as Gundolf or Staiger, have done much to boost the almost metaphysical *Eigengesetzlichkeit* (having its own inner laws) of 'Dichtung als Dichtung'. This in turn has given rise to a whole terminology of modern German literary criticism—viz. 'Erlebnisdichtung' (based on valid personal experience), 'reine Dichtung' (pure and uncontaminated by non-formal factors), 'Wortkunstwerk' (ditto) or 'Hochliteratur'. Not to mention, conversely, such pejorative terms as 'Trivialliteratur' or 'Gebrauchslyrik' ('utility poetry'). 'Literat', like men of letters', comes in this context to denote someone clever with the pen and writing primarily for money—viz. Hofmannsthal's famous 'philologischer Feuilletonist', or Thomas Mann's hybrid, neither *Dichter* nor *Bürger*.

Such attitudes die hard, and they have given rise to some distorted value judgments. A writer, however manifest his literary qualities, who does not fit the preconceived notion of a pure *Dichter,* has always tended to suffer a sad loss in status. As Robert Minder, a well-known French authority on German literature, has said, the novelist Heinrich Mann was one of the few critical minds and rare stylists of his epoch, but to say this were sacrilege, for in the eyes of time-honoured German *Geisteswissenschaftler* he was no *Dichter*. Similarly, Kurt Tucholsky, a first-rate satirical writer of the inter-war period, a masterly handler of the German language who had, according to Professor Minder, more political good sense in his little finger than the whole George circle put together, was at best regarded as a high-class journalist. Even Heine, one of the greatest thinkers ever produced by Germany, and after Goethe the only nineteenth century German writer with an international reputation (except for the popular Romantic E. T. A. Hoffman, would have ranked at best as a brilliant *Publizist* amongst his own countrymen, but not as a *Dichter,* had he not also written 'pure' poetry of the 'Du-bist-wie-eine-Blume' kind.

Not only did these writers favour such unpoetic genres as the essay or the satire, not to mention newspaper articles, but they were also politically committed, and 'engagierter Dichter', besides forming an odd linguistic misalliance (the one partner French, the other so very German) has in many quarters tended to be regarded as a veritable contradiction in terms. Symptomatic of this have been attempts to separate the social and political views of a writer from his 'Dichtertum'. Thus the poet Mörike was able to speak of Heine as a '*Dichter* through and through', whilst vehemently rejecting what he called 'the lie of his whole being'. In our own time, Brecht is no doubt the most striking example of how the artist is played off against the doctrinaire, the poet against the fighter (even Martin Esslin found it necessary to give the German version of his book on Brecht, *A Choice of Evils,* the sub-title *Das Paradox des politischen Dichters*).

Brecht, as is well known, had nothing but contempt for such an attitude and spurned the title *Dichter* for this very reason (he is said to have winced every time the communist poet Becher—of all people—prefaced a remark with 'ich als Dichter'). But in this he merely signals a general trend: after 1945 the word started to fall irrevocably into disrepute amongst German writers. Hölderlin's rhetorical 'Und wozu Dichter in dürftiger Zeit?' ('Wherefore poets in meagre times?') would, after the holocaust of World War II, have appeared even more of a painful paradox than in 1801. How could the poet aim at aesthetic distance, at formal excellence, in a world in which not only people's lives, but, as many felt, the very language itself had been shattered? The reaction on the part of the young generation of post-war writers was violent, not to say exaggerated. 'We do not', declared Wolfgang Borchert in his little *Manifesto,* 'need *Dichter* with good grammar. We lack the patience necessary for good grammar.' He might long to nurse his 'sensitive German Rilke heart' (and sometimes did!), but that was an outdated luxury—so was composing beautiful verses in the manner of Rilke. Hence the word 'Dichter' in this period of so-called 'Trümmerliteratur' ('literature of wreckage'—Böll) and of the 'Kahlschlag' ('*tabula rasa*') became almost synonymous with 'Belletrist' or, more scathing still, 'Kalligraph'.

The position today is that the word seems to be regarded by the majority of writers themselves as inappropriate and out of date—as much a 'bourgeois invention' (Martin Walser) as those plaster cast busts of the two 'Dichterfürsten' (poet princes) Goethe and Schiller, which used to adorn every self-respecting middle-class German drawing room. As Hans Mayer has put it, 'Which writer of today, who attaches importance to the composing of "texts" could dare, without loss of respect, describe himself as a "*Dichter*?" ' The word, with all its nebulous connotations, lingers on in the popular imagination, and in German critical jargon—but amongst the *Dichter* themselves its use tends to be restricted to denoting '(lyrical) poet'. Thus in a recently published collection of so-called 'Workshop Interviews' (*Werkstattgespräche*) with a number of the more important of them, the word is used in its wider connotation only in two instances, and then either apologetically or with considerable qualification. Thus the novelist Gerd Gaiser, who is said to use it more frequently than any other present-day prose writer, declares:

> I don't like the word. Rather, I regard it as an honorary title, which at best time can bestow. I would never use it in connection with my own literary efforts.

Like virtue to Büchner's poor Woyzeck ('Es muß was Schönes sein. Aber ich bin ein armer Kerl'), *Dichtung* to the contemporary German writer is beautiful, but irrelevant. Dürrenmatt writes that

> A *Dichter* is certainly something beautiful—but the term has become so muddled and vague that it can now only be applied in closed circles . . . not publicly, not as a description of profession.

Used 'publicly', it has become suspect. 'If you hear someone call himself a *"Dichter"*,' the novelist Hans Nossack has remarked, 'you may be sure that he isn't one . . . rather an empty phrase-thrasher and windbag.' When Karl Kraus, the great Austrian satirist, uttered the dictum that it was 'not enough to have no ideas in one's head : one must also be incapable of expressing them', he was in effect giving a definition of all those who, to quote Dürrenmatt again, 'zwar dichten, aber nicht schreiben können'. The aim of any writer, whether of a poem or a *Lehrstück,* an essay or a short story, must be not to write 'beautifully' or 'profoundly' (that is, 'dichterisch') but, as Borchert put it in *Der Schriftsteller,* 'legibly' ('es ist egal, ob er groß oder klein schreibt. Aber er muß leserlich schreiben').

The primacy of clarity of thought over beauty of expression has, of course, always been the concern of all really great German writers, from Lessing onwards. Of him the poet, journalist and moralist Erich Kästner has said :

> Das, was er schrieb, war manchmal Dichtung,
> doch um zu dichten schrieb er nie.
>
> (That which he wrote was sometimes *Dichtung*, yet it was not to this end that he wrote.)

As is well known, Lessing himself categorically denied being a *Dichter* or *Genie,* saying with characteristic modesty that whatever was 'tolerable' in his dramatic work was due solely to the faculty of criticism ('Kritik').

The current preference for terms such as 'Schriftsteller', 'Schreiber' or 'Schreibender', 'Prosaist', 'Stückeschreiber' and even 'Stückezimmerer' reflect a similar modesty (the East German 'Arbeiter der Feder' and 'Werktätige der Literatur' border on self-effacement). Coupled with it, one finds a marked emphasis on the sheer craft element in the creative process—the 'Handwerk', which implies something very solid and respectable. As Max Frisch has pointed out, to speak of a work of art in terms of an artefact or 'Mache' (that is, 'something made') used to amount to almost as unambiguous a criticism as to call it 'intellectual'. Yet one after another, from Zuckmayer to Uwe Johnson, contemporary German writers have testified to the importance of craft in their own work—the word 'Eingebung' (inspiration) is either taboo or replaced by the more prosaic 'Einfall' (bright idea).

More important still—a point already hinted at in the above Frisch quotation—is the general acceptance of a synthesis between the apparent irreconcilables, imaginative writing and the intellect. Günter Grass is by no means the only one writing in Germany today whose lyric poetry, strictly controlled as it is by the intellect, is the joint product of the *Denker* and the *Dichter*. But heaven preserve such writers from 'the nation of poets and thinkers'—the misguided critics and the well-meaning public who cling to the time-honoured image of the German *Dichter* as dispenser of sensibility rather than sense! As Dürrenmatt has complained, they simply spoil the climate in which the writer today has to work—'Incense befogs the intellect, it does not clarify!'

The kind of climate which still allows what Ingeborg Bachmann, one of the great living German poets, has referred to as 'the sentimental division between *Dichtung* and literature' is no longer in keeping with the demands made on the mid-twentieth century writer—and the demands which he tends to make upon himself. These may perhaps best be summed up in the word 'commitment' —not in the sense of commitment to the dogma of the East or the dogma of the West, to a particular party or creed, nor yet to the task of 'changing the world' (Brecht) through literature. The contemporary German writer is too sceptical and too realistic to 'take sides', as Frisch has put it, 'over alternatives which are no alternatives'. In the creative process, the *sine qua non* must still be the imaginative writer's 'Spieltrieb' (Schiller's 'innate instinct for play'), the joy of shaping, the urge to 'faire l'image'; yet this can no longer take place in an ivory tower, but (to cite the title of a speech by Frisch), with 'the public as partner'—if necessary in the street (viz. Peter Handke's *Straßentheater*). The motive force today is not self-expression, but communication, borne of a sense of social and moral awareness. As Dürrenmatt has put it, the writer cannot unfortunately 'bale out in order to satisfy the demand for pure *Dichtung* made by all *non-Dichter*. Fear, concern and above all rage makes us cry out'. *Dichtung* is no longer 'the most innocent of all pursuits (Hölderlin): the German writer is as never before, at any rate since the age of enlightenment, aware of the *effect* of his work, both in depth and in breadth, as a social, not an individual phenomenon.

> The author of our time [writes Professor Walter Jens] is a sober, modest person, inclined towards 'the social', unassuming, conscientious, critical, politically awake, a craftsman who receives his commissions from the publisher and from the radio, and who presents the commissioned piece of work on time.

In this the contemporary German poet, novelist or dramatist is no exception. He has become, like his West European counterpart, a public figure, a man, as has been said, 'with dinner jacket and engagement diary, little time and many duties, secret telephone number and public distinctions'. What shall we call him? 'I think you will agree,' said T. S. Eliot in the address quoted at the beginning, 'that the claim to be a man of letters is, after all, a modest pretension.' It is a happy thought that, in an era when even the most otherworldly of German novelists, Hermann Hesse, once again adopted the title 'Literat', few German writers—like the best of their predecessors, would aspire to any loftier title. They would like to be called 'German Men of Letters'.

PART THREE

Translations into English

I

THEODOR FONTANE ON LAURENCE STERNE

By D. Turner

The following essays—if such they can be called—were written in 1873, during a period when Fontane was concerning himself with a number of English novelists (including Fielding and Smollett as well as Scott, Dickens and Thackeray, with whom he was already acquainted), but when the appearance of his own first novel was still some five years off. The two pieces were never published in his lifetime; indeed, apart from partial reproductions, they have become available to the public only in recent years.[1] They will probably strike the reader as undisciplined pieces of writing, with a tendency to diffuseness and—especially in the comments on *The Sentimental Journey*, where there is a marked slackening of interest—to repetition. Fontane himself was aware of this,[2] and one can be certain that, had he ever seen fit to publish them during his lifetime, they would have looked very different; the famous file would have been at work.

It is not altogether easy to understand what interested him in Sterne to the extent of causing him to put down on paper his response to both *Tristram Shandy* and *The Sentimental Journey*. For it is not merely the hundred or so years of calendar time that separate the two writers. To judge from their personal lives, they can scarcely be called kindred spirits. The 'high priest of sentimentality',[3] who could fluctuate between the extremes of mockery and feverish emotionalism, seems a far cry from the restrained and emotionally discreet German. In their social habits, too, they are worlds apart. It is difficult, for example, to imagine Fontane being lionised in Berlin society in the way Sterne was in London and Paris, still more to imagine him enjoying it. And although both men had their 'clubs', one could hardly have transplanted 'Lafontaine' from the 'Tunnel über der Spree', with its serious literary pretensions, to the 'Demoniacs of Skelton Castle', where 'The Blackbird' (the parson Sterne) enjoyed the delights of wine, sport and bawdy talk as well as disputation.

As novelists the two men also appear to have little in common :

the Englishman deliberately discursive, full of erratic flashes of humour, treating both plot and characters in a wilful manner, for ever reminding us of his presence as narrator; the German generally more economical and controlled, more gentle in his humour, more serious in his approach to the business of narration, with a greater respect for literary manners and conventions, keeping himself well in the background. Nevertheless there are similarities, however few. Both men were keen observers of human life: Sterne, it has been suggested,[4] because he was also a painter, concentrating more on the outward appearance as an expression of the inner life; Fontane, as a result of his years as a journalist both at home and abroad, looking beneath the surface of human activity and social behaviour. Both shared an interest not only in human foibles, but also in the apparent trifles of life, in what Walter Shandy calls 'la bagatelle' and Professor Schmidt (*Frau Jenny Treibel*) calls 'das Nebensächliche'. And, for all the difference of their finished products, both novelists were careful stylists, given to much polishing. Finally, although Fontane cannot have realised it, both had the experience of finding their true literary outlet as novelists only late in life.

To turn now to the essays themselves, among the points Fontane selects for comment are some in which his own artistic creed, as yet of course untried in major narrative works of his own, comes into play. First of all there is the question of reality and realism. In discussing characterisation, for example, he is disturbed by Sterne's tendency to caricature, which threatens to rob Uncle Toby and Corporal Trim of their truth. Leaving aside the question of whether these two characters are in fact more 'overdrawn' than Walter Shandy, it is interesting to observe Fontane's concern for verisimilitude. He returns to it again towards the end of the second passage, though in a rather different connection, this time dealing with some of the erotic adventures in *The Sentimental Journey*. He makes an important distinction here between art and life; for him art has its own laws, so that what is possible in life is not necessarily possible or desirable in art. It is this same basic conviction that led him to advocate the poetic refining or 'transfiguring' of ugliness in art[5] and—another aspect of the same truth—will later allow him to defend certain errors of detail in his *Irrungen, Wirrungen* by pointing to the *total* effect, which is realistic.[6] Realism for him, in other words, is not identical with a detailed, photographic reproduction of what we choose to call 'real life'. Again, when he commends Sterne's handling of Lieutenant Le Fever's death or the characterisation in *The Sentimental Journey*, achieved by light brush-strokes, one can already observe the preference for understatement that will later become a mark of his own novels. Similarly, the comments on Sterne's 'art of suggestion, of interruption, of dropping hints, and often of dropping matters altogether' read in retrospect like a manifesto for Fontane's own subsequent practice.

Finally, there is the question of the so-called obscenities. Here again the transfiguring power of art is brought into play, since he emphasises how the comic treatment of the subject dissolves the ugliness. But the prurience remains. Now of course Fontane himself was by no means as squeamish in sexual matters as his discreet literary practice may suggest. Indeed one wonders whether there was not just a little of the novelist himself in some of those characters (Kommerzienrat Treibel and Herr von Briest, for example) who love to indulge in risqué conversation. Nevertheless, in the last analysis, he can give his blessing to Sterne's subject-matter—as also to his wayward humour[7]—only as an exception; it is ultimately alien to his own manner. And yet it is a mark of his unbigoted approach to new literary experience—he seems quite unaware of the considerable interest Sterne held for eighteenth-century Germans such as Lessing, Wieland, Herder and Goethe—that he should show understanding for something so foreign to him. His response to Sterne in the following two extracts makes it easier for us to appreciate his unbigoted, though by no means uncritical approach to the phenomenon of Naturalism towards the end of his life.

Laurence Sterne: Tristram Shandy

Tristram Shandy relates his history. It is a history of his procreation, birth, christening and circumcision, the last of which is effected, when Tristram is about five years old, by a falling sash-window.

At the moment of his birth and christening the novel is already half completed; when the said circumcision takes place, we are already three-quarters of the way through the novel, for all that we still have to learn is that Tristram is probably given young Le Fever as a tutor, later becomes consumptive, and undertakes a journey to the South of France. This journey is described. On the Languedoc Plain he goes on to relate the history of his Uncle Toby's wooing of the beautiful Widow Wadman, and before this history (which incidentally took place five years before the birth of Tristram) is completely finished, the whole story is over.

The novel therefore ends with events that took place five years before the birth of the hero, while on the other hand the death of the parson, Yorick, and the burial of Uncle Toby, which did not occur until Tristram was at least twenty years old, are narrated at the beginning, long before Tristram manages to complete the story of his birth.

Of Tristram's life we learn little or nothing; all the author's art of representation is concentrated on the above-mentioned description of or philosophical reflections on Tristram's procreation, birth, christening and circumcision. In doing this the novel now and again or even frequently regales us with Tristram's own views, but by and large he is treated as an object, who is there merely in order to enable other characters to develop their views and personalities. These other characters are, first and foremost: his father (Walter Shandy) and his uncle (Tobias Shandy, Uncle Toby); then his mother (Mrs. Shandy), the parson, Yorick, rector on the family estate, and Corporal Trim, servant to Uncle Tobias; and finally, Doctor Slop, Obadiah (Walter Shandy's servant), Susannah (Mrs. Shandy's maidservant), Widow Wadman, whom Uncle Tobias woos, and Bridget (Widow Wadman's maidservant).

In actual fact the whole novel consists of three characters: Tristram Shandy's father, Uncle Tobias and Corporal Trim (I reckon the latter high-relief figure among the fully rounded ones). All the other figures—masterful as they are—are merely sketched.

Of the three main characters Tristram's father seems the most perfect to me, although in England Uncle Toby and Corporal Trim are more popular. Both of these are in my opinion a little 'overdrawn', border on caricature, and thereby lose something of their truth and individual life. Nevertheless this loss is only quite small; in the eyes of many people the loss does not exist; it all depends whether one regards these characters as possible or not. I have my doubts, though I cannot absolutely deny their vitality.

A major part of the novel is taken up with interpolations, which, for all their apparent or perhaps even real arbitrariness, are always so skilfully woven into the texture that they serve to characterise the main figures. Sterne could have chosen a thousand and one other things, but even what he has chosen serves his purpose and enriches not only the content in general, but also the characterisation. Among these interpolations are the following: (1) a discourse on baptism in the womb ('par le moyen d'une petite canulle', as three Sorbonne scholars have suggested); (2) a discourse on cursing, including information about a model curse by Bishop Ernulphus of Rochester, if I am not mistaken; (3) a sermon on conscience; (4) a discourse on noses (sixty to eighty pages long); (5) a discourse on the importance of names; (6) a discourse on whiskers; and many more besides. All these things are not only amusing in themselves; they also complete the picture of the main characters, especially that of Tristram's father, who is altogether a man of intellectual ventures, of hypothesis, of debate at any price.

The novel is the product of an extraordinary genius. He makes no attempt to disguise his indebtedness to Cervantes (*Don Quixote*) and Rabelais, yet everything appears perfectly original. He has drawn his inspiration, discipline, control from these great models, but he does not copy them; all his characters have a completely independent existence both in time and space: they are Englishmen, and Englishmen of the last century. They are British Nationalists, British Rationalists, i.e. atheistic in philosophy.

Tristram Shandy, then, is an uncommonly original novel, and all the modern novelists (Walter Scott, Dickens, Jean Paul) have made great use of it, though fortunately none has copied it. A hundred more examples could probably be cited. Jean Paul comes closest to him in his manner of writing, but without actually equalling him. And it would be interesting to trace the reasons for this. I see them first of all in the following: Jean Paul, for all the talent he displays and his equally abundant wit, is nevertheless more affected, more sentimental and even more arbitrary. Jean Paul's characters and situations, inasmuch as they are humorous, seem less natural; one rarely succumbs to hearty laughter; one feels a sense of irritation more often than admiration. So much for naturalness and affectation. The same superiority is also evident in the matter of sentiment. Sterne is very rarely emotional; and where he is, it is always with extraordinary power. The simple story of Lieutenant Le Fever, who dies in a tavern, destitute and deserted, and whose last moments are transfigured by the appearance and magnanimity of Uncle Toby, is among the finest pieces of emotional writing one can read. The greatest possible effects are achieved with the simplest means, with just a few strokes. Here is a demonstration of complete genius. The hand of a master plucks at the strings of our heart and beneath the gentle touch of this hand we experience in rapid succession joy and pain or, with both sounding together, a sweet sorrow. Of sentimentalities à la Jean Paul not a trace; it is the very absence of all high-sounding phrases that has such a powerful effect. What it comes down to is that Jean Paul is also more arbitrary. Not in the composition of the whole—here he takes fewer liberties and observes a *kind* of regular procedure. But he is much more arbitrary in detail. He writes down everything that comes into his head, while Sterne—however abstruse the things may seem at first sight—always keeps before him the question, 'Does this serve your purpose, your artistic intention?' It will always be possible to discover why a particular passage is included; but with Jean Paul the bits of nonsense, the oddities, the figures of speech, the episodes are there by and large for their own sakes. Indeed, for all the madness of Sterne's composition there is such a high degree of method in the madness that what appears to the naïve beholder as a playful caprice is in fact an accomplishment of the greatest artistry. Jean Paul observes the traditional laws of narration and deviates from these laws only in detail, wherever it suits him. But in this respect he operates in a really arbitrary fashion. Sterne only appears arbitrary, and while it seems that he not only breaks the laws of narration, but turns them upside down as if he were mad and blind, he observes them most strictly—only, of course, in his own manner. This manner, which he invented for himself and then put into practice, is a stroke of genius through and through. There is no end to one's amazement and admiration, and yet it is a book that should not be repeated. Apart from the enjoyment it gives, one can learn a great deal from it, but imitation is impossible, in both form and content.

Both form and content.

But for all the artistry, all the masterful brilliance of this apparently arbitrary form, for all the admirable boldness of structure it displays in building the house roof first, in burying characters in the first chapter whom we observe in the last chapter just beginning their courting, for all the humorous and marvellous effect of having half, or almost half the book behind us when the hero is finally born, so that we have actually more interest in the unborn hero, the hero in the womb, than we have left for the hero after his birth—marvellous as all this is, superior as the talent it displays may be, it does not nevertheless warrant imitation. In his correspondence with Schiller Goethe makes the fine point: 'In the epic or narrative the art of retardation is displayed'; but here this art is taken to excess. The skilful interruption of the narrative and the interpolation, the shuffling around of descriptions, the simple delaying tactics, so that the journey and not the arrival is the main concern—all that is very fine. Yet Sterne no longer practises this art merely as an artist, but as a conjurer; it assumes the character of hocuspocus; things are no longer subject to a grand aesthetic system, only to a brilliant whim, which in spite of its brilliance remains a whim. Art should be an aesthetic game, but this is a wanton game, graceful, charming in its madness, but still—madness. One such object is a gem, as a species it is anathema.

Much the same is true of the content. Many passages are obscene, prurient; they should by right be excised; but ignoring these isolated and at least questionable passages and concentrating on the cardinal points, which can be heard like a ground-bass running through the whole work, it can be said: one such is excellent; even in duplicate it is questionable; as a species it is abominable! To recapitulate, then, it is a matter of the comic content of an act of procreation, a confinement, an eventual delivery by means of forceps, a circumcision with the aid of a sash-window, a flat nose of which no good can come, since happiness in life and love is to be found only among the big noses. Then comes Uncle Toby with his 'shattered pubic bone' and suspicion of impotence, and finally Widow Wadman with her investigations to clarify this obscure but important point (the pubic bone and the question of impotence). And scattered in among all this those discussions, which do stick to the limits of what is seemly about 'big noses', 'whiskers' and—convent tales of all kinds. As far as content goes (apart, that is, from the mere gossip of the author), any further comic situations there are have not very much significance and can be reduced to Uncle Toby's hobby horse: war, siege, military architecture. These passages are quite excellent and form a pure, harmless accompaniment to the comic impropriety, although they definitely represent the weaker tendency. Thus the subject-matter of the novel can be described as the saucy, humorous treatment of every possible situation deriving from sexual life: virile and decrepit intercourse, the lasciviousness of widowhood, the shyness and clumsiness of bachelorhood, the ever ready servant, the connection between 'chambermaids and button-holes', the cynical remarks of a philosopher who stands *above* it all and an *accoucheur* who operates in the *middle* of it all, the abbreviated or damaged genitalia of a child, the misery of impotence or incapacity and the enviable good fortune of possessing a big nose. This, and much more in similar vein, forms the content.

The boldness, the comic power and the charm with which—apart from a few exceptions—all these matters are treated make the book a joy to read, even as far as content goes; but, truth to tell, it is *not* the content, but the way it is garnished and served that endears the subject-matter to us. Undoubtedly these matters possess a certain natural comicality in themselves, but there is still more about them that is ugly and disgusting. The enormous difficulty lies in submerging this ugliness beneath the comicality. This Sterne has managed to do, and so his novel will always remain a masterpiece. A masterpiece, but not a model or pattern, at least not directly. This sort of thing has not only a right to exist, it has a duty to do so; but it must remain by itself. If it begets a species, it is to be resisted. Such a novel must itself remain a bachelor, an Uncle Toby with a shattered pubic bone; it is a bad mistake for it to have intercourse with the lascivious Widow Wadman and beget children.

All in all I would say that the good and the best works of Fritz Reuter are in my view superior. Sterne's genius is undoubtedly greater, but his caprices spoil it and make it unpalatable for the majority.

A Sentimental Journey through France and Italy, by Mr. Yorick

Yorick, the same parson Yorick who has such a genial part to play in *Tristram Shandy*, makes a journey through France as far as Italy in his younger years, and Sterne presents us here in the form of passages from a diary, so to speak, the jottings of one of his favourite characters (Yorick). Yorick sojourns in Calais, narrates his encounters here, passes quickly through several areas of Northern France, visits Paris and Versailles, where he makes his major jottings, and then travels through Bourbonnais and by way of Moulins to Savoy, and thence to Turin. Everything revolves around his experiences in Calais, Paris-Versailles and Moulins; the rest occupies only a few pages.

Not a trace of actual itinerary. Any expatiation on landscapes or, still worse, churches is abhorrent to him; only man is of interest to him; and in this connection he is of the opinion that people are more easily recognised from small, even minute characteristics and better depicted in small rather than large brushstrokes. All quite correct of course.

So the whole thing is a succession of small encounters, neatly painted vignettes from the sphere either of the picturesque, sometimes idyllic, sometimes coarse, or of aristocratic society. We get to know a considerable number of characters, various noble ladies, chambermaids, landlords, a French count, an old French colonel, a virtuoso beggar, a *valet de chambre* (Lafleur), a Parisian *grisette*, a country girl who has gone out of her mind at the loss of her beloved. All these characters are amiably drawn, and Yorick himself, who narrates all this, is likewise amiable. On the point of talent, much of what is narrated, although perhaps first rate, is not always admissible *in spite of* this talent (I will return to this later). This is true, for example, of the encounter with the beautiful Flemish widow in Calais, the scene with the *grisette* in the glove-shop, the meeting with the chambermaid on the Quai Conti, the visit to the French count in Versailles, also of the visit to the theatre with the French colonel, the adventure with the noble lady with whom he collides on the steps of the concert-hall, the bedroom scene with the beautiful Piedmontese lady and her maid, in part also of the encounter with maid Maria near Moulins. Added to this is a peculiar art of suggestion, of interruption, of dropping hints, and often even of dropping matters altogether; and as always a wealth of learning, practical wisdom, and knowledge of human beings.

Nevertheless this *Sentimental Journey* seems to me considerably inferior to *Tristram Shandy*, and for the most varied of reasons. One reason may be the fact that much of what on first acquaintance seems a *brilliant* caprice, so that emphasis is placed on brilliance, can afterwards, when one gets to know a second work, produce only the effect of a brilliant *caprice*, with the stress more on the capricious arbitrariness than on brilliance. But even apart from the fact that this form, as I already indicated in connection with *Tristram Shandy,* can be accepted and fully relished only once, the subject-matter or the spirit of which this subject-matter is born is also of such a kind that it can obtain a legitimate place in literature only as an exception and under special conditions. *Tristram Shandy* is a brilliant and unsurpassed attempt to regard and represent sexual matters from the comic point of view; the aim it sets itself is both colossal and bold, and the power of invention, the courage and the charm with which Sterne solves his problem is astonishing. That a genius should ever set himself such a task I regard as fortunate; it filled a gap. Even this sort of thing must exist. But only once. Now the *Sentimental Journey* is of course not a repetition of *Tristram Shandy*, and yet Sterne again introduces into the *Sentimental Journey* all those ambiguities, sensual capers, and delicate situations that were present in *Tristram Shandy*; and it can properly be said that they are out of place here, or that they would be better absent. In *Tristram* the task, magnificent in its way, lay in this direction; here it does not. Here he could content himself with depicting scenes such as that with the beautiful Flemish woman, the *grisette*, the French colonel, the count at Versailles, and the like; but he could not resist his penchant for the sensual and prurient, and so there arose scenes such as that with the noble lady on the steps of the concert-hall, with the chambermaid in the hotel and with the beautiful Piedmontese lady in the Italian inn. I can quite well appreciate his intention. He takes as his starting point the fact that life is like that; whoever describes it differently is a liar or a hypocrite; anyone who finds himself alone with a chambermaid has in the natural course of events the desire to possess her, and if matters stand favourably and virtuously, he will struggle to control his senses. All that I can concede. But if I am making a journey, there is no necessity for me to get into such situations, and if I nevertheless do get into them, there is no necessity to describe them. In *Tristram Shandy* the task in hand demanded this and similar matters; in the *Sentimental Journey* the task did not demand this at all, and Sterne described this sort of thing not because he *had* to in order to fulfil his aim, but because his nature and inclination led him to *want* to. Here lies the mistake from our modern point of view. It is very probable that the previous century felt differently, and yet, I believe, our view is more correct, even from the aesthetic point of view* —to say nothing of the moral point of view.

* The final scene in the Italian inn, where the chambermaid is suddenly standing between the two beds, has perhaps even more truth than comicality, and yet ultimately it is nothing more than a piece of obscenity on the level of indecent French pictures which one cannot deny a certain wit, comicality and virtuosity.

NOTES

1. Notably in Theodor Fontane, *Sämtliche Werke*, Vol. XXI, i, 'Literarische Essays und Studien', ed. Kurt Schreinert, Munich, 1963, and Theodor Fontane, *Aufzeichnungen zur Literatur: Ungedrucktes und Unbekanntes*, ed. Hans-Heinrich Reuter, Berlin/Weimar, 1969.
2. On the cover of the folder in which the manuscript is held Fontane has noted: 'Sehr zu kürzen und einheitlicher zu machen' (see Reuter's notes in *Aufzeichnungen zur Literatur*, p. 342).
3. Cf. Peter Quennell, 'Laurence Sterne', in *Four Portraits: Studies in the Eighteenth Century*, London, 1947, The Reprint Society, p. 148.
4. Ibid., p. 159.
5. Cf., for example, his early essay, 'Unsere lyrische und epische Poesie seit 1848', in *Sämtliche Werke*, vol. XXI, i, pp. 9–12.
6. Letter to Emil Schiff on 15 February 1888.
7. Later he was to say it was a question of wit rather than true humour (letter to his wife on 20 June 1879).

OPHELIA: VARIATIONS ON A THEME

By Ian Hilton

The theme of the drowned maiden goes back in literature a long time. It was to prove popular with German poets in the early twentieth century. Georg Heym's poem was composed on 20 November 1910 and appeared in the verse collection *Der ewige Tag* (1911). It is characteristic of the work of one who has been described as the German Rimbaud. Certainly he seems here to have taken up the theme of Rimbaud's 'Ophélie'. Heym stresses the decomposition of beauty (cf. G. Benn's 'Schöne Jugend', B. Brecht's 'Vom ertrunkenen Mädchen'). The opening line is immediate and drastic in its effect. The rats in her hair and the eel gliding over her breast (in the final stanza) produce a lasting macabre vision. The poem's overall mood is of loneliness, darkness and death. The poet himself seems to maintain a somewhat detached air, emphasised perhaps by the formal appearance of the original poem with its regular metrical and rhyming scheme, though in fact the poem has considerable emotional force.

Peter Huchel, one of East Germany's best lyric poets and former editor of *Sinn und Form*, updates the Ophelia theme in his own poem which first appeared in *Neue deutsche Hefte* 1/1968. In these lines he gives poetic expression to a present-day situation and experience in the border region. As in Heym's poem, nature enters here; the landscape is the scene of catastrophe. The impersonal element (boots wading, the thrust of poles, some harsh command) and the naked cruelty of 'Stacheldrahtreuse', 'zersplittern' serve actually to accentuate Huchel's sad concern over the human condition. The simple and precise language and the straightforward use of free rhythm combine effectively to create a poem of intense atmosphere.

GEORG HEYM : *Ophelia*

Im Haar ein Nest von jungen Wasserratten,
Und die beringten Hände auf der Flut
Wie Flossen, also treibt sie durch den Schatten
Des großen Urwalds, der im Wasser ruht.

Die letzte Sonne, die im Dunkel irrt,
Versenkt sich tief in ihres Hirnes Schrein.
Warum sie starb? Warum sie so allein
Im Wasser treibt, das Farn und Kraut verwirrt?

Im dichten Röhricht steht der Wind. Er scheucht
Wie eine Hand die Fledermäuse auf.
Mit dunklem Fittich, von dem Wasser feucht
Stehn sie wie Rauch im dunklen Wasserlauf,

Wie Nachtgewölk. Ein langer, weißer Aal
Schlüpft über ihre Brust. Ein Glühwurm scheint
Auf ihrer Stirn. Und eine Weide weint
Das Laub auf sie und ihre stumme Qual.

PETER HUCHEL : *Ophelia*

Später, am Morgen,
Gegen die weiße Dämmerung hin,
Das Waten von Stiefeln
Im seichten Gewässer,
Das Stoßen von Stangen,
Ein rauhes Kommando,
Sie heben die schlammige
Stacheldrahtreuse.
Kein Königreich,
Ophelia,
Wo ein Schrei
Das Wasser höhlt,
Ein Zauber
Die Kugel
Am Weidenblatt zersplittern läßt.

GEORG HEYM : *Ophelia*

Her hair a nest of baby water rats,
Her ringed hands stretch'd in the water's flow
Like fins, she drifts thus through the forest's shade
So great and primal resting down below.

The final sun, that in the darkness strays,
Sinks low down in her shrinal cerebrum.
Why did she die? Why does she so alone
Drift in the water tangling ferns and weeds?

In clumps of reeds the wind is caught. It scares
Just like a hand when raised the twitchy bats.
On sombre wings, to which the dampness sticks,
They hang as smoke above the sombre flow,

Nocturnal clouds. A slimy long white eel
Glides wet across her breast. A glowworm shines
Upon her brow. A weeping willow sheds
Its leaves on her and muted silent pain.

PETER HUCHEL : *Ophelia*

Later that morning,
Towards the pallid dawn,
Boots wading
In the shallow water,
The thrust of poles,
Some harsh command,
They raise the muddy
Barbed-wire trap.
There's no kingdom,
Ophelia,
Where a cry
Hollows the water,
Where a spell makes
The bullet
Splatter against the willow leaf.

3

GERTRUD VON LE FORT AND GRAHAM GREENE

By J. Foster

Not long before Oswald Wolff died he asked me if I would be interested in revising and expanding a little book I had written some years before about Christian literature; he expressed the view that the Church had not always received due credit for the good it had done over the centuries and said that he would like to do something to redress the balance. So when I was invited to contribute to this memorial volume I felt at once that something connected with 'Christian literature'—if I may be allowed provisional use of this piece of question-begging shorthand—would be particularly appropriate (though what I have chosen is far from being merely an encomium of the institutional aspect of Christianity).

The following essay by Gertrud von le Fort (whom Wolff had met, he told me, at Berlin University many years ago) originally formed the preface to a collection of Graham Greene's occasional pieces published in German translation in Switzerland in 1952 under the title *Vom Paradox des Christentums.*[1] It also appears in the collection of Gertrud von le Fort's own essays called *Die Krone der Frau.*[2] The interesting, indeed profound, notion that all literature is fundamentally akin in spirit to Christianity is repeated and developed in Gertrud von le Fort's later essay 'Vom Wesen Christlicher Dichtung'[3] ('On the nature of Christian literature'), which ends with the assertion that 'it is from the *anima Christiana naturaliter* that all true literature springs'.

The Paradox of Christianity (An essay on Graham Greene)

If we had to find a motto for the work of Graham Greene we should choose the saying of St. John, 'God is greater than our heart'. For Greene's work is a ceaseless and often absolutely breath-taking struggle with this very saying—breath-taking if only because it is naturally also a continual struggle with the pettiness, the limitations and the fearfulness of our own hearts.

That this struggle takes place not in the realm of dogmatic or moral theology but exclusively in the realm of literature makes Graham Greene's work a breath-taking event in an even wider sense, for it runs into the difficult problems connected—at any rate for a Catholic—with the relationship between literature and theology, particularly moral theology. There is no writer who faces these problems with such boldness as Graham Greene. He represents a previously unknown kind of Catholic writer or—as Greene prefers to have it—writer who is a Catholic. The distinction between these two definitions already makes the essential point: the first definition implies that the banner of the Church waves over the writer, the second implies that it is absent. This means that Graham Greene assumes the right to be as sovereign in his own domain as any profane writer. And indeed no unbeliever could take the world more seriously than he does. In him we find all the aberrations, all the boundless distance from God, all the naïve and perfidious vices, all the earthly, purely materialistic attitudes that the image of contemporary humanity displays. Graham Greene by no means gives his characters the peace of Christ to help them on their way, nor does he let them attain this peace; they remain, as he himself says, 'bound to the end to this world, and share its passions and weaknesses'. Yet they also share in the redemption. For the amazing thing about Graham Greene is that this writer, who spares us the sight of no abyss of human depravity and does not allow us to retain any illusions at all, is nevertheless in a position to reject the reproach that he is a pessimist with amazement, indeed almost with anger. In a very instructive conversation with some French priests printed in the present volume he confesses to an overflowing optimism, though this obviously does not draw its nourishment from man. And this is where the writer Graham Greene shows himself a Christian: the amazing and comforting surprises which he gives us in his work always tend to imply that God is in fact greater than the human heart.

But let us look at this work itself. The very language of these books shows the curious disenchantment of the modern world; it is related to poetry as the merciless brightness of electrically lit cities is related to the moonlight of a romantic landscape. But in the midst of the trivialities and bareness of these dialogues we come across sayings of such compulsive truth that they almost sound beautiful. This beauty, which is really truth, communicates itself to the characters as well as to the language.

Take for example *The Power and the Glory*, a book set in Mexico during the persecution of the Church and dealing with the last priest alive in his country, whom nicely brought-up Christians would like to see measuring up, in ascetic self-sanctification and enthusiastic courage for martyrdom, to the grandeur of his situation. And the fulfilment of this wish, one might think, would also be appropriate to a Christian literature. Instead of this we see a man degenerate in every way, called 'the whisky priest' by the people, who is constantly at the bottle, who trembles like a coward for his life, and whose existence embraces pretty well everything calculated to disgrace a spiritual mode of life. Yet the priestly conscience is the last thing in him to be destroyed, or rather it is not destroyed at all. Indeed it is almost as if this disreputable figure wished to remind us of the very fact that, according to the Church's teaching, the priestly office is indestructible. When it comes to the pinch, this poor, unworthy priest is capable of uttering, under the worst and most painful prison conditions or during a confession heard in a stable, Christian words that are unusual but amazingly profound. The deeply moving result is that he himself is astonished to find how his own inadequacy and disreputableness render him more merciful, but also more sensitive and vulnerable to those false notes of which the so-called pious in particular are often guilty. When the betrayer asks him to go to a dying person he follows him obediently, if trembling, although he suspects that his priestly conscience is being abused in order to lead him to death. And he suffers this death, but again not in the way that our idle wish desires. Whilst in the same town at almost the same hour a pious woman reads aloud to her children the elevating description of a martyr's death, Graham Greene's poor hero, supported by two policemen, totters towards the wall in front of which the fatal bullet is to strike him. The cry 'Viva el Cristo Rey' with which his spiritual brothers died is denied him in his fear of death. Two worlds are revealed: the elevating one of pious deceptions, of noble wishes and noble demands, and the illusion-free, shaming, yet humanly so moving reality. This priest, so disappointing in life and so wretched in death, does in fact die for his holy office after being the last guardian of his people: God confirms him as such—

immediately after his death the first priest sent from abroad treads the soil of Mexico.

The situation is even more dangerous, indeed frighteningly dangerous, in the novel *The Heart of the Matter*. Even in the first part of the book summer lightning flashes across the sky when we hear the hero of the novel, the police officer Scobie, say in front of the corpse of a young suicide of whose salvation the priest present despairs: 'Even the Church can't teach me that God doesn't pity the young.' Scobie here pronounces unawares the judgment of mercy on himself, for it says in the Gospel, 'with what measure you measure, it shall be measured to you'. When he utters these words Scobie does not yet suspect that his own life will end one day through suicide—through a suicide committed out of love of God, after he has previously committed adultery out of pity. It is difficult to re-read this tremendous concept in Graham Greene and then to oppose it with confidence—no one will deny its dubiousness; even Greene does not. In the conversation with French priests mentioned above he admits that pity can be the occasion of serious sin. But as a writer he is less concerned, he says, with the sin than with the depth of abandonment of the sinner, with the dreadful hopelessness of his situation. And we may add that he is also concerned with the motive of the sin. 'The Church knows all the rules,' says Father Rank to Mrs. Scobie, 'but it doesn't know what goes on in a single human heart.' Even in pity that has become sinful the heart of all things is still revealed. 'For', we read again in that same conversation, 'who could understand his fellow men without pity?' Scobie, whose pity will not let him part either with his wife or with his beloved, yet to whom it also says inexorably of God, 'I love you and I won't go on insulting you at your own altar', finds no other way out but the self-slaughter condemned by his Church. But the words 'I love you, God' imply to Greene the possibility of forgiveness. 'It may seem an odd thing to say—when a man's as wrong as he was,' says Father Rank to the widow of the suicide, '—but I think from what I saw of him, that he really loved God.' And the certainty of forgiveness comes home to us, if anything even more movingly, in the wonderful scene in which we meet for the last time poor little Helen, whom Scobie saved, by his adulterous acquiescence in her liking for him, from falling into the hands of a wastrel. Is it not as if the sympathetic Scobie were endowed with the grace to protect, even from beyond the grave, the again grievously endangered girl, indeed to save her once and for all? The seduction to which the despairing Helen has already consented does not come off. 'Do you believe in God?' she asks the man as he is about to leave. And she adds: 'I wish I did, I wish I did!' There now follows a conversion of great simplicity, quite unlike any conventional one. The girl, left to herself, clasps her hands to say the 'Our Father' again for the first time after an infinitely long gap, but she can only remember the words 'For ever and ever, Amen'. Here too, as in the novel about the poor priest, a mysterious confirmation has resulted, a confirmation, it is true, that only the writer can provide.

This brings us back to the tensional relationship of which we spoke at the start. Graham Greene would be the last to deny it. So let us turn once more to the man himself. In a very bold, very candid letter to Elizabeth Bowen he comes to speak of the duties which society imposes on the writer, or rather would like to impose on him, for Graham Greene asserts that the writer has the privilege of evading these duties or, as he puts it himself, of being disloyal—a privilege which, he knows very well, people are unwilling to grant him. Thus he is perfectly well aware that for him, particularly as a Catholic writer, difficult conflicts can arise. We do not need to waste any words over these conflicts, for their nature is sufficiently well known. They are based on the misconception that writing exists to edify, to create, models worthy of imitation, and that—in so far as it deals with problems of the Christian religion—it must champion the laws prescribed by moral theology and help them to triumph. Graham Greene does not hesitate to recognise that these laws are lofty and worthy of respect, indeed loftier and worthier of respect than the laws of writing, but he also recognises that they belong to an utterly different function, to a different sphere of being. Moral theology is concerned with the realm of obedience; writing—like everything creative—with the realm of freedom. We do not mean freedom of will, but freedom of mind and conscience. If you rob writing of this you are cutting a stream off from its source; writing that is not free is condemned to impotence. All guided art displays a curious powerlessness; its products are patchwork rather than art. But freedom of conscience is an inalienable part of Catholic doctrine—thus it cannot possibly be denied to the writer from this quarter. In his letter to Elizabeth Bowen, Graham Greene rightly asks, '[Otherwise] how is one freer than the Leningrad group?'.

The fundamental division between the two functions and spheres of being gives rise to a series of further differences. Morality is concerned with the universally valid, literature with the individual. Morality erects laws, literature depicts people. Morality is obliged to make theoretical claims, literature to portray concrete cases. Its roots lie not in what should be, but in what actually is, and therefore in the human element, with all its inadequacies. In short, it has to do with life itself, not with advice about living—life is always something more or less irrational. In the last analysis no one knows this better than the moral theologian, for after all in his practical work he is as much concerned with the relativity of phenomena as the writer is. Nevertheless, his demands are perfectly comprehensible to the writer, and not only because of the dignity of his function. For even in an age of cultural decay literature still wields over human feelings a great power of suggestion, which with good reason one would like to enlist for educational purposes. But this wish is based on a fallacy, for literature exerts its power precisely because it is not concerned with the triumph of the laws—though certainly not with the relaxation of the laws either—but with the relaxation, the softening of human feelings. Literature does not plead in favour of the recognition of morality; it pleads that our hearts should be moved. If morality's formula says 'Either—Or', in other words 'Either guilty or innocent', literature's famous device is 'guilty *and* innocent'. Every great work of literary art is based on this principle, which was the formative element in Greek literature and has remained valid ever since. Without it there can be no tragic hero nor any hero of a novel in the grand style; every one of them is simultaneously guilty before the bar of morality and innocent in relation to the laws of his own psychology and the forces of his destiny. It is on this double outlook that literature's power to move us is based—the vagueness of its point of view is the very thing that constitutes the magic of its immediacy and its closeness to life.

There is indeed a way in which literature can serve an educational purpose, but it lies in a totally different direction from the one demanded. In the letter to Elizabeth Bowen already mentioned, Graham Greene suggests to Catholic writers that they should choose the great Cardinal Newman as their patron, for he has left us some very instructive remarks on the relationship between literature and morality. When one reads these remarks, one cannot help wondering how it is that doubt and grotesque errors could still arise in our day about the point in dispute. 'It is a contradiction in terms,' the Cardinal says, 'to attempt a sinless literature of sinful man. You may gather together something very great and high, something higher than any literature ever was; and when you have done so, you will find that it is not literature at all.' With the last sentence the Cardinal hits the nail on the head—art that is directed, as we have said already, does not produce literature but only patchwork concoctions. Guided by a deep knowledge of human nature, the Cardinal then goes on to say: 'Cut out from your class books all broad manifestations of the natural man; and those manifestations are waiting, for your pupil's benefit, at the very doors of your lecture room in living and breathing substance . . . To-day confined to the Lives of the Saint, to-morrow thrown upon Babel . . . You have refused him the masters of human thought, who would in some sense have educated him, because of their incidental corruption.'[4] But, people will doubtless object, the stumbling block lies not only in the fact that the writer takes the depiction of the sinful world seriously. What is much graver is that he puts the sinner in that dubious light already mentioned, that the latter remains thus blurred right to the end, and that nevertheless he can be saved and can save others, as we have seen in the cases of the poor whisky priest and the suicide Scobie. And it is true that here Graham Greene goes far beyond the great cardinal. He has made a breach in much profounder scruples, much more deeply rooted resistances than those assailed by Newman, a breach that it will be difficult to close up again. He has been able to do this not because the grandeur and boldness of his conception have overpowered its opponents—these opponents cannot be overpowered, for from their own point of view they are perfectly right—but rather because the time has become ripe for such a breach to be made.

No one who keeps his eyes open can be in any doubt that we are faced today with the complete collapse of so-called bourgeois morality; and it is becoming apparent that this morality was widely assumed to be Christian morality. But this is an error. We are not saying anything against bourgeois morality; law and order are needed—how badly they are needed! We are simply saying that it is not identical with Christian morality. Bourgeois morality is the morality of the righteous of this world; but Christian morality is embraced by the saying about publicans and sinners, namely that they are nearer than the righteous to the kingdom of God. They are also nearer to the heart of the writer: literature has an irresistible inclination to concern itself with questionable characters, people assailed by temptation, people indeed who have come to a tragic end—untempted, morally safe existences hold little attraction for the writer. At this point the real paradox of literature becomes clear; but is it not at the same time the paradox of Christianity? And does it not fall in line with that very saying about publicans and sinners, who are nearer to the kingdom of God than the righteous? But who then is really righteous, and who belongs to the publicans and sinners? If we look deeply enough, even the Pharisee appears only as a poor sinner, indeed probably the most pitiable of all. We are indebted to Graham Greene for this perception, for he demands sympathy even with the adversary, a sympathy which his work does in fact evoke—one has only to think of the figure of the lieutenant who guards the poor whisky priest during his last night on earth. In a letter to V. S. Pritchett containing some remarks as important as those in the letter to Elizabeth Bowen, Greene asserts yet again that it is the writer's first duty to be disloyal—and for Greene 'disloyal' means 'free'. The letter to Elizabeth Bowen deals more with the conflict with ecclesiastical morality, the letter to Pritchett discusses the conflict with the demands of the state and of society. The loyal writer, Greene explains, can have neither understanding nor sympathy for the nonconformist, the outsider; therefore the writer cannot be loyal, for he must demand sympathy for every creature—a creature who evokes no kind of sympathy is a failure from the literary point of view. We can see that here 'the heart of all things' becomes visible not only in the writer's work but in the writer himself. And here too we have reached the point at which we can see how the time has become ripe for the writer Greene; for what does this age really lack? What failing distinguishes it from all other ages? Is it not simply the death of the heart, even deep in the ranks of those regarded as pious Christians? Indeed, perhaps it is precisely here that we find the really dead point in the contemporary world, for however far we look love is the only creative principle known to us. And from whom is the re-creation of our old world to proceed if not from Christians? The only thing certain is that:

> Der Dichter kann nicht verarmen;
> Wenn alles um ihn her zerfällt,
> Hebt ihn ein göttliches Erbarmen—
> Der Dichter ist das Herz der Welt.[5]
>
> Joseph von Eichendorff

Therefore let us no longer strive to reconcile irreconcilable opposites, for although such a reconciliation is certainly possible it lies beyond our earthly task. The tensional relationship between writing and morality reflects an opposition that extends far beyond the human sphere. Writing is governed by mercy, morality by the need to pass judgment; this means that in the last analysis the tension between the two is a metaphysical one—it is the tension which leads deep into the very concept of God and which to the finite mind is insoluble. We are left only with trust in Nicholas of Cusa's *coincidentia oppositorum*: in God himself opposites coincide, though to our minds they are poles apart. Morality and literature will never be in complete harmony with each other; one will unhesitatingly represent eternal justice, the other the infinite nature of grace. Yet is not the unshakable insistence on grace demanded by literature nevertheless the very point at which it makes contact with the profoundest utterances of theology? In the final analysis Graham Greene's figures, who cause morality such grave doubts, are surely covered by that saying of the greatest theologian of the West, St. Augustine: 'Love and do what you will'.

NOTES

1. Zürich, 1952. The collection contains the letters to Elizabeth Bowen and V. S. Pritchett originally published in *Why do I write?* (London, 1948) and a number of other essays which, as far as I have been able to discover, are not at the moment in print in English in any collection of Graham Greene's prose.
2. Zürich, 1952.
3. *Woran ich glaube und andere Aufsätze,* Zürich, 1968.
4. Cardinal Newman, *Discourses on the scope and nature of university education,* Dublin, 1852, pp. 356–60.
5. [The poet cannot be impoverished;/When all around him crumbles,/He is borne up by a divine pity—/The poet is the heart of the world.]

4

KOEPPEN: RED BUSES IN AN ENCHANTED FOREST

By M. A. L. Brown

The passage which follows is an extract, about half the length of the original, from Koeppen's essay on London in the volume *Nach Rußland und anderswohin*. This collection of five 'sentimental journeys', as they are sub-titled by the author, was written as a series for broadcasting, then published in 1958. By this time Koeppen had already established a reputation as a novelist, based principally on his three post-war works—*Tauben im Gras* (1951), *Das Treibhaus* (1953), and *Der Tod in Rom* (1954). He has continued writing as a journalist and broadcaster, producing two further travel books, *Amerikafahrt* and *Reisen nach Frankreich*, and a selection of poems by Shelley, but not so far another novel. In 1962 Koeppen was awarded the Georg Büchner prize and in 1967 the Immermann prize of the city of Düsseldorf.[1]

The selection of this particular extract for translation and for inclusion here is not intended to suggest that Koeppen has any 'special relationship' to England. The other essays of the volume describe journeys to Spain, Holland, Russia and Italy, all undertaken with the same restless appetite for impressions and sensations, the same curiosity to discover whether experience measures up to expectation or reality to fable, and all related with the same brilliance of style. It is suggested, more simply, that this view of London, the London of the mid 1950's, as seen through the eyes of a sophisticated, widely-travelled German observer, may have a special interest and some surprises for the English reader.

Koeppen's technique is to present a rapidly moving sequence of pictures, unfolding almost cinematically before the eye of the traveller as he looks out through the window of his taxi, bus, ship or plane. Speed is necessary to this traveller if he wishes to keep up with the pace of mid twentieth-century life and, used in place of a narrative thread, it also provides Koeppen with the appropriate literary style to mirror a life-style characterised by swiftness of movement and change. It might seem at first that

Koeppen, for the purposes of his travel-books, is assuming the role of that well-known figure of the contemporary landscape, the globe-trotting tourist; and indeed the mass tourist, cellophane-wrapped and celluloid-minded, is conspicuous wherever Koeppen goes—for instance, soaking in the Elizabethan atmosphere beneath the smoke-blackened beams and galleries of the George Inn, Southwark (in a passage not included here). Koeppen, however, specifically dissociates himself from their kind as he wishes to remain, in his schedules and his reactions, a private individual, 'der unzeitgemäße Individualist',[2] the awkward outsider in an age where even non-conformity is no longer an individual matter. Some of the few expressions of anger and scorn in this book are reserved for the 'blindness',[3] the unawareness of the tourist herd who are perhaps in this respect more similar to their less travelled contemporaries than they think.

It is clear from the opening paragraphs of this essay that Koeppen sets out for England, as for all his destinations, with certain quite definite preconceptions of what he will find there. These preconceptions are derived in part from naïve childhood memory and cliché, in part from widely scattered literary reference and allusion, ranging in the case of London from Chaucer to T. S. Eliot and from Elizabethan drama to Lawrence's 'The Mint', in part from events and developments of recent history and in part from classical myth. These all go to form a highly personal system of cross-references which is then tested against the sights, sounds, tastes and scents of the actual visit. Some of these may give the English reader of 1970 a shock—to some extent of recognition but also of disbelief: are we really little more than a decade away from this post-want but still pre-Quant London? And we may be tempted to proceed from this question to blame Koeppen's naïveté or nostalgia or fantasy or sheer bias for a view of London which emphasises so lovingly its nineteenth-century period charm.

On comparing the London essay with the others in the volume this impression seems to be confirmed—the new, modern aspects of the other cities are given more prominence. What fascinates Koeppen, however, is not the old or the new for its own sake, but rather the manner and the effect of their juxtaposition. The relationship of past and present in the lives of mid twentieth-century Europeans and their cities is one of Koeppen's main concerns, here as in his novels, and as one reads on through these essays it increasingly gives thematic unity to the sharply contrasted observations of individual countries. It is a mistake to read these essays as the harmless sentimental journeyings of a non-political man, far removed from the more problematic world of his novels.[4] Koeppen can testify that modern cities, the faces of their crowds, are equally international, in Moscow and East Berlin no less than in Rome and London. What gives them an individual atmosphere is not so much the new, shining cosmopolitanism, but the place of an older, national past in relation to it. He must find out in visiting a new country whether the past has been obliterated or hidden, whether it is allowed to exist in an uneasy, precarious balance with the present, or whether past and present can coexist in unproblematic harmony. It is because he finds this last in London alone of the cities described in this volume that his eulogies may seem backward-looking; the English sense of historical continuity accepts without violence, if not entirely without humbug, that Imperial and Victorian grandeur has given way to an era whose virtues are more domesticated.[5] Nowhere in London is there a sense of agony, trauma, or nightmare, of the past rearing its ugly head from the waters, such as confronts him predictably in Stalingrad, but also in Rome in a memorial to 350 Italian civilians rounded up and shot as reprisals for an attack on a German army lorry, in Madrid where the 'German' restaurant helps to keep old memories alive, and even in Holland. In all these places the period of the 1950's is separated from the past of ten or twenty years before by catastrophe and horror, for so much of which his country was responsible and Koeppen, travelling as a German with his country's past as part of his own, can see the lasting wounds in every country he visits, even when they are not deliberately pointed out to him. The nightmare has not been forgotten—except, he finds in London. The scars left by the blitz have healed and by some magic the English are not haunted by the past, so neither, on these shores, need the German visitor be. It is an unexpected sidelight on the familiar theme of 'Bewältigung der Vergangenheit', of overcoming the past, more familiar from its fictional treatment in numerous novels of the period. Ironically, however, it is London which brings back another special memory to Koeppen. The opening comparison with Berlin hardly reads like a serious observation and its force is not felt till later in the laconic words, 'Wir haben nichts dergleichen mehr'. The fact that Berlin, as one city, no longer exists is for Koeppen both a private wound and a permanent reminder of the breach between past and present that exists in mid twentieth-century Germany.

Red Buses in an Enchanted Forest

My grandfather—or perhaps it was Fritz Reuter—used to say 'Berlin is a village, but London—London is a city!' However, as my grandfather was a native of Anklam and Fritz Reuter belonged to Stavenhagen, rural communities in the depths of Mecklenburg-Pomerania, remote from the world, they were perhaps not ideally qualified to assess the relative merits of large cities, but Fritz Reuter had the penetrating vision, the precise intuition and the magical word-power of the poet and my father was a sea captain with North German Lloyd who had to navigate proud paddle-steamers across the seas, so that maybe after all their judgment carried some weight.

England is an island. A fact every schoolboy knows—or thinks he knows; only by going there does one discover what it means. One has to leave terra firma behind—despite all his inventiveness the element with which man has most affinity—and commit oneself to air or water. No more than thirty years ago Channel steamers stirred the imagination of little boys and confidence men. Hanging below the local time-tables in small German railway stations there used to be white and blue posters with a picture of a bearded mariner in bad weather rig embracing the Hook of Holland and Harwich in his brawny arms, while between his massive hands the wide ocean rippled and the trusty steamer of the company in question crossed from the continent to the island. The posters have vanished, the dreams of little boys and bank clerks are about aeroplanes flying over the Atlantic or the North Pole, but the Channel steamers of today look exactly as they did in the old pictures, clean and safe, as they lie alongside the quay in the Hook, the trains from Germany and Austria stop at the foot of the gangways, and navigation lights, foghorns, screaming gulls and salt air give the land-dweller a taste of sea-travel, the adventure on which he is about to embark for a few hours.

With the first step aboard one is on English soil and in the nineteenth century. The captain could pass for Joseph Conrad and the stewardess for Queen Victoria. The purser—ship's accountant, money changer, and head of the office staff—stands in front of his lit office, in which the pound has been queen of the currencies since time immemorial, like the first Lord of the Admiralty in person. At any moment someone may bring off a coup on the Stock Exchange, conquer an Empire, win or lose the Battle of Trafalgar. In the saloon, natives of Klagenfurt tell stories in the manner of Kipling, and ladies and gentlemen from the valleys of the Rhein and Main promenade on deck in the cool of the night, forget all about business for a little and feel that they are en route for India. Rudolf Diesel, the inventor, could not forget his cares, perhaps the future raised its ugly face from the waters and terrified him, Rudolf Diesel vanished from this deck one night and was never seen again. The whisky, ordered in the bar with man-of-the-world nonchalance, turns out, amazingly, more expensive than in Germany. At this anyone standing nearby who has lived in England for a long time will complain about the rates and taxes there. A true Englishman will say nothing but go on drinking his beer. The beer is dark, thick and bittersweet, the very look of it enough to tire the foreigner. Queen Victoria has the energetic manner of a conscientious corporal and looks ready to cope—even with shipwreck. She shows passengers the life-jacket under their pillow, explains the rules in case of emergency and bids them good-night. In these circumstances one has no desire for a bed, but instead like Masterman Ready falls cosily into a bunk and yields to the gentle, if possibly nauseous, rocking motion and the exciting lullaby of the waves against the iron of the ship's side. It is a fine way to travel, giving time to feel the distance as it is covered and to move with it. The cabin window, referred to of course by the nautical term of port-hole, is round, screwed down, with brass fittings, and with luck if the moon is shining one can look through it on to the vast sea, a field of rolling green, but with something, yes something slightly uncanny, about the foaming white crests.

In Harwich the human race is divided into British citizens and aliens. The Englishman who the evening before was just another fellow-traveller has awakened this morning as a British citizen. He is more cheerful, pinker in the face, and taller. His clothes have acquired an unheard-of, inimitable dignity. With head held high he stalks past the foreigners and on to a door open to him alone; it is a return of the prodigal and the other travellers stand waiting, suppliants, at the door, which is shut and under police guard. The foreigner is distrusted in England as in Spain; best of all, so it seems, simply not to admit him to the promised land and the regrettable necessity of having to let some of these undesirables in is dealt with by bureaucratic procedures. The traveller waiting to get in at the English door cannot understand how it was that Casanova and Karl Marx and revolutionaries and regicides without number fled to England as the island of freedom. Once on the other side of the door, actually in England, the reason becomes clear again. The police officer, a woman, directed me to an immigration officer who was enthroned like a teacher at a high desk but who, like all English officials, was agreeable, quiet-spoken and of the utmost civility. Unfortunately he seemed to take me for a prophet. He inquired as to my business in London, where I should live, whom I should see, and how long I should be staying. Who knows such things in advance? How could I tell whither fancy or passion might take me? To pacify the kindly gentleman I named a hotel which I remembered from Virginia Woolf. I could just as easily have said that I would be staying in Baker Street with Sherlock Holmes. To my shame the nice polite official entered the name which I had so lightly given on a card which I had to sign; after this formality I was free; England trusted me, it put me on my honour and I resolved to show myself worthy of this trust.

The cheerful, pink-cheeked Britons, while their visitors had been waiting at the high desks of the immigration officers, had taken possession of the boat-train to London. The train looked very high class. It reminded me rather of the Moscow-Leningrad express except that the Russian train was much, much higher class. Even so, blue upholstered seats and tables with white cloths offered the traveller, as he stood on the platform still shivering a little in the cool morning-air, a promise of warmth, well-being, refreshment and repleteness. But unfortunately this handsome conveyance had no seats left for such foreigners as had been admitted to the country and they were relegated to a later, slower, and much less comfortable train. It could have been most upsetting; however, my problem was solved, as problems are the world over, by a porter who severed the invisible Gordian knot of amazement by elevating me to the status of one of the conquerors —he took me into the train, sat me down at one of the ready laid tables, pushed my cases beneath it and winked at me encouragingly. Thus Fortune favoured me with breakfast in the company of three cheerful, pink-faced Britons.

This breakfast ceremonial did a lot to endear Great Britain to me. It was a good sound foundation for existence on the island and in London. Bacon, fish and hot milk smells wafted through the coach. It was a meal straight out of Dickens. The tea was as black as the Indian night, the porridge had the grey warmth of a foggy day, and both bacon and eggs were as English as can be —like bacon and eggs in a Lyons restaurant, that remarkable institution where the gastronomic dreams of the island race come true. No one need be surprised that my companions read *The Times*, remained as agreeably silent as the kippers they were consuming, and that after the end of the meal they lit short-stemmed pipes with honey-scented tobacco.

Liverpool Street Station is a pantheon of the Steam Age. Black and sombre yet daring, this iron edifice is an interwoven canopy of progress and homely charm. Civilisation here shows its motherly side; one might speak of the station as the bosom to which she holds her children to protect them from the rain; beer and spirits are dispensed at this international cross-roads with old-world kindliness; even the murderer whom Sherlock Holmes observes leaving the case with the body at the Left Luggage office has civilised features and plays the game according to the rules. My friend the porter, a different one of course, put me in a taxi, but before I had time to admire this old-fashioned, ordinary-looking, but practical and fast-moving vehicle an extra-ordinary thing happened: two gentlemen joined me, taking their seats in the back. The driver, to whom, in order not to let down the friendly official in Harwich, I had given the name of the hotel in Bloomsbury, the name associated with Virginia Woolf, was clearly, if not in league with the new passengers, entirely happy with their presence; he drove off into a swirling mass of traffic, double-decker buses pounded round us like red elephants, while we made our way through a magic forest—in terms of relative height—like an agile tortoise—yes, London is a city! I was about to shout it out, but the taxi was already rattling through back street after back street, or so they seemed to me, brick buildings like late nineteenth-century factories, monotonous, dilapidated, lining the streets, in the evening gaslamps could have burned here, and the gentlemen sitting opposite me on this journey through unknown regions in an unknown direction now looked like criminals out of Edgar Wallace, vicious crooks, the one fat and brutally jolly, the other small and sly with a rat-like mouth, and they smiled and I smiled and we drove on and on and London was an immense city of endless, battered brick rows, shabby people, smoke-filled air and wind-blown refuse, when suddenly the adventure evaporated into nothingness, the gentlemen got out at a dreary-looking station, paid the driver his due, and he then changed course for Bloomsbury, the sacred preserve of friendship and culture in the midst of the big city. I could see the revered poetess wandering round the familiar squares deep in thought in a world all her own, Victorian houses rose up, then a concrete colossus, the new university, trying to match the tower of knowledge in Moscow, small green lawns, the shade of trees, deckchairs, all human and friendly, intellectual Negroes, intellectual Indians with turbans, some of the students women in gaily coloured tropical costumes, in fact the whole Commonwealth, then the British Museum with its columns, we stopped at my hotel, oh! if only the immigration-man in Harwich could have witnessed it—the unexpected can cancel best-laid plans as well as entries in the records of foreigner visitors—the Virginia Woolf hotel was full and the taxi-driver advised me to try two houses further on and there I found a room.

It looked out on a small garden. There in the centre of London was a wooden arbour, crumbling and askew, and perhaps jasmine would flower here in summer, and a rococo chair stood there dreaming among the neglected flowerbeds, and so this garden too had the urbanity and the homeliness of detective stories, fictitious and real, the chair might have been put there by Hitchcock, a masterly touch, one would have said, and Christie, who was hanged, the real London murderer, might have buried his victims in this patch of nature behind the British Museum and beneath the bare branches always kept in motion by the wind.... The residents here were not exactly middle-class in their ways, but as they were familiar neither with the flame of the spirit nor with the fire of revolt they were not Bohemian either, nor angry young men—presumably young schoolteachers accompanied by pale young women who wanted to see London, with now and again a sinister moustachioed individual on unidentifiable business. They were all domineering to the friendly, frightened landlord and scared of his wife and the maid who insisted on breakfast being eaten by nine o'clock—when the house exuded the odour of rancid bacon, the sound of British frying arose from dirty frying-pans and in the basement sitting-room, the twilight gloom of these nether regions penetrated by a beam of pale light filtering from the street through the grating of the windowshaft, with the radio on and the scorching, sweet smelling gas fire switched on, warm bluish milk was poured into tea the colour of dish-water.

Like every continental the first time I went out I was almost run over, I looked left and the car approached from the right, but in London the pedestrian is king and the driver, instead of cursing, said 'sorry'. Nowhere can one cross the street more safely than in the densest traffic stream of the English capital. And then there are the yellow globes, eternally glowing moons, which show the traveller the safest places to ford this stream, the crossings which restore to him his human right—one which is always respected in this part of the world—to priority over the motor vehicle. I went to the Strand, it was mid-day, I was approaching the city when I saw them, the gentlemen in black suits with the stiff black hats, the knights of the Royal Exchange, the courtiers of the Bank of England and a hundred other banks with names steeped in tradition, and the honourable company of lawyers and judges was taking a walk in the thin sunshine, in momentary escape from the administration of justice with its wigs and gowns, and now and again there was even a glimpse of a high priest of the pound and the interest rate bearing proudly on his head a dignified, upright top hat. No one should think that the scene was comic; they wore their city costume soberly and matter of factly and the sight of them immediately gave one confidence, confidence in the English currency, confidence in the British Empire, and the conviction that, never mind India and Suez or Malta and Cyprus, the lion will live on. It was mid-day, the time for the clerks, they poured forth from offices, from bank-counters and legal chambers, they emerged from the editorial offices of Fleet Street with world events still ringing in their ears, the streets were full of them, it was a world of men, in which typists and secretaries had the role of vestal maidens, without sex or thought of love, in a business-like rite practised by men, quite unlike Paris and its mid-day scene, say, in the Place Vendôme, with all the bright stars of haute couture—a Milky Way of erotic suns. These clerks now queued up, they stood patiently in long queues at eating-places, some large, some small but all hopelessly full at this time of day, some of the queues were for restaurant meals but mostly for sandwiches of deathly pallor. This could well have been depressing. But there were pubs and inns, reserved for the top men, the senior appointments and for casual strollers—these were temples of homely comfort full of smoke and stained wood, looking, even when they were built yesterday, like something from before the Fire of London. There they all stand in their pubs, with their bowler hats and their dignity, their pink faces and their self-confidence, each a gentleman among gentlemen, with scarcely a woman to be seen, dark brown beer is pulled at the bar, whisky and gin are there to revive the spirits, and broad slices of roast lamb to restore the body, and there is always a healthy smell of curry because India once belonged to the crown; even more inviting are the old port and sherry houses, massive oak casks which once crossed the seas under sail are filled with dark or light coloured liquids, the bouquet from which conjures up in these rooms the picture of Iberia, severe, chivalrous, and sweet, as though a catholic majesty had paid welcome tribute to the English crown.

I looked for a restaurant to have lunch, soon found one and even, after a short wait, a free chair, but the meal that was served confirmed the bad reputation of English cooking, which is not to be dismissed as a myth. The soup was made from a strange, completely tasteless powder, the flavour had been assiduously removed from the vegetables and replaced by bright green dye, the roast beef, which one is surely entitled to think of as an English national dish, had the consistency of rubber and the dessert consisted of mysteriously jellified red ink. I looked all round and saw to my surprise that there were no open coffins set up by the side of the diners and that there was no question of an evacuation of the city, as in the time of the Black Death. I later experienced a similar meal in the dining room of a first-class, even a famous hotel, this time gentlemen and ladies wore dinner-jackets or seemingly unpretentious evening-dresses, and were served the wretched food with the utmost ceremony by brigades of starchy waiters whereupon the diners assumed enraptured expressions as though to say (and indeed they did say): Aren't we having the most delicious dinner? A wicked fairy must have put a spell on the cookers of England, even good cooks who come to London in droves from Paris, Italy, India, Java, China in no time lose their skill completely. But later, in the vicinity of the Old Bailey, the criminal court dealing with capital offences, I found a pub where the worshipful judges took lunch, in it there was traditional English fare, mutton pies and kidney puddings, prune sauces and pasties, all deliciously prepared, I was almost led to believe that in England working with criminals must go hand in hand with the enjoyment of creature comforts.

The best way to see the sights of London, really to get to know it, is to take one of London Transport's red buses, climb to the top deck, and go off into the unknown. The buses go everywhere; their routes open up the enchanted forest of this immense city; they are a willing, safe form of transport. But first the queue at the bus-stop. Every Englishman queues, with single-minded dedication, and though, anywhere else, constant queuing frays the nerves badly, in London it is relaxing. One waits in line, in a line of well-balanced, solid common-sense. Even the self-centred submit to the rules and benefit from the smoothly running mechanism of a mass society. Heinrich Heine called London a forest of houses; it is an enchanted forest where the whole world comes together and where, at any moment, things can happen by magic. On the top of a red bus one swoops down streets, glides through openings, swims at the bottom of shafts and thinks as all around millions of wheels turn—this is a city, this is a city, this really is a city. We have nothing like it now. London is an entity, a capital, a cosmopolitan city, a metropolis with one centre and many centres, with strongly marked, highly charged contrasts of rich and poor, high and low, noise and quiet, of public life and bustle on the one hand and private hermit-like seclusion on the other.

The Thames bisects London as the Seine does Paris, but there is no Left Bank, which here would have to be the right one. There are plenty of fine bridges over the river but where do they lead to? No one really knows. Not only foreigners but also many natives have never set foot on the right bank, except perhaps for Waterloo Station, the point of departure for pleasures and also on two occasions for death in France. The route to Wimbledon is across Chelsea Bridge, and the Royal Family, the 'Royalties', the Knights of the Garter, or of fortune or talent drive in the drawing-room interiors of their noiseless Rolls Royces to the grass courts and the lace panties of Wimbledon Park, passing on their way brick built houses and factories which stand there blackened with soot and dust, the bare brick work not so much dilapidated as sad and hopeless. But no bombs are thrown or even stones. The revolution is in the person of the fiery-tongued Bevan, soon to be one of the Queen's ministers. In Battersea Park British army veterans dodder along with the help of sticks but wearing splendid scarlet jackets and a chestful of medals—another sad sight. In India, the Sudan, by the Yellow River, beyond the statue of de Lesseps, in the green of Ireland and the heat of Africa, in Flanders their life was with the guns and now they are fading away, spared alike by martial fire and tropical or desert heat, in the pale light of home and of her majesty; these men, who took on all races, are now occupied with the welfare of the children playing in the park, and *they* look on the old soldiers with the unimpressed arrogance of a young generation which is ready to conquer the moon but not to fight the Mahdi or Nasser. Nobody does the Lambeth Walk in Lambeth and even the Festival of Britain failed to give the area any lasting glamour. . . . The river is a disappointment. At low-tide it flaunts the rubble and filth in its bed. The banks are without anglers or bouquinistes, and the port area is quite lacking in Hamburg's all-embracing cosmopolitanism; it is swallowed up in the black isolation of the docks where the ships lie hidden.

Everything that goes to make the *rive gauche* in Paris, the Latin quarter, Bohemia, the nightlife, is to be found in London on the main bank, immediately adjoining officialdom and commerce, in Chelsea and Soho, and in the university museum sector. Chelsea is English to the core, it is friendly, sometimes rural, with small houses as evidence of its respectable, cultured, middle-class past, of family life by the domestic hearth. Just now Chelsea is a vogue, an expensive young people's vogue; they are called and they sometimes act 'angry', but they rarely are. The houses still have simple, old-fashioned fronts as though lost in a dream, but the rents have shot up like skyscrapers, the interiors have been rebuilt, studios constructed, every room an image of the modern way of life, a coloured photograph for an expensively produced architectural journal. Actors, night club owners, young people with titles have their bachelor flats here and the young intellectuals strain their talents trying to keep up with the snobs in their lavish display. Part of this display is beautiful girls and old cars. The effort is worth it. The girls are extremely beautiful and the cars extremely old. Both are taken out along the King's Road, Chelsea's boulevard, on Sunday afternoons. The cars have lots of polished copper and the girls lots of shining, often red hair. Chelsea is the district for showing off neat well-proportioned bottoms, for skin-tight trousers and heavy woollen sweaters which look as though they were intended for rounding Cape Horn. Sometimes there are children clinging to mother's trouser seams. Even the 'angry' generation has offspring, spurning the ways of Dr. Malthus. Here as elsewhere in London, everyone is hungry for the sun; whenever it shines varnished hoods on prams and tattered ones on expensive old cars are taken down and faces held up to the light. Another pastime is to drink milk or beer on the pavement outside shops and pubs. The professional outsiders stand at the counters inside, the conformist scorners of conformism with their short pipes, short hair and short beards, like characters out of John Osborne, Colin Wilson or Dylan Thomas : they read the thick Sunday newspapers with an expression of loathing, finding no new slogans there to banish the tedium of general threats to world survival, red moons, western rocket failures and the social security of the increasingly comprehensive Welfare State.

Soho, situated between Oxford Street, Regent Street, Shaftesbury Avenue and Charing Cross Road, that is between department stores, shops, offices, mass eating places and main traffic arteries, is an oasis of leisurely charm. Soho has the name (Soho is a hunting-cry, 'so ho' was a call to the hounds in the hunting grounds once situated here) of being a foreigners' quarter; foreigners do live and make their living here, but the atmosphere of domesticity is English. Soho Square is old trees and aristocratic narrow houses and wrought iron railings and such silent windows that one could imagine Thomas Carlyle sitting behind them and then, in the evening after writing about heroes in revolutions, taking a walk round the square hand in hand with his maidenly wife. In the window of a publisher's shop the memoirs of eminent personalities with a distinguished record in world affairs are on display. Until now the charm and wit of the squares have been perfectly in keeping with the girls out looking for custom in the narrow streets nearby and their knife-happy boyfriends. But recently, unfortunately, film companies have discovered this idyll. They either tear down the old houses or tart them up barbarously and from the concrete fortresses of their new head offices the bust of Jayne Mansfield is displayed on enormous posters which are lit at night; it weighs heavily on the aristocratic charm of the area, on the unyielding, idealistic spirit of Carlyle and on the memories and justifications of disappointed statesmen. In the evening the streets have something of the Reeperbahn, but much less respectability. This was once the home of French émigrés, refugees of conscience and exiles of royal birth and even if, today, this area is a kingdom of waiters, bar attendants and Italian traders it has still preserved freedom of conscience and refinement of manners. . . .

In an Oxford Street store I saw palm trees and waterlilies and tropical lagoons, all synthetic and all ready for purchase, and I wondered whether retired Indian Army colonels are in the habit of having a 'jungle room', decorated in weird green, ghostly blue and demon white. Also available are synthetic apes and stuffed elephants and living lions and genuine safari-outfits, dangerous big game rifles, camping gear for comfort at the Poles. In Bond Street, the celebrated Bond Street, a school-uniform shop has a horse in its window, public school caps and boarding-school hats are made to lift their wearers into the saddle, to elevate them above their fellows, but the shopkeeper's Rosinante looked distinctly jaded. Despite occasional covetous glances in the direction of the New World, inherited wealth reigns here supreme, a preference for the well-made and the tasteful, the fame of a shop lies often not in the wares on show, but in some fact of which one must have prior knowledge, perhaps that Beau Brummell brought his custom here or Edward the Seventh, the brilliance of some pieces is legendary, these diamonds are said to be the finest ever found in Sir Ernest Oppenheimer's South African mines and those sapphires and emeralds to come from the treasure-chests of a fairy-tale prince. The shops are guarded, or so it seems at first glance, by the English army in person, the porters are former N.C.O.s in most genuine-looking uniforms—their present duties, for which decorations are worn, are clearly nothing less than the defence of Society. Savile Row houses the tailors, more exclusive by far than their customers, it is they who create the gentleman and their professional name-plates are more discreet even than those of medical specialists. On the ground floor are piled the stocks of cloth, a client's measurements and often those of his great-grandfather are stored in old-fashioned safes, the manager is the very picture of decorum. The assistants and the women work in the basement. They are to be seen in house after house, through uncurtained windows, sitting on tailor's tables, in permanent artificial light, like the poor seamstress in Oscar Wilde's fairy-story of the happy prince. A gentleman's head receives its crowning glory from a hat-maker in St. James's Street, where the seemingly careless window display is a carefully calculated collection of battered, dusty headgear, such as may be found, if it escapes the rag merchant, in the attics of old families; this shop keeps a coach and every hat is taken on completion by coach and pair to the appropriate customer whose address may on occasion be Buckingham Palace. . . .

The hundred or so green parks stand out on the street-plan of London like airy tabernacles, each with its grass, its stretches of water, its swans, fish and sheep. The parks are places of refuge. One may walk on the grass, set up deck-chairs, have long picnics, tumble about with the dog, kiss and embrace—London's public parks are everyone's most private garden. The English are said to be stiff. I find them kindly. Their distinguishing feature is tolerance. Even the city gentleman with the round hat and the formal umbrella finds nothing to take offence at as he sits on a park seat studying the financial press. A lot of love-making goes on in the grass and it is the girls who take the initiative, they are by far the more active partners, trying everything they know to excite their rather stolid lovers, they play at Ophelia and Hamlet, 'A fair thought to lie between a maid's legs', but once the man has begun to pluck up courage the girl sits up and pushes him away. At the highest social level the debutantes give the dances, it is the girl who issues the invitation, who takes the young man out, dines and wines him, who pretends on the way home to be ready to give him everything, only to laugh at his disappointment as she leaves him on the doorstep. Hyde Park is no more than a few minutes removed from the heart of London's bustle, and yet Hyde Park is away from it all, is the country, is England with gentle green slopes, beautiful and open, as far as the eye can see. By the entrance the orators are up on their stands, they too enjoying the benefits of freedom. They fling accusations and abuse, taunts and contempt at each other and the bobby listens peaceably. What an intelligent way to wield power! And what insight into human folly to let every fool have his way here. Everyone speaks on behalf of everyone else and this seems to me to function as a natural means of releasing complexes. The ornamental gates of Hyde Park bear the royal arms, but the kingdom as a whole, by giving human shortcomings their due, is a true democracy.

On the way to Hyde Park stands the mighty, if somewhat fraudulent Marble Arch, designed as a triumphal archway for the outings of George the Fourth, but built too narrow for the gold state-coach to pass through, this archway in marble stands endearingly as a monument to a very human act of folly. Opposite it is a Lyons Corner House, where social distinctions are levelled out by the palatial décor and cheap prices—the gastronomic paradise of the Londoners. I saw them standing in long queues at the gates of bliss, well-behaved, patient, and completely free, and through a window I could see chefs, for all the world like real chefs, like the chefs of a fairy-tale king, with enormously high hats, tell-tale corporations and dazzlingly white aprons and every-one of these regal chefs placed two thin slices of streaky bacon in a frying-pan, broke a couple of eggs on top, then placed the pan on the gas, over and over and over again. Just that and nothing more.

NOTES

1. A useful bibliography can be found in D. Weber, *Deutsche Literatur seit 1945*, Suttgart, 1968.
2. Cf. *Nach Rußland und anderswohin*, paperback edition, Fischer, 1961, p. 11.
3. Ibid, p. 10 and p. 60.
4. Cf. M. Reich-Ranicki, *Deutsche Literatur in West und Ost*, Munich, 1963, p. 52, speaks of a 'Rückzug ins Unverbindliche'.
5. Though Koeppen does not relate his picture of London—and by extension of English life as a whole—to any English writers of the 1950's it is worth noting the remarkable similarity between the attitudes and behaviour he notes and those expressed in the poetry of the Movement.

5

ELIOT, POE AND USINGER

By R. W. Last

Fritz Usinger (b. 1895) is particularly known among German scholars for his studies on a wide range of subjects, and for his editions of writers such as Hölderlin and Schiebelhuth.[1] Less widely recognised is his own poetry which spans a half century of steady productivity. In his latest collection, *Canopus*, Usinger writes

> Einen Brief wollte ich dir schreiben.
> Ich begann ihn unter der Petroleumlampe
> Mit ihrem schön gerundeten Glasschirm,
> Ich schrieb ihn weiter bei Gaslicht, lange, lange . . .
> . . .
> Nun schreibe ich weiter bei der
> Elektrischen Stehlampe auf meinem Arbeitstisch . . .[2]

Usinger's whole work, poetic and critical, is characterised by this patient, humble search, and the urge to communicate to the reader, not by propagandising from the rooftops, but by writing in an intimate, private form such as the letter in the poem quoted.

Roddewig has pointed out that one should not expect to find the latest poetic fashions in a writer of Usinger's generation;[3] and indeed Usinger attacks most of the current generation of writers, but not because they are too modern—on the contrary, he argues that they are not modern enough.

> We no longer inhabit earthbound space and dimensions, but are living on the threshold of infinity. . . . By some means or other we must come to terms with the vastness of infinity which is there right outside our front doors and can no longer be pushed to one side or ignored. . . . Open books by Böll or Grass, Krolow or Celan, or any writer of the Gruppe 47 : we find no reference to this fact in their work.[4]

He accuses his contemporaries of having such a myopic fixation on the immediate social and historical environment that their world view is, if anything, less enlightened than that of their predecessors. It is not enough, argues Usinger, to set man in his immediate context; he must be viewed in the context of the cosmos as a whole, in the full light of human knowledge. The Second World War appears to have wrought fundamental changes in our awareness of the universe; but the real revolution took place centuries before as a result of the discoveries of men such as Copernicus.[5] With very few exceptions, Usinger argues, Western literature still acts as if the earth were the centre of a fixed universe, and not an infinitely small and insignificant speck in an infinitely vast universe.[6] He singles out the German expressionist poet Alfred Mombert[7] as one significant exception: Mombert recognised the immediate confrontation of man and the cosmos, and explored without fear the deeps of the universe, seeking to come to terms with this new situation in his enormous cycles of mythical poems by translating the remote abstract concept into tangible, physical terms.[8] And, at first sight somewhat surprisingly, he singles out Edgar Allan Poe as well.

Usinger points out that Mombert has been ignored because of his positive recognition of the new human condition;[9] and that part of Poe's work which to Usinger is the most significant has equally been neglected, not least by T. S. Eliot in his essay 'From Poe to Valéry'.

Eliot is offended by Poe's 'carelessness and unscrupulousness in the use of words';[10] suspicious of his assertion that the long poem is an impossibility; and sums him up as a man of great imaginative potential but deplorably lacking in 'maturity of intellect'.[11] For Eliot, Poe's influence in France is in no small measure attributable to an inadequate command of English on the part of his most ardent admirers;[12] and this, together with a combination of his curious qualities and defects of mind, his poetic theory, and the compelling fascination surrounding his work, has accorded him this special place in literary history, even if it is unwarranted on strictly literary grounds.

Usinger's counter-arguments are important in that they seek to draw on a more complete picture of Poe's work than does Eliot. The latter makes no reference to Poe's *Eureka,* which Usinger regards as the key to his achievement and the culmination of his work. Usinger is not primarily concerned with literary merit[13] but with the breadth of Poe's vision. *Eureka*, which has been 'denounced as a farrago of nonsense or the last maudlin ruminations of a diseased Romantic mind',[14] attempts a redefinition of the nature of the universe. Essentially, Poe conceives the universe in terms of divine heart-beats, of an alternation between unity and multiplicity:

> A diffusion from Unity, under the conditions, involves a tendency to return into Unity—a tendency ineradicable until satisfied.[15]

The universe commences in a state of 'Material Nullity',[16] expands to its maximum dimensions, and then returns to its initial state:

> But are we here to pause? Not so. . . . Guiding our imaginations by that omniprevalent law of laws, the law of periodicity, are we not, indeed, more than justified in entertaining a belief—let us say, rather, in indulging a hope—that the processes we have here ventured to contemplate will be renewed forever, and forever, and forever; a novel Universe swelling into existence, and then subsiding into nothingness, at every throb of the Heart Divine?
>
> And now—this Heart Divine—what is it? *It is our own.*[17]

Poe operates by a strange blending of intellect and intuition, and it is this, coupled with the essential nature of his vision, which renders him so attractive to Usinger.[18]

Edgar Allan Poe.

Essentially, Poe was no storyteller. One could hardly describe any of his tales as exemplary. They all possess quirks of theme and structure which reveal that the author's main concern was not the narration of events, but rather something quite different: as a consequence he is not really telling a story at all, but most often weaving a web of theories; he is mindless of motivation, breaks off his tales in the most unpredictable fashion at the climactic point of some revelation or other, giving the reader no indication of how he should react to the circumstances, nor how they might be extrapolated and guided back into the sphere of reality. Poe has no consideration for his reader. He is concerned solely with himself, with his own ideas, with what preoccupies him and seeks articulation.

Attitudes to his work tend to take extreme forms. We have one prominent witness to this fact in T. S. Eliot, who wrote an essay entitled 'From Poe to Valéry'. In it he states that Poe's works and theories had a far-reaching influence in France but found no echo in England or America. It would be difficult to name a single poet in the English-speaking world whose style has matured through a study of Poe's style. In Germany Poe has been esteemed solely as a writer of horror stories. His poems have remained without influence and no one has devoted any attention to his theories. Poe's greatest impact was upon France, where three great poets made him famous and proclaimed his greatness: Charles Baudelaire, Stéphane Mallarmé and Paul Valéry. Baudelaire saw in Poe the archetype of the *poète maudit*, the social—and spiritual—outcast, but also the creator of a poetry which existed for its own sake; Mallarmé was impressed by Poe's artistry and the magical power of his poetry, and Paul Valéry found in Poe's famous and infamous essay on the philosophy of composition, the first description of that arbitrary and artificial mode of poetic production to which he himself adhered.

To be fair, Eliot does concede the possibility that the French saw in Poe something which eluded English-speaking readers. But what could that something be, apart from the factors enumerated above, which completely failed to convince England and America? There he was regarded as no more than an insignificant hanger-on of the Romantic movement, and in particular of Byron and Shelley. His work, says Eliot, was touched with provinciality, in a sense in which—to name a contrasting figure—Walt Whitman was never in the least provincial. Poe's provinciality is that of a man who is not at home where he belongs, but who is incapable of feeling at home anywhere else. He is a kind of displaced European. Anglo-Saxon criticism, Eliot continues, regards Poe as a dabbler in verse and various prose forms who never brought off anything of significance in any one of these media. Not one of the French poets who adulated him, says Eliot, had a good command of English, not even Mallarmé, who may have taught English in various French schools, but demonstrated by his book on English that he had no real scholarly knowledge of the language. Eliot states that if someone reads something in a language which he knows only imperfectly, then there is a distinct possibility that he will find many things which are not in the original at all. It is true that Eliot does conclude his observations by remarking that, if he looks through the eyes of Baudelaire, Mallarmé and Valéry, he becomes increasingly convinced of the importance of Poe's life's work as a whole (a pronouncement which, it must be confessed, is vague in the extreme). In spite of this we are left with the impression that the critical dicta of Eliot's essay, couched in terms of prudent decorum and ironic tactfulness, represent the most destructive kind of criticism that one great writer can perpetrate against another.

. . .

Only gradually did Poe come to recognise that Heaven and Hell are indissolubly bonded together, that the earth is no more than an accretion of the two. Poe's acrimony slowly evolves in the direction of recognition and affirmation of the true reality. Out of the world of the maelstrom and the prisons of the Inquisition there develops at a later stage a cosmos of supreme divine laws which he never tires of exploring. People only read Poe's tales of horror. But these represent only one phase in the development of his world view. No one sees his pondering spirit, groping its way slowly upwards from riddle to riddle, from solution to solution, to emerge out of the realms of horror into an endless sphere of knowledge and understanding. It is not enough to be aware of this: in addition, one must study in depth his last completed work, his great cosmological study *Eureka*, and it is not exactly light reading. Only from this extreme standpoint can the threads that hold Poe's life's work together be recognised.

He had previously sought to penetrate beyond the frontiers of death, he had investigated the uttermost limits of the shadowy realms of horror, he had sought the edge of the physical world in fantastical novels of travel . . . None of these shocks and experiences brought him illumination. And then suddenly came the flash of insight into what he had himself termed cryptology, the study of riddles, the science of mysteries. He began with the interpretation of ciphers and ended with the interpretation of the universe. In such terms can the genius of Edgar Allan Poe be defined. It can only be recognised if it is seen in the context of its development. He has constructed a stairway which continues into the heights and beyond the limits of human vision. The mystery is layered through the world in many stages, from the riddles which are concealed in the human subconscious, in the vaults of the individual mind, to the mysteries of the astral spiral nebulæ. All are subject to a law of gradation, a cosmic interrelationship.

Poe had no interest in democracy. It was utterly foreign to him. In this as in every other respect, he is the complete opposite of his great contemporary Walt Whitman. The coexistence of these two opposite poles at the beginning of the history of the American spirit is a phenomenon of impenetrable profundity and significance. This does not mean that one of these two great men is any more important for the history of America than the other. America followed the path of Walt Whitman. But this does not imply that Edgar Allan Poe was pushed into the background. On the contrary: the influence of his spirit over most contemporary American productions is more clearly in evidence than that of Walt Whitman. Both men, Whitman and Poe, are two source phenomena, two archetypes, to which the spirit constantly returns, whether it will or not, whether it knows it or not.

He demonstrates that the cosmos originated in a particle so minute as to be to all intents and purposes non-existent, grew outwards in every direction and continues to grow today, and the resultant cosmos is boundless but at the same time finite. He resolutely denies the concept of an infinite universe. Rather, the universe is spherical in shape. All this corresponds in a striking fashion to the latest theories of the cosmology of our age, founded as it is upon quantum mechanics, which states that space, time and matter grew from a microphysical germ, a so-called Riemann quantum, whose dimensions in the first elemental time-span of 10^{-23} seconds occupied only 10^{-13} cm and was 10,000 times smaller than the diameter of a hydrogen atom, that is about a billionth of a millimetre in size, and contains just two elementary particles, the building bricks of the whole universe. Out of this beginning the cosmos has grown to its present vast size, whose total mass can today now be calculated at 10^{80} elementary particles. Even contemporary science denies the concept of the infinity of the universe. Out of the hypothesis of the bending of space comes at the same time the limitlessness as well as the finitude of the universe, in precisely the same way as Poe had already conceived them. In one respect Poe even reaches beyond this newest cosmic theory. When the cosmos has evolved to the limit of its development, he postulates a corresponding retraction of material and space until the starting point has once more been reached, and then a new process of creation will take place. According to Poe, the cosmos is not a unique, but a cyclical, phenomenon. The universe comes into being and fades again in an eternal sequence. Such a concept is to be found in no other writer or researcher anywhere.

With this interpretation of the universe Poe's cryptology celebrates its greatest triumph. Acuity of mind and intuition conspire in perfect harmony and prove Poe to be a figure of a modernity which could, even after over a hundred years, readily absorb himself into the most radical intellectual position.

Eliot saw none of this, and therefore his criticism of Poe is invalid in the crucial issues. He is unaware of an analytical problem such as Poe's, or he dismisses it as outmoded, a thing of the past. When Poe presented this analytical principle of cryptology it was utterly new in both the European and American worlds. It was a consolidation of methods pioneered by antique philosophy, sharpened by medieval scholasticism and attuned to mathematics and science by modern philosophy since Descartes. Poe the artist reconciled and brought together analysis and intuition. Therein lies the special quality of his methodology. His literature belongs in the great European tradition of the understanding spirit. It cannot properly be judged on purely literary criteria. His life's work was the development of a universal intuitive analysis, which went from the synthesis of the poem, thence to the analysis of a criminal case, until finally he arrived at an insight into the mystery of the creation of the universe. And when the significance of this achievement is fully realised, then it must be stated that Edgar Allan Poe is one of the most astounding writers the world has seen.

NOTES

1. For a bibliography of Usinger's work, see his retrospective collection of poetry *Pentagramm*, Wiesbaden, 1965, pp. 101–102.
2. 'Der Brief', *Canopus*, Wiesbaden, 1968, p. 12.

   I wanted to write you a letter.
   I started it under the paraffin lamp
   With its finely rounded glass shade,
   I wrote on by gaslight, on and on . . .
   . . .
   Now I still write on by the
   Electric lamp on my study desk . . .

3. *Nachwort* to *Pentagramm*, p. 93.
4. *Tellurium. Elf Essays*, Newied am Rhein/Berlin, 1966, p. 137.
5. See, for example, *Tellurium*, p. 138.
6. These two standpoints Usinger calls 'tellurisch' and 'planetarisch' respectively.
7. For example, in 'Das Lebenswerk Alfred Momberts' in: U. Weber, *Alfred Mombert. Ausstellung zum 25. Todestag*, Karlsruhe, 1967, pp. 13–14.
8. 'Alfred Mombert ist der erste Dichter der Welt, der das menschliche Leben nicht nur tellurisch, sondern planetarisch erfahren hat.' 'Das Lebenswerk,' p. 13.
9. *Tellurium*, p. 145. Mombert himself acknowledges this: 'Ich erlebe es nun seit vielen Jahren: je mehr man aus dem Ganzen heraus für ein Ganzes dichtet, aus der Menschheit heraus für eine Menschheit, aus dem All heraus für das All: um so kleiner wird der Kreis der Aufnehmenden' (E. Herberg (ed.), *Alfred Mombert. Dichtungen*, Munich, 1963, ii, 611).
10. 'From Poe to Valéry' in: E. W. Carlson (ed.), *The recognition of Edgar Allan Poe*, Ann Arbor 1966, p. 218.
11. Ibid., p. 213.

12. Baudelaire's knowledge of English is the subject of critical discord. At one end of the spectrum, P. M. Wetherill (*Charles Baudelaire et la poésie d'Edgar Allan Poe*, Paris, 1962), in his discussion of Baudelaire's poetry, says that Baudelaire 'travaillait à coups de dictionnaire' (p. 157) and had '[une] connaissance insuffisante ... de l'anglais' (p. 167); on the other hand, P. F. Quinn (*The French face of Edgar Poe*, Carbondale, Ill., 1957), concentrating on the prose, states that, whereas Baudelaire's first efforts at rendering Poe into French were somewhat inadequate, 'by dint of serious study, carried out not through books alone but pursued actively, wherever he could hear English spoken, he earned the right to act as the authoritative translator of the work of Poe' (p. 98).
13. Writing about the Brazilian poet Pereira Lima, Usinger makes the case for his critical standpoint in these terms: 'Ob man von diesen Gedichten ergriffen wird oder nicht, ob man sie für gute Gedichte hält oder nicht, das ist nicht entscheidend. Wichtig ist, daß sie genau *die neue menschliche und dichterische Situation* treffen, die für uns alle gegeben ist, auch wenn sie uns noch nicht recht zu Bewußtsein kommt.' *Tellurium*, p. 150.
14. E. H. Davidson, *Poe. A critical study*, Cambridge, Mass., 1957, p. 223.
15. J. A. Harrison (ed.), *The complete works of Edgar Allan Poe*, vol. XVI, Reprint, New York, 1965, p. 207.
16. Works, p. 311.
17. Ibid., p. 311.
18. The translations are from the essay in *Tellurium*, pp. 8–9, pp. 16–19.